THE CELTIC CHURCHES
A HISTORY A.D. 200 to 1200

John T. McNeill

THE UNIVERSITY OF CHICAGO PRESS
CHICAGO AND LONDON

JOHN T. MCNEILL is professor emeritus, Union Theological Seminary. He is a well-known scholar in various areas of church history and has published many books and articles.
1974

The University of Chicago Press, Chicago 60637
The University of Chicago Press, Ltd., London
 Published 1974
Printed in the United States of America
INTERNATIONAL STANDARD BOOK NUMBER: 0–226–56095–3
LIBRARY OF CONGRESS CATALOG CARD NUMBER: 73–84193

This book is dedicated to the memory of
NETTA HARDY MCNEILL 1890–1970
who first suggested it and shared in its beginnings

Contents

Preface
xi

1. The Pagan Celts and Their First Contacts with Christianity
1

2. Christianity in Britain to the Anglo-Saxon Invasions
15

3. Monastic Saints of the British Church
35

4. The Christianization of Ireland: St. Patrick
50

5. The Flowering of Irish Monasticism
69

6. The Christian Mission in Scotland: St. Columba
87

7. Irish Saints and English Kings
102

8. Learning, Art, and Worship
120

9. Founders of Christian Brittany
137

10. St. Columban and Other Missionary Peregrini
155

11. Irish Scholars in European Lands
177

12. The Celtic Churches Incorporated in the Western Hierarchical Church
193

Retrospect
223

Abbreviations
227

Notes
229

Bibliography
273

Index
281

Maps

Celtic Monastic Sites of Scotland, Wales, and England
34

Ireland: Early Monastic Foundations, with a Few Additional Places
68

Early Christian Brittany
136

Principal Irish Monastic Foundations in Continental Europe, with Some Other Ecclesiastical Centers
176

Preface

In the winter of 1908, when I was an undergraduate at McGill University and residing in the Old Presbyterian College, Montreal, something happened to me of which this book is a sequel. One day, kept indoors by a slight illness, I explored the unused "tower room," where I found the floor strewn with damaged and discarded books and pamphlets. I lifted a small dishevelled volume, lacking covers, title page, and author's name, and stood motionless for an hour reading a popular account of early Irish missionary monks at work in the Scottish islands and highlands. The incident so impressed me with the fascination of the Celtic religious world that it led to my specialization in areas of Celtic church history in preparation for the B.D. degree at Westminster Hall, Vancouver, in 1912 and for the Ph.D. at Chicago in 1920.

Although most of my published work has ranged through later periods, the Christian history of the Celtic peoples has never lost its attraction for me. At every opportunity I have given attention to aspects of the field in lecture courses and seminars, and, in addition to some minor articles and book reviews, I have put my studies on record in my dissertation, *The Celtic Penitentials* (Paris, 1923), and in *Medieval Handbooks of Penance*, an annotated translation of the Penitential Books, published in 1938 in the Columbia University Press Records of Civilization series and in 1965 by Octagon Books. As joint author of the latter book, the late Dr. Helena M. Gamer made a distinguished contribution by her work on the early manuscripts.

In 1966 my wife, having come upon a manuscript of early date in my files, seriously proposed the preparation of a general book such as is now presented. A plan was then formed and the work begun. In 1968 she joined me in a busy course of reading in the National Library, the library of Trinity College, Dublin, the library of the British Museum, and the university libraries of Edinburgh, St. Andrews, and Glasgow. She lived to see, and to talk over helpfully with me, the first draft of the manuscript. It has since been extensively rewritten and much enlarged in the light of wider reading. The task has taken me repeatedly to the libraries of Harvard University and Divinity School, those of Union Theological Seminary and Columbia University, Regenstein Library and the Divinity School library at the University of Chicago, and the library of the Lutheran Seminary, Chicago, as well as that of the Bellarmine School of Theology now housed with it. There have been short forays to the libraries of Hartford Theological Seminary, Yale University, McGill University, and Dartmouth College. A good many books have been obtained by interlibrary loan through Middlebury College Library, to whose shelves I have also had constant access. In the preparation of a book such as this, one tests the patience and competence of countless librarians: they have earned my gratitude and unqualified admiration.

Some teachers and scholars no longer living have had an indefinable but quite real part in the making of this book. These include Professor James Stalker of Aberdeen and Professor Alexander R. MacEwen of Edinburgh, both of whom I first met when they taught small classes in Vancouver; James Westfall Thompson, professor of medieval history and my supervising professor at the University of Chicago; Thom Pete Cross, professor of Celtic studies there, and Professor Shirley Jackson Case, head of the department of church history at the University of Chicago Divinity School. My debt to an uncounted number of contemporary scholars is, as far as possible, acknowledged in the footnotes. To my great regret, most of them are not personally known to me. But I have gained help from conversations with a few who are masters in this or related fields. Interviews with Professor Ludwig Bieler of University College, Dublin, and with Professor J. H. Baxter of St. Andrews University proved especially stimulating. The advice of my son, Professor William Hardy McNeill of the University of Chicago, who read the manuscript throughout, has led to a number of stylistic improvements and a change in the sequence of chapters. The maps were prepared by my granddaughter Deborah McNeill Van Koughnett.

The purpose has been to provide an introduction to Celtic Christianity for students and other readers who are not specialists. Though a more ample book has emerged than was at first intended, it retains the character of an introductory text. It attempts a proportionate treatment of the entire field with attention to the information needed by beginners. I hope too that it may commend itself to teaching scholars as a useful handbook for students.

The admirable work of Dom Louis Gougaud, *Les Chrétientés celtiques* (Paris, 1911), translated in a revised form by Maud Joynt as *Christianity in Celtic Lands* (London, 1932), well represents the state of scholarship more than forty years ago. In the interval archaeological findings have helped to clarify or correct many points in the story of Celtic Christian beginnings, some new documents have come to light, others have been subjected afresh to searching examination, and many new veins of interpretation have been explored. Debate among the experts has been animated and has extended to all the Celtic areas, especially with reference to the earlier stages of the history. A lull in these amicable contentions seems now to be discernible, and this may make more opportune the appearance of a new book of generalization that takes account of the accumulating body of discussion.

JOHN T. MCNEILL

One | The Pagan Celts and Their First Contacts with Christianity

In ancient times the far-ranging tribes called *Keltoi* by the Greeks and *Galli* by the Romans drew the attention of numerous classical authors. In the Graeco-Roman world they were thought of with some apprehension as impetuous and militant barbarians menacing the frontiers of civilization. Early in the sixth century B.C. they were known to have reached the Atlantic coast of Spain and made settlements on a strip from Cadiz southward. In a work of about 500 B.C. attributed to Hecateus of Miletus, Narbonne is spoken of as a Celtic town. About 440 B.C. Herodotus reports the presence of Celts on the upper Danube and in Spain. Plato mentions them in a list of nations addicted to drunkenness, and Aristotle notes their reckless indifference to danger, even of earthquakes and raging seas. Gradually the classical writers show an increasing familiarity with the qualities and social life of the Celts. Polybius (d. 122 B.C.) refers to incidents in their expansion, including their campaigns in Thrace and Macedonia a century before his time. Writers of the first century B.C. treat Celtic matters with greater intimacy than their predecessors, and have left for us invaluable descriptions of Celtic customs and of Celts in action. Livy in his *History* has a vivid account of the invasion of Italy by the Gauls and their siege and occupation of Rome in 390 B.C. Julius Caesar, their discerning enemy in Gaul and Britain, made intimate observations on the Celts and their ways. A more disengaged and academic writer, the influential stoic teacher and historian Poseidonius, in works not now extant furnished descriptions of Celtic society in Gaul that were soon extensively used by Diodorus Siculus and Strabo. Both these writers provide substantial materials, Strabo as a well-traveled geographer and Diodorus with some interest in history. Diodorus narrates the incursions eastward of some Celtic tribes early in the third century B.C. and their exploits in Greece and Asia Minor.[1]

The Greeks and Romans knew that Celts came from over the Alps, but gave little thought to the question of their ultimate origin.

Scholars today have reached no certainty regarding the original matrix of a distinctly Celtic tribal society. Some hold that this is to be sought in the primitive, contentious, partly nomadic life of ancient tribes north and east of the Black Sea. Arguments for this view, which rest largely on the similarity of tribal and local names, cannot be said to be conclusive. To trace a line of descent from the Cimmerians, some of whom were pushed out of the Caucasus and Black Sea region by the Scythians in the sixth century B.C., to the Cimbri who emerged from Jutland to play a troublesome rôle at the close of the second century B.C., has been a tempting hypothesis. But the Cimbri may have been more Teutonic than Celtic, and the hypothesis rests upon fragile arguments. Henri Hubert, a highly respected Celticist in his day, called it "a confusion that has raged like a pestilence among modern historians." Yet it has been revived with variations, notably by Calvin Kephart in a book of impressive learning (1960) in which we are led back for Celtic origins to the Caucasus highlands.

Most scholars remain uncommitted on the remote beginnings of Celtic existence, and keep within the certainties provided in our century by archaeology. This makes it clear that the Celtic motherland for European expansion lay in a wide region north of the Alps and south of the upper Danube, embracing territories now within Germany, Austria, and Switzerland. The area corresponds roughly to that which archaeologists call, from bronze funereal urn findings, the northern Alpine urnfield, where no doubt something of a common culture prevailed in very ancient times. It may have been in this area that the earliest Celtic speech came into use and a recognizably distinct Celtic people emerged. Whatever our view of the place of origin, long centuries must have elapsed within what was still prehistory during which variant Celtic dialects developed and early Celtic art forms were evolved.

It was important for the expansion of the Celts that for them the age of iron came relatively early. By about 700 B.C. Celtic smiths at Hallstatt in Upper Austria had become skillful pioneers in ironwork, providing utensils and war equipment, notably the great two-handed and two-edged swords that were to be wielded victoriously in many a battle. The argument for an Asian Celtic origin has found some support in the similarity of some Hallstatt animal patterns in metal ornamentation to those employed by Scythians and Sarmatians. But we more and more realize the great fact of the interpenetration of peoples through traveling salesmen and buyers in the ancient world, and it is questionable how far the imitation of art patterns implies that adjacency of two peoples. Like Asiatic tribesmen too, the Celts made constant use of horses. They come into history in chariots or on horseback. It was recognized in Roman times that they were superior in horsemanship, but it does not follow that this expertness was acquired from imitation of Asiatic neighbors rather than in practical response to a Western environment. Certainly their long, heavy swords had no counterpart among warriors of the Steppe. Horses were used by the Celts for work as well as for war; but the ordinary work animal was the ox. In the earliest era of their expansion the Celtic tribes were so habitually in motion that little attention could be given to agriculture. But well within pre-Christian times, without giving up their readiness for war, they had become farmers, tilling the soil with oxen and harvesting grain for human and animal food.

At La Tène, by the eastern end of Lake Neuchâtel in Switzerland, a more advanced Celtic culture flourished about 500 to 100 B.C. Here there were borrowings from Greek and Etruscan art patterns together with the elaboration of earlier Celtic ones, all treated with originality and wrought with ingenious intricacy. In metal work a great variety of form and color was cultivated, with a skillful use of gems and enamel. La Tène art was applied to utensils and tools in common use, and widely cultivated for centuries through the Celtic world. Mere utility was never satisfying to the Celt. The hilt of his great sword was richly decorated with gold inlay; his horse-trappings flashed with ornaments in metalwork; even the linchpin of a cart axle and the handle of a cooking pot must bear an ornamental design, the creation of artistic hands.

The Greeks and Romans came to know the Celts only after the latter had spread widely. The first active period of their expansion may have been about 1000 B.C. They came early enough to give enduring place names to many spots in central and western Europe and to many of its familiar rivers such as the Seine, the Rhine, the Inn, the Shannon, and the Boyne. We do not know the circumstances of the earliest Celtic expansion, or the degree to which it was military or the result of any sort of planned enterprise. Later the settled communities seem to have broken forth in warrior companies large or small, or undertaken tribal armed migrations, as impulse or opportunity drew them, with such frequency and force as to change the demographic and to some extent the political map of Europe.

The early history of Rome is marked by a crisis of Celtic invasion which almost brought to an end the rise of that city of destiny. In 390 B.C. a Celtic host from Gaul defeated a Roman army at the Allia River and plundered Rome. Only the well-provisioned fortress of the Capitol continued to resist. After a seven-month siege of this stronghold the Celtic commander, Brennus, accepted a large ransom and withdrew with his followers to settle near the mouth of the Po, where other Celtic immigrants were their neighbors. The whole Po valley was then beginning to be infiltrated and dominated by Celtic tribesmen who kept coming over the Alpine passes. Thus a predominantly Celtic expanse of territory rich in natural resources lay across northern Italy. It was known to the Romans as Gallia Cisalpina, or Hither Gaul. It long remained hostile to Rome and an obstacle to Roman expansion in Transalpine Gaul. By 222 B.C. the Romans brought it under subjection, and colonization by Latin-speaking immigrants followed, bringing its mixed population into the domain of Roman culture. Among the eminent Latin writers born in Cisalpine Gaul was the supremely gifted Vergil; of his ethnic ancestry nothing conclusive can be said. The early Gallic invasion dispersed itself also in raiding companies over much of the Italian peninsula and entered Sicily.

A few years after the siege of Rome, as Xenophon reports, Dionysius of Syracuse secured Celtic and Iberian troops, including cavalry, to aid the Lacedemonians in the Peloponnesian War (369 B.C.). These were brought by ships, doubtless from Spain. It was in this period that the Celts dispersedly overran the Balkans and spread into southern Russia. We learn from Strabo that Alexander the Great, nearing the height of his power about 335 B.C., was interviewed by some Celtic chiefs from the Adriatic coast. When he inquired what they feared, they surprised him by answering that they feared no man but only that the sky might fall. He thought them arrogant in not fearing him; but an agreement was reached in which they pledged their faithfulness to him unless the sky should fall upon them. This expression, a form of solemn oath, recurs in Christian Ireland. In the next century B.C. adventurous tribes from Gaul and northern Italy threw Macedonia and Achaea into disorder and sacked Delphi (279 B.C.), but soon suffered a crushing defeat. A year later three other Gallic tribes, numbering twenty thousand in all pushed eastward over the Hellespont into Asia Minor, where, after extensive depredations, they established a principality with its chief stronghold at Ankara, the ancient Ancyra, now the Turkish capital. This center was held by the leading tribe of Celtic invaders, the Testosages, who according to Strabo and Pliny had formerly occupied a wide area in southern Gaul. The name Galatia, a varient of Gallia, Gaul, was applied to this state. With enlargement southward it became in 25 B.C. the Roman province of Galatia. So firm were the Celtic characteristics of the people of Galatia that nearly 700 years later St. Jerome, commenting on St. Paul's Galatians 2:3, observes that in addition to Greek they used a Celtic speech, a little corrupted but similar to that which he had heard spoken by the Treveri in Gaul. This statement has been treated skeptically by some writers; but Jerome was in a good position to know the facts. In early manhood he had spent about four years in Gaul, mostly in the area of Treves, and soon thereafter he wrote to Rufinus reporting travels in Asia Minor which included "journeyings through Galatia."[2] We have numerous modern examples of the protracted survival of an indigenous speech under an alien government; Celtic instances are Irish and Scottish Gaelic, Welsh, Cornish, and Breton, all of which, including the now extinct Cornish, have endured through longer periods under alien pressure.

No attempt to mark in detail the limits of Celtic expansion before the Christian era is needed here. Many Celtic artifacts have been found in Hungary, Czechoslovakia, and Denmark, and there and elsewhere in Europe local names of Celtic origin suggest the temporary ascendancy of Celtic invaders where we have no other evidence. In Spain the Celtiberians, an alliance which became a fusion of two peoples, after participating somewhat ambiguously in the Spanish phase of the wars of Rome and Carthage, were with the whole peninsula nominally subjected to Rome about 201 B.C. In later decades they frequently revolted, until the capture of their stronghold Numantia in 133 B.C. Thereafter the Celtic element gradually became merged with the population of Spain.

A map of the ancient Celtic world would give the impression of a vast empire. But the Celts were, as Caesar said, "too much given to faction" to erect a political structure on a grand scale. Their political achievement was, nevertheless, far from despicable. With loose federations of tribes, and despite incidents of internecine strife, the Celts of Gaul, Britain, and Ireland long maintained territorial sway, and subsequent invasions have left in these countries a large admixture of Celtic blood. The prehistoric dates of their first coming to these lands have not been determined. The earliest penetration may have long antedated the principal migrations, which were in all probability subsequent to 500 B.C.

It is sometimes argued that the word Celtic is properly applicable to the aggregation of those who spoke a Celtic language rather than to a racial entity. The half-dozen Celtic languages that have been used in different communities are classified by philologists on the basis of the use of *p* or *c* to represent the Indo-European *qu* sound. The C-Celtic languages—Irish in its early and later forms, Manx, and Scottish Gaelic—were developed from a speech designated Goidelic, the ancient Irish having called themselves Goidels. The ancient Gaulish speech, together with Welsh, Cornish, and Breton, are P-Celtic or Brythonic languages. These language variations must have been developed through long centuries of local separation. Yet a sense of racial affinity was always felt by the severed language groups. The classical writers make only occasional reference to Celtic speech, different forms of which were apparently equally barbaric and incomprehensible to them. But they observed and described closely the racial characteristics common to the Celts, their bodily stature and facial features, their clothing and war gear, their religion, habits, and temperament. The picture is consistent and convincing. The Celts were for these observers not a miscellaneous aggregation of peoples with what was basically a common language, but essentially a single people. As T. G. E. Powell has written: "The term Celts is therefore justifiable in a proper ethnological sense, and should not necessarily be restricted to mean Celtic-speaking, which is a concept of academic thought of quite modern times."[3] There seems no basic reason for a dispute between the philologist on the one hand and the archaeologist and historian on the other.

The ancient Celts are described as a race of tall, fair-haired warriors, strong and agile, easily provoked to battle, boastful before combat like the Homeric heroes. They come to the battlefield in two-horse chariots driven by subordinates, and leap from these (sometimes stark naked) upon their startled foemen with loud shouts, brandishing their great swords. The severed head of a slain enemy might be taken away in triumph to decorate the victor's humble dwelling. Their barbarous rites include human sacrifice and vaticination from the convulsions of a dying victim. In their feasts they serve to war heroes the choice portions of meat; and they are charged with habits of gluttony and intemperance. But they are also a people fond of song and music, talented and capable of higher learning, and even their chiefs honor and obey the learned druids and bards.[4] Of the Celtic expansion the historian Gibbon characteristically remarks: "Spain, Gaul and Britain were peopled by the same hardy race of savages." But their civilized contemporaries thought of them with a certain respect, for their talents and aptitudes no less than for their prowess in war.[5]

Religion played a large part in the social life of the Celts. We have numerous early accounts of their religious practices and beliefs, and modern research, with intensive study of the legendary material and with the aid of archaeology, has shed fresh light in this area. But the study is handicapped by the absence of descriptive texts by any of the participants, and consequently the range of assured knowledge is strictly limited. While more than 400 names of deities have been identified, these include multiple local names for the same god; and not all the gods were revered by all the Celtic tribes. Caesar thought the religious notions of the Gauls "much like those of other nations." Like the Greeks and Romans, the Celts had gods to preside over many special human concerns. There were gods of fertility and of the fruitful earth as Mother; gods of the animal species familiarly known, such as the bull, the bear, the horse, and the stag; gods of rivers, groves, and meeting-places; gods of eloquence and poetry; gods of art and craftsmanship; gods of war and victory. In Ireland Dagda, whose name means "good for everything," was more than other deities a divine factotum to be called upon at need. The great god Lugus, or Lug, was honored in widely distant place names. Lugdunum (Lyons), Léon, Leiden, Liegnitz, and some places in Switzerland and Spain were named for him. His feast day, August 1, was kept as a harvest festival (Lughnasa) in Ireland until recent times. Moreover, since Lug was also known as Find, place names containing the syllable Vind such as Vindobona (Vienna) should be linked with the cult of this widely worshipped deity. But worshippers of Dagda or of Lug were not on their way to become monotheists. No god was more real to the Celt than the sid-folk or fairy beings who issued from caves or mounds on errands of bane or blessing to mankind.

The mythology was as complicated as life itself and as vivid as the Celtic imagination.

The religious rites were performed in the presence of the druids, who though recruited from the aristocratic layer of society were not a strictly hereditary caste. Men were admitted to the order only after long training in druidical schools where the youth were orally instructed in a body of traditional lore. Great numbers are reported to have attended these schools; but little is really known of them. In the early Irish tale, the *Tain bo Cualnge* (Cattle-Raid of Cooley) it is incidentally said that a famous druid, Cathbad, had 100 pupils, a modest number. More liberal estimates may be quite fanciful. The druids were not merely priests but personal and political advisers who spoke with authority. They were teachers of moral philosophy as well as of scientific and theological ideas. Poseidonius, Diodorus, and Caesar believed that they taught a doctrine of the transmigration of souls like that of Pythagoras, and to this belief Caesar attributed the indifference of Celtic warriors to death in battle. Recent studies, however, tend strongly to discount the classical ascription to the druids of a doctrine of transmigration. This is now regarded as a construction placed by Greek interpreters upon their reported teaching on immortality. They believed in survival after death, but they may have held no elaborate views of a future life or other recondite dogmas. They flourished before the art of writing came to their people, and though some of them seem to have written down fragmentary formulas using the Greek alphabet, we are handicapped by the lack of a single authentic sentence of their traditional teaching, the bulk of which was so great as to require many years of study. Pomponius Mela, a contemporary of St. Paul, states that "they profess to know the size and shape of the world, the movements of the heavens and the stars, and the will of the gods." It is to Pliny the Elder that we owe the earliest reference to their magical use of the mistletoe, which they climbed great oaks to obtain, detaching it with golden sickles.[6]

Druids were active functionaries in the tribal life and were often deeply involved in political affairs. In Gaul their annual convocations, attended by tribal deputies, framed decisions that had controlling force for public policy. In an age of frequent tribal discords, these synods may have been the one unitive element among all the tribes of Gaul. Something parallel to this is indicated in

Ireland and Britain. One of the few druids known to us by name is Divitiacus, brother of Dumnorix, a chief of the Aeduans, a powerful tribe in what was later Burgundy. Toward the Romans the two brothers took different courses of action. After temporary submission to Caesar, Dumnorix defected from him and was slain. Divitiacus, fearing German aggression as a greater danger to the tribe than Caesar's legions, firmly espoused the Roman cause and rendered to it indispensable services. Later in Italy he became well known in the intellectual circle of Cicero, who in his *De Divinatione* refers to him as professing the science of nature called by the Greeks "physiology" and as claiming power to predict events. Caesar's account of the wide activities of these Aeduan leaders makes it appear that both were able men and shows that a druid of high family could readily take a leading role in the gravest political matters.[7]

There may have been from early times differences in function between the druids of Gaul and those of Britain and Ireland. It is in Ireland that the order of bards (*fili*) is most clearly defined, and there also flourished the order of brehons or legal scholars. Within the Roman Empire druidism was virtually suppressed well before A.D. 100, but Ireland saw no suppressive imperial power that would destroy the native professional classes. It was the coming of Christianity that ended the supremacy of the Irish druids. The lives of certain Irish saints play up alleged confrontations between these and druids of local eminence, in which the latter are discomfited or have their lives snuffed out. The legends give St. Patrick miraculous powers by which he can unfailingly overmatch druidic opponents. Columba counters druid spells to gain control of the weather. Similar instances are numerous. But more authentic is the record that Columba was at one stage a pupil of a Christian bard, as is also the incident in which on revisiting Ireland he eloquently defended the Irish bards who were under indictment for their satires. His championship of their cause was suitably praised in bardic verse by Dallán Forgaill (below, p. 93). Columba is also said to have prayed, in a battle, to Christ as "my druid, Son of God."[8] But even if this were true it might not necessarily involve any approval of druids as he knew them. In general, it would appear that the druids (Latin, *magi*) were thought of by the Christians as in their priestly functions anti-Christian magicians, while the *fili* and *brehons* were made at home in the Christian society. This view presupposes, however, a degree of differentiation among these pre-Christian clerical orders that some would question.[9]

From the very beginning of the Christian infiltration of the Roman provinces it is inherently probable that some persons of the then widely distributed Celtic race were hearers of the Gospel. By the time of Christ's ministry there were in the Roman Army legions that had been recruited in Gaul, but it is not known that these were represented among the detachments stationed in Palestine. Whether the "churches of Galatia" to which Paul wrote an important epistle about A.D. 50 were situated in the Celtic northern area or in the southern cities of that wide province is still an unsettled issue in New Testament research. There is no mention in the epistle of any specific location. We know from the Book of Acts that, whether before or after Galatians was written, the Apostle preached in the populous cities of the south. Yet he addresses his readers as "Galatians" (3:1), suggesting that they were a people, not just the inhabitants of a province. From the early centuries the interpreters of the epistle associated it with the Celtic area. There the great Celtic stronghold had been Ancyra (Ankara) and it was in Paul's time the capital of the Roman province. But the traditional view has been vigorously assailed by some modern scholars, and the problem remains unresolved. We may no longer with assurance link St. Paul, as author of one of the early fragments of Christian literature, with a body of readers who were bilingual Celts. But in any case we may be sure that the Celtic-founded provincial capital, Ankara, came within the Christian mission area during Paul's lifetime. New Testament scholars are uncertain, too, about the mission field of Crescens who is mentioned in I Timothy 4:10 as having gone "into Galatia," or, with equal manuscript authority, "into Gaul." Western tradition made him the founder of the church of Lyons and Vienne.[10]

We know that Paul intended to visit Spain, and the supposition—vaguely supported by Clement of Rome in about A.D. 96—that he actually preached there is still held by some as a possibility, though it is not doubted that he was executed in Rome. Similarly the Apostle James was credited in seventh-century legend with a period of preaching in Spain though it is not questioned that he was martyred in Jerusalem. On the assumption that his relics were, miraculously or otherwise, brought to Compostella, it was supposed that his Spanish mission was in the area of Galicia. In this north-western hill country of Spain the Romans had encountered the Celtic Gallaci. It is incredible that James ever saw these highlanders. But since from Phoenician times the region was open to the world through the busy port of Corunna, an actual entry of Christianity there in apostolic times is by no means an impossibility.

Some element of Christianity is likely to have touched the Celtic population of Gaul much earlier than specific evidence shows. This is an inference from the active traffic between Italy and Gaul during the early spread of the Christian teaching and not from medieval legends that make France a mission field in apostolic times. Such legends are generally of late origin. From the eleventh century it was firmly believed that Mary and Lazarus of Bethany and Mary Magdalene brought the faith to Provence, and that St. Martial, supposedly a Jew who served Jesus and the apostles at the Lord's Supper, was sent from Rome by Peter to convert the Gauls; while the wholly legendary St. Angélique came to live and die at Soulac in the Médoc district on the Gironde. Many art representations helped to fix these fantasies in popular belief. It is reasonably conjectured that the actual entrance of Christianity into Gaul was by way of Marseilles and the Rhone valley, where the population was largely Greek. When this beginning was made cannot be known, but the Mediterranean traffic was such that it was a possibility in the first century. The fact that records from that time fail us does not compel us to deny this possibility.

The earliest reliably recorded Christian mission to Celts in western Europe is associated with the eminent church father Irenaeus, for many years active in southern Gaul until his death in about 202. He had been ordained by Bishop Pothinus before the time of the persecution at Lyons and Vienne in 177. In that year Irenaeus was in Rome, sent on an errand by his bishop, who was soon to be a martyr and whose successor Irenaeus became. He was then in his forties, and his mission to Celtic communities had probably begun at a somewhat earlier date. At any rate, in his new office he diligently pursued this mission. A native of Asia Minor and a friend of Polycarp of Smyrna, who had been a disciple of St. John, Irenaeus exemplifies the type of Christian scholar who is also animated by apostolic pastoral and missionary zeal. Not content to shepherd the Greek- and Latin-speaking community, he went with his message among the native tribes of the region.

Lyons had been an important center of Celtic paganism until the Romans made it an administrative capital and headquarters for the emperor cult. Its name, "Lugdunum," means "stronghold of the god Lug." Under a Roman government hostile to Christianity, Irenaeus carried the faith to this populous Celtic area, no doubt amid discomforts and dangers. In the preface to his best-known work, *Against Heresies*, written about 190, he adds to a conventional disclaimer of rhetorical skill the excuse that he is among Celtic people using a barbaric tongue.

Prominent among the Lyons martyrs of 177 was a young Gaul, Vettius Epagathus, who seems to have come from the territory of the Bituriges between the Cher and the Loire. This strong tribe had long held sway in an extensive area between Bourges and Bordeaux. Conquered in bitter fighting by Caesar, the Bituriges had obtained the designation "liberi," and were permitted to exercise some self-government. During the trials at Lyons, Vettius behaved with great boldness, as appears from the letter of the survivors recorded by Eusebius.[11] Here he is highly praised for his courageous example and for the love of God and neighbor previously exemplified in his life, young though he was. He loudly protested against the "savagery" of the governor, became "exceedingly angry" at the irregularity of the proceedings, and was eager to defend his brethren. Asked if he too were a Christian, he loudly declared his faith. It may perhaps be assumed that the steadfast Blandina, young household servant of another martyr, was of Gaulish origin. She was among those who, not being Roman citizens, were thrown to wild beasts. What other Celtic Christians suffered among the 48 known victims at Lyons and Vienne cannot be known. The text of the martyr acts was written in Greek and the form of a name given in it does not prove ethnic origin. A short time afterward occurred the martyrdom of St. Symphorian at Autun, former capital of the Aeduans and by this time the site of an important Latin school. The statement in the *Life of St. Symphorian* that as he went to his death his Christian mother called out to him words of encouragement in Celtic speech (*voce gallica*) points to an early planting of the faith in the Celtic uplands of eastern France.[12]

From a notable passage in Gregory of Tours it appears that in about A.D. 250, numerous bishoprics were established in Gaul. Gregory states that at the beginning of the reign of Decius seven bishops were consecrated in Rome by Pope Fabian and severally commissioned to Tours, Arles, Narbonne, Toulouse, Paris, Auverne, and Limoges.[13] Of these, Paris is the most northerly and Tours is nearest to Brittany, the most permanently Celtic part of France. Gatianus, the first bishop of Tours, according to his remote successor, Gregory, suffered much hostility and hardship during an episcopate of forty years but won enough converts to form a church. The bishop sent to Paris was Dionysius. It was natural that later legend-makers should, with characteristic indifference to chronology, identify him with his namesake the Areopagite, Paul's Athenian convert (Acts 17:34). From the time of Charlemagne this identification passed for history, and served to provide the French church with an enviable claim to antiquity. Well before the ninth century the Areopagite was fully accredited to the medieval mind as the author of the influential pseudo-Dionysian writings. When Paris became the capital of Western learning and theology, what could be more fitting than to celebrate its Christian founder as the Athenian believer and presumed scholar? The story of the bishop's martyrdom on Montmartre was embroidered with the (not unique) miracle of the severed head carried by the martyr to his burial place—where stands the church of St. Denis. The Dionysius of A.D. 250 may indeed have been the founder of the episcopate, though it is most unlikely that he was the first Christian there. The presbyter Eleutherius and the deacon Rusticus are said to have been martyred with him, but it is possible that they suffered "a little earlier or later." Graveyards containing Christian burials of undetermined early date have been found in the Paris area.[14]

According to Gregory, another of the seven bishops sent by Pope Fabian, Saturninus of Toulouse, suffered martyrdom. But each of them seems to have labored effectively for sufficient time to form a permanent community of Christians. Gregory selects for high praise Martial of Limoges. The Spanish poet Prudentius, in *Peristephanon*, a work of about A.D. 400, mentions as a martyr another of the seven, Paulus of Narbonne.[15] Amid such perils, schism also troubled the Gallic church. At the beginning of the pontificate of Stephen I (254–57), Cyprian of Carthage wrote to urge the pope to excommunicate Marcianus, bishop of Arles, as a Novatianist.[16] Apparently the schismatic prelate had soon replaced Trophimus, the Arles appointee of Gregory's list. As a contemporary document Cyprian's letter has an authority that can hardly be claimed for Gregory's late sixth-century account. Gregory's scheme of seven papally appointed bishops well distributed geographically may seem too neat to be other than somebody's invention; but who can say that it was not Pope Fabian's own well-thought-out project? Gregory's unadorned plainness and his avoidance of marvels in the passage tend to confirm its credibility.

But even if it is taken as reliable, the passage is all too meager to form a picture of third-century Christianity in Gaul; and indeed no such picture can be drawn. It is unlikely that Gregory's seven form anything like a complete roster of the Gallic bishops at mid-century. Estimates based on local tradition raise the number to about thirty. Moreover, as in other parts of the Empire, many places of worship were in all probability being formed all the while in rural districts outside the episcopal towns. We may assume that the membership of the worshipping groups in such localities embraced a large percentage of native Celts. This would accord with the general trend in the society of Gaul, in which the Celtic population with surprising alacrity acquired the essentials of the Roman Latin culture. In the churches Latin and Celtic folk readily commingled. In most areas the Gaulish language rapidly yielded place to Latin, the language of the schools. In their eagerness to pursue Latin culture, Gauls assumed Latin names. Their freedom to participate in the schools and in public affairs facilitated the blending of the two peoples. Thus in most of Gaul those factors that might have nurtured a church distinctively Celtic were obliterated. Instead, the Christian Celts of Gaul were from the first incorporated in what was becoming the imperial and papal church of the West. In the pages to follow the references to Gaul will be largely confined to matters connected with the travels and missions of Irish and British monks on the Continent. Any attempt to trace the upgrowth of the church of France would be extraneous to our purpose. Except the large racial element in its membership, little that is recognizably Celtic can be found in it.[17]

There is one important exception to this generalization: ancient Armorica, which became Brittany. In this province the imperial authority was never secure, and the predominantly Celtic character of the population was confirmed in the fifth century by a large migration from Britain. The church of Brittany was for centuries far more closely linked with that of Wales and Cornwall than with the hierarchical church of France and was a minor member in good standing of the family of Celtic churches. Its history will be sketched in chapter 9.

Two | Christianity in Britain to the Anglo-Saxon Invasions

"I FROM OUT this northern island, sundered once from all the human race" wrote Tennyson, remembering Vergil's First Eclogue, which casually refers to the Britons as "quite severed from all the world." We are told by Dio Cassius that when Aulus Plautius was under orders to invade Britain his soldiers protested that they were asked to "make war beyond the habitable world." But historians of our time present ample evidence of traffic between continental ports and the harbors of Britain and Ireland from remote ages. With little notice by their learned contemporaries, fearless sailors made the seas their pathways in small ships laden with ornaments, utensils, and wine from the Mediterranean, gold from Irish mines, copper from Wales, tin from Cornwall, iron ore from the Severn valley, hides of cattle and deer from Britain and Ireland, and Baltic amber. In very early Christian times the Roman rulers of Britain brought that island into the cultural as well as the military and economic nexus of the wide Empire, making it subject to the religious currents of the age.

Roman Britain (ca. A.D. 43–410) was roughly England and Wales, with a shifting fringe of southern Scotland which at its fullest expansion reached to the Forth and the Clyde. Tacitus, writing shortly before A.D. 100 notes that the Britons bore their burdens cheerfully, being subjected but not enslaved, and this may be taken as a valid generalization for the entire period of the Roman occupation. Two walls were constructed to protect this Roman province from the unconquered northern Celtic tribes: Hadrian's Wall, laboriously built of stone in the third decade of the second century stretching from the Tyne to the Solway, and the earthen Wall of Antoninus Pius built in the 140s, extending from the Forth to the Clyde. The more northern barrier could not be defended; but after a disastrous incursion, that of Hadrian was consolidated by the Emperor Septimius Severus who died at York in 211. Local disturbances within the province were not infrequent, but these were kept in check by means of garrisoned forts linked by an elaborate network of military roads. In the fourth century a new chain of forts was established to protect the southeast coasts from Saxon invaders. Towns were growing up in which ex-soldiers and civilians made themselves comfortable in Roman fashion, building spacious houses, baths and temples, and providing schools in which many Britons mingled with their Roman masters and became Latin-speaking. But the Romans were not given time enough to complete the task of Romanization, and much that was Celtic besides the population strain existed still. Certain British tribes had won a recognized identity and constituted units of local government within the province. The enduring strength of the Celtic element is shown by the simple fact that when the legions were withdrawn, the common use of Latin soon ceased and the native Brythonic speech again prevailed.

In view of all the possibilities, it need not surprise us that we cannot know how or when Christianity first appeared in Britain. The recorded data for the early spread of Christianity are almost everywhere so meager that we can only resort to conjecture. We are justified in assuming that in Britain as elsewhere there was much early Christian activity that remains undocumented. St. Paul has high praise for Epaphras as the teacher of Christianity to the Colossians (Col. 1:7), but gives us no narrative of this pioneer mission. There must have been many an Epaphras whose name and work went wholly unrecorded. Apart from any purposeful mission, there is every probability that in the ordinary course of interprovincial migration, Christians would be among those who were constantly entering Britain and would early form a recognizable element in civilian communities that gathered about military and administrative posts there. We should also make allowance for the possibility of planned missions to the province of which we have neither record nor legend, while treating warily those invented tales of origins circulated in the Middle Ages, in which some credible items may have been preserved.

The statement of Gildas that the Christian religion entered Britain in the reign of Tiberius (who died in A.D. 37) is not verifiable, but when we realize the busy traffic on Roman roads and western seas, we can hardly think it certainly false. Christians of Tiberius' time were too early to be converts of St. Paul, but according to the Book of Acts there were many of them, and "they that were scattered abroad went everywhere preaching the word" (Acts 8:4). In A.D. 57 Pomponia Graecina, British wife of the

famed Roman commander Aulus Plautius, who had gone with her husband from Britain to Rome about A.D. 50, was there accused of a "foreign superstition." That her heterodoxy in Roman eyes was Christianity is mere conjecture; quite as likely it was some druidic cult practice. More probability attaches to the case of Sergia Paula, wife of Gaius Fronto, commander at York in A.D. 79. She was supposedly the daughter of Sergius Paulus the proconsul of Cyprus, who listened favorably to Paul and Barnabas at Paphos and became a believer (Acts 13:7, 12). The apostles Peter and Paul were both taken to Britain by the legend makers, and Caesare Baronius in his celebrated *Ecclesiastical Annals* (1601) under date of A.D. 58 affirms on the authority of Symeon Metaphrastes (ca. 950) that while the Gospel was being carried by others through eastern provinces Peter enlightened the West, and in proclaiming the Faith went "as far as to the Britons [*usque ad Britannos*]."[1]

The well-known legend, employed by the English representatives to confound the French at the Council of Constance in 1417, that Joseph of Arimathea was sent by St. Philip to Britain in A.D. 63 as head of a band of missionaries, and that he established a church at Glastonbury, erecting an oratory of wattles and daub, is first recorded in the twelfth century. It appears in an anonymous insertion of the work of William of Malmesbury entitled *The Antiquity of the Church of Glastonbury* (ca. 1126). William himself, in writing this book, had access to local monastic sources, and the unnamed author of the Joseph story may also have gleaned traditional material similarly available. Without regarding Joseph as the founder, Malmesbury was convinced that the church at Glastonbury was the earliest to be planted in Britain. After his time the Glastonbury legend became increasingly fantastic and complicated. Features of it are the story of the Holy Grail, the identification of Glastonbury with Arthur's Avalon, the miraculously flowering thornbush, and the residence of St. Patrick there. Patrick is represented as reorganizing an earlier-formed ascetic community into a monastery with himself as abbot. Pilgrimage to Glastonbury was popular and has been intermittently maintained to our century.

The antiquities of Glastonbury have attracted much study. About 56 B.C., during the Roman invasion of Gaul, the area was occupied by refugees from Armorica (Brittany). There was a small population in two villages residing in crannogs (artificial islands). Keepers of cattle and sheep, they used wheeled carts for hauling field crops and were skilled makers not only of implements and weapons but also of ornamented bowls and utensils. With the coming of Christianity, Christian and pagan themes began to appear together in their ornamentation. Some of their wares were exported to settlements in Britain and Ireland. Although the Joseph legend must be held to be fiction, Glastonbury, from very ancient times an active seaport on the Severn estuary, was well situated to be the entrance point for a new religion into western Britain. It was most likely "trade-borne," as Margaret Deanesly suggests, and may have come as early as the second or even the first century. Miss Deanesly notes "the curious appositeness of the site selected by tradition as that of the oldest church in Britain."

At Constance the English spokesmen, claiming Joseph of Arimathea, were one-up on the French bishops whose boasted Dionysius had to do with Paul, not with Jesus himself. Similarly, in the Reformation the prevailing name of Joseph was invoked by Archbishop Parker in his *De antiquitate ecclesiae Britanniae* (1572) in disproof of the papal origin of the Church of England.[2]

Reliable written sources of Christianity in Britain before Constantine are meager, and the archaeological evidence is still not abundant. Bede was wholly misguided in saying that a British king named Lucius in the year 156 sought and obtained Christian baptism from Eleutherus, bishop of Rome.[3] Eleutherus was not then bishop, and there never was a king of Britain named Lucius. The story comes from the paragraph on Eleutherus (170–85) in the *Liber pontificalis*, written about 550, and apparently involves a confusion with the legend of Abgarus of Ephesus. The date is, however, set in an era when Christianity may well have made a substantial beginning among those Latin-speaking Britons who had traffic with the occupying Romans.

After the conquests of Agricola (78–85) and the building of the Wall of Hadrian (142) a time of relative stability ensued favorable to the upgrowth of elemental Christian organization. We cannot dismiss as fanciful the famous boast of Tertullian: "In all parts of Spain, among the diverse nations of the Gauls, in regions of the Britons beyond Roman sway but subjected to Christ . . . the name of Christ now reigns."[4] This is part of a paragraph listing about twenty-five areas or peoples, with the addition, "and many islands unknown to us," into which Christianity had penetrated. The treatise was written between the years 200 and 208. Allowing for the exuberance of Tertullian, we must also remember that he was one of the best-informed persons of his time. His "Britannorum inacessa Romanis loca" is a studied phrase. It may well represent a report he had heard from a Christian traveler, conceivably one who had been himself displaced from somewhere in the Scottish lowlands where the Romans had then recently lost a wide territory to the Picts. In A.D. 196 Pictish forces drove far southward into the province past the Wall of Hadrian and into what later became northern England. The territory overrun had been "Britannorum loca" under Roman rule for two generations, during which the spread of Christianity in the Empire was a feature of the times. It is highly credible that Christian groups had arisen in the environs of Roman settlements there, that these survived the defeat and departure of the legions, and that Tertullian was making a brief allusion to ascertained facts. Since the Pictish campaign of 196, the "places" were "inaccessa" not necessarily in the literal sense of "unreached" but, as often translated, "inaccessible" to Roman armies. In affirming the existence of Christianity on the frontier of the province, Tertullian undoubtedly assumed its existence within the province itself.

This impression is supported by a rhetorical question in a homily of Origen[5] which implies that in Britain Christianity had become a unifying force: "When before the coming of Christ did the land of Britain agree on the worship of one God?" This is vague enough, but at least he had, and assumed in his readers, a settled impression that a considerable community of Christians had arisen in the province. Eusebius in a little-known work, *Evangelical Demonstrations,* states that "some apostles passed over the ocean to what are called the British isles"[6] but this reads like a mere echo of some fragment of early legend. And Bede's assertion that the Britons kept the faith in peace from its introduction to the time of Diocletian is a mere flourish to round out his erroneous Lucius story.

Bede supplies no names of British Christians prior to the era of Diocletian (284–305), during whose reign he places the martyrdom of St. Alban of Verulam. Of this incident he gives substantial details with some ornament of miracle. Among Bede's sources here is the *De excidio Britanniae* of Gildas, who admits uncertainty regarding the date and has no real identification of the locality. The date usually assigned in accordance with Bede's account is 304; but at that time Constantius Chlorus, whose non-persecution principles were well known, and whom Bede himself elsewhere commends for his "singular clemency," was Caesar of Gaul and Britain. How Diocletian contrived to override his tolerant policy in a distant province remains unexplained, although scholars have pointed to similar severities in Spain where Constantius ruled through a deputy. Bede lays direct responsibility on an unnamed "wicked prince," obviously local. But even if we dismiss doubts of the historicity of the martyrdom, we cannot trust Bede's dating. Suggestions have been made to set the date at a time before the promotion of Constantius (293), although Diocletian's real persecution began later, or to carry it back to the reign of Decius (249–51), where it would fit well into the general picture. Some would now dismiss as a fabrication the statement of Constantius of Lyons that the visiting bishops Germanus and Lupus in 428 made a pious pilgrimage to the tomb of Alban at Verulam. But it remains certain that Alban had long been venerated at Verulam (St. Alban's) in Bede's time, and we can hardly doubt that he was a martyr of the era of imperial persecution. It seems unnecessary to discard the main features of Bede's detailed account—that he was a householder who sheltered a Christian cleric through whose witness he was converted from paganism, and that he tried to save his guest by himself wearing the cleric's hooded cloak (caracula). Nor is it in the least degree incredible that his bearing before the judge was haughty to the degree that he refused to declare his ancestry and family name yet unhesitatingly announced himself a Christian. In martyrdoms such conduct was hardly exceptional. It is usually assumed that he was a Roman, but his refusal to disclose his family connection may suggest that he was a Briton. The district around Verulam had been occupied by Belgae before Caesar's time, and he may well have been of Belgic stock. In any case we must regard Alban only as the most distinguished among numerous martyrs in different parts of the province at the same period. Gildas and Bede alike refer to widespread persecution, with martyrs of both sexes. Bede supports this by a quotation from the poet Venantius Fortunatus of Poitiers (d. 609), and both authors name two of the sufferers, Aaron and Julius, citizens of Caerleon-upon-Usk, who like Alban were tortured and beheaded.[7]

The probability that the persecution was fairly extensive supports the conjecture that Christianity had become a noticeable element in Roman Britain well before the era of Constantine. The absence of substantial evidence in the nature of ecclesiastical buildings and Christian art objects does nothing to prove the nonexistence of Christian churches. We may be sure that early Christian buildings in Britain were not of durable structure. Christians might be fairly numerous without being rich enough, or secure enough in the community, to erect and adorn great buildings. If they were Celts, they had no ancestral tradition of large edifices for worship; the pagan Britons had worshipped not in temples but in groves. From the megalithic era to Roman times structural remains other than fortifications are never imposing.

But soon after Constantine's edict of liberation (313), churches arose bearing some resemblance in materials and architecture to the shrines of Mithra and other pagan Roman temples. At Lullingstone in Kent, about 337–40, Christian and pagan groups seem to have shared for worship one building of modest size, the Christians using the upper story. The most complete known British church foundation of Roman times is that of Silchester in Hampshire, the Roman Calleva. The Christian use of this building has been placed beyond doubt by the piecing together of wall paintings found in the debris of the fallen structure and, notably, by the Alpha-Omega symbol on a leaden seal with the Chi-Rho emblem set between the Greek letters. The church was apparently built in the fourth century, and may have been one of the earliest of British stone churches. The main building was only 30 feet by 10, but the length was extended by a semi-circular western apse and an eastern narthex, and there were short transepts, bringing the overall measurements to 42 by 33 feet. It stood in the heart of the little city, adjacent to the southeast corner of the forum. In structure it shows a marked resemblance to the Mithraeum, which was one of the four pagan temples in that community of perhaps 2,000 inhabitants. In a field beside the village of Hinton St. Mary in Dorset a mosaic pavement 28 by 19 feet was discovered in 1963; it may now be seen in the British Museum. It shows an impressive combination of pagan and Christian themes. There are other instances in which this artistic syncretism appears, often clearly with intent to make the pagan mythological figures favor Christian beliefs. In the pavement pattern the representation of Bellerophon slaying the Chimaera, set to match the Chi-Rho symbol behind the head and upraised arm of Christ, bears a suggestion of Christ's victory over death.[8]

The church among the Roman Britons took its place with the continental churches through the attendance of British bishops and other clergy in various fourth-century synods. When the Donatist schism arose in North Africa and threatened to disrupt the church in the western provinces, Constantine the Great, realizing the perils involved, called a council at Arles to settle the controversy (A.D. 314). In addition to the bishops of North Africa, bishops and other clergy representing thirty-five sees in Gaul, Britain, Spain, Italy, and Dalmatia were present. The council adopted a series of twenty-two firmly phrased disciplinary canons. The signatories include three bishops from Britain—Eborius of York, Restitutus of London, and Adelphius, whose see may have been (depending on readings of the codex in which the document appears) either Lincoln or Caerleon-upon-Usk, or, as some now believe, Colchester. A presbyter named Sacerdos and a deacon named Arminius were also in the deputation from Britain.[9] It would be wholly unjustifiable to assume that Britain had only three bishops at the time. The bishops of Gaul then numbered thirty-six, of whom only sixteen were present at the synod, and it is reasonable to suppose that the three British bishops constituted an even smaller proportion of their colleagues. Since only one year had then elapsed from the Edict of Milan, the episcopate must have come into existence in Britain, as in Gaul, at a considerably earlier period than that of Constantine. We are safe in assuming that in Britain, as elsewhere in the Empire, Christianity had gradually been embraced by increasing numbers, despite opposition and danger from environing paganism, until by about A.D. 300 an organized church had taken shape in most parts of the province. The robed clergyman who appears in the Alban incident is not to be thought of as a figure new and strange.

We are given no information of early episcopal consecrations in Britain or for British sees. The pioneer bishops may have been designated and consecrated in Gaul or in Rome. The names of those who were at Arles are in Latin form, but this tells us nothing of their racial origin, and we have no knowledge of their personal histories. The intimate relations of the British church with that of Gaul, and specifically with the diocese of Auxerre, in the fifth century, may have been anticipated in the fourth, but nothing can be affirmed of this.

There is evidence that certain British bishops made the journey to Sardica (Sophia) to attend the council held there in 343. We know too that a considerable number of them attended the Council of Ariminum (Rimini) in 359, an unhappy chapter in the Arian controversy. Sulpicius Severus made note of the information conveyed to him personally by a member of this synod that the bishops from Gaul and Britain declined the payment of their expenses from the imperial treasury, with the exception of three of those from Britain who by reason of their lack of funds (*inopia proprii*) and not wishing to burden church friends with the charges, accepted the public provision. Sulpicius has heard criticism of this, but expresses his approval of their poverty, apparently thinking of this as the voluntary poverty of ascetic piety. But Sulpicius is perhaps importing into a pre-monastic era the sentiments of his ascetic generation. We should at least remember that at Ariminum Britons were farther from home than most of the other bishops, and that the sessions lasted from May till October. It is not remarkable that three of them became embarrassed for funds. The fact that the other British members paid their own expenses by choice seems to dispose of the supposition by some writers that the acceptance of help by the three should be taken as evidence that the British church was impoverished.[10]

The later fourth century saw the rise of Western monasticism with Martin of Tours (d. 397) as its eminent leader, whom St. Ninian, a Briton by race, is alleged to have visited before founding his mission at Whithorn in Galloway. To mention Ninian is to enter a realm of historic uncertainty and debate. Our earliest notice of him is a brief statement by Bede written about 731, three centuries after Ninian's lifetime. Other Ninian materials of Bede's century are: a now lost account of his life and miracles, thought by some scholars to have been written originally in Irish; a document dependent on this, entitled *Miracula Nynie Episcopi*; and a poem on St. Ninian apparently written at Whithorn. These materials were available to St. Aelred (d. 1167), Cistercian abbot of Rievaulx in Yorkshire, whose uncritical and imaginative *Life of Ninian* is, in the words of its editor, A. P. Forbes, "almost worthless as a historical tract." An illuminating study by Nora Chadwick points to some probabilities regarding origins and motivation of the eighth-century items.[11] Bringing the Ninian passages into comparison with the two slightly earlier accounts of the life of Patrick, written in the interests of Armagh, and with that of Kentigern, which asserts the claims of Glasgow, Mrs. Chadwick presents strong evidence for the view that the *Life, Poem*, and *Miracula* of Ninian were ecclesiastical and political propaganda pieces designed to promote the leadership of the newly established see of Whithorn as against the claims of Iona. This was a policy of Bernicia, and it was adopted by King Nechtan IV of the Southern Picts, who was instrumental in reducing Iona to submission (718) on the issue of the substitution of Roman for Celtic usages (see below, pp. 117–18). As for Aelred, he was brought up at the court of King David I of Scotland, and was no doubt impressed by David's program of restoring or creating bishoprics in his realm. His aim is to magnify Ninian's person and work, and for this he employs eloquent and fervid language with little basis of fact. Ninian goes forth to rescue the Picts from Satan, draws throngs of old and young to belief and baptism, ordains presbyters and consecrates bishops, builds basilicas and plants monasteries, and finally returns to Candida Casa to live out his days in tranquility, "perfect in sanctity and glorious in miracles." All this without a single place-name in the Pictish area. If Ninian research has been in our time a tournament of scholars, this is due to the inexplicitness and tendentiousness of the written sources.[12]

Bede's few sentences on Ninian contain the substantive statements that he was a bishop, by race a Briton, and trained at Rome, that his "White House" (*Candida Casa*) was so named because it was built of stone, a thing unfamiliar among the Britons, and that his preaching caused the Southern Picts to abandon idolatry. Bede inserts at the outset a phrase which makes us feel that he is not very certain of his facts: *"ut perhibent,"* "as they say." His informant seems to have been Pecthelm, bishop of Whithorn, who is elsewhere referred to by Bede as reciting to him personally the troubled vision of an unrepentant theyn. It is unfortunate that the Englishmen Bede and Pecthelm had so little interest in matters concerning Britons and Picts that they failed to search out Ninian's story or explain the geographical setting of his work. Since Whithorn was surrounded by Britons, the "Southern Picts" converted by Ninian's preaching were evidently somewhere else. Bede does tell us that they were separated from the Northern Picts, whom

Columba later evangelized, by a range of steep and forbidding mountains. It has been suggested that he was misled by a map of the world emanating from the school of the second century mathematician and geographer Ptolemy of Alexandria, in which Scotland is seen leaning far eastward so that the true east becomes south and west becomes north. But this may not have been the case. Ninian's Picts probably dwelt north of the Forth and south of that rugged highland belt known as the Mounth, which extends eastward to Aberdeenshire from the north-south range which Adomnan of Iona called Drumalban, the Spine of Britain.

While the written sources fail to give specific details of Ninian's mission, the meager archaeological evidence has been closely examined, though with varying results, and much has been made of church dedications to Ninian as witness to extended missionary travels and church plantings. The reputation of Ninian has been brought into collision with that of Columba of Iona, who has been traditionally regarded as the principal founder of Scottish Christianity. G. A. Frank Knight, in a two-volume work which appeared in 1933, professed to show that more than 80 men and women who were missionaries before Columba "covered the land with hundreds of churches," and on the basis of early crosses and inscriptions, he ascribed to Ninian many places of labor. But Knight's elaborate work has been judged tendentious and has no acceptance among scholars. More respect is paid to the studies of W. Douglas Simpson as champion of Ninian's apostolate. In two impressive books (1935, 1940) and other writings, Simpson made masterly use of crosses, inscriptions, and dedications, brought to light by archaeologists, to trace the supposed footsteps of Ninian in Pictish Scotland, reaching into the northern countries of Caithnesshire and Aberdeenshire, and to claim his influence upon the beginnings of Christianity in the Orkney and Shetland Islands. Consistently with this enlargement of Ninian's mission, Simpson would reduce what in his view is the greatly overrated work of Columba, whom he represents as "a politician first and a missionary afterwards." For that matter, he does not detach Ninian from the political world, either. The inception of his work is connected with the attempted revival of the rule of the now Christian Roman power in the time of Stilicho, who made southern Scotland again for a short time firmly Roman. The legions, as we know, departed in about 410, but Ninian's work continued till about 432.

Simpson's construction of the history has been assailed both by admirers of Columba and by initially uncommitted scholars. John MacQueen, in a small but well-documented book (1961), rejects the connection of Ninian's mission with the many sites associated with him by Simpson. Father Paul Grosjean, in a series of articles in *Acta Bollandiana* (1944–68), has learnedly deflated the expanded image of Ninian. The searching critique of the sources by Nora K. Chadwick, referred to above, while not, like Simpson's work, concerned with archaeological evidence, tends to undercut his thesis. A more recent study by A. C. Thomas contains an adverse treatment of Simpson's theory. Thomas reminds us that Bede does not call Ninian the first bishop of Whithorn and, with support from archaeology, gives the impression that Christianity was spreading in the region before his coming. Father Grosjean calls in question even Bede's short notice of Ninian, in important particulars. That Ninian was trained in Rome he regards as "almost certainly imaginative propaganda from the Anglian clergy." He points out that Bede did not say that Ninian himself dedicated his center to St. Martin; such a dedication could not, he believes, have taken place, as alleged, at the time of Martin's death (397), since Martin was not a martyr. (In the *Miracula* iv it is said that Ninian "dedicated it to the Lord with the name of Martin.")[13]

It is not Simpson's research that is discounted, but his rather strained construction of the evidence. At present Ninian's reputation is perhaps more impaired than brightened by the controversy. But it would be unjustifiable to dismiss him as an inconsequential figure. He remains for us the most eminent pioneer of the Christian mission in southern Scotland.

Apart from Bede's mention of St. Martin, a connection of Ninian with Martin may not be wholly legendary. Martin (d. 397) was very influential in his late years, and was active in missions among Celtic tribes in the diocese of Tours. His younger fellow bishop and personal friend, Victricius of Rouen, imitated his work among Celts in northern France and in about 395, as he himself relates, paid an extended visit to Britain on some mission of ecclesiastical pacification. He reflected Martin's interest in monasticism. Whether, as has been suggested, he had something to do with Ninian's foundation at Whithorn or not, his admiration for Martin probably found frequent expression in British church circles and helped to awaken there an interest in monasticism, and in Martin as its famous pioneer in Celtic Gaul.[14] It is uncertain whether we should regard Ninian as a monk. But it is clear from Irish sources that a monastery and center of learning flourished at Whithorn in the fifth and sixth centuries under his successors. It was called, like that of St. Martin, "the great monastery," and by the Irish, "Rosnat," from the "little cape" on which it stood, and was a training school for monastic missionaries and monastic founders.[15] Ninian's eighth-century poetic panegyrist makes him the founder of many communities of monks that were still flourishing in the poet's time; but no foundations directly by Ninian can be identified. Some Irish monks of note, however, were certainly trained at Rosnat; a few of these will be mentioned in our next chapter. Within Scotland, Caranoc—Ninian's pupil and successor whose name remains in Curnoch, Stirlingshire—is thought to have engaged in missions to Pictland and to Dalaradia, the Pictish district of Ulster (below, p. 91). More widely celebrated in dedications is St. Blane, who for some time labored in Strathclyde. Thus it remains that if Ninian was not the pioneer of Christianity for all Scotland, he may at least be regarded as a leader of immense importance for the Celtic churches.

The weakening and final extinction of the Roman power in Britain gave opportunity to the forces of disruption and invasion. The fifth century has usually been regarded as an era of bitter strife and anguish for the people of the former imperial province. From the disorderly materials offered by Gildas, Bede, the Anglo-Saxon Chronicle, and the *Historia Brittonum* of Nennius, and with eager attention to archaeological findings, our diligent historians have endeavored to present the events in sequence, but we follow them with unsure steps. Scots from Ireland and Picts from the north harried those parts of the province to which they had access. The extent of their depredations is variously assessed. However, most of the country was under the fairly secure and orderly rule of independent British chiefs who were called *reges*, or kings. The term apparently corresponds to the Welsh word *teyrn*, which later came to be rendered into Latin as *tyrannus*, a word of similar form. Possibly the so-called *tyranni* in the sixth century were not thought of as tyrants in our sense of that word, though a number of them were charged with misrule. The shadowy figures of Vortigern, Ambrosius Aurelianus, and Arthur, magnified in Welsh legend, seem to represent political and military personages who tried to rally the

Britons to their own defense. It would seem that after some success in this they were assailed by increased invading forces, and as a desperate measure Vortigern, with the consent of other princes, invited Saxons from the Elbe basin to join the Britons in defense against their insular enemies. Gildas, whose *Downfall of Britain* refers gloomily to these events, blames Vortigern, but in the circumstances his policy may not have been unpatriotic. The first coming of Saxons was probably not later than 428. After some years as allies they became hostile, demanded higher rewards, and began to dispossess the Britons and push them westward. They were in turn attacked by Ambrosius, in legend the sometimes unfriendly nephew of Vortigern, and were hurled back toward the eastern coast. Meanwhile, menaced and displaced Britons began to migrate in considerable numbers to Armorica (Brittany), where in time they subjected the earlier population to their sway. The main invasion of Angles, Saxons, and Jutes was still to come, perhaps not suddenly but as a series of armed immigrations through nearly half a century, roughly 449 to shortly before 500. Arthur is the legendary victor in a series of twelve battles culminating in that of Mons Badonicus, which J. R. Morris now dates within the 490s.[16] It is to the Welsh author Nennius that we owe much of what is known or guessed about Arthur, who became in legend the most celebrated folk hero of the Britons, but whose true character and precise role remain undetermined. It does not appear that the Celtic population was exterminated in any considerable part of Britain. Gildas speaks of slaughter indeed, but also of enslavement, migration, and retreat to mountain regions. It was only in areas roughly comprising, in later geographical terms, Wales, Cornwall, and Strathclyde, that Britons remained in control. Before 500, many Scots from Ireland infiltrated into these areas. They became a dominant element in parts of South Wales, and, moving in force into southern Scotland, they wrested from the Picts an area almost identical with Argyleshire, to form the kingdom of Dalriada. Strathclyde occupied an embarrassed position with these Scots on the northeast, Picts on the north across the Forth, and the still pagan Angles of Northumbria to the east and south.

That the British church had in early times a reputation for orthodoxy is attested by Chrysostom, Jerome, Bede, and others. But early in the fifth century, it produced the most famous of all western heretics. The life story of Pelagius cannot be told, but we have such writings by him and contemporary references to him as to bring him into clearer light than the political leaders. He was evidently a man of high abilities and good learning, though in what degree he obtained his learning in Britain cannot be known. It is certain that he was born in Roman Britain late in the fourth century and that as a young man he traveled widely,[17] residing for some time at Rome and later visiting Egypt and Palestine. The fact that Jerome in the prologue to his *Commentary on Jeremiah* refers contemptuously to Pelagius as *"pultibus Scottorum praegravatus"* (stuffed with the porridge of the Scots) has led some to suppose that he was an Irishman, but it is known that for Jerome the word "Scot" was sometimes merely a term of abuse and that he thought of Britain and Ireland alike as remote and barbarous nations. Pelagius had as his ally in controversy Coelestius, who on fallacious evidence has been regarded as an Irishman. In the year 413, according to the chronicler Prosper of Aquitaine, Pelagius uttered his "dogma against the grace of Christ," and in 429 Agricola, son of a Pelagian bishop Severianus, corrupted the British churches with his heresy. Bede adds to this that the orthodox Britons were unable to confute the Pelagian teachers and sought aid from the bishops of Gaul. The latter, holding a council, deputed two of their number, Germanus of Auxerre and Lupus of Troyes, to visit the British church and contend with the heretics in public debate (429). Following the *Life of Germanus* by Constantius of Lyons (ca. 480), Bede describes the miraculous escape of the ship that bore the emissaries to Britain, and a great assemblage of men, women, and children that gathered to hear them. After the Pelagians had addressed the multitude with "empty words," Germanus and Lupus, "pouring out torrents of eloquence," confounded the heretics and won the verdict of the people. When orthodoxy had, according to Constantius, been thus vindicated, the visiting bishops went to St. Alban's tomb, where Germanus left precious relics and took away a portion of the martyr's dust still miraculously red with his blood. Apart from the typical miracle, there are other improbable features of Bede's account. We learn of no part taken by British bishops in a great debate on heresy, but Bede, following Constantius, makes the decision rest on the people's acclaim (*populus judex; populus arbiter*). The story continues with the fascinating incident of the "Alleluia Victory" just after Easter. Germanus, who has been plagued by a sprained foot, becomes the inspirer and commander of the Britons when they are assailed by joint forces of Scots and Saxons. Germanus conceals chosen soldiers, who are newly baptized converts, on mountainsides around a valley, with instructions to shout "Alleluia" in unison at his signal. As the enemies move confidently in, the thunder of the shout, re-echoed from enclosing hills, strikes such sudden terror through their ranks that they drop their weapons and take to ignominious flight.[18] Some plausibility is lent to the role of Germanus as military commander by the fact that in early manhood he had been a Roman dux, an administrator with military duties, in Armorica and Aquitania. And perhaps he had expert advice about the terrifying echoes of a sonorous word in a deep Welsh glen!

Our chronicler Prosper, however, attributes the initiative in combatting Pelagianism in Britain and commissioning Germanus (Lupus being omitted) not to a Gallic council but to Pope Celestine I (422–32), the chief papal contender against this heresy.

The time of Germanus' visits to Britain is that of the rising peril of the Germanic invasions and the end of an era in which the still-elementary Christian culture of the Roman province outlived the vanished imperial power. The century between Constantine and the withdrawal of the legions, while not a period of stable peace and security for the Britons, had at least given opportunity for the upgrowth of a regularly organized church, which, with some peculiarities, resembled in essentials the churches of Gaul and Italy and was able without embarrassment to participate in important synods with the continental churches. The rising disorientation and disorder of the fifth century, and the expansion of the Anglo-Saxon domain in the former province, which largely depopulated the towns that had been flourishing episcopal centers, could not but impair the British church in its inner life and outer relationships. Already in the latter part of the fifth century the bishop was yielding leadership to the new order of monastic apostles, and intercourse with continental Christians was becoming confined to the travels and migrations of monks and the flight of British refugees to Brittany. Changes in worship and discipline that were being made on the continent and the tightening solidarity with Rome on the part of the provincial churches were not reflected in Britain. Instead insular Celtic church customs became endeared by inveterate use; though not unchallenged, they would long prevail. Toward Rome there was no antagonism, but respect without obedience. While the Germanic invaders of Britain, on becoming Christian, were to come within the expanding sway of the papacy, Christians of British race in Wales and Cornwall, whose ancestors had been fairly content under imperial Rome, remained aloof from Rome ecclesiastical and formed instead close fraternal ties with their Celtic brethren in Ireland and Brittany.

A link between the two accounts is supplied by Prosper's mention of Palladius the deacon as having proposed to the pope the sending of Germanus. Palladius may have been deacon at Rome or at Auxerre, and neither connection would preclude his identification with the Palladius who according to Prosper was sent in 431 as bishop to Irish Christians.[19] Prosper writes sentences where a modern historian would write pages, omitting much of what he must have known, thus inviting interesting but hardly convincing conjectures from present-day scholars. The discussion of these would be tedious and inadmissible here. But it seems easiest to suppose that Palladius had before 429 acquired knowledge of the state of Christianity in Britain and perhaps in Ireland, that he had visited Rome from Auxerre before the anti-Pelagian mission of that year, and that a council was indeed held in Gaul in support of the pope's action in which Lupus was appointed as Germanus' companion.

Constantius and Bede report a second visit (ca. 444?) of Germanus to Britain, with a disciple of Lupus named Severus, to combat a new wave of Pelagianism. By miracles and preaching he is said to have won the Britons back to the Catholic faith and procured the banishment of the heretics. If this visit is historical, it may point to an endemic strain of Pelagianism in Britain during the fifth century. It has even been argued that Gildas (who wrote a century later), with his emphasis on good works, was unconsciously a Pelagian. The early fifth-century Pelagian bishop Fastidius, called "Fastidius Brito" by a writer of his century, was probably a Briton, though the writings ascribed to him were written on the Continent. Better known is the British-born semi-Pelagian Faustus who having been abbot of Lerins became bishop of Riez about 460. Certain seventh-century Welsh materials incorporated in the *Historia Brittonum* of Nennius make Faustus the son of Vortigern by an incestuous union, and a disciple of Germanus who becomes the censor and adversary of Vortigern. The inference that Vortigern was the political champion of the British Pelagians is held "fantastic" by R. P. C. Hanson, and indeed any confrontation between him and Germanus may be purely imaginary.[20]

Britons of the time of Germanus and Vortigern confronted only the vanguard of the great host of Anglo-Saxons by whom they would soon be assailed and ultimately overwhelmed. They would be able to defend from the invaders only some western and northern regions of Roman Britannia, with its Christian culture. Yet for Christianity among them an era of vivid activity was about to open.

Celtic Monastic Sites of Scotland, Wales, and England

Three | Monastic Saints of the British Church

THE TURBULENT and unstable condition of early medieval society was partly offset by the retreat of piety and culture into ascetic communities, large and small. For centuries these were to constitute the abiding-places and centers of energy of Christianity in the West, leavening a barbarous militarism with spirituality and learning.[1] The diffusion of monasticism through Western Europe followed rapidly after the circulation of Athanasius' *Life of Anthony* in Latin (361), the communities established by St. Martin of Tours between 360 and 397, and the foundation by St. Honoratus in about 410 of the monastery of Lerins in an island off Cannes. As we have seen, it is probable that Ninian organized a monastic institution at Whithorn. Otherwise it is hard to account for the known existence of a vigorous monastery there some decades after his death (432?), honoring his name as its founder. His career comes so early in the westward expansion of the movement that he may have had no predecessor in British monasticism. If there were contemporary or earlier founders, they met with no such success as to be remembered.

The monastic ideal was soon to lay hold of the British church so strongly that a century after Ninian all British churchmen of note were monks, including those who were also bishops. In Wales the most eminent figure of the fifth century is St. Illtud (ca. 425–505). Too young to have known Ninian, he is represented as a disciple of Germanus. Illtud—if not, as a Breton legend says, Germanus himself—founded the long-famous monastery of Llantwit (Llanilltud) Major on the coast of Glamorganshire on the Bristol Channel. After his death he was lauded as the most learned of the Britons not only in Scripture but also in geometry, rhetoric, grammar, arithmetic, and philosophy; moreover, he was credited with magical powers. In early life a soldier and a married man, Illtud is said to have, at the command of an angel, put away his wife as well as his weapons in order to become a monk. The good woman, Trinihid, did her part by founding an oratory on a mountainside and caring for nuns and poor widows. Llantwit was a seminary of learning, though not to the neglect of physical labor, and it trained numerous able monastic leaders and founders in the sixth century. Illtud's successor as abbot was Dubricius, allegedly a descendant of a line of Caernarvon princes and consecrated as bishop by Germanus. The accounts of Dubricius indicate an awareness of the rapid rise of monasticism, for he is credited with founding a prosperous community at Hentland, Hertfordshire, and with overseeing no fewer than nine other institutions. A younger contemporary of Illtud, he seems to have lived well into the sixth century. He is represented as ordaining St. Samson to the priesthood in 504 and to the episcopate in 521. Dubricius was to be profusely celebrated in Welsh legends, and he is the "Dubric, chief of the church in Britain" who crowns King Arthur in Tennyson's *Idylls of the King*.[2]

The British church in Wales, Cornwall, and Strathclyde produced in the early sixth century a bewildering brood of monastic saints who were held in memory in local tradition. Their written "lives" are replete with surprising incidents and extravagant miracles. The urge to enter monastic life seems to have been epidemic and irresistible, often affecting several members of one family together. An extreme instance is that the children of Brychan at Brychaniog or Brecknock. Brychan is credited with fathering thirteen sons and twenty-five daughters, most of whom "entered the desert," adopting a life of strict asceticism. A number of them founded monasteries in Wales or Cornwall, one, St. Josse, even going as far afield as Picardy. It is impossible here to separate fact from literary invention, but the idea of a large family ending its family existence in dispersed monastic enterprises was apparently congenial to Welsh piety. Somewhat less fantastic is the legend of St. Teilo, pupil and successor of Dubricius at Llantwit Major and alleged supervisor of all the latter's ten monasteries. He was probably in fact a monastic administrator of importance, residing chiefly at Llandeilo Fawr in Carmarthenshire. His fame in Brittany is associated with a sojourn there, begun when he took flight from a visitation of plague in Wales. In an attempt to make him an equal of St. David, legend has it that he accompanied David on a pilgrimage to Jerusalem. In the early twelfth century, Teilo's name was made to do duty for the Norman policy in Wales. A Norman bishop of Llandaff wrote a *Life of Teilo* in order to persuade readers that the saint had been a bishop of Llandaff and in obedience to Canterbury. The so-called *Book of Llandaff* in which this is preserved bears the marks of Norman propaganda for a plan to take over the Welsh church; but it stands also as evidence that Teilo was still regarded as a popular saint at that period. According to Wade-Evans, "Llandaff was not even church property till after Teilo's death."[3]

St. Samson of Dol deserves attention as a vivid personality and as linking the Welsh church with those of Ireland, Cornwall, and Brittany. His *Life* was written perhaps as early as 610 by an anonymous Breton who had traced his footsteps and consulted some of his surviving acquaintances in Wales and Cornwall, and who had an appreciation of Samson's humor and other personal qualities. Samson may have been a compulsive wanderer, and he had odd ways; but we are assured that "nobody ever saw him drunk," and evidently his activities were highly productive toward the extension of monasticism. In the *Life* he becomes a monk under St. Illtud and is for a short while abbot of Ynys Byr (Caldey Island). On invitation from some Irish monks who pay him a visit on their way back (be it noted) from Rome, he leaves his task for a stay in Ireland. He there becomes head of a monastery whose abbot has gone insane. But Samson soon returns to Britain, accompanied by the now-restored Irish abbot. Next he sets up an oratory with his two brothers and their father, Amon, in a cave beside the Severn. He is now commanded by a synod to become abbot of Llantwit Major and to take episcopal orders. But after being thus promoted he is prompted by a divine voice to go on pilgrimage "beyond the sea," a phrase that meant for him beyond the Severn estuary, into Cornwall. There, amid incidents of conflict, he founds four monasteries, in one of which his father is installed as abbot. The biographer may have been somewhat credulous of the materials made available to him; but the main outline of the life-story as he gives it is hardly questionable. It is undoubted that Samson in later years crossed to Brittany and there continued his strenuous monastic labors, as we shall see in a later chapter (pp. 144–45). If even half the episodes reported of him are historical, St. Samson was an extremely energetic and versatile Welshman whose achievements as a monastic leader and founder were on an impressive scale.[4]

By the middle of the sixth century the British church, now contained within a territory shrunken by the Anglo-Saxon conquests but still called "Britannia," had entered on a stage of history marked by the ascendancy of monasticism. Bishops were retained, and their functions in ordination were honored, but the effective leadership was in the hands of abbots whether they happened to be bishops or not. About this time three leaders emerged in Wales—each a monk, a saint, and a scholar—whose names have never ceased to be familiar in the Celtic realms: David, Gildas, and Cadoc.

St. David (Dewi), famed in later ages as the patron saint of Wales, was probably the eldest of the three; but no historian will vouch for the life-dates of any of them. The dates most favored for David are 462–547. His life was written by Ricemarchus (Rhygyvarch) (d. 1099) of Menevia (St. David's), whose aim was by magnification of the founder to promote the claims of St. David's, as the primatial see of Wales, against the claims of Canterbury. A century earlier an Irish *Life of St. Finnian of Clonard* represents Finnian as deciding in favor of David, from among the three Welsh worthies just named, for that place of leadership which is described as "the abbacy of the island of Britain." David was born at Mynyw on the coast of Cardigan, and according to Rhygyvarch was descended from royal personages of southern Wales. His father, Sant, and his mother, Nonn, sent him to be trained by Paulinus (Peulin), a Welsh disciple of Germanus of Auxerre. In time he went forth to found a monastery and after some delay was guided by an angel to "the valley of the little bog," which he renamed after his birthplace, Mynyw, Latinized as Menevia. Here later arose the Cathedral of St. David's. The situation is a commanding one near the westernmost point of Wales in Pembrokeshire, with ready access by sea to ports in Ireland and western Britain.

In the severity of his discipline David was thought extreme, and he is hardly surpassed by the monks of Egypt. No meat was permitted and bread was measured out to each monk. Farm work was rendered harder by having monks do the work of oxen. David was dubbed "Aquaticus," the Waterman, because he required total abstinence from alcoholic drinks. A medieval codex contains a set of penitential provisions under the title, "Certain Excerpts [*Excerpta quaedam*] from a Book of David." These seem to reflect his abhorrence of drunkenness in that the first four canons assign penalties for offenses connected with "wine or strong drink." The regulations are chiefly for clergy who are not monks, and no doubt David wanted to extend this abstinence beyond the monastery. The man who craftily induces another to get drunk "for the sake of good fellowship" (*humanitatis gratia*) does the same penance as the drunken man. David took a stern view of what may have been a social problem in his time. He likely knew the scandalous case of St. Piro, Samson's predecessor at Ynys Byr, who is said to have met his death by falling into a well while inebriated.

The hagiographer inflates the fame of David by taking him on a pilgrimage to Jerusalem. He is said to have presided in two synods, at places called by Rhygyvarch Brefi and Victoria. The dates of these were set by the Bollandist editors as respectively 519 and 529; the date 569 given by Haddan and Stubbs for the later synod would place it beyond David's probable span of life. The sixteen canons of these two synods are extant in the same Paris codex as the *Excerpta*. Rhygyvarch, who did not see the canons of these synods, mistakenly thought that they were concerned with the suppression of Pelagianism and with full adherence to Rome. Instead they provide severe penalties for monks guilty of sexual offenses, theft, sacrilege, perjury, and affording guidance to "barbarians" (Anglo-Saxon pagans?) who would slaughter Christians. Amid remaining uncertainties, the figure of the patron of Wales emerges from the shadows of history not as a commanding prelate but as an exemplar and promoter of austere monasticism.[5]

Since St. Cadoc is represented as at some time the spiritual director or soul-friend of the father of Gildas and of Gildas himself, it may be assumed that he was older than Gildas. The *Life of Cadoc* was written by Lifris, an archdeacon of Glamorgan, not long before 1100. Even apart from its five chapters on miracles, it is somewhat detailed and, while liberally sprinkled throughout with strange wonders, seems to provide the outline facts of his career. His principal monastic foundation was Llancarfan (Nantcarfan), five miles from Llantwit Major toward Cardiff. Lifris tells us that he was born in a village in Monmouthshire west of the Usk, and that his warrior father had obtained his wife, Cadoc's mother Gladys, by snatching her from the family of a local king. The parents sent Cadoc to be educated at Caerwent in Gwent under one Tatheus (Tathai)—an Irish founder in Wales, alleged son of a king. On reaching manhood, Cadoc built, largely with his own hands, the essential structures of a monastery at Llancarfan; but soon many "from all Britain" came to join him. Seeking better instruction, he went with some of his adherents to Ireland; and it is alleged that he came under the instruction of St. Mochuta (Carthach), the celebrated abbot of Lismore. He is said to have founded a monastery by the Liffey. Having made friends among monks and scholars and "acquired complete knowledge of the West," he returned to Wales, bringing with him three Irish disciples, one of whom was Finnian, later founder of Clonard. He further studied rhetoric at Llanspyddyd under a master named Bachan, alleged, probably in error, to have come from Italy. He is also credited with journeys into Scotland where, with Caw, father of Gildas, he is said to have founded a monastery at Cambuslang, and to have preached to heathen folk and healed their sick at Bannock, planting another monastery there. Travels to, and foundations in, Cornwall and Brittany are also credited to Cadoc, and Lifris takes him on pilgrimage to Jerusalem, perhaps in imitation of Rhygyvarch's David. The fanciful account of his martyrdom at "Civitas Beneventana" seems to bring him at the end to Italy, but the place may have been, as Wade-Evans holds, Llansannor, not far from Llancarfan.

The view has been expressed by J. R. Morris that the "aristocratic abbots," Cadoc and Gildas, opponents of harsh asceticism, planted in prosperous former villa areas a monasticism different in temper from the austere type formed under "plebeian ascetics." The latter, represented by David, arose in poorer districts where Irish settlers were numerous.[6] Cadoc indeed appears as a rather liberal man of letters. But his discipline seems to have been severe enough. At least he evidently practiced, and exacted of his disciples, a regimen of physical labor. As in David's case, certain writings are, not without question, ascribed to him. He is said to have been a friend of the bard Taliessin, who, like many of the saints, is almost lost to us in a mist of legend. *The Wisdom of Cadoc* is the title of a seventeenth-century collection of Welsh sententious and didactic sayings that are dated early enough to be his. Examples are:

> No man is the son of knowledge if he is not also the son of poetry.
> No man loves poetry without loving the light,
> Nor the light without loving the truth,
> Nor the truth without loving justice,
> Nor justice without loving God.
> The best of patriots is the man who tills the soil.
> No man is pious who is not cheerful.

Love is heaven, hate is hell.
Conscience is the eye of God in the soul of man.

What we know of Cadoc, and what was in early times believed about him, would lead us to suppose that, like many Celtic monks, but with a peculiar vividness, he combined the qualities expressed in another connection by Jean Leclercq in his title "The Love of Learning and the Desire for God."[7]

In Gildas we have a writer of distinction whose life-story is nevertheless largely unknown. He says he was born in the year of the Battle of Mons Badonicus, which scholars are now dating not later than 500. A date of about 570 for his death seems to be gaining acceptance. Gildas never calls himself a Briton, and there is some reason to regard him as of Pictish origin. He was born in the Clydesdale region of southern Scotland, his father, Caw Prydyn, having migrated to that area from near Bannockburn in northern Stirlingshire. The *Life of Cadoc* makes Caw a monstrous and wicked giant, but this late characterization of him may simply reflect the resemblance of his name to the Welsh word for giant. Another tradition brings Caw and his family southward to Anglesey during the boyhood of Gildas, and this would more readily account for Gildas' attendance at the school of the learned Illtud. There, and possibly in a subsequent period in Ireland, he became a scholar and one of the most fluent Latin writers of his century. It is believed that he had been married when young, and that he had two sons who obtained recognition as saints, as did also one of his brothers.

It was probably while in retirement on the island now called Flatholm, in the Bristol Channel—a retreat also, at times, of his master Cadoc—that he wrote the *De excidio et conquestu Britanniae (The Ruin and Conquest of Britain).* Doubts were long ago raised about his single authorship of this work. Bishop James Usher in his *Britannicarum ecclesiarum antiquitates* (1639) distinguished Gildas Sapiens from Gildas Badonicus, the latter being the author of the historical part of the work, chapters 2 to 26. It was the contention of the late A. W. Wade-Evans that this portion was written by an early eighth-century author whom he designates as "Auctor Badonicus"; but his labored argument[8] has not gained assent. Studies by C. E. S. Stevens and F. Kerlouégan have shown convincing evidence that the book is a single whole. For his use of mordant and unrestrained language of condemnation Gildas has been compared with St. Jerome, and the influence of Orosius, who similarly excoriated the half-Christian Romans of an earlier century, is recognizable in his work. Gildas views favorably the former Roman authority in Britain, and attributes the widespread evils later prevailing primarily to the perversity of the Britons themselves and only secondarily to the devastations of the invaders—the Picts, Scots, and Saxons. In a period of relief from war, the Britons fell into luxury, drunkenness, and strife and were ruled by wicked kings. They rallied, however, against the Saxons, and won a victory at Badon Hill, only to fall under new misrule and degradation. He especially reproaches the five contemporary kings who bear rule in Cornwall and Wales, including the "dragon" Maglocunus (Maelgyn Gwynedd) of North Wales, famous descendant of Cunedda who a century earlier had come from a spot near Edinburgh to dominate a wide province of Wales, including Anglesey. Gildas is aware that some good men exist, but they are few and powerless. He condemns the priests and kings without exception, leaving an impression of his alienation from them all. The book, he tells us, is written "out of zeal for God's church and his holy law," which are flouted by the men in power. He excoriates bishops who buy their offices and engage in secular pursuits. Notwithstanding the upgrowth of monasticism, it is clear that the church on which he sits in judgment continued to be in structure episcopal, and to retain the subordinate clerical orders. While on the side of a moderate asceticism, Gildas is passionately concerned for a high morality in church and state. Whereas in the previous century the church has suffered from the fierce assaults of pagans, in his time it suffers rather from a decadence that arises from ease, from "levity" and a certain unawareness which he calls *insipientia.* He is an aroused and indignant critic of a decadent establishment, but eager to reform it if he can gain a hearing. "Kings hath Britain," he laments, "but they are tyrants; judges she hath, but they are impious; priests hath Britain but they are unperceiving [*insipientes*]; pastors so-called, but they are wolves alert to slay souls." Hurt and angry, Gildas seems a reincarnation of a Hebrew prophet, an Amos or Jeremiah.

Gildas' authorship of two sets of disciplinary canons is regarded as probable. One of these is his "Preface on Penance," extant in one Paris manuscript only. It assigns penalties for twenty-seven offenses of monks and clergy. The sentences are generally milder than those assigned in later penitentials. The other set of canons is associated with his Irish sojourn. The unnamed monk of Rhuis in Brittany who wrote a *Life of Gildas* has him go to Ireland as a youth for study and return on the invitation of the High King Ainmere to amend a deplorable condition in the Irish church and restore faith and order. Welsh and Irish sources also allude to his presence and influence in Ireland. The eighth-century *Catalogue of the Saints of Ireland* states that the Irish saints received a Liturgy from David, Gildas, and Cadoc. One of the "Epistolary Fragments" ascribed to Gildas blames the British clergy for practicing in their liturgy and tonsure what is "contrary to all the world and inimical to Roman custom," and according to the *Life of Cadoc* Gildas presented to Cadoc a missal that he had written. The *Life* was earlier than the *Catalogue* and may have been known to its author. (See below, p. 72.) The Rhuis author has him tour Ireland on his reforming mission. These documents, while not independently reliable, seem together to attest the fact of an early tradition that for some years he gave his services to the Irish church. The *Catalogue* referred to may have been prepared as an instrument of reform in this connection, and intrinsically it is of interest. Its provisions are as much opposed to a meticulous and extreme asceticism as to the lack of good discipline in the church. Abstinence without charity is placed under penalty, and it is an offense to leave a community ruled by an abbot for more austere solitary devotion. Monks who replace oxen to draw the plow (as was required by David) may be doing this from presumption and pride.

His eleventh-century Breton biographer, a monk of Rhuis in southeast Brittany, makes Gildas the founder of that monastery and takes him to the lonely island of Houat off Quiberon Bay for his final retirement and death. Most scholars are extremely skeptical of this chapter of the story; and obviously the writer may have had motives other than historical truth for connecting a celebrated saint with his community. Some have been led to conjecture that our Gildas had a namesake to whom this narrative should be applied. But at the present stage of research it seems unwise to regard it as pure fiction. Nothing is more characteristic of Celtic saints than *peregrinatio*, going to live in foreign parts for religious reasons, and it may be argued that such a course would be the more probable in the case of Gildas who wrote as one alienated from the rulers and clergy of Wales. In the *De excidio* he speaks of the migration of Britons to Brittany; is it not possible that he lived to join this movement? We have no record or tradition in insular sources of his last days and place of death. And it was in Brittany, not Britain, that he was remembered in dedications.

The Latin of Gildas was admired from his own time and has been recently much commented on and acutely studied by experts in early medieval Latin. Unlike many of the Irish scholars, he is not under the influence of classical Latin writers. His style is an outgrowth of familiarity with the Latin Bible and knowledge of the Latin church fathers. Some passages of the *De excidio*, however, show an acquaintance with the affected style called "Hisperica famina" (below, p. 122) later practiced by a number of Irish monastic writers and their English pupils. Gildas used Latin with great fluency and vehemence; not, however, as one to whom it is a native speech but as one to whom it is a language acquired in diligent study.[9]

Cornwall and Devon, forming one peninsula like a great limb stretched out between Wales and Brittany, were traversed and evangelized by Welsh, Irish, and Breton monks at an early period; but dates and details largely elude us. In his study of the saints of Cornwall, Canon Gilbert H. Doble threads his way through local legends which have their own charm but which provide little reliable information.[10] Paul Aurelian, a Welsh disciple of St. Illtud, spent a period in Cornwall but left a greater reputation for his work in Brittany. St. Budoc is remembered in St. Budeau, Devon, but apparently his chief contribution was made in Brittany, as was that of his Irish associate St. Mawes. There is a similar legend of St. Sezny, or Sithney (original of the name Sidney), who ends his travels at Kerlouan in Brittany. The legend of St. Breaca brings this Irish nun of Kildare to Cornwall in company with numerous Irish saints of both sexes, some of whom are later active in Brittany.[11] Whatever of true history lies behind the fiction in these instances, the common note on the part of the hagiographers, a period of labor in Cornwall and Devon followed by some notable activity in Brittany, has significance. It is assumed that the geographically distinct parts of the Celtic Christian world have such spiritual unity that there takes place a natural and unhindered circulation of monastic clergy among them. And the prevailing direction of this movement, from Ireland and Wales to Cornwall and thence to Brittany, can be safely taken as historical.

A century before St. Columba and King Brude MacMalchon, Nechtan Morbet reigned over the Picts (457–81) from his capital at Dunnichen (Dun Nechtan) near Forfar. A Pictish chronicle makes him the first of his line to adopt Christianity; but the circumstances alleged are chronologically impossible. His conversion is associated with his exile as a young prince to Ireland, where he is befriended by St. Brigid, who was actually less than ten years old at the beginning of his reign. He is said to have bestowed on St. Brigid the city of Abernethy, in the presence of St. Darlugdach, Brigid's successor at Kildare (ca. 525), who is represented as a missionary to the Picts of Scotland. An equally romantic account in the *Life of St. Boite*, narrates that St. Boite, founder of Monastirboice (see below, p. 75), came to Nechtan Morbet's court and, finding that the king had died, raised him to life and received from him the gift of a royal castle. The story continues that after some years with his teacher, St. Teilo of Llandaff, St. Boite returned to the east coast of Scotland by sea, leading sixty "holy men and virgins" whose ranks included twenty "Germans," a designation sometimes used of Anglo-Saxons in Britain.[12] Since Boite died (allegedly on the day of Columba's birth) in 521, he was not too late to have received royal favors from Nechtan Morbet, and it is conceivable that when Nechtan was a boy and both were in Ireland, St. Boite "raised him to life" by baptism. Such tales seem to point to an early tradition in Pictish Scotland that missionaries had come to their country from Irish monasteries; but no decisive confirmation of this can be adduced.

Strathclyde in the sixth century saw the work of at least one eminent religious founder in the person of Kentigern, whose most probable dates are 518 to 603. But for his career we have to draw conjectures from the fanciful twelfth-century *Life* by Jocelyn of Furness.[13] Lake many saints, he is represented as an illegitimate child. His mother, Thanau or Thaney, daughter of a king of Lothian, having been violated by Prince Owen, is by her father's command thrown down a steep bank on Traprain Law, a little mountain in Huntingdonshire, but unharmed by this is set adrift in a coracle which takes her to Culros on the north shore of the Forth. There St. Kentigern is born in a wood. We are told that he was reared and educated under St. Serf[14] whom late legend makes an eminent missionary north of the Forth. Serf, it is said, affectionately addressed him as Mungo (Dear Fellow), the name by which he has always been popularly known in Scotland. Grown to manhood, St. Kentigern goes to preach in the region of the "Cathures," Glasgow. Jocelyn ties his work to that of St. Ninian by having him occupy the spot where, as he states, Ninian had consecrated a cemetery. The improbabilities here may be measured against Jocelyn's claim, made in his prologue, to have used an early account of Kentigern "composed in Irish style" (*stilo scotticano dictatum*). Otherwise we have no clue to the source of this alleged Ninian connection. W. Douglas Simpson regards the item as fully historical but A. C. Thomas takes the view that its source is to be connected with the later Ninian tradition that was taking shape in the seventh century. Ninian, he thinks, may not have gone to Strathclyde, but any Christian activity in Strathclyde before Kentigern may have been "within the sphere of the Whithorn episcopacy."[15]

The outline of Kentigern's career as missionary is far from complete. Apparently he was induced by the local king, clergy, and people to become bishop of Glasgow (ca. 583), and an Irish bishop was brought in to consecrate him "according to the custom of the Britons and Scots." This is usually said to mean that he was consecrated by a single bishop, but Jocelyn seems to have been thinking instead of the manner of anointing.[16] Some time later he encountered the hostility of a "tyrant" named Morcant or Morken (who probably represents a pagan reaction) and was driven out. He turned toward Wales, but on his way is said to have preached through the Cumberland mountains, converting many. Welsh legend of late date makes him the founder of Llanelwy, and its first bishop, but it is now known that the bishopric of St. Asaph was founded at the former Llanelwy at a much later date, and in fact we have no certainty that St. Kentigern ever was in Wales. Strathclyde was long in civil strife before the battle of Ardderyth in 573, after which King Redderch the Bountiful received the kingship. Redderch, who may have become a Christian in Ireland, pursued a Christian policy in Strathclyde and at once recalled Kentigern. The saint returned, says A. R. MacEwen, "deliberately and with distinction" through Dumfriesshire, pausing for a preaching mission at Hoddam before taking up his work in Glasgow. There he remained active, probably exercising a wide authority in Strathclyde, until his death, which, it is thought, occurred in 603 when he had reached the age of eighty-four. Jocelyn tells a fine story of an arranged meeting of St. Kentigern with St. Columba (ca. 584). The two leaders, both in their sixties, approach the meeting place with psalm-singing retinues of monks and clergy, and the alliance is confirmed in an exchange of crosiers.[17] Kentigern's success as a bishop is somewhat clouded by the fact that the bishopric of Glasgow has no recorded history for some centuries after him, and that he is not mentioned in the lives of Columba and David, or in that of Asaph, whom Jocelyn makes Kentigern's pupil. His reported missionary excursions to eastern Scotland and the northern islands are probably unhistorical.

A younger contemporary of Columba and Kentigern was St. Blane. He was born about 565 near Kingarth, now a town and parish in the southern part of the island of Bute, five miles distant from Rothsay. There, it seems, his uncle, St. Catan, founded a monastery of some importance. Blane's best-known foundation in Bute was, says Dorothy Marshall, "in a lovely spot in a valley above Dunagoil."[18] This is within the parish of Kingarth in the south-western sector of the island where Dunagoil Bay opens on the Sound of Bute. It is uncertain whether Blane was a Pict or a Briton, or of mixed race. He was trained as a monk at Bangor in Ulster under the eminent founder of that monastery, the Dalaradian Pict Comgall, and the latter's associate, Kenneth. St. Blane gained wide repute and is remembered in church dedications in Strathclyde, eastward to Dunblane in Perthshire, and thence northward in the Pictish highlands. James Hutchinson Cockburn takes these numerous dedications as indicative of a correspondingly wide and effective ministry.[19] Dunblane, where Blane spent his late years, was in a Pictish area. He may be thought of as renewing the Christianizing process among the Picts where St. Ninian and St. Serf had been his predecessors. His life apparently extended well into the seventh century. In 790, under his seventh successor, the monastery buildings at Dunblane were burned by Norse raiders.

It was about two centuries after Ninian's mission, and in the year of Columba's death (597), that Augustine, the tall monk of Marseilles who had become prior of the Benedictine monastery of St. Andrews in Rome, sailed into the Thames estuary with forty monks and landed on the isle of Thanet. He came under appointment of Pope Gregory the Great on a well-prepared mission to Anglo-Saxon England, where paganism still prevailed. How much of British Christianity may have been alive in the British remnant left within Anglo-Saxon kingdoms can never be known. But Bede tells us that at Canterbury "a church built in ancient times in honor of St. Martin" was available for the Roman mission. Probably the Celtic members of this church had been slain or scattered. In Kent a royal marriage had opened the way for the missionaries. King Ethelbert was married to a Frankish Christian princess, Bertha, whose Frankish chaplain, Liudhard, had been using St. Martin's church and had no doubt already acquainted the king with some elements of Christian teaching. Bede has much to say about Augustine's early acts and problems in his post at Canterbury[20]; with these matters we need not concern ourselves. Later he comes to an event of major importance for this history, Augustine's conference with "bishops and teachers" of the British church. The date is probably 602; the place, known to Bede as Augustine's Oak, cannot now be identified. There were in fact two conferences, or sessions, and it is uncertain whether both were in the same place. According to Bede, seven British bishops and numerous scholar-monks from the large monastery of Bangor-is-Coed (Bancornaburg) met Augustine and his associated clergy. Dinoot, the abbot of Bangor, had sought in advance the advice of a highly esteemed recluse, who said that they should watch for proofs that Augustine was meek and lowly in heart, something that would be evident if he should rise to greet them. But Augustine remained seated when they entered his presence. It is not unlikely that by this he meant at the outset to serve notice that he felt called upon to assert the authority of Rome and would accept from the Britons only acquiescence and obedience. Some exchange of views followed, but the record is too meager for us to reconstruct the arguments. We know that Augustine invited the Britons to join with him in efforts to convert the Anglo-Saxons, but on prior conditions: they were to adopt the Roman date of Easter and the Roman rite of baptism. In the end they declined his terms, saying that since he had not risen to greet them, they knew that he would despise them the more if they should yield to him. Bede falls below his usual level of Christian feeling in what follows. He tells how Augustine threatened the Britons that if they refused peace with their friends, they would suffer the consequences in war with their enemies, and he sees in the subsequent massacre of 12,000 monks of Bangor-is-Coed by Ethelfrith "the workings of divine judgment" for their recalcitrance.[21] We have too little information here to give anything like an adequate account of the arguments exchanged and the temper of the debaters. But it is clear from Bede that the Roman position was flatly laid down as not debatable, in a way that was rather tactless if not arrogant, and that the British monks and bishops—not perhaps duly interested in the eternal salvation of their English ravagers—were antagonized rather than conciliated. It is an unhappy hour for the churches of Britain. The history of an era turned on this fruitless ecclesiastical confrontation. Centuries were to elapse before the triumph of Augustine's and Pope Gregory's plan for the church organization of Britain.[22]

Four | The Christainization of Ireland: St. Patrick

Knowledge of the first entrance of Christianity into Ireland quite eludes us; but it is certain that the Apostle of Ireland, Patrick, was not the first Christian to set foot on the island. The intimate, if sometimes hostile, relations of Ireland with Britain, and its active sea trade with Gaul, both reaching back to remote antiquity, make it antecedently likely that some infiltration of the new religion took place as soon as it became dispersed in these nations. It is worth noting that the age which celebrated Patrick in a prodigious body of legend testified in no less fantastic tales to a belief that the Christian faith had come to Ireland centuries before his mission. An extreme instance is the legend that Altus, an Irish centurion in the imperial army, witnessed the Crucifixion and returned to his own country to proclaim the Gospel.[1] Among the popular stories about Cormac mac Airt, alleged high king of Ireland (ca. 227–66) and founder of the Tara dynasty, it is said that he "turned to the adoration of God," thereby offending his druids who brought it about by their spells that he choked to death on a salmon bone.[2] His burial at Rosnaree beside Tara was regarded as instituting a Christian burial place of kings. It would not be in the least unlikely that the very numerous British and Gaulish captives he is said to have taken on his sea raids included some Christians, from whom he might have become informed of, and favorable to, the Christian faith. Raiding the accessible British and continental coasts was a favorite enterprise of Irish chiefs, and among their captives put to service in Ireland may have been a Christian element from an early date. Patrick himself first saw Ireland as a young captive taken, as he says, with many thousands; and though their story is not recorded, many of these must have been, at least nominally, Christians.

We have also the legendary lives of men represented as Patrick's predecessors and occasionally associated with him in his labors. It is difficult to make much historically of the lives of Kieran, Ibar, Abban, and other shadowy figures of this class, but they were credited with planting churches in the southeastern counties of Waterford, Wexford, Wicklow, Tipperary, and Kilkenny, localities which Patrick may not have entered. A rather extreme view of the extent of pre-Patrician Christianity in Ireland was put forth by Heinrich Zimmer in 1901. The learned Celticist conceived a low opinion of Patrick as a self-important, narrow-minded zealot who accomplished little, Christianity having been widely diffused in the island before his time.[3] Zimmer's brilliant but slanted interpretation served to stimulate the more balanced work of others in which we find recognition of a considerable pre-Patrician Christian community in the southeast region.

We move out of the realm of mere conjecture and probability by means of a document which immediately precedes the inception of Patrick's mission. Under the date 431 Prosper of Aquitaine entered in his *Chronicle* the typically condensed sentence: "Ad Scottos in Christum credentes ordinatus a Papa Caelestino Palladius primus episcopus mittitur." (Palladius, ordained by Pope Celestine, is sent to the Scots who believe in Christ as their first bishop.) Prosper does not here mention Ireland, the primary homeland of the Scots. Some Scots had already begun the invasion of a region north of the Wall of Antonine, part of the latter kingdom of Dalriada, where they formed a settlement under a king named Saran (425–51); and somewhat earlier invaders who were refugees from Ireland had gained a foothold in Wales. The question therefore arises whether Pope Celestine's "Scots believing in Christ" were living not in Ireland but rather in an area surrounded and influenced by Christian neighbors in Britain. It has been argued by J. Gough Meissner that Palladius went first to the Scots in Scotland and made only a brief visit to northern Ireland before his work was cut short by death.[4] But Prosper, in his *Contra Collatorem*, written about 434 when he was residing in Rome, seems to imply that Palladius' mission was to Ireland itself. Here, referring to Celestine's anti-Pelagian policy in Britain and his appointment of a bishop for the Scots, he comments that "while he strove to make the Roman island [Britain] Catholic he also made the barbarous island [Ireland] Christian,"[5] Prosper alone gives us contemporary statements, and he was in a position to know the facts. Clear certainty in this matter is made difficult for us, however, by the meagerness of early Irish notices of Palladius, while a number of dedications to "St. Paldy" in southern Scotland seem to attest his presence there.

It is natural to suppose that we have here the deacon Palladius who, as we have noted, had recommended the action taken against the Pelagians in Britain two years earlier. Linking this identification with Palladius' mission to the Irish, Zimmer contended that the Christian communities in Ireland had become infested with Pelagianism and that Palladius, with his known concern over this heresy, was sent to reclaim them.[6] But Prosper speaks of making Ireland not orthodox but "Christian"; it was Britain that was being delivered from heresy. In 613 St. Columban, writing to Pope Boniface IV, remarks: "We are the disciples of Saints Peter and Paul, all the Irish dwelling at the ends of the earth; no one of us has ever been a heretic [but all have kept] the Catholic faith as it was first transmitted by you."[7] Whether this has any reference to Palladius' work or not, it runs counter to the supposition of Pelagianism in Ireland. Muirchú maccu Machtheni, in his seventh-century *Life of Patrick*, makes Patrick the successor of Palladius, sent, however, not from Rome but by Germanus of Auxerre when that prelate received word of Palladius' death. One of the lives of Patrick in John Colgan's *Acta Sanctorum Hiberniae* (1647), of date not later than the ninth century, say that Palladius landed at Wicklow, only to withdraw after leaving relics and scriptures. Nennius in the early ninth century, whether filling by guesswork a gap in his information or reporting an earlier tradition, states that Palladius was prevented by storms from his intended mission and soon after died among the Picts. Ludwig Bieler, on the basis of Prosper's phrases quoted above, thinks Palladius was "still successfully active" in Ireland at least two or three years after his commission. He observes that the leader of a papal mission would come "with a retinue of clerics of every grade" and that this large-scale effort would be reinforced by new missionary personnel.[8] Something like this may have taken place, but if so the effort seems to have had only limited success. Patrick, in his *Confession* (Conf. 51), shows himself aware of a ministry functioning in some places, conferring ordination, baptism, and confirmation; but he does not mention Palladius, or any other missionary predecessor. Prosper's "first bishop" was apparently no celebrity in the parts of Ireland visited by Patrick, and he cannot have achieved a widespread organization of churches. Patrick clearly regarded himself as essentially a pioneer, and not as anybody's successor. Even when we recognize his intense consciousness of divine authorization, his silence about predecessors must be held significant.

It seems necessary here to introduce some notice of the "Patrick problem" as it appears in recent studies. The unclarified relation between Palladius and Patrick embarrassed early writers on Patrick. One of these, Tírechán, refers to "Palladius who is called by the other name Patrick," an identification that has often since been adopted. The slightly later "Hymn of Fiacc" (ca. 700) refers to "the other Patrick" as joining his greater namesake in heaven. A century later, in the *Martyrology* of Oengus, Palladius is called "the Old Patrick" (Sen-Patraic), and under date 457 the "repose of the Old Patrick" appears in the Annals of Ulster. Taking up this theme, T. F. O'Rahilly in 1942 learnedly challenged the reigning interpretation of Patrick by identifying the Old Patrick with Palladius and bringing Patrick the Briton to Ireland only in 462, more than thirty years after the sending of Palladius. James Carney in 1961 and D. A. Binchy in 1962 presented, with fascinating detail, variant responses to O'Rahilly's thesis. Carney argues for, and Binchy tentatively favors, a much later date for the coming of the British Patrick than the commonly assigned 432, and both scholars hold that some areas of southeastern Ireland had been Christianized before the mission of Palladius. Ludwig Bieler, in a fresh examination of the sources bearing on Palladius, thinks that "the odds are against" identifying him with the Old Patrick, but argues for his presence over some years in the Wicklow region where after founding three churches he probably suffered martyrdom. When J. B. Bury, historian of the later Roman Empire and editor of Gibbon's *Decline and Fall*, turned his research upon Ireland and produced his *Life of Patrick* (1905), he created in his readers a gratified sense of finality. But this once convincing biography has in the past two decades, at the hands of the authors mentioned, become an antiquated book. Nor can it be said that a firmly outlined narrative of Patrick's career emerges even from their work. This is more nearly achieved, though with less assurance than Bury showed, by R. P. C. Hanson.[9]

In these and a great number of other studies, our awareness of the difficulties has been increased, but not without some enhancement of our understanding of the man and his mission. It will be best to present here the few assured biographical facts mainly from the saint's own writings, with necessary help from his modern interpreters and from some of the early documents in which the Patrick Legend had its written beginnings. It will be convenient to refer to the latter before coming to the main sources, his own writings.

The reference is to certain late seventh-century "lives" of Patrick written less to provide ascertained facts about him than to confirm or heighten his repute as a miracle-working saint and extraordinary missionary apostle; and by this portrayal to promote the ecclesiastical claims of Armagh as Patrick's foundation. Muirchú maccu Machtheni of Sletty, Queens County, represents himself as the first to write a life of Patrick, but Bieler takes the view that the work of Tírechán of Tirawley is earlier.[10] Both are probably to be dated between 664 and 700, and both make use of materials, oral and written, that are not available to us. Muirchú's greater use of Patrick's statements commends him to some scholars as the superior authority. This is asserted by John Morris, who is followed with some modification by Hanson[11]; but Bieler gives a good deal of weight to Tírechán. Both seventh-century writers are partisans of Armagh. Tírechán indicates an element of conflict arising from the aggressive spread of a monastic association, presumably that of the Columba monasteries, threatening the supremacy of Patrick, and both authors present Armagh as the administrative center of a wide-reaching *paruchia*, or diocese, rightfully owing allegiance to Patrick. In a familiar literary affectation of the time, Muirchú disparages his own competence before giving proof of it. He has launched the frail rowboat of his slender talent on the surging and perilous sea of sacred history where none but his "father Cogitosus" has preceded him. Cogitosus was the author of a well-known life of St. Brigid, and was Muirchú's "father" probably in the sense of soul-friend or personal adviser. Actually Muirchú's concern for historic fact is far greater than that to be discovered in his master's diverting account of St. Brigid. Despite his credulity with regard to rumored miracles, we detect a certain conscientiousness and something of human interest in his presentation of the meager body of data at his disposal. Some of the strong expressions he attributes to Patrick in critical situations seem to have the ring of reality as if faithfully transmitted from those who heard them. He represents Patrick as not only the authoritative ruler of the church but also the preeminent teacher of all Ireland. Tírechán relies largely on a now lost text by Ultan, bishop and abbot of Louth, who died about 630, and utilizes other material derived from local memory or tradition. We have no knowledge of any writer on Patrick before Ultan, and his work is absorbed into Tírechán's and not separately known. Both these accounts of Patrick are preserved in the Book of Armagh (ca. 800). This treasury of texts has also the *Tripartite Life of Patrick*, a somewhat later composition designed to enhance further the image of Patrick as the touring and wonder-working apostle and national prophet of the Irish.[12] It contains, too, *The Book of the Angel*, a short document apparently completed in the eighth century, a pamphlet in the guise of an angelic revelation.[13] The angel visiting Patrick declares, "The Lord God has given all the tribes of the Irish by way of *paruchia* to you and to this city of yours which is called Armagh." A great body of legendary material highly seasoned with astonishing marvels was now gathering about the name of Patrick, whose true figure was so obscured as to become almost indiscernible. Even today the popular image of Patrick partakes largely of the legend and bears little relation to the historical person.

Yet from his own writings, which have been several times edited in our century,[14] the man himself is revealed with an intimacy comparable to that which characterizes Augustine's *Confessions*. Not that Patrick has anything of Augustine's searching self-analysis or disclosure of inner struggle. Instead, he often reminds us of St. Paul when the Apostle affirms his divine call and the sincere motives of his ministry. Patrick is the unquestioned author of two short Latin works, both of which have autobiographical content and were written in his later years: the *Epistula ad Coroticum* (or *ad milites Corotici*) and the *Confessio*. The purpose of Patrick's Confession is to vindicate against defamers his missionary calling and career. The *Letter to Coroticus*, intended for the eyes of the soldiers and clerical subjects of that British kinglet, is written in unmeasured indignation and grief provoked by an act of barbarity of which many of the author's beloved converts have been victims. It is the Confession which, though the later of the two, furnishes the chief facts about his early life. It must be dated very near the end of his labors.

The title *Confessio* reflects the use of the cognate verb "confiteor" in the Latin Psalter to introduce the psalmist's thankful testimony to the goodness of God; and a note of thankfulness keeps recurring in the book. But its main purpose is apologetic. Patrick aims to persuade his readers that he has exercised an authentic and effective ministry in Ireland and to refute derogatory charges and rumors, circulated by persons unnamed, obviously in Britain. He is anxious to explain his motives to his "brethren and kinfolk" (Conf. 6). He intimates that at the time of writing he is in advanced years (*in senectute mea,* Conf. 10), and the book closes with the solemn words: "This is my confession before I die." From these phrases it has been suggested that the book was dictated during his last illness, and such a view might in part account for the disorderly sequence of materials that makes it so difficult to use as an historical source. Certainly he looks upon his career in retrospect. While making no attempt to write an autobiography, he holds in view his entire life.

Patrick writes in the Latin of one whose study of the language has come too late for mastery. His weakness in Latin is a point on which he is almost pathologically sensitive. His sentences show that he often found it difficult to make even simple thoughts intelligible in a still foreign tongue. His opening words are: *"Ego Patricius peccator, rusticissimus et minimus omnium fidelium* [I Patrick, a sinner, quite illiterate, and the least of all the faithful]"; and from his pen these words are by no means merely conventional. He several times reverts to the theme of his handicap through lack of early schooling, remorsefully attributing this to his own willful negligence.

Patrick's boyhood (ca. 390–405) was spent in a frontier area of Roman Britain at a time when the imperial power was withering. Of his birthplace it is certain only that it was near the exposed western coast of the province. He names his home village Bonnavem Taburniae—or as some amend the text, Bonaventa Berniae (or Burniae)—adding, "where three roads meet." He repeatedly refers to his relatives as living in Britain, without any hint of a more exact location. Muirchú adds "not far from our sea," an observation which is obvious from the story, and says the place was otherwise called Nemtrie. This name takes many forms; and attempts to determine the place are unconvincing. Bury identified Bonnavem Taburniae with Banwen in Glamorganshire, and various writers have pointed to the possibility that he was descended from Irish invaders of Wales. It is well known that many Irish settlements had been made in Wales in generations before his time, including that of the Dessi, a Munster tribe, who, banished from Ireland, entered South Wales in about 368.[15] Perhaps a dozen spots along the British Coast from the Severn to the Clyde have been learnedly treated as possibilities for Patrick's birthplace; but certainty has not been attained, and informed scholars have little or no expectation that it will be. The poem *Genair Patraic* (Birth of Patrick), attributed to St. Fiacc, his alleged contemporary, but probably written in the eighth century, says he was born at Al-Cluaide, that is, Dumbarton. The strongest objections to this identification are made on the ground that certain terms used by Patrick—*vicus, villula, decurio*—are said to be inapplicable to Dumbarton as it then was. However, Patrick's letter to Coroticus of Strathclyde, whose capital was Dumbarton, seems to imply that this miscreant prince was his fellow countryman. A location in Cumberland, within the region called Rheged in Welsh documents, has also been proposed. It will be recalled that both this and the Dumbarton area quite possibly felt the missionary influence of St. Ninian. We must here remind ourselves that Ninian's work probably had its beginning only when Patrick was a young boy, and the Christian family background indicated by him certainly drew from earlier British church sources.

Hanson, in the work cited, has closely re-examined the controverted issue of Patrick's dates. He cautiously offers for the saint's life-span the dates 390–460, and for the inception of his mission "some point between 425 and 435." If, however, as is widely agreed, Palladius preceded him, Patrick can hardly have begun his work before 432; and this date, which has early support in the Annals, remains as likely as any. Patrick tells us that his father, Calpornius, was a deacon, his grandfather, Potitus, a priest (Conf. 1). Elsewhere he says Calpornius was also a decurion, a minor local magistrate. For good measure an eleventh-century chronicler gives him a great-grandfather, Odissius, who is also a deacon. Though Patrick himself was undoubtedly a celibate, no special opprobrium was associated with clerical marriage in the less ascetic age of his parents' generation. He makes no mention of his mother, who may have died in his early years; but Muirchú names her Concessa, and later legend made her a sister of Martin of Tours.

Notwithstanding his clerical background, the boy's religious education was neglected. He kept the company of ungoverned youths who were alienated from their priests, and to the time of his capture he "knew not the true God" (Conf. 1). Thus he is very different from those who have studied Holy Scripture from infancy and "have never changed their speech" (Conf. 9). From what followed, however, it is plain that some commonplaces of Christian teaching were early lodged in his mind, and formed the basis of his conversion.

He was about sixteen years old when, together with "many thousands" of British captives from the district, he was snatched away from his father's farmstead close to the village and carried off to Ireland. The date was about 405, the year of the death of the "High King" Neill of the Nine Hostages. Whether, as is sometimes supposed, Neill was the commander of this large-scale raid, Patrick does not say. Undoubtedly Neill would have been fully capable of such grand piracy, but it was hardly beyond the enterprise of any maritime Irish chief strong enough to raise a fleet. How little did Patrick's barbarous captors guess what they were doing to their country when they hustled into one of their ships amid a throng of bound captives this badly brought up and bewildered teenager and gleefully sailed away!

Six years of captivity followed, during which his task was to tend flocks (*pecora*), probably of sheep (Conf. 16). The early writers make him the slave of one Miliucc of Slemish in Antrim. This location has been questioned in the light of Patrick's own words where he describes a vision that he experienced some decades later while in Britain (Conf. 23). One Victorinus comes to him bearing innumerable letters and hands him one of these, entitled "the voice of the Irish," whereupon he "heard the voice of those who were by the Wood of Voclut by the western sea," calling to him: "Come, we pray, holy youth, and walk among us once again [*adhuc*]." But the meaning of "adhuc" in this context is questionable and it has been variously rendered. Many efforts have been made to explain this puzzling passage, including that of placing the Wood of Voclut in eastern Ulster, the "western sea" being the Irish Sea as viewed from Britain where he saw the vision.[16] But it is significant that Tírechán, who adopts the Slemish location for Patrick's captivity, nevertheless regards Voclut as his own birthplace, Tirawley, near Kilala Bay on the Atlantic. It is well to remember that Patrick is here describing a vision experience, and that he was without doubt a highly imaginative person. Moreover, he was extremely conscious of the "far west" situation of Ireland, his mission field. Ireland was for him, as for some classical writers, the outermost west of the habitable world. He tells us that he had been "predestined to preach the Gospel even to the ends of the earth" (*Letter to Coroticus*, 6). He will never leave the people whom the Lord has "purchased in the farthest ends of the earth" (Conf. 58). Matching the geographical uniqueness of his mission is his scripture-based eschatology. From Matt. 28:19–20 and parallel passages drawn from both Testaments, he sees his work as culminating the expansion of the Faith begun by the Apostles, to be followed by the coming of the end. He gives thanks to God, who heard his prayer, so that, ignorant though Patrick was, "in the last days" he undertook "such a holy and wonderful work, imitating those who [were sent to] preach the Gospel for a testimony to all nations before the end of the world." This prophecy is now fulfilled: "The Gospel has been preached to where there is nobody beyond [*usque ubi nemo ultra est*]"—as he phrases his naïve claim (Conf. 34). His exaltation at the singular role appointed to him is unmistakable. It does not destroy his humility, but it endows him with dauntless courage. It is probably in this context that we should read his report of the vision of the people of Voclut in the west. There is nothing to suggest that during his captivity he could have "walked among" Irish people as a "holy youth." The vision has all the waywardness of dream life. What reader has not, at least in youth, envisioned in dreams so vivid as to be long remembered towns and peoples, coasts and harbors totally beyond his experience when awake, but suggested by some floating fragment of hearsay information or incidental reading? It is safest to dissociate Voclut from his place of captivity.

We return to the captive lad. His master, a man of some property, sent him to tend flocks alone. In his loneliness he sought relief in prayer. "Many times a day I used to pray," he tells us, and as he prayed "the love and fear of God increased," his faith was strengthened, and he was so moved in spirit that he would say a hundred prayers in a day and remain for prayer in the woods and mountains at night. "Before daybreak I used to be roused up to pray, and I felt no harm whether there was snow, frost or rain, nor was there any sluggishness in me, because, as I see, the Spirit was then glowing [*fervebat*] within me" (Conf. 16). In his ecstatic fervor he longed to escape to the Roman Christian world. Six years of servitude had passed when a heavenly voice in a dream comforted him with the assurance that his prayers were heard and that he was soon to revisit his fatherland (*iturus ad patriam tuam*). Soon afterward the voice announced to him that the ship that was to carry him was ready and lay some 200 miles away. Was the voice in reality that of a friend who knew about seaports and was perhaps conducting a secret escape route for British captives? Leaving his master, he set forth and reached the ship's anchorage unharmed (Conf. 17). This would naturally be one of the southeastern harbors of Ireland, say Wicklow or Wexford. The captain of the ship at first brusquely refused him passage, but when he turned away, praying as he went, he heard himself suddenly called back. He steadfastly declined to make a solemn pact with the sailors by the pagan rite of sucking their breasts, but was accepted on his own terms as a Christian and went with them hoping that some of them would be converted (Conf. 18).

Three days at sea brought them to their destination. Was this a port on the Bay of Biscay, or in Brittany, or in Britain? The whole subsequent career of Patrick is involved in the answer to this question. If the landing was at some port in Gaul, say Bordeaux or Brest, the contacts with persons in Gaul, at Lerins, and at Rome, alleged in late documents, are given some color of probability. If it was on the coast of Wales or of Southern Scotland, the supposed continental phase of Patrick's career is brought under the greatest suspicion, and may have to be almost entirely cancelled out. Much research has been devoted to an intense restudy of the documents that bear upon this issue, and on the continuation of Patrick's story after the sea voyage away from Ireland. The date would probably be about 410.

For half a century the view of T. Olden,[17] elaborated by Bury, obtained general acceptance. The path of Patrick's journey of twenty-eight days overland (Conf. 19), by this interpretation, lay across Gaul southeastward toward the Mediterranean, through territory then recently devastated by Vandals and Suevi so as to be depopulated and without food supply. Patrick tells of the peril of starvation, relieved by the appearance of a herd of swine (*grex porcorum*) in answer to his prayers. The slaughter of the pigs provided a feast of pork, after which the journey was resumed. In most manuscripts the word *canes* (dogs) enters here, somewhat surprisingly; the dogs, half-dead (*semi-vivi*, like the Good Samaritan's wounded traveler in the Vulgate), were revived by the pork. Bury gives a plausible construction of the phrase. The men were in charge of a shipment of Irish wolfhounds, known since the time of Suetonius to be in demand on the continent for hunting and for the sanguinary sports of Roman amphitheaters. (Though near starvation themselves, the dog-drivers apparently had no thought of eating dog meat.) Anyway, the word "canes" had to be explained. Professor Carney, however, found a manuscript that had instead the form *carne*, not dogs but meat, an alteration which makes the passage readable in a new sense. It was the men themselves who had been "half-dead"; they were now replete with pork, and after a stay of two nights resumed their journey.[18] Professor Bieler, claiming the superiority of the manuscripts with "canes," keeps the dogs, but with a slight emendation and an adjustment of punctuation makes *"semi-vivi"* apply to the men.[19] Professor Hanson, on the other hand, accepts Carney's reading and remarks that "the whole story of the dogs has an air of improbability, not to say of absurdity."[20] What is clearly improbable is Bury's picturesque "Irish wolfhound" elaboration. What Patrick wrote, or intended to write, may never be known with certainty.

Carney could find no evidence for a continental port of landing, and numerous scholars now join him in setting the land journey in Britain. Bieler retains a continental setting for the journey, without following the whole course of Bury's account, which takes Patrick to Lerins and Rome. He argues that the "porci" of Patrick's "grex porcorum" would be not wild hogs but farm stock allowed to stray, as would happen in a cultivated area disturbed by war, such as Gaul was at the time. One is reminded, however, of Patrick's own experience some twenty years earlier; a farm near the British coast could be disrupted by raiders, the animals presumably being left to range untended. In accordance with his dream, Patrick had doubtless started out hoping to come to his native place (Conf. 17), and if he had been so far diverted as to find himself in a devastated region of Gaul, it is strange that he does not refer to this. The weight of argument seems to favor some sparsely inhabited part of northern Wales or of Cumbria or Strathclyde. Carney makes it appear not improbable that the second part of the sailors' land journey was a return to their ship. They had come to unfamiliar ground, and the captain's words to Patrick would suggest that his plans had gone awry. Perhaps they had missed their way to some undisclosed destination. After the incident of the swine, the sailors thanked Patrick's God, and he himself was in high esteem among them. But he soon took an opportunity to slip away from their company, presumably heading for his old home. He does not say how his disengagement from them came about; instead he inserts a paragraph (Conf. 21) about a subsequent captivity of sixty days which cannot be set into a narrative sequence.

If Patrick ever went to Gaul, it was probably during the two decades and more for which we have no record of his life. Both the *Confession* and the *Letter to Coroticus* mention Gaul once. In the *Confession* (Conf. 43) Patrick expresses an unfulfilled desire "to go as far as Gaul to visit the brethren and to behold the face of the saints of my Lord." In the *Letter* (14) he refers to "a custom of the Roman Christians of Gaul," that of ransoming Christian captives taken by the Franks. Neither passage indicates more than a knowledge by report of the Christians of Gaul, yet both could have been written by a man who had been among them.

In this connection some notice of the minor texts traditionally attributed to Patrick must also be made, since if they are genuine they have some significance for his career. There are three "Sayings of Patrick" gleaned by Tírechán from sources available in the seventh century. The first is: "I had the fear of God before me through Gaul and Italy and in the islands of the Tyrrhene sea." If accepted this would make more probable a stay at Lerins, the famous monastery of St. Honoratus founded in 410. The second brief saying makes use of the pious ejaculation "Deo gratias," several times found in Patrick's acknowledged writings and easily copied from these. The third commands the singing of the Kyrie at each (monastic?) hour of prayer in "the Church of the Scots, in order that you may be Christians as are the Romans." While Patrick's authorship of the third of these *Dicta* is defended as a possibility by Bieler, all three are on various grounds disallowed by Binchy and Hanson. From various utterances it is evident that Patrick equated "Christian" with "Roman." To make Ireland Christian was to bring it into the nexus of the now Christian Roman Empire and culture. Bury confidently took him to Lerins for training, and believed that he visited Rome; but both these allegations have been generally abandoned. Other short writings later ascribed to Patrick include: (1) the *Lorica* ("Patrick's Breastplate"), a beautiful Christian poem in the style of bardic verse; (2) a letter allegedly addressed by him to two bishops; (3) the disciplinary canons attributed to him together with the bishops Auxilius and Iserninus, supposedly promulgated in a synod; and (4) the canons of an alleged second synod of Patrick.[21] All of these in their extant form seem later than his time. If in addition to obvious quotations there are in them genuine Patrician elements, these cannot now be identified.

All the annals and other documents that allege continental associations for Patrick, including the hymns in his honor ascribed to Secundinus and Fiacc, were written centuries after his time, mainly as contributions to the Patrick legend. That he owed his appointment as a missionary to Pope Celestine; that he was in 441 "approved in the Catholic faith" by Pope Leo I; that he spent many years in study under Germanus of Auxerre and was consecrated either by bishop Amator or by Germanus—all are late additions to the legend. It is next to incredible that an old missionary whose credentials were attacked would in writing his defense have remained silent on his authorization either by a pope or by Germanus, the most eminent ecclesiastic of Gaul. There is nothing in the evidence to preclude his original appointment by British bishops and subsequent responsibility to British church authorities. It is certainly to British readers that he addresses his apologia in the *Confession.* Here he devotes several sections (Conf. 26–32) to a distressful experience in which a close friend betrayed to his accusers some boyhood offense of Patrick which he had later confessed in secrecy, and makes reference to what appears to have been a deputation sent to Ireland to investigate his "laborious episcopate." Only in Britain could a boyhood sin of Patrick have been known and subsequently recalled. It seems highly probable that after some twenty years of training and service as a British cleric, and following the inner dedication associated with the vision of Victorinus and the pleading Irish, he received his commission and episcopal consecration from some British church authority.[22]

Patrick does not write as one who had learned his Latin in a monastic or episcopal school. Christine Mohrmann, in a searching study of his style and vocabulary,[23] takes the view that his Latin has affinities with the colloquial Latin spoken in Gaul in the fifth century, and she notes that it is "unbookish" and that the vocabulary is not monastic. Patrick "lives with the Bible, his only book," and is particularly fascinated by St. Paul's Epistles and by the sayings of Jesus. Others have pointed to evidence that he had read some of the Church Fathers, so that "man of one book" is not quite applicable. Some doubt about his debt to a vulgar Latin spoken in Gaul is raised by Dr. Hanson's proof from numerous inscriptions and graffiti that a vulgar Latin was in use in Britain.[24] Certainly Latin was the language of the British church. It is thus not improbable that in a British church connection before his call to Ireland he acquired the meager Latin he later used. His quotations of Scripture reflect familiarity with both Jerome's Vulgate and the Old Latin version. He relied upon the Bible in a remarkable degree for his phraseology; in some instances his memory of biblical language seems to come to his aid when he is embarrassed for lack of appropriate secular vocabulary. In Ireland he encountered scorn for his deficiency in Latin from certain critics whom he calls, in the text as we have it, *"dominicati* [or *domini cati*] *rhetorici"* (Conf. 13), which seems to mean "lordly rhetoricians." Heinrich Zimmer supported from this passage the view that Latin learning had already gained a foothold in Ireland before Patrick's mission. He used a sixth-century gloss of a fifth-century text which purports to record the migration of "all the learned men on this side of the sea" chiefly to Ireland, making their escape from the disorders in Gaul caused by barbarian invasions. The glossator adds that the migrating scholars "brought about a great advance of learning to the inhabitants of those regions."[25] Hanson proposes to read *domini cata rhetorica* (or *rhetoricen*), *cata* meaning "according to" as it does in the Old Latin Bible.[26] On any interpretation, Patrick seems to have reference to rhetoricians, masters of Latin style, who were unfriendly or contemptuous toward him. Whoever they were, they used their standards of literary education to wound Patrick at a vulnerable point. There were also accusations of simony, and to these he replies spiritedly, indicating his meticulous refusal to accept gifts for his ordinations or other episcopal acts: "The Lord ordained clerics everywhere through my unworthy person, and I conferred the ministry upon them free" (Conf. 50). To guard against any occasion of defamation he had returned the gifts laid on the altar by pious women even though the givers were offended by this (Conf. 49). From some source not indicated probably the churches in Britain, he was evidently provided with funds, which he used liberally to gain from local authorities permission to preach and protection from harm. He speaks repeatedly of persecution, but he appears to have suffiered relatively little serious hostility. In one instance mentioned, he and his aides were thrust into prison, and the missionary band spent fourteen days in fetters until released through the intervention of "dear friends" (Conf. 52). Neither defamation nor personal danger can dismay the dedicated evangelist, who is always inwardly assured that he has the approval of God and is happy in the fruits of his labor. "God," he says, "granted me such great grace that many Christians through me should be regenerated to God and afterward confirmed, and that clergy should everywhere be ordained" (Conf. 38); and he speaks of "Christians in countless numbers whom I begot to God and confirmed in Christ" (Letter 2). It is his joy that countless "sons of the Scots and daughters of princes have become monks and virgins of Christ." There are several passages of this sort, which show clearly that Patrick promoted the beginnings of celibate religious communities.

Thus Patrick's writings indicate something of his achievement. A Christian church strongly colored with asceticism had arisen, and he writes as if it extended over Ireland. Modern writers, in accord with Muirchú, tend to limit his actual missionary journeys largely to the northern half of the island, but it was certainly of wide extent.

Patrick felt very keenly the affection of a pastor for this large flock. An atrocity committed against his converts brings a note of anguish in his *Letter to Coroticus*. Coroticus was apparently one of the princes called Ceretic in Welsh genealogies, probably Ceretic Wledig of Strathclyde. Although nominally a Christian, he led a ruthless raid on the Irish Coast, aided by some "Scots and apostate Picts," at a spot where Patrick had just baptized a company of new converts. The soldiers burst upon them, slaying and capturing many. Patrick treats the raiders and their prince as Christians by profession who have denied their faith by an atrocious deed. Having declared himself "a bishop appointed by God, in Ireland," he excommunicates all who have had anything to do with the massacre (Letter 7), urges good Christians to shun them until they repent, and calls for the liberation of their captives. The pastor suddenly bereaved of his flock by a deed of revolting cruelty pours forth his outraged soul in bitterness. "Lord, I am greatly despised; around me are the sheep torn to pieces and driven away . . . by those robbers." The letter is sent to the Christian subjects of Coroticus in the hope that they will bring pressure to bear on their king and that the women captured in the raid may be released. The document vividly reveals the deep emotional involvement and commitment that gave strength and quality to Patrick's mission to the Irish.

Patrick's religious testimony is extremely personal, and it is a warm piety rather than an emphasis on formalized belief that pervades his writings. In one section, however, he so summarizes his doctrines as to show that he taught the essentials of Nicene trinitarianism (Conf. 4). But since the important Nicene phrase "of one substance with the Father" is not used, he was evidently under the influence of writers of earlier date than Nicea. The intense reality of his faith is conveyed through abundant use of biblical phrases. He has invited comparison with St. Paul, and with John Bunyan. Like Paul he is obedient to heavenly visions and voices, and such experiences he seems to have felt to be normal. At the end of a vision, after words not understood have been spoken, he hears the divine commendation: "He who laid down his life for thee, he it is who speaks in thee" (Conf. 24). There is no arrogance here, but an amazed gratitude for the bestowal of a potent grace that makes his work effective: "I was not worthy . . . that He should bestow upon me such great grace toward this nation" (Conf. 15).

It would be unprofitable here to attempt an account of the extent and limits of his missionary tours in Ireland. The seventh- and eighth-century documents that try to trace his steps are tendentious and unreliable. As bishop of the Irish, Patrick shows no awareness that other bishops shared his work. If he consecrated other bishops, or, as seems probable, was associated with others who came from Britain or Gaul, he has no occasion for mentioning this. In the Annals of Ulster it is stated that in 439 three British bishops—Secundus, Auxilius, and Iserninus—were sent to join him. Muirchú largely confines Patrick's labors to Ulster, while Tírechán has him visit numerous places and meet tribal kings in Meath and Connaught. Muirchú says that Patrick loved Armagh above all other places, and there is some probability that he founded a church in Armagh. Annalists give for this the dates 441 and 444; but Patrick has no mention of Armagh. His place of burial was not Armagh but, according to Tírechán, Saul in County Down. Three centuries after his time, the image of Patrick conveyed by his own writings was hardly recognizable in the growing legend. He had become a magician confounding the assembled druids at Tara, and at the same time a powerful ecclesiastic. In the *Tripartite Life* he is represented as exercising from Armagh the authority of a primate, consecrating hundreds of bishops, and his missionary itinerary over most of Ireland is plotted in detail. No doubt the expanding legend is motivated by the desire to magnify Armagh, as against a monastic "parochia," the connection of houses associated with the name of Columba. But any geographical restriction of his ministry to northeast Ireland seems to come under question from Patrick's own habitual reference to "Ireland" as his province and "the Irish" as his beloved people, as well as his incidental claim that grace was given him to ordain clergy everywhere (Conf. 28).

With many questions still unanswered, scholars have nevertheless led us back from the unsafe world of legend and tradition to the sure ground of Patrick's writings. The miracle-worker of the hagiographers, who Christianizes Ireland by a series of dramatic demonstrations before princes, gives place to the warm-hearted, alert, zealous, diligent, and courageous biblical preacher, and the faithful bishop intensely conscious of his unique mission and pastoral responsibility. In this role Patrick was indeed the Apostle of Ireland.

Ireland: Early Monastic Foundations, with a Few Additional Places

Five | The Flowering of Irish Monasticism

THE CHRISTIANIZATION of Ireland took place within the period of that powerful and surprising movement, the rise of monasticism and its spread from Egypt, Palestine, and Asia Minor to all parts of western Europe. In Gaul the first great monastic personality was St. Martin (325–97), a native of Pannonia (Hungary) who, having left the Roman army, founded a monastery at Ligugé in about 360, and in 371 (despite objections by neighboring bishops on the ground of his crudity, sordid clothing, and neglected hair) became bishop of Tours. Martin was soon famous and influential in all western regions, not least in Britain and Ireland, where his name entered into the legendary lives of numerous saints including Ninian and Patrick. Although it is unlikely that Patrick had any ties with Martin's foundations, he can hardly have been unaware of the impulse toward monasticism associated with his name. Assuredly, too, the influence of Ninian cannot be ruled out as a factor in Patrick's promotion of asceticism. There is no reason to doubt that Patrick formed groups under vows at some of the numerous churches he established. The "monks and virgins" of whom he speaks with gratification must have been drawn away from family ties into communities of some sort. It may have been the normal thing for a monastic unit to grow up beside each of his churches. These, however, would usually be quite small, offering little promise of the populous monasteries of the sixth century that were to be of supreme importance for the Irish Church and to yield a unique service to Christian life in Europe.

Unquestionably there lies here a hiatus difficult to bridge. It would seem that Patrick aimed to establish in Ireland a ruling episcopate such as existed in Roman Britain and elsewhere, monastic elements being subject to the bishops. But by the time of Brigid, the Finnians, and the Brendans, the Church of Ireland was under the leadership of abbots who were secondarily bishops, or had bishops attached to their monasteries and under their jurisdiction. There was no repudiation of bishops as essential functionaries in the church; they alone could ordain to clerical office, confirm the faithful, and consecrate church properties. There were important duties, and bishops were held in honor, as we see from the heavy penalties for injury to them prescribed in the *Penitentials* and in the Brehon laws. But there is much to show that bishops who are not abbots appear as agents of abbots or of monasteries; and bishops in such subordinate position seem not to have contended for control. Diocesan episcopacy did not flourish, and what promise there was of it at the early stage faded as monasticism mounted in importance. It may have been the tribal and rural character of Irish society that chiefly prevented the permanent establishment of episcopal jurisdiction after Patrick. Elsewhere the diocese was organized with a town of some political importance as its center; but Ireland had no such towns. The transition to monastic leadership may not have seemed startlingly abrupt. John Ryan saw evidence of episcopal jurisdiction being long exercised independently of monasteries; and he observes that while in the Annals of Ulster the successors of Patrick at Armagh are called bishops, in the Book of Leinster the same persons are abbots.[1] Kathleen Hughes sees a long-continued control by bishops over a class of clergy who were detached from monastic communities, and notes the legal authorization of episcopal visitation in the *Crith Gablach*, an eighth-century law tract.[2] But such functioning by bishops seems to have been unusual. From the sixth century the leaders of the church were abbots and learned monks.

However social conditions may have affected this strange inversion of jurisdictions, what most arrests our attention is the astonishing flow of youth into the monastic life, which drew men with irresistible attraction. In many cases what the founders sought was a retreat with few companions in some remote spot, but they found themselves pursued by throngs of young men eager to follow their example and to obey their rules. Such had been, to be sure, the experience of Anthony in Egypt, of Martin in Gaul, and of Illtud and David in Britain. But it is possible that in Ireland a larger percentage of the whole population than anywhere else entered monastic communities. Nowhere else in Christendom was the culture of a people so completely embraced within monasticism. The Irish Christian youth felt with peculiar force the urge to ascetic devotion, and the busy life of the monasteries offered an outlet to native talent and energy in art and learning and missionary adventure by which Ireland was to make its great medieval contribution to the Christian West.

How the new tide of monastic activity in sixth-century Ireland began cannot be fully stated, but there is clear evidence that Ninian's successors at Candida Casa maintained a strong community there, in which certain Irish monastic celebrities spent years of training. The institution was called Rosnat by the Irish and was sometimes referred to as "The Great Monastery." The late fifth- or early sixth-century Irish founder, Enda, was an alumnus of Rosnat and in legend ranks among the foremost monastic teachers of the time. Finnian of Magbile (Moville) is believed to have been trained under Mugint, a successor Ninian. In a biography of this Finnian we are told that when he was in the monastery of Nendrum on Strangford Lough, ships came thither from "Nennio" (apparently the contemporary abbot, Mugint) in one of which Finnian was carried over the sea to the "Great Monastery." A strange and incredible tale of Finnian's involvement there in a love intrigue between another Irishman and a high-born British girl takes it for granted that early in the sixth century Candida Casa had become a double monastery. One may ask whether this offers a clue to the later appearance of like coeducational institutions in Ireland (Kildare) and northern England (Whitby). In the same general period Tighernach of Clones received training there, and Brignat of Killeavy is said to have gone to Rosnat at the bidding of St. Darerca to obtain a monastic "rule."

Better known is the monastic contact of Ireland with Wales in the era of the great Welsh saints (see chapter 3). Father Ryan notes that "in the sixth century the Irish were the borrowers" in this relationship, and he gives special prominence to Gildas.[3] The statement in the Life of Gildas by the Monk of Rhuis that he was invited to Ireland by King Ainmere to "restore ecclesiastical order" (chapter 3) implies a state of disorder in the Irish church of which no sufficient evidence has been shown. No doubt there were perils in the transition that led to the ascendancy of monasticism, and the age may have witnessed unusual strife among the clans and kings. The survival of pagan beliefs and practices is attested, and while this did not amount to a repudiation of Christianity, it may have been alarming. Ainmere may have sensed a growing deterioration when he called the Welsh leader to his aid.

In balance the flow of influence was probably as Ryan states it; but in large degree the stimulation of monastic life and learning was mutual and continuous. A large part of South Wales had been populated by Irishmen, and intercourse was freely maintained by ships that went and came. The traffic of saints, as the hagiographers constantly remind us, moved in different directions about Ireland, Wales, Cornwall, and Brittany, assuring a spiritual interdependence that was taken for granted. Samson of Dol, as we saw, accompanies some Irishmen from Wales to Ireland, labors in Cornwall, and spends his late years in Brittany. Cadoc's teacher in Wales is the son of an Irish king. British St. Carranog, called Cernach in Irish documents, is alleged to have joined Patrick, formed with him a sort of comity of missions, and "converted districts of Irishmen" in Leinster, despite the hostility of "magicians." St. Padarn, of Breton birth, is chiefly active in Wales; but his father, at the time of Padarn's birth, goes to pursue a holy life in Ireland where after some decades he is visited by his now eminent son. St. Finian, before founding the great monastery of Clonard, is brought by Cadoc to Wales, where with other Irishmen he was to pursue his studies. Such notices, however questionable in detail, go to show how naturally the Celtic churches shared a common tradition and experienced a habitual interchange and cross-fertilization in monastic discipline, learning and spirituality.[4]

The Catalogue of the Saints of Ireland is a ninth-century writer's wayward construction of Irish church history in three stages prior to the plague years 664–65.[5] The "First Order" of saints, ending in 544, consists of noncelibate bishops, 350 in number and by race Franks (Gauls), Romans, and Scots. Their one chief is Patrick, and they have one liturgy and one tonsure "from ear to ear." This order is pronounced most holy (*sanctissimus*), while the Second Order (544–98) is only relatively holy (*sanctior*). It is composed of bishops and presbyters who are rigidly ascetic, "avoiding the society of women" and "excluding them from their monasteries." The subsequent Third Order, practicing a further extreme of asceticism, is rated merely *sanctus*. It consists of desert dwellers "living on herbs and water and from alms" and shunning private property. By his characterization of the three orders, the author stresses his rejection of the ascetic ideal, and his categories undoubtedly misrepresent the actual evolution of Irish church leadership. No such abrupt transformations are credible, nor is the progressive triumph of extreme asceticism to be regarded as historical. It is permitted to suspect that the writer, in thus shrewdly grading the holiness of the saints, is consciously playing the role of a satirist rather than offering a sober and straightforward interpretation of history. Even his somewhat graphic phrase to describe the Celtic frontal tonsure, *"ab aure usque ad aurem,"* may have been penned in a humorous mood. Writers on medieval Irish literature have made us aware that there were those among his contemporaries for whom the austere life had no appeal, and it is to this company that our author belongs.

Incidentally, it is of some interest that he subscribes to the traditional prominence of Gildas and his Welsh colleagues as reformers of the Irish church and liturgy. Here he is in general accord with statements about Gildas in Ireland made by the Monk of Rhuis. But we have no contemporary corroboration of this or of the adoption in Ireland of any new liturgy of the Mass in Gildas' time. If such a reformed liturgy was introduced, its adoption may have been gradual rather than by action of a synod affecting the whole church.

As schools of learning the monasteries must have had a more than accidental relation to the well-developed colleges of pre-Christian Ireland in which druids, bards, and brehons underwent exacting courses of instruction. In the druidic schools the successful completion of a twelve-year period of disciplined study earned the rank or degree of Ollam, signalizing the highest attainment in learning. The instruction was oral, and of its content only traces are left in heroic tales, poems, and law tracts. In Ireland, as not in Britain and Gaul, the druidic culture was never destroyed by force. While druidism as a religion yielded to Christianity, bards and brehons continued to function. The bards were numerous and influential through early monastic times, and some of the saints were their pupils. After his adoption of the monastic life, St. Columba went for instruction to the bard Gemman and resided for a time with him in Leinster. Late in his life he championed the cause of the Irish bards when their guild was under attack. In Wales, too, the bardic tradition survived so strongly as to contribute in the twelfth century to a newly affirmed national consciousness. In that century Ireland saw a revived interest in bardic education with a plan for a curriculum comprising twelve years of adult study. The Irish church never repudiated the early cultural heritage, least of all the ancient concern for mature and protracted study; and this could flourish only where students and masters were assembled in considerable numbers.

It was the monasteries that provided the opportunity for a higher education long cherished in Ireland. The vigorous new monastic communities soon far outclassed in significance the pre-Christian institutions, but the latter long continued to receive support from the *Túaths*, or clan districts, which were the units of local government; and peripatetic bards continued, under conditions prescribed, to instruct and train groups of pupils. "Each *fili*" says James Kenney, "was expected to maintain and teach a number of pupils, and in some places there were large schools of *filidecht* (bardic lore) with a nation-wide reputation."[6] Similarly a close relation was usually formed between the monastery and the *túath* within which it stood, based on an original transfer of land from the clan chief to the monastic founder.

Whether Tírechán was soundly informed or not in his report of Patrick's foundation of Trim near Tara, he was probably describing what by his time (ca. 675) had become a familiar pattern. Fedilmid, son of King Loeghaire and lord of Trim, makes a gift of land on which a church is built. In the lives of the saints similar transactions enter into many accounts of monastic foundations. Mutual obligations were involved, of which we have evidence in many passages of the *Senchus Mór*, the great collection of Irish legal determinations. Purporting to be a fifth-century compilation in which Patrick cooperated with the court poet Dubhthach and other eminent persons, the *Great Senchus* really belongs to a much later era, when the relation of monastery and tribe had become stabilized through time. The monastery is obligated to provide instruction for children of the *túath*, and one in seven of the young men is to become a recruit to the monastery. The latter provision was hardly requisite in the early period, when the monastic urge was sufficient to bring voluntary recruits in embarrassing numbers. Succession to the abbatial office was restricted to members of the founder's family wherever such a candidate was available; hence the abbot was designated "*comarba*," or *co-arb*, successor by family inheritance. A hundred years ago the Count de Montalembert was so impressed by the close alliance of clans and monasteries in Ireland that he described the latter as nothing else than "les clans réorganisés sous une forme religieuse."[7] Yet their concerns were never merely local. In a great many cases they formed units in a confederated series, the whole connection being regarded as the *paruchia*, or province of authority, of a single founder and his successors. There was evidently much intercourse among monasteries, many individuals being permitted to move from one to another almost at will. Irish monks who went abroad were apt to think of themselves with pride as Irish, without calling attention to their former local attachments.

Mention has already been made of certain Irish monastic founders whose training had been at Candida Casa. One of the earliest of this group was St. Mochaoi of Nendrum on Strangford Lough. His death has been placed as early as 497, with the improbable claim that he was ordained by Patrick. Excavations of the site have revealed a considerable establishment with vallum, church, refectory, kitchen, guesthouse, library, and workshops.[8] More celebrated is St. Enda, born in the Pictish area of Ulster, who chose for his location a storm-lashed island off Ireland's western coast. It is the largest of the Aran islands, now called Inishmore. The date of Enda's settlement there may have been before 500 and cannot have been much later. It is not known whether Enda deserved his later reputation as a founder of other monasteries and a teacher of saints of the next generation; but he must have carried to that far-out haunt of fishermen (whose descendants people John Synge's *Riders to the Sea*) the treasures of monastic learning, and been accompanied across Galway Bay by a courageous band of disciples.

Our attention has been called to some unverifiable features of the *Life of St. Boite* (see above, p. 45); but his achievement in founding the important monastery of Monastirboice in County Louth is not in doubt. One of the earliest of the Irish monasteries, it also became one of the largest. Its beginning must be dated shortly after 500. Ciaran (d. 548?), founder of Clonmacnois in Offaly, is reputed a disciple of St. Enda and thus an heir of the Whithorn school of learning. He is also in the honors list among the alumni of Clonard. Building, with eight companions, a primitive shelter at Clonmacnois, he soon found himself at the head of some thousands of volunteer learners of the monastic way; and Clonmacnois maintained a front-rank position in Irish monasticism to the age of the Vikings. Finnian, abbot of Clonard in Meath, seems to have established that monastery about 520; it was apparently later that he was associated with the Welsh saints (see chapter 3). Until his death from the plague in 549, Clonard was regarded as preeminent in learning. Finnian's reputation remained very high among Irish abbots, and through the subsequent distinction of those of his disciples known as "the Twelve Apostles of Ireland" his influence was great throughout the century.

Included among these twelve celebrities are St. Columba of Iona, St. Ciaran of Clonmacnois, St. Brendan of Birr, and St. Brendan of Clonfert. The latter is known as Brendan the Voyager, from the marvelous legend of his quest, with thirty (in some texts, sixty) companion monks, of the far-off ocean Isle of Promise, or of Paradise. In the ninth or tenth century the earlier reported ventures of Brendan on sea were elaborated with vivid imagination, apparently with some awareness of the actualities of Atlantic seagoing. The historical possibilities here have been probed by many writers, with the object not so much of becoming acquainted with Brendan as of learning something of the history of navigation. Had the legend-makers some knowledge from unpublished sailor lore of spots on the American continent? This has been made to seem not improbable; but if accepted, it does not extend Brendan's own explorations to our shores, but merely sets back a century before Leif Ericson the traversing of the Atlantic. Some stone structures found in North Salem, New Hampshire, bear a puzzling resemblance, as Geoffry Ashe and others have pointed out, to the walls of early Irish corbelled huts; but the *Navigatio Sancti Brendani* offers no clue to this. The tale is a tissue of extravagant marvels shot through with poetically phrased descriptions of ocean scenes, in which experience and invention mingle. There are strange trees and fruits, beasts and birds and sea-monsters, and meetings with departed humans. Conversations with St. Ailbe and St. Patrick are suitably included, and there is a vivid interview with Judas Iscariot during one of his periodic releases from torment. The thrice repeated celebration of Easter on the motionless back of a cooperative whale, Jasconius by name, is an unforgettable fragment of pious extravaganza. The story belongs in a class of voyage fiction which the Irish called *Imrama*, and has affinities with the voyages of Bran and of Maeldune; but unlike these it is remarkably devout in tone, and makes frequent use of elements of monastic psalmody, with Brendan on occasion singing at the top of his voice.

Brendan's true life story can be traced with some assurance. He came from County Kerry, and it was in the Dingle peninsula that he was first active, setting up a number of small communities there and in the neighboring islands. He is credited with a foundation on Inishglora off the Mayo coast, and with establishing a nunnery at Annaghdown on Lough Corrib in Galway, which he placed under his sister Brig. He was a friend of St. Comgall, with whom he visited Columba at Iona, and in the course of some journeyings among the western islands he probably formed a community on Tiree. The extent of his actual sea travels cannot be determined; it is believed that at some time he reached Iceland. He was in his seventies when he founded Clonfert in Galway. In old age he joined his sister at Annaghdown; and he spent his last days under her care. He died there in 578, supposedly at the age of ninety-two.[9]

In Brendan's time and in later generations, a great number of corbelled huts arose, chiefly by the shore, in Kerry County, the homes of lone seekers after God who left no record of their piety and hardships other than this work of their hands. The area at that time was forested, save for their small clearings, and the much-indented shorelines at many spots afforded shelter for small boats. Long centuries earlier megalithic builders left numerous monuments in that region of Ireland; as elsewhere, their burial places but not their dwellings remain for us to see. The fifth- and sixth-century anchorites and monks built their beehive huts so well that many of these stand securely still. On the Dingle peninsula in Kerry is located Dunmore Head, the westernmost point of Ireland; the spot is locally dubbed "the next parish to America." Seven or eight miles away to the northeast is Mount Brendan, on whose summit, at an elevation of more than 3,000 feet, Brendan had a retreat and an oratory. On the peninsula stands, too, what is perhaps the best-preserved of all corbelled stone churches, the Gallerus oratory, a shapely building which still retains the regularity of its structure and has been likened to an inverted boat. A remarkably similar structure of the same era is located on the island of Inchcolme in the Firth of Forth.[10] In some instances numerous huts were set close together and the colony was surrounded by a wall. If wooden buildings were also used, they have disappeared. On the lofty island rock of Scellig Michael, eight miles out in the ocean from the coast of Kerry, unnamed heroic pioneers formed a small community, whose corbelled huts and leaning cross remain, a marvel and a testimony.[11] Here as in countless seaside settlements on Ireland's coasts and islands and among the Hebrides, men went alone, or in small groups, to live in great simplicity a life of prayer. The hardy saints drew their sustenance mainly from the sea, and they made the shores echo with their psalms, until their voices were silenced by Norse invaders.

In the generation after Brendan's came Comgall who, like Enda and Finnian of Moville, was an Irish Pict. Dr. Ryan calls Comgall the greatest of the sixth-century founders,[12] a tribute earned by the extraordinary importance of his monastery of Bangor, founded about 558. Thronged by great numbers of monks, Bangor was unmatched as a nursery of scholars and missionaries. Even before Comgall's death in 603 many of these had become distinguished in service on the Continent (see chapter 10). Hardly less renowned and perhaps more beloved in later times was his contemporary, St. Coemgen (Kevin), a descendant of kings of Leinster, who was sent as a boy to study at Kilnamanagh near Tallacht, County Dublin. Here he was instructed by St. Petrock, a Cornwall monk and scholar. Fleeing the advances of an amorous girl, Kevin settled in the picturesque solitude of Glendalough (Valley of the Lakes) in County Wicklow. He proposed to live as a hermit in uninterrupted devotion, but he soon found an eager multitude of admirers about him. Kevin established there a community that was to be influential and enduring. The monastery was set between the upper and the lower of the two lakes, and most of the marvelous anecdotes told of Kevin have to do with boats and fishing. Like many Irish monks he cultivates the friendship of beasts and birds: A friendly badger brings him a salmon daily, and once rescues from lake waters, unharmed, his precious psalter. Flocks of birds sing about him as he prays, and in a late story a blackbird builds its nest on his extended palms while he stands in prayer, and he keeps this posture till the birdlings are hatched. Nearer to plain fact is the story that as the monks became numerous he would slip away to "St. Kevin's bed," a grotto by the upper lake, where he could be alone with God. Neither the little stone church known as "Kevin's kitchen" nor the other ruined structures that meet the visitor's eye today were built in his time, but they are older than the tall and well-preserved round tower to the north of the monastic settlement. He may have been a centenarian when he died in about 615.[13]

Women, too, had prominence in Irish monasticism, and some of them were admired for maternal and practical qualities in their good works and services to the social community. St. Ita (d. 570), in her nunnery at Kileedy, kept a school for young boys and numbered among her pupils such future leaders as Brendan of Clonfert. He is alleged to have sought her counsel when he was troubled about the accidental death of a youth, and again in connection with his second voyage. Early among the great foundations was that of Brigid at Kildare in the valley of the Liffey. Brigid was born at Faugart in County Louth about 450, some years before the death of Patrick, but anecdotes of her association with him are fictional. Her death date is placed at 523 or 528. The *Life of Brigid* written about 650 by Cogitosus weaves a delightful chain of miracles, and the half-dozen later "lives" continue to multiply pleasant fictions; but undoubtedly the legend affords some glimpses of her personality and career. She is represented as the daughter of Dubhthach, King Loeghaire's poet-laureate, by his concubine Brotsech, and as spending her years of childhood in a druid's household. She takes part in the lowly tasks of the house and farm. Her numerous childhood miracles include the multiplication of milk and butter for the relief of poor folk. Having returned to her parents in her teens, she is commanded to marry; but she avoids that misfortune by disfiguring her face (certain references to her later appearance would suggest that the effect of this was impermanent!). She takes the vow of virginity, and according to one author receives the veil from Macaile, a bishop in Westmeath. Gathering women about her, Brigid founded the nunnery of Kildare (Church of the Oak) where, it is believed, a pagan sanctuary featuring an oak tree had long existed. A competent, vigorous, and prompt personality is reflected in the accounts of Brigid. Since the institution needed the services of a bishop, she induced Conlaed, head of a group of anchorites in the neighborhood, to receive episcopal consecration and move with his followers to a site adjacent. This is the only authenticated example in Ireland of the "double monastery," a type which had a considerable vogue elsewhere. Brigid appears in policy-forming conferences with abbots and bishops, and as a person of influence in Irish church affairs; and she became the head of a connection of nunneries. She is driven about in a carriage on her errands of benevolence. On one occasion, when the driver tries to save distance by crossing a fallen fence and the vehicle is overturned, Brigid rises from her fall with the pithy remark, "Short cuts make broken bones." A note of compassion runs through the Brigid legend, matched by a talent for taking practical measures of relief for the unfortunate. Her beneficiaries include victims of violence and poverty, and a surprising number of lepers, some of whom impose upon her kindness. She has remained through the centuries Ireland's beloved and motherly household saint. As St. Bride in Scotland and as St. Ffraid in Wales, she was locally venerated and beloved. In the Hebrides (Uist) she is invoked in a song by women tending cattle, and elsewhere in Scotland she is "St. Bride of the Kine."

Brigid bore the name of the ancient pagan goddess Brigit, daughter of the good-for-everything god Dagda (see chapter 1), who was herself revered as the heavenly patron of poetry and the useful arts. Apparently derived from the cult of this goddess was the sacred and perpetual fire maintained at Kildare, which was tended daily in turn by twenty nuns (after Brigid's death, nineteen) to the time of Giraldus Cambrensis, who saw it in 1186. The Irish came near to making a goddess of the saint, often identifying her with the Virgin Mary. In popular lore she is "the Mary of the Gael," celebrated in poems as "Mother of the High King of Heaven." Her foundation at Kildare prospered under royal favor in the seventh century when its church was probably the most magnificent in Ireland. Kildare was for three centuries an institution of high rank; but it later became injuriously involved in political strife and suffered repeated violation from both Irish and Danish soldiery.[14]

Characteristic in the rise of Irish monasticism is a modest beginning in the founder's desire to practice with a small company a devotional asceticism, followed by an unforeseen inrush of recruits from which a community of hundreds or even thousands was soon formed, living in obedience to the founder abbot. Once established, the great monasteries must have lived a prosperous, self-sufficient, and extremely busy life, almost oblivious of the little, dispersed companies that we have noticed in remoter regions, shorelands, and islands. The large communities formed more or less stable relations with the local rulers, and each obeyed the written or unwritten rule of its own abbot. When we read of 4,000 monks at

Bangor and 3,000 at Clonmacnois, we may at least be sure that these round numbers represent very large aggregations, and we can in some measure appreciate the firm discipline and unfailing loyalties that made their peaceable existence possible.

The discipline of the Irish monasteries bore a close resemblance to that of the contemporary Welsh communities, perhaps with a more general accent on austerity. In both countries there was variation at the will of the founder and his successors, and much sheer individualism among the anchorites and solitaries. There existed no Celtic monastic rule in general use, and it is doubtful if any rule in early days was circulated in written form. Yet there was evidently a fairly close resemblance among the major monasteries in the routines followed and in the degree of austerity required. St. Benedict of Nursia was a contemporary of such Irish abbots as Comgall and the Finnians. His celebrated rule offers a far more moderate discipline than theirs. The written rules attributed to Columba, Comgall, Ailbe of Emly (Imlech) in Munster, Carthach (familiarly called Mochuta, of Lismore), and others of their time are all products of the eighth century and written in the interests of the Culdee revival of discipline led by Máel-rúain of Tallaght.[15] This reformer's death in 792 was followed by the Viking raids, which in large degree annulled the effects of his work. There is extant a metrical rule for Culdees attributed to St. Carthach (d. 637), founder of a once-celebrated monastery at Rathen in Offaly from which he and his monks fled to Lismore a year before his death; but the text is of much later date. It gives some details on the worship and work of the members. The translation by Reeves as repeated with alterations by MacEwen contains the lines:

> We watch, we read, we pray,
> Each according to his strength . . .
> Labour for the illiterate,
> Guided by pious clerics:
> The wise man's work is in his mouth,
> The unlearned work with their hands.[16]

The short Rule attributed to Columba is one for anchorites rather than for an organized monastery; the anchorite, however, here has with him a discreet servant. The discipline involves "a mind prepared for red martyrdom . . . fortified and stedfast for white martyrdom." White martyrdom was that of austerity or of death in a foreign land. The anchorite is also enjoined to pray constantly for those who trouble him.[17]

The actual rule of Comgall as practiced in Bangor is thought to be reflected in the *Regula coenobialis* of St. Columban written at Luxueil (see below, p. 165). Its ten short chapters are on the topics: obedience; silence; food and drink; the suppression of greed; the suppression of vanity; chastity; the sequence of the Psalms; discretion; mortification; and (borrowed from Jerome) the perfection of a monk. Features of this exacting rule are the requirement of complete submission to superiors, strenuous toil, and meager food. It is impossible to believe that the merciless rules of Columban and Máel-rúain afford an adequate index to life as it was lived within the monasteries. The men who wrote and embellished the Irish illuminated manuscripts and those who chiseled elaborate interlaced patterns in profusion on grave-slabs and crosses were free men who took delight in their skills and were able to call their souls their own. They were such men as could pause in their tasks to scribble verses devout or amusing. Even a heavy assignment of psalm-singing must often have had its reward in a musical experience and an exaltation of devotion. We have abundant evidence that abbots were not only obeyed but beloved, and that ordinarily monks lived together in brotherliness and friendship. They entered the monasteries with no illusions about its demands, but came from a secular society that could offer them little of comfort and ease. The recruits who came in years of manhood were volunteer soldiers prepared for an exacting but withal rewarding life, eager for the contest of the soul against the flesh, and for the knowledge that was available from scholar-monks only. Many also came to a monastery in childhood on action of their parents or from early piety of their own, and grew up in the stimulating atmosphere of an institution where men in earnest were always at work with hand and brain or engaged in acts of prayer and holy song. The growing lads may often have suffered from the meagerness of the diet, the lack of play, and the pressure of school tasks; but we see no evidence of recalcitrance on their part. Monks of all ages who were physically able engaged in the farming, gardening, and fishing tasks that were necessary to their subsistence. In some monasteries only one meal a day was eaten, and the sleeping hours, broken by the night office, were passed in conditions of studied discomfort. That vivacious Celts in large numbers subjected themselves to these inconveniences remains something of a wonder. It is a lesson in the possibilities of human nature under the impulse of devotion.

A forbidding aspect of the discipline is documented in the series of Penitential Books which, coming out of Ireland and Britain, virtually set the pattern of private confession and penance for the Western Church. The *Penitential of Finnian* (probably Finnian of Clonard)[18] lists proportionately measured periods of penance for many offenses of both clerics and laymen. The layman in each case draws a much lighter penalty than the cleric, since "his reward is less in the world to come." Thus a cleric who starts a quarrel with intention to strike or kill his neighbor must do penance for a year, while a layman so offending pays a fine at the discretion of a priest or judge and does penance for forty days. Murder by a cleric is penalized by a ten-year term of exile including seven years of penance. Offenses of a sexual nature, practices of magic, perjury, covetousness, and spoliation of churches receive similar attention. Penances are assigned with concern for motive and intention rather than the bare act of the offense.

A century after Finnian, a certain Cummean, or Cummine, probably Cummean the Tall (Fota) wrote a penitential which is similar in character but far more detailed and searching. It is arranged methodically on the basis of the deadly sins. Between these two writers in date was Columban (see chapter 10), whose penitential regulations are severe in prescribing floggings for the minor infringements of the discipline by monks.

The compilers of these handbooks were somewhat inventive in requiring curious penitential acts. They show a familiarity with John Cassian's account of the Desert Fathers of Egypt and with other sources for early monasticism. But some austerities voluntarily practiced by early Eastern ascetics are here prescribed as penalties for specific offenses. The cross-vigil is occasionally required for the sins of monks. It consisted of standing with the arms extended while singing an appointed number of psalms; and there were a number of variations of this posture, such as leaning forward with the hands upheld. Often the prescribed psalm is the *Beati*, Psalm 119 (with its 176 verses in modern Bibles), and in some cases it has to be sung not only once but as many as four or even seven times. Many of the documents require terms of "exile," a penalty used and dreaded in the Celtic world from druidic times.

Needless to say, fasting is constantly prescribed, often as an accompaniment of other penalties.

In the Penitentials we frequently find expressed the principle of the "contraries" derived from the medical schools. It is this principle that characterizes the Methodist School of medicine that originated with Themison of Laodicea about 50 B.C. and was greatly promoted by Soranus of Ephesus shortly after A.D. 100. "The duty of a physician," wrote a sixth-century Methodist, Alexander of Tralles, "is to cool what it hot, to warm what is cold, to dry what is moist and to moisten what is dry." The phrase *Contraria contrariis sanantur* (contraries are cured by their contraries) is many times repeated in the Penitentials from Finnian down. The medical analogy is habitually employed in the interpretation of penance. Sins are diseases of the soul, and specific penances are prescribed to counter the variety of maladies. In adopting the medical principle of contraries, the authors do not, however, draw directly on medical treatises. Their sourcebook is that compendium of monastic lore, John Cassian's *Colloquies*, with which the Irish monks were familiar. In the texts we can see that often penance is thought of not as penalty justly due but as medicine for the malady of sin and for the restoration of moral health and social acceptance.

An impressive feature of these guide-books for administering penance is their ingenious combination of elements from the social and legal heritage with scriptural morality and severe ascetic practices. Some of them introduce prominently the substitution of money payments for bodily penances in accordance with the system of fines and recompenses employed in Celtic and Germanic secular law. In Ireland everybody had his *enech-lann*, or honor-price, measured by his social rank, in addition to his *éric*, or body-price, which is common to all. Payments are sometimes reckoned in *cumals*, originally the price of a female slave and equal to three cows; more often in *solidi* or other units of money.

The "seal of confession" was strictly required in Celtic penance long before that phrase became current. According to *The Martyrology of Oengus* (ca. 800), one of the four sins for which no penance avails is to disclose what has been secretly confessed to one's *anmchara*, soul-friend or father-confessor. Relations with the *anmchara* appear in the "lives" as more or less permanent, and the saying occurs repeatedly, "Anyone without a soul-friend is like a body without a head." The wide circulation of the Penitentials on the Continent through the activities of the *peregrini* (see chapter 10) made them highly influential in the formative state of penitential discipline in the Western Church.[19]

The more intense form of ascetic life is that of the anchorites, and there were many of these. Characteristically they were not in entire detachment from the organized communities but were under the jurisdiction of an abbot, though living and praying apart from the fraternity. According to the late rule erroneously ascribed to Columba, the anchorite is to "live alone near a great monastery." The lives of saints have many references to hermit life, revealing different degrees of detachment from the monasteries. The *Catalogue of the Saints of Ireland* represents the spread of anchoritism as a late perversion of Irish Christianity; but no reliance should be placed on this document. The influence of Egyptian and Syrian asceticism in Ireland and Britain, while not fully explained, cannot be denied. But here resemblance is not mere duplication. Differences in climate and terrain made Irish hermitages no exact imitation of those of Egypt and the Near East, where there was little rain and much warm sand. But some imitation was intended. Wherever the hermit was, he called the place a desert (disart). The saints' lives show many departures to a "disart" by earnest monks, and this is no late development. In this connection George T. Stokes remarked that "from the earliest times the anchorite system formed an essential part of Celtic monasticism."[20]

The unhesitating commitment and powerful energy that marked the Irish monastic movement can hardly be exaggerated. It drew off from secular activities and the rampant violence of clan feuds a large percentage of Ireland's vigorous youth and potential warriors. It was an affirmation on a vast scale of the supremacy of spirit and mind over material interests, and of a realized need, in a primitive society troubled by strife, to obtain at any cost access to the faith and culture in which lay what hope there was of a better life for the Irish people. The monks believed indeed that by their austerities, studies, and prayers they were in some sense securing their own eternal happiness. But they were also lovers of their country and of its people and eager to testify to spiritual values too little recognized in lay society. Their life was not one of irresponsibility or of immunity from struggle. Monasteries were sometimes mauled by contending Irish chiefs and, from about 800, by ruthless Norse marauders; and in some instances they were themselves drawn into warfare. But on the whole they were able to achieve their destiny as a Christian leaven in a rude society, to implant and preserve a Christian culture like a cultivated garden amid a wilderness of disorder—to the measureless advantage not of Ireland only but, as we shall see, of Western Europe.

Six | The Christian Mission in Scotland: St. Columba

On 5 December 521 a boy was born to a princely family amid the "thousand hills" about Gartan Lough in northeastern Donegal in Ulster. He was christened Colum (Latin *columba*, "dove"), possibly with a memory of Matt. 3:16, where the Holy Spirit descends *"sicut columbam."* His father, Fedilmidh, or Phelim, was a great-grandson of the celebrated King Neill of the Nine Hostages, and his mother, Ethne, was alleged in later legend to have been a descendant of Cathair Mór, a king of Leinster. Columba spent his early years, as was customary among families of high rank, in fosterage, his foster father, Cruithnechan, being the priest who baptized him, and under whose guidance he became acquainted with the elements of Christian learning. It is said that he was affectionately called Colum Cille, "Colum of the Church," by his young companions who used to watch daily for his emergence from the little church in which it was his habit to read the Psalms. Since he was closely related to the reigning King of Tara, Ainmere, there was a possibility that he would succeed to the Tara throne; but while still quite young he chose a monastic life. It was probably under Finnian of Moville, an alumnus, as we have noted (above, p. 71), of Candida Casa, that he had his introduction to the monastic experience. While at Moville he studied the Scriptures under Finnian's guidance and became a deacon. At some period of his youth, as already noted, he received instruction in bardic lore from the Christian bard Gemman who taught in Leinster (see above, p. 9).

The other eminent Finnian had been building up his monastery at Clonard, which was illustrious as a fellowship of scholars and missionary founders, and Columba, now in his middle thirties, joined this elite company. Apparently he soon drew Finnian's attention and received preferred treatment, which became an occasion of complaint by some of his fellows. He was singled out for clerical advancement. We are told that Finnian wished to have him made a bishop (who in the Irish manner could be attached to a monastery) and for this purpose sent him for consecration to one Etchen, a bishop at Comfled in Meath, and that through an inadvertence Etchen ordained him to the priesthood only. Columba, seeing in this an intervention of Providence, announced that he would remain always a presbyter. An eleventh-century writer refers to him as "the arch-presbyter of the Island of the Gael." At Clonard he was in the company of those disciples of Finnian who were to be known as "the Twelve Apostles of Ireland," and there he seems to have formed a friendship with Kenneth (Cainnech, Canice) and with Comgall—both of whom were to be associated with him at Iona—as well as with Brendan the Voyager and others of the apostolic twelve. One of these, St. Mobhi, left Clonard to found the monastery of Glasnevin on the Liffey, and thither Comgall and later Columba followed him. But this institution was abandoned in a visitation of the Plague in 543, and the founder died at that time. Columba now returned to Ulster and founded the monastery of Derry on Lough Foyle, at the royal fort of Aedh, son of Aimmere, who deeded the ground to him in 545.

Despite his frequent changes of monastic residence, Columba apparently was constant in his attention to monastic duties and studies. Adomnan, his biographer and ninth successor as abbot of Iona, in a laudatory passage lays stress on his studious habits:

> Devoted from childhood to the Christian novitiate and the study of philosophy, preserving by God's favor integrity of body and purity of soul, he showed himself, though placed on earth, ready for life in heaven; for he was angelic in aspect, refined in speech, holy in work, excellent in ability, great in council.[1]

Columba founded other monasteries in Ireland. Later legend multiplied these to a hundred, but we have certainty regarding only two in addition to Derry: Durrow in Offaly and Kells in Meath. It is now believed that all three of these Irish foundations were formed before his departure from Ireland at the age of forty-two. Whether he did found any others can neither be affirmed nor denied.[2] Possessed of ardent zeal and gifted with a ready mind and a powerful and pleasing voice, Columba must have readily attracted people wherever he went, some of whom would be easily persuaded to take up the monastic life. He might well have carved out for himself a monastic career within Ireland unsurpassed by any of his teachers and associates. Instead he was to spend thirty-four of his mature years mainly on an island three miles long nestled in the Inner Hebrides—but engaged in activities momentous for Scottish history.

Columba's departure from Ireland is attributed by Adomnan to his own decision: in his forty-second year, "planning to become an exile for Christ [*pro Christo peregrinari volens*], he sailed away." But the date of this action is given as "the second year after the battle of Culdrevney," and the allusion to this battle (461) seems to show that Adomnan was aware of another story, not so creditable to his hero, that comes to us in a much later document. It is to be noted also that in the same context Adomnan refers to an unjustified excommunication of Columba in a synod held at Teltown, the verdict being at once withdrawn on the intervention of St. Brendan of Birr and the commendation of Columba by Finnian of Moville, the offended party. Eager for Scriptural knowledge and for the best Bible texts, Columba is said to have copied without permission a manuscript of Jerome's text of the Psalter and Gospels which Finnian had brought from Rome. Finnian, learning of this, was bitterly angry and demanded the copy. This was refused, and appeal was made to the high king at Tara in Meath, Diarmit, head of the southern Hy-Neill. Following a stuffy maxim of the Brehon law, Diarmit gave the verdict, "to every cow belongs her calf"; the copy must be returned to join the original. Columba was incensed and roused the clansmen of the northern Hy-Neill to attack the forces of Diarmit. In a sanguinary battle at Culdrevney near Sligo, the party of Columba was victorious. Thereafter St. Molaise (Laisran) of Devenish, as Columba's soul-friend, assigns to him the penance that he should depart from Ireland with the task of converting to Christ as many souls as the number slain in the battle.[3]

From the story of the copied book, which it is assumed remained in Columba's possession, comes the traditional identification of the "Cathach" of Columba (see below, p. 124) as the one in question. It is of the Psalter only, and it bears some marks of haste in writing, as would be expected in the circumstances alleged. It would, of course, be naïve to accept this tale as authentic history. Even if Adomnan knew it about 690, he may not have believed more of it than that Columba was in some way involved in the battle. In a hundred and thirty years the Irish imagination could easily have invented it. But it is at least a revelation of what men assumed to be the tumultuous state of society, and of the recognized authority of the *anmchara* or soul-friend among Irish Christians. We have much else to show that Columba was a man of vehement temper, and whatever his connection with the cause of the battle of Culdrevney, it may well have represented for him a crisis between monastic missionary dedication and a return to the mores of his warrior ancestors. Such a view does not exclude the likelihood that he had long felt a desire to undertake a "peregrination" and devote his life to a mission beyond the shores of Ireland. A time of remorse for his participation in the conflict, and the advice of a trusted counselor, may well have furnished the occasion of his momentous decision.

Whatever the immediate circumstances, there can be no doubt that Columba's ruling motive in leaving his beloved Ireland was truly expressed by Adomnan in the words "to become an exile for Christ." He went forth to enlarge the kingdom of Christian believers. Like other missionaries of his time, he made use of contacts with political personages who could aid his approach to their subjects. By his royal lineage and his superior personal gifts he was well qualified for the political aspects of his role, and his Christian devotion naturally accorded with a pacifying function such as he seems to have exercised between the Pictish and Scotic powers. To say that his mission was political is to refer only to what was strictly a minor, though not unimportant, aspect of his work.

In his forty-second year, a tall man of noble bearing and unusual physical strength and endurance, highly endowed by nature, well instructed by the best teachers and fully trained in the monastic discipline, Columba brought away from Ireland a combination of qualities hardly surpassed in any man of his age. There is good evidence that the wrath and violence to which he was prone gave place to a saintly gentleness that endeared him to his younger associates and caused him to be remembered with peculiar affection in the Celtic churches. The coracle of wicker and hides on which he sailed forth from Derry must have been a large one, for he took with him twelve companions and presumably some supplies and implements. One of the twelve, Ernan, was his uncle, two were his cousins, and one, Mochonna, was the son of a king. Columba sought an island that would offer no haunting view of his beloved Irish hills. But first, for reasons not fully known, he paid a call on his royal cousin Conall, ruler of Dalriada in Scotland. This was at Conall's fortified capital, Dunadd, near the coast of Kintyre at the head of the Sound of Jura.

A century earlier Dalriada in Scotland had been settled by invaders from Dalriada in Ulster, and the little kingdom so formed had been expanding at the expense of the Picts until it embraced the area of modern Argyll. But Conall was now in trouble with a revived Pictish power. Brude mac Maelchon, whom Bede calls "a very powerful king," ruling the northern Picts from Inverness, not only had effectively stopped the expansion of the Irish kingdom in Scotland but also had regained some territory on its northern frontier and reduced Conall to vassalage. However, the island of Islay was ruled by another Dalriadan chieftain, and the Scots seem to have remained in the ascendant in the Inner Hebrides. W. F. Skene, G. T. Stokes, and others have regarded Columba's enterprise as in some sense a response to Brude's challenge to Christian Dalriada, and Isabel Henderson suggests that Conall may have made Columba his agent in a conciliatory approach to the Pictish monarch, to whose fortress at Inverness he was soon to journey.[4]

Leaving Dunadd, Columba and his twelve found Islay and Jura and even Oronsay and Colonsay still within sight of an Irish skyline. They sailed on northward to the little isle of Iona located "seaward from the westernmost projection of Mull" from which it is separated by a sometimes turbulent sound half a mile wide. The weary band drew their boat to shore on a terraced beach shining with many-colored pebbles, at Port à Churaich, the Port of the Coracle, 12 May 563.

Iona, then called Hy, was potentially disputed ground between the Scots and the Picts. Bede and the Irish Annals respectively assert that it was granted to Columba by Brude and by Conall. Can it be that both are right, and that some agreement between Brude and his unwilling vassal had been reached to make it a Christian sanctuary for Columba's mission? This would be the more likely if, as Miss Henderson thinks "perfectly possible," Brude mac Maelchon is Brude mac Maelgwyn, son of Maelgwyn king of North Wales, whose family came from Scotland, and who was a Christian convert and a patron of monks.[5]

There are roughly 2,000 acres of land on Iona, 500 of which are arable, but little can be known of the earlier population of the island and of their use of the soil. Some have suggested, indeed, that it was quite unoccupied, but this seems improbable. On the analogy of neighboring islands, the Iona farmers and fishermen would be Irish Scots and not Picts. They appear to have neither welcomed nor opposed the new settlers. It is probable that they had seen men in the same garb before, for the island held the Reilig Oran, the sacred burial ground of the kings of Dalriada, instituted by, or dedicated to, St. Oran, who had died in 549. A later legend has Columba confronted by two bishops, whom he did not recognize as such, who tried to get him to leave the island at once; and again these predecessors have been turned into druids.

It was beside the Reilig Oran that Columba, having surveyed the terrain, decided to build his monastery. For Irish monks this was not a great undertaking. They were not concerned with enormous edifices erected at heavy cost of time and labor. Each of them had his own hut, and these were arranged in an irregular circle around that of the abbot. Columba's hut was larger than the others, and prominently placed at the top of a knoll, Tor Abb. Other necessary buildings were soon erected: a refectory with a kitchen; a scriptorium with a library; a guesthouse (*hospitium*) for the use of the surprisingly numerous visitors from near and far; a smithy, a kiln, a mill, and two barns; and a small church, later enlarged and strengthened with oak beams brought by sea. A thick earthen wall was constructed, surrounding the whole compound. Probably help was received from some of the original inhabitants, from whom also milk and cereal foods could be obtained until the monastic farms were in production. As the monastery grew in numbers, it became necessary to bring some supplies from the farmlands of Tiree and from the nearby island of Mull. Some Britons and even Saxons joined the Irish beginners, and there was a flow of recruits from Ireland. When the community numbered 150, additions were discouraged.

Although each monk slept alone under his own roof, they all worshipped, worked, and ate together. The monks were classified into three groups, largely by age, each of these having different activities. The Seniors were employed in worship services and in the transcription of manuscripts; the Workers were both teachers and laborers engaging in such outdoor work as farm labor, fishing, and obtaining seal products at the shore of Erraid, an island two miles away; the Juniors were the young learners who had not yet taken vows, and who in addition to their studies performed minor duties under direction.

The brethren of Columba's "family," like Irish monks everywhere, wore garments of undyed wool: a long tunic with an undergarment almost as long, and a hooded cloak. They slept in these habits, ready to go to the church promptly for the night hours. In severe weather sealskin coverlets were laid over the beds. It was no mere token austerity that was practiced, but a regime of simple and scant meals and hard beds. Adomnan with admiration tells us that Columba used "for straw mattress a bare rock, and for pillow a stone," and gives evidence that his sleeping time was minimal. The base of what is believed to have been Columba's cell has been excavated (1957) and lends corroboration to this reputed austerity. Adomnan had seen Columba's stone pillow; it was faithfully preserved by his grave in Adomnan's time (*Vita* III, 23). An oval granite slab one foot seven inches long, found a short distance away, is thought to be this precious relic, and may be seen in a brass case in the museum at Iona today. Although, as we have seen, the Rule attributed to Columba is not his, its precepts are not foreign to his spirit. There is a strain of anchoritism in his piety. He often retired to a lonely spot within a mile of the community, and occasionally to a more distant retreat on the island of Hinba (Elachnave), one of the Graveloch Islands in the Firth of Lorne.

Undoubtedly the monastery was strictly ruled and Columba was its unquestioned master. Monastic offenders were sometimes sent to Tiree, twenty miles off, for a period of penance. But insubordination was not a problem, since obedience was seasoned by affection. Their abbot was always painstakingly concerned with what the monks were doing, participant as well as director. The Iona community was a hive of constant activity in "work, prayer and reading." The mere physical labor was demanding and varied. The monks were accustomed to the handling of boats and had no dread of the sea. There were many errands over the often turbulent waters to nearby islands and there was fishing in the bays and on the sound. There were cows to be tended and milked, and milk products to be processed. The cattle were pastured on the *machair*, a stretch of sandy plain covered with grass and clover. Nearer to the monastery were fields on which barley and oats were grown.

Carts and horses were in routine use for the farming and harvesting. These manual tasks were conducted in an atmosphere of religion. Columba was accustomed to make the sign of the cross to banish demons and to speak a word of blessing over the common tasks of the field, the dairy, or the barn. Wednesdays and Fridays were days of fasting, and Saturday was a day of rest. The Eucharist was celebrated regularly on Sundays and occasionally on other days by special decision of the abbot. The duty of hospitality was so sacred that the coming of an eminent guest might occasion the breaking of the ordinary fast. The day and night hours of worship were strictly observed, and, as elsewhere, consisted largely of protracted singing of the Latin Psalms.

Adomnan's *Life* gives historical details in the framework of an abundance of miracles. It is in three sections, entitled respectively "Miracles of Power," "Miracles of Prophecy," and "Apparitions." Not all the miracles are beneficent. St. Columba could be wrathful against those guilty of injustice or oppression. In one incident he "casts down to hell" the despoilers of his friend's house. But there are many instances of the healing of sick persons by his touch or prayer, and in one case he restores the lost affection of a wife for her husband. He has frequent visits from angels and is instructed by them on public actions. Telepathic advices reveal to him the outcome of a battle in Ireland. While at prayer he becomes aware that a bishop who is trying to reach Iona in a boat has been caught in a whirlpool and is praying in fright. Columba announces that the voyager will be delivered and will be the better for the experience. We are insistently informed that Columba possesses "the divine gift of prophecy," by which Adomnan means what in Celtic Scotland is called "second sight." Asked to explain this, the saint is made to answer: "There are some, though few indeed, to whom divine favor has bestowed the gift of contemplating clearly and very distinctly, with scope of mind miraculously enlarged, in one and the same moment, as though under one ray of the sun, even the whole circle of the whole earth, with the ocean and sky about it" (*Vita* I, 43). But the passage is indebted to Gregory's *Dialogues* and has little bearing on the incidents reported.

Iona was the center of an active mission to the Scots of Dalriada and the islands, and to the northern Picts. The extent of this missionary enterprise is still a topic subject to disagreement and uncertainty. Reference was made in chapter 2 to the relative extent of Ninian's mission and that of Columba. Unfortunately, Adomnan makes no attempt to present a systematic record of Columba's travels and preaching tours. From place names and local traditions, W. Douglas Simpson tentatively ascribes to his influence thirty or more church foundations in the isles and in mainland Scotland west of the Drumalban range of hills. Most of these localities are in the Inner Hebrides, a few others in Skye, Harris, Lewis, and Uist. He lists also a score of sites east of Drumalban but is very skeptical of Columba's connection with them or with the half-dozen locations in Strathclyde that bear his name.[6] We must rest content without exact knowledge of the geography of Columba's mission area and foundations, and recognize that he was less of a pioneer in the absolute sense than has been popularly believed. Nevertheless he must still be esteemed a great and powerful Christian leader who made an immeasurable impact on western Scotland and ultimately on the whole Celtic Christian world.

His first move from Iona was his visit to King Brude in 564. Bede regards this visit as significant for the conversion of Brude, and Adomnan presents it in the light of a Christian and not a political mission. But in the circumstances it would not fail to have also some political significance. Adomnan, unfortunately, in this connection obscures the actual events behind a cloud of miracles. Columba took with him some companions who spoke the Pictish language (we are elsewhere told that these included his friends Comgall, abbot of Bangor, and Kenneth, who was later to found Agaboe). During their journey they witness on the Ness River the recovery of a corpse mangled by a water beast (the original Loch Ness monster); nevertheless Columba sends a monk, Lugne, swimming across the water to bring back a boat from the farther bank while he himself holds off the raging beast by the sign of the cross (*Vita* II, 27). The same potent gesture is used in other instances. When the gates of Brude's fortress are found closed to Columba, using this sign he knocks for admission, whereupon the bars are drawn back and the doors are "opened of themselves." Brude is alarmed at this, but receives Columba and his companions graciously and greatly honors him thenceforth (*Vita* II, 35). A fantastic contest between the saint and the court druid, Broichan, for control of the weather enters the story, to the exclusion of any report of the conversation between the abbot and the king. Columba then gaily sails away against a contrary wind but is called back to minister to Broichan, who is in a grave condition, having been laid low by an angel for his sin of holding an Irish girl in slavery; on her release the act of healing is accomplished (*Vita* II, 34). The druids try to outshout the singing of the monks, but Columba drowns their din by chanting Psalm 145 "like a peal of thunder" (*Vita* II, 37).

It would appear that Columba replaced Broichan as Brude's soul-friend and left Brude friendly and cooperative, ready to countenance the Iona mission and the Christianization of his own people. In 693 another powerful Pictish king named Brude was to be buried at Iona.

Adomnan gives us only glimpses of Columba's later missionary travels. We know that on occasion he talked with Picts through interpreters. In one account, in which he pays a visit to Skye, an old enfeebled Pictish captain, hitherto a pagan, lands there and is ministered to by Columba. Repenting of his sins, he is baptized and remains to die (*Vita* II, 33).

Evidently Columba's relations with the Dalriada kings remained intimate, and much of his work was done within their domain or sphere of authority. There he could preach and converse without an interpreter, as he could not do among the Picts. On the death of King Conall in 574, Columba, then in his retreat at Hinba near the Argyle coast where he repeatedly experienced mystical visions, was commanded by an angel to consecrate to the kingship Aidan, son of Gabran, instead of Aidan's brother, whom Columba had initially preferred (*Vita* III, 5). The act of consecration took place at Iona; it is the earliest of such ceremonies in British history. Aidan proved an able and enterprising king. He threw off the Pictish yoke of vassalage and extended his sway to the Orkneys as well as to the Forth. In his time Cormac, a voyager monk like Brendan and later a bishop to Durrow, carried on from Iona a mission to the Orkneys and Shetlands and sailed northward "beyond the bounds of human enterprise," where, according to Adomnan, his ship was attacked by froglike creatures, perhaps stinging jellyfish. Columba, becoming mystically aware of his friend's plight, obtains by prayer a wind from the north that brings Cormac safely to the home port (*Vita* II, 42).

Adomnan has unfortunately no interest in setting such events in historic sequence or in telling the whole story of other sea-roving evangelists. But we may be sure that Irish monks based on Iona played a large role in bringing the Christian message to the northern and western islanders. The records of this expansion are inadequate, and no reliable list of Columba's Hebridean foundations can be made. These apparently include monasteries on the islands of Hinba, Tyree, and Skye. In one instance we know of a prosperous beginning made by one of his Iona family that was soon followed by tragedy. St. Donnan came from Iona to form a monastic community on the island of Eigg about fifty miles to the north. At Easter, 617, all the fifty-four brothers then on the island were massacred by sea rovers, possibly at the instigation of a local enemy. The incident probably marks the first appearance of Viking raiders in the Hebrides, where generations later their descendants would extinguish many little monastic communities.

It is possible, however, to claim too much for the extension of the Iona mission. Monks of Pictish race from Dalaradia, a small district in Ulster, roughly County Down, which was inhabited by Picts, must be credited with significant missionary activity in the islands. Dr. Simpson treats their work as independent of Iona; but the best known of them, Comgall, accompanied Columba, as we have seen, on his visit to King Brude. Comgall's foundations apparently included not only a church on Tyree but others in the Hebrides. St. Moluag, another Pict, after wide-range travels settled on Lismore Island in Loch Linnhe, planting there a monastery of historic importance. St. Maelrubha, an alumnus of Bangor, labored in Pictish areas for nearly fifty years (673–722), founding Applecross in Ross-shire and leaving his name in Loch Maree and traces of his work in Sutherlandshire and Banffshire. St. Drostan, alleged founder of the monastery of Deer in Aberdeenshire was probably a contemporary of Columba, but his association with Columba in this foundation has only the doubtful attestation of the twelfth-century *Book of Deer* in a charming story which is probably fictitious.

In 575 Columba revisited Ireland in company with King Aidan of Dalriada to attend a national convention at Drumceatt (Mullagh) near Londonderry. The docket of business included action on the claim of Dalriada (not improbably Dalriada in Ulster) to exemption from tribute to the Tara kings; and on the proposed suppression of the order of bards, whose damaging satires and exorbitant fees had aroused hostility. Columba's influence in this assembly was evidently dominant. Despite some opposition from King Aedh mac

Ainmere of Tara, he won, in substance, the argument for the Dalriadans; and he eloquently and convincingly defended the bards as an essential element in Irish society. At his proposal, however, they were subjected to discipline, and were commanded to attend to the work of teaching. According to the verses of Dallán Forgaill, 1,200 bards entered the meeting and lauded in song the embarrassed saint, who covered his face with his cowl.[7]

It is clear that the return of the most famous native son was triumphal. When he paid a visit to Clonmacnois, where Alither had succeeded Ciaran as abbot, all the monks thronged from the fields and buildings to greet him, hailing him as "an angel of the Lord," and with exultant hymns escorted him to the church (*Vita* I, 3).

Columba lived to a good age, sustained, says Adomnan, by the prayers of the community. In his early seventies he began to have premonitions of death. When he prayed for this, he was told that he was to remain with his people four years more. Adomnan surpasses his usual style in the closing section (*Vita* III, 23), in which he describes Columba's last days and the circumstances of his death. Having said farewell to the brethren working in the fields, and to the beloved pack-horse used by the monks to bring in the milk, he took up for the last time his favorite task of transcribing a Psalter. At the words of Ps. 34:10, "But they that seek the Lord shall not want any thing that is good," he laid down his pen, saying, "Let Baithene write what follows."[8] That night Columba rose as usual from his hard bed to join his brethren at the midnight office, and hastened to the still unlighted church, followed anxiously by his personal attendant, Diormit, who found him lying, in a state of rapture, before the altar. As lights were brought and the monks gathered, he was able only to bless them with upraised hand as he drew his last breath. It was now a new day, Sunday, 9 June 597.

A further word about the *Life of Saint Columba* and its author, Adomnan, may be in order. It is clear that Adomnan conceived of his task as that of furnishing abundant evidence from miracles to attest Columba's sanctity. To this end he was industrious in making use of oral and written sources, to most of which we have no access. He incorporated in his work testimonies from some individuals whose memories reached back to acquaintances of Columba, and to an unknown degree he made use of the *Book of the Miraculous Powers* [*De Virtutibus*] *of Saint Columba* by Cummene the

White, abbot of Iona 657–69. From this document he quotes a dire prophecy ascribed to Columba against King Aidan and his descendants if they should "practice deceit" against him and his successors (*Vita* III, 5); but suspicion arises that this passage is a timely invention of Cummene. As a biographer in the modern sense of the word, Adomnan has no claim to recognition. The work is frankly about miracles and visions, and with the exception of some passages at the beginning and the end, events are jumbled without reference to their time sequence. In clothing incidents in a mist of miracle and affirming to his own generation of readers the supernatural powers of his hero saint, he has surpassed the work of such preceding hagiographers as Sulpicius Severus on St. Martin and Constantius on Germanus of Auxerre. To the modern mind it is hard to realize that such a collector of miracles was also a scholar acquainted with the higher learning of his time. But the same incongruity appears in other instances. Alcuin, a more renowned scholar than Adomnan and commended for his contribution to a revival of learning a century later, wrote a "life" of St. Willibrord similarly fortified with supernatural improbabilities.[9] We have to make use of such material with discrimination and with appreciation of our author's good intentions.

Adomnan left to modern scholars the difficult task of reducing Columba's career as far as possible to a dated narrative and evaluating it in historical perspective. It must be said, however, that despite his lack of historical skill, he leaves us with the assurance that we have come to know the man Columba, a masterful, practical, kind-hearted, and deeply religious personality, devoting extraordinary gifts and energy to a mission of epochal importance.

Of Adomnan's other writings the best known is the *De locis sanctis*, on the Holy Places of Palestine and Christian sites of Syria, Constantinople, Alexandria, and Crete. That a guidebook of this sort, long regarded as authoritative, should have been written by a man who had never traveled beyond a narrow corner of the West is remarkable enough. It grew out of the peculiar circumstance that the Frankish bishop Arculf, having paid a visit to Palestine and the eastern Mediterranean, came to the Scottish isles as a result of a shipwreck, and was entertained at Iona. He was closely interrogated by Adomnan, who recorded on wax tablets and later wrote on parchment the somewhat credulous traveler's report on his tour. Aided by knowledge of the Bible and the writings of Jerome and other patristic works, Adomnan was able to produce an essay that was widely circulated for centuries. It was highly regarded by his younger contemporary Bede, who gives it an extended notice in his *History*.[10] The treatise was personally presented by Adomnan to King Aldfrith of Northumbria at his court in Bamburgh in 686, and was given wide circulation by command of the king.

The *Câin Adamnáin* (Law, or Tribute, of Adomnan)[11] is remarkable as a document in Christian humane legislation. The Old Irish text is dated in the ninth century, but its editor, Kuno Meyer, thought it possibly framed under the influence of Adomnan in the Irish national synod held at Birr in 697. Heavy penalties are assigned for death or injury inflicted on women and children, and women are freed from the obligation to serve in war. A similar measure had been sponsored by Columba at the assembly of Drumceatt but had not been adopted. For his achievement Adomnan was hailed as "by the gift of Christ the liberator of the women of the Gael." To him are also ascribed the *Canones Adomnani*, of date early enough to be his. These twenty canons are concerned with the distinction between clean and unclean meats. Primitive conceptions of taboo seem reflected in some of the regulations. They also repeat restrictions from Exodus, Leviticus, and Deuteronomy, and offer commonsense prohibitions of tainted meats.[12]

It is not unlikely that Adomnan, like his hero Columba, was prone to vision experiences; but his authorship is not to be claimed for the tenth century Irish text, the *Fis Adamnáin* (Vision of Adomnan) which contains a vivid Dantesque representation of heaven and hell.[13] Apart from his writings, Adomnan played a key role in the Easter controversy (see below, p. 117). As both scholar and leader he was the most eminent of the series of abbots in the Columba succession. Bede as a youth probably saw the venerable Irishman when during a visit to Northumbria Adomnan conferred with Bede's own abbot Coelfrid at Jarrow; and Bede's testimony is that Adomnan was "a wise man, admirably [*nobilissime*] learned in the Scriptures."[14]

Iona remained for centuries an active center for the propagation of the Gospel and an outpost of the Irish church. It was also an influential member of a widening circle of monastic communities owing allegiance to Columba in Ireland and Scotland and among the Angles and Saxons of northern and central England. In general the seventh-century abbots were men of competence but not of genius.

They were called upon to participate in the troubled affairs of their era, including the controversy with the Romanizing party over the date of Easter and other issues, and to respond to the opportunity presented through a turn of events in Northumbria. These matters call for review in a wider perspective.

Seven | Irish Saints and English Kings

THROUGH THE energy of the Christian movement in Britain and Ireland, the old deep-rooted Celtic paganism was totally eclipsed and as a system exterminated. At the same time Germanic paganism took root in a large part of Britain through the invasions of Angles, Saxons, Jutes, and smaller tribal units from northern Germany, to whom Christianity was virtually unknown. Their spreading conquests left Christian Britain reduced mainly to Wales, the Cornish peninsula, and parts of Scotland. The British Christians, mauled and dispossessed by the invaders, were in low morale and incapable of an effective mission to their conquerors. It was from other sources that Englishmen were to receive the Faith: from the Roman mission of St. Augustine and his successors and, to a greater extent, from Iona, the outpost of Irish monasticism in northern Britain. Discord between the Irish and the Roman missioners, and conflicts of interests among English kings, impeded but did not prevent the Christianization of the English people.

The coming of Augustine with forty Benedictine monks to Thanet and Canterbury (597) marks the first important Christian approach to the pagan English, but not the absolute beginning of the conversion of Englishmen. Even if we discredit the hagiographer's "twenty Germans" (Saxons) accompanying St. Buite, we know that a few English monks had somehow entered Irish monasteries. Columba's family included a Saxon named Generus, who was baker to the monastery, and another Saxon brother named Pilu.[1] It was important for Augustine that Ethelbert, king of Kent, had obtained some knowledge of Christianity from his Christian wife, Bertha, daughter of the Frankish King Charibert II (d. 632). As administrator of Aquitaine, Charibert played a secondary role to his brother Dagobert I. The princess, as was noted in chapter 3, brought with her a bishop, Liudhard, who made use of an old church of Celtic origin at Canterbury. John Godfrey, impressed by the peculiar readiness of the English to desert their old religion for Christianity, gives some countenance to Hunter Blair's suggestion that Christian Britons still in their midst may have already disposed them favorably toward Christian conversion. But he finds no specific evidence for this view, and it must be taken as conjecture only.[2] A situation parallel to that in Kent came about from another royal marriage in 625, when Paulinus, formerly one of Augustine's aides and now made a bishop, escorted Ethelberga, daughter of the now deceased Ethelbert, to Northumbria to be the bride of King Edwin, who had hinted that he too might become a Christian.[3] Paulinus, at the direction of Pope Boniface V, preached to the pagans at the court, and finally won Edwin himself, who was baptized at York. Bede's lively paragraphs on these events leave an impression that some of the pagan English had grown weary of their old, unprofitable religion and were ready to be taught a better one. In an assembly called to decide the religious issue, an unnamed counselor in a memorable oration likens man's life in its brevity and mystery to the flitting of a sparrow through the fire-lighted assembly hall "from winter unto winter," and craves any guidance on human destiny that the missionary stranger may have to give. Edwin's own high priest, Coifi, becoming an anxious inquirer and a convert, mounts the king's stallion and with sword and spear rides forth in command of a company of warriors to destroy the idols he has served.[4]

Bede treats Edwin's conversion and baptism as the work of Paulinus alone. But there is a strong tradition, resting on Welsh sources earlier than Bede, that the baptizer was the Briton Rhun, son of Urien, a warrior who, like many others, had become a priest. This account is favorably examined by Kenneth Jackson and by Nora K. Chadwick.[5] Jackson even suggests, in view of Bede's account, that both Rhun and Paulinus participated. Nothing conclusive is claimed by these scholars, but the question remains an open one. It should be remembered that Bede's oft-expressed low opinion of the British (as distinct from the Irish) Christians would make him antecedently indisposed to acknowledge any part taken in this event by a British priest, especially one who had earlier been a fighting enemy of his own people, the Northumbrian Angles. And with the intervening changes before Bede's time he may have found it difficult to ascertain the facts.

Paulinus was a zealous missionary bishop for eight years in Northumbria. But soon after the battle of Heathfield and death of Edwin in October 632, he abandoned his see and accompanied the widowed queen and her children back to Kent. One of his clerics was left at York, James the Deacon, who lived out his days in a nearby village, instructing his converts in Gregorian plainsong.[6] Otherwise the Roman mission in Northumbria, begun with bright hopes six years earlier, collapsed through the death in battle of the Christian king. The kingdom was now divided between two relatives of Edwin. Bernicia, the northern section, extending from the Tyne to the Forth, was ruled by Eanfrid; Deira, which reached from the Tyne southward to the Humber, was under Osric. Both these princes turned away from Christianity and encouraged a pagan reaction; but very soon both were slain by the fierce British warrior Cadwallon. Presently, however, Cadwallon was himself defeated and slain by the new contender, Oswald, at the Battle of Heavenfield (St. Oswald's) near Hexham in Bernicia (633).[7]

This rapid series of changes brought Iona's opportunity for an effective mission to Northumbria. Oswald was the son of Ethelfrith, the ruthless prince who had first united the two Northumbrian provinces. His successor, Edwin, had made refugees of Ethelfrith's family. Unlike his father, Oswald was a Christian. His wanderings in exile had led him to Iona, then ruled by the abbot Seghene (623–52), and there he imbibed the teaching of the heirs of Columba. Adomnan tells us that on the eve of the battle of Heavenfield Columba appeared in a vision to Oswald, promising him the victory, and Bede describes him as fighting the battle from the location of a wooden cross that he had set up. Oswald was undoubtedly one of the most genuinely devout of the Christian kings of history. To have his people taught the Christian faith was his great desire. Instead of reviving the Roman mission, he appealed to "the elders of the Scots" at Iona.[8] It was thus not, so far as is known, on their own initiative, but on a royal invitation, that the Irish came to Northumbria.

In point of time, the Iona mission to Northumbria was not the earliest Irish attempt to bring Christianity to the English. A halting effort to introduce the new faith from Canterbury to the East Angles under King Redwald had been followed by some success under King Sigebert who while an exile in Gaul had come into the sphere of labor of St. Columban (see chapter 10). A Frankish disciple of Columban, Felix, already a bishop, followed Sigebert back to East Anglia and, under obedience to Archbishop Honorius of Canterbury, pursued a successful missionary career for seventeen years (ca. 630–47). During this time there came also to East Anglia the vivid personality of St. Fursa, an Irishman of high lineage and a sensational preacher who had already become a celebrity in Ireland. There he had founded a monastery, fled to a lonely island to escape the throngs attracted by his apocalyptic preaching, and resolved (in Bede's words) "to go on pilgrimage for the Lord wherever opportunity might offer." He came to East Anglia with a few companions, including his two brothers (ca. 633) and soon established a monastery at Burgh Castle near Yarmouth. Fursa was famous for his extraordinary visions, and these he so described in sermons that generations later the memory of them was reported to Bede by "a certain elder brother of our monastery" who had heard Fursa preach. As in the later *Vision of Adomnan* (see chapter 6), Fursa's visions were to him authentic revelations of the joys of the blest and the torments of the damned. Unlike Dante, he has no departed human to guide him; all is revealed by angelic visitants.[9] After ten years in East Anglia, fear of a military invasion from the Mercians, which Sigebert, who had become a monk, was in no position to repel, and an urge to begin a new pilgrimage for Christ, occasioned Fursa's departure to Gaul, where the third phase of his career unfolded in the monasteries of Lagny and Péronne (see below, pp. 169–70).

Far more significant was the coming of St. Aidan from Iona to Northumbria in response to Oswald's appeal. The council of monks at Iona at first appointed a certain Corman to the mission. He went forth, but soon returned in discouragement. When in a long session he reported his difficulties to the brethren, another spoke up with the suggestion that too much had been expected of the intractable Angles and that St. Paul's principle of "milk for babes" (I Cor. 3:2) should have been followed.[10] The speaker was Aidan, and his words at once made him the choice to lead a new effort. He was consecrated a bishop and despatched to Oswald's court. By arrangement with the king he chose Lindisfarne, an island at low tide, not far from Oswald's capital at Bamburgh, as the headquarters of his mission. He was soon joined by "many of the Scots" who, says Bede, preached the Word throughout Oswald's domain. While deploring Aidan's Celtic errors on Easter and the tonsure, Bede pours forth his admiration for the exemplary piety and dedicated labor of the great missionary. Bede's sketch is directly biographical, but it reminds us of the idealizations of Chaucer's "poure parson" and of Goldsmith's pastorally minded village preacher and counselor. Bede lived within the area of Aidan's labors at a time when his ministry was still remembered; his own grandparents may have been among Aidan's auditors and converts. Aidan shared with Oswald Bede's profound admiration: they are alike holy men, and the conversion of Northumbria proceeds through their combined efforts during the nine years given them to be together.

Wise and competent as he was considerate and humble, Oswald gained ascendancy in all England, rivaling the sway of Ethelbert or Edwin before him. Among his own people he was ready to serve. Having acquired the Scotic tongue while in exile, he was glad to act as Aidan's interpreter on his journeys. The robust English thanes who gathered at the king's table may have been bored by the ascetic abstemiousness of the monk, but on festive occasions it was understood that Aidan might leave the feast for his devotions. Oswald himself was known to give away to the poor a good dinner that had been set before him. From Bede's glowing account of Aidan's ministry we realize that the conversion of Northumbria was no merely nominal acceptance of beliefs and rites but the leavening of life and the adoption of a new culture. A corps of associate Irish monks contributed in the effort, "preaching the word of faith" throughout the kingdom and establishing churches and schools. When Oswald fell in battle at Maserfield in 641—Penda, lord of the Mercians, having surprised his forces—the Christian order that had been created was by no means shattered. Pious hands recovered Oswald's head from the battlefield, and Aidan solemnly interred it at Lindisfarne.

Aidan was now to renew his work with little encouragement from Oswald's brother Oswy, who ruled in Bernicia, but with the full support of Oswy's cousin Oswin, who was King of Deira, a man possessed of every grace of body and mind. With Oswin Aidan enjoyed a relationship similar to his former association with Oswald. Bede has an anecdote that illustrates both Aidan's unworldliness and Oswin's generosity. It was Aidan's custom to travel on foot, the more readily to converse with the people he met. But the king presented him with an exceptionally fine horse for use on bad roads. One day while thus mounted Aidan met a beggar and impulsively gave him the valuable animal with all his trappings. Oswin in some displeasure called him to account for this, but Aidan responded with the question: "O, King, is that son of a mare dearer to you than that son of God?" At this Oswin repented of his anger and promised "never again to ask how much of our money you give to the sons of God."

Oswin fell victim to the dagger of an assassin in the employ of Oswy, and twelve days later on 31 August 651, Aidan himself succumbed to age and grief. Bede lingers over his memory with peculiar attachment. He condones the Irishman's imperfect understanding of the Easter date, affirming that Aidan "kept in his heart, revered and preached nothing other than we do, that is the redemption of mankind through the passion, resurrection and ascension of the mediator between god and man, the man Christ Jesus."[11]

At Aidan's death the tide had definitely turned against paganism. The perceptive if unscrupulous Oswy, having added Deira to his realm and thus ruling all Northumbria, returned to the policy of his brother Oswald and became a powerful champion of the Christian cause against military foes. He dedicated his daughter Elfled from her cradle to perpetual virginity, endowing her with lands for a community of nuns: she ended her life service as abbess of Whitby. In 654 Oswy won a decisive battle against Penda the Mercian; that now aged scourge of Christians was slain, and his son Peada was a committed Christian. Oswy now used his advantageous position to promote the adoption of Christianity in adjoining kingdoms. He won over Sigebert the Little of the East Saxons and sent to him Cedd, a Northumbrian trained under Aidan, who had already pioneered the cause in Mercia, where he would later found the monastery of Lastingham. Finan, bishop and abbot at Lindisfarne after Aidan, with two other bishops, consecrated Cedd bishop for the East Saxons; and Cedd vigorously labored in that office, founding numerous churches and monasteries in Essex, where the work of Mellitus, Roman bishop of London, had long before been crushed by royal hostility. Cedd died while visiting Lastingham in 664. His work in Mercia was carried on by his brother Chad, another alumnus of Lindisfarne and pupil of Aidan. Peada had been baptized (653) by Finan, and, having gained authority in part of Mercia, had invited and supported there English and Irish monks even while his father still lived to menace Christian kingdoms. He gave all possible encouragement to Chad and other Lindisfarne men, including Diuma, an Irishman who became the first bishop in Mercia, having also been consecrated (or, as Bede says, "ordained") by Finan. Diuma was followed by another Scot, Ceollach, whose successor, Trumere, was an Englishman "ordained by the Scots."[12]

Thus it had come about that by 663, the revised date of the Synod of Whitby, what was by far the greater part of England, a stretch of territory greater than the whole of Ireland, had become permanently Christian under the influence of the Celtic mission and was being served by preachers and bishops trained under Irish teachers at Lindisfarne. The part played by a surviving British Christian element especially in the north should not be overlooked;[13] but the conversion of the English was mainly the result of the sustained effort of the Lindisfarne men, their dauntless zeal and singular persuasiveness with all classes of Englishmen from kings to the lowliest cottagers. From the coast of Bernicia on the Firth of Forth to the shores of Essex on the Thames, there existed a fraternity of churches and monasteries looking toward Lindisfarne and the Celtic religious world beyond. The tiny island, formerly the haunt of sea adventurers and strange wild fowl, had become, in thirty years, without quite knowing it, the capital of Christian England. "Not St. Augustine, but Aidan," wrote bishop J. B. Lightfoot in 1890, "is the true Apostle of England."[14]

With the flight of Mellitus from Essex, and later to the Continent soon after 616, the Roman mission begun by Augustine had, after short-lived incidents of expansion, shrunk back into Kent. Another Roman-based missionary bishop came to Wessex in about 633. This was Birinus, whose origin is unknown, but who was commissioned by Pope Honorius I to work in outlying parts of the English domains. He was soon successful in the conversion of King Cynegils, at whose baptism Oswald of Northumbria was present and "lifted Cynegils up as he came forth from the laver." Birinus founded the see of Dorchester, and "brought many to the Lord."[15] The cause was impaired by the death of Cynegils in 543, his successor Cenwalh remaining a pagan. Soon after, however, having been driven into exile in East Anglia, Cenwalh there received baptism (648). He returned to institute a Christian regime in Wessex. The Frankish bishop Agilbert, who had studied in Irish monasteries, exercised a brief leadership in the Wessex mission, but failing to make his teaching understood by the English, he returned to Gaul (660) and was later in Northumbria (see below, p. 112). Cenwalh also brought in the English-speaking Wini, a bishop trained in

Gaul, but after a few years expelled him. Again the unsuccessful missionary proved a successful ecclesiastic. From Wulfere, king of Mercia, and a brother of Peada, Wini "bought with money" the bishopric of London.[16] During the years 681–86 Wilfrid, foe of the Celtic practices, who nevertheless had been a novice at Lindisfarne in his teens, became the pioneer of Christian preaching among the South Saxons. Even here he had an Irish predecessor, one Dicul, who had planted a little monastery on a woody shore at Bosham near Chichester.[17]

"With that singular fatality which has dogged the Celtic races," says a facetious historian, "their form of Christianity, however pure in doctrine, varied in certain ceremonial trifles of the most essential importance, from the Christianity of the Western Church."[18] Matters which in the abstract may seem trifles often assume central importance when they are bound up with the sacred traditions of a people, or become the symbols of a certain ecclesiastical attachment. Actually the issue between the Romans and the Celts went far deeper than the recorded exchange of arguments would indicate. The arguments were about the date of Easter, a variation in clerical tonsure, and certain differences in the rite of baptism and in the consecration of bishops. The ultimate issue was that of Celtic ecclesiastical autonomy as aganst integration within the Roman ecclesiastical system. To some degree the participants were aware of this, and understood the implications of what they were arguing about. But the main discussion took place over the individual points of difference; and in these particulars the Celts were overmatched.

The stage was already well set for their failure at the Synod of Whitby in 663.[19] On the Easter question more than half of the Irish churches had already yielded to the Roman arguments. Following Augustine's futile attempt to reduce the British clergy to obedience (see chapter 3), his successor Laurentius of Canterbury in 605 addressed to the Irish bishops and abbots a circular letter presenting the Roman position on the Easter question. He was apparently moved to this action by the refusal of an Irish bishop, Dagan, on a visit to Britain, so much as to eat with the Roman clergy at Canterbury. To Laurentius this is disquieting evidence that "the Scots do not differ from the Britons"; and he refers to the attitude of Columban who was then at work in Burgundy and in controversy with the bishops there. No immediate results were obtained from this overture, but it may have prompted some rethinking of the received tradition by Irish clerics. The next approach came from Rome itself. In 628 Pope Honorius wrote to "the nation of the Scots," reminding them that they were few in number and "at the ends of the earth" and ought not to claim a wisdom above that of all the churches in the world regarding the celebration of Easter. Twelve years later Pope John IV, just before his consecration as pope in 640, wrote to certain named Irish bishops and priests, and to the "doctors and abbots of the Scots" in reply to inquiries that had been sent from Ireland to his predecessor. He erroneously charged the maintainers of the Celtic Easter with reviving the heresy of the Quartodecimans, a second-century Asia Minor sect who, following the Jewish date of the Passover, celebrated Easter on the fourteenth day of the moon following the spring equinox (that is, the 14th of the month Nisan).[20] On the other hand, the Celtic Easter, like the Roman, was always on Sunday. The complicated nature of the calculation of Easter and the historical phases of this were often not fully grasped by the disputants themselves.

The problem had its sources not only in ecclesiastical history but in the very structure of the solar system in which the moon's phases are not timed with the earth's daily rotation or with any twelve-month calendar. Easter had always, like the Passover, been regulated from the full moons. A number of attempts had been made to devise a cycle of a definite number of years at the expiration of which the date for the festival would begin to repeat itself, and thus to furnish in advance a definite fixation of dates over long periods of time. One of the earliest of these was an eighty-four–year cycle, based on Jewish usage. A nineteen-year cycle had been invented in the third century, and in 457 Victorius of Aquitaine had improved on this, producing what is called the Victorian Pascal Table for the years 28–559, which implied a cycle of 532 years. A new table, the work of Dionysius Exiguus, was promulgated in Italy about 525. But our Celts "at the ends of the earth" had not kept up-to-date on these changes. They used the antiquated eighty-four–year cycle, which it is thought the British bishops brought home from the Council of Arles in 314.[21] The limits within which Easter day could fall also differed. The Roman and Gallic churches observed the first Sunday after the first full moon following the vernal equinox, the date of the equinox being March 21. The Celtic feast fell on the Sunday which occurred between the fourteenth and the twentieth day after the first full moon after the vernal equinox, which for them was on the 25th of March. Occasionally that Sunday was on the fourteenth day after the full moon, the day of the Jewish feast, which was scrupulously rejected by the Western church elsewhere.

As a result of this aggregation of differences, the dates of Easter in the two systems rarely in fact corresponded, and they were often weeks apart. A commission of research scholars not antecedently committed to one or the other side might have pointed the way to agreement; but in England resort was had instead to claims and counterclaims of apostolical authority which could only cloud the issue. As might have been expected, the Celtic churches, having no central authority, were converted to the Roman practice in segments and not without internal strife. The definite erosion of Celtic solidarity on the issue came in southern Ireland in the 620s and 630s, with a movement led by the abbot Laiserian of Leighlin and by Cummian, who was probably abbot of Durrow. In 633 Cummian sent a revealing letter—conveying his judgment, with something of factual background, to Seghene, abbot of Iona—in which we find echoes of the then recent letter of Pope Honorius cited above. A number of those involved had been paying visits to Rome and had held conversations with learned clergy there over the disputed usages. Continental journeys were always more frequent from southern Ireland than from the north, and Cummian reflects a familiarity with Roman practice hitherto hardly known in Ireland. He looks on the problem definitely from a Roman viewpoint. "What can be felt worse for Mother Church than to say: Rome is mistaken (*errat*); Jerusalem is mistaken; Alexandria is mistaken; Antioch is mistaken; all the world is mistaken; the Scots and Britons alone have sound wisdom?" While meticulously courteous to the abbot of Iona, he is an apostle of Romanization and has no patience with the reactionary insularity to which the northern Scots adhered. He makes a point of his study of the earliest Irish church, and firmly claims St. Patrick for the Roman Easter, calling him "*Patricius noster papa.*" (Bede does not quote this; he never mentions Patrick's name.) Cummian had already promoted the meeting of a synod at Mag Léne (near Durrow) which had decided to introduce the Roman Easter, but an opponent, Fintan, an Ulster man whom he scornfully calls a whited wall, had partially rendered void this decision. From this synod emissaries had gone to Rome for protracted conferences and these had now returned, having joyously attended Easter services there in 631.[22] As a result of their inquiry, the reformers were successful in having the Roman Easter generally adopted in South Ireland by 636.

In England at that time matters still stood as they had been left after the conference at Augustine's Oak. The Easter issue caused remarkably little friction until it was made critical as a result of a royal marriage, something so often noteworthy in Anglo-Saxon church matters. The wife of Oswy of Northumberland was the princess Eanfled, daughter of Edwin of Northumbria and his Queen Ethelberga of Kent. She had been born and baptized by Paulinus on the Roman Easter day 627, which may have made the date of Easter especially important to her. At any rate, while her royal husband kept the Celtic date, she with her own chaplain Romanus steadfastly adhered to the Roman, which she had learned from Paulinus and practiced with her mother after their return to Kent. Thus it happened, says Bede, that "when the king had ended his fast and was keeping Easter, the queen and her followers were still fasting and celebrating Palm Sunday."[23] This was scandalous, confusing the minds of new converts, disturbing the royal household, and causing public agitation. Amid this stir, an enthusiastic Scot named Ronan who had learned "ecclesiastical truth" in France and Italy plied Finan of Lindisfarne with arguments. But Finan, angered and unconvinced, died in the error of his brethren and was succeeded by Colman, a no less determined Irishman (661). Under the influence of the brilliant English cleric Wilfrid, the king's son Aldfrith, though indebted to Irish teachers, joined the party of change, and did much to bring about the decisive meeting at Whitby. Another figure of importance here is Agilbert, whom we met as an early bishop of Wessex and who would soon be bishop of Paris. He was at this time in Northumbria and eager to cooperate with Aldfrith and Wilfrid. At Aldfrith's bidding, Agilbert ordained Wilfrid, and the prince bestowed on him the abbey of Ripon with a great acreage of land. Oswy himself was disinclined to break away from the Celtic usage, but was in some degree pressured by his aggressive son.

The place of meeting was the double monastery that had been founded by St. Hilda at Whitby, then known as Streanaeshalch, about 20 miles northward from Scarborough on the North Sea coast. Hilda was of King Edwin's kindred and played a notable role as abbess of Hartlepool and later of Whitby, where she helped to nurture the future leaders of the northern Church. She owed her first opportunity in Northumbria to Aidan, who in about 640 invited her back from East Anglia; and she was so heartily loyal to the Celtic cause that despite her gentleness she later showed some hostility to Wilfrid. Though present in the conference, she does not seem to have entered the discussion. She was, however, a personality of importance as head of the monastery in which it was held.

At the meeting Colman of Lindisfarne was accompanied by some of his monks, and had the support of the venerable Bishop Cedd, who acted as interpreter. On the Roman side were Wilfrid and Agilbert; a companion of Agilbert named Agatho; the now aged James the Deacon, who had waited long for this; Romanus, the queen's chaplain; and the sub-king Aldfrith. Oswy himself presided. Colman was asked to state his position, which he did in simple words, as reported by Bede. He follows the practice of his predecessors, men beloved by God, for whose Easter calculation he claims the authority of St. John, the beloved disciple. The king then called for a statement from Agilbert, who, no doubt remembering his old trouble with the English language which had lost him a Wessex bishopric, asked that Wilfrid be his substitute, using "the very tongue of the English." (The royal personages may not have understood Latin). Wilfrid invoked the alleged practice of Peter and Paul and the contemporary custom of all churches, as he had himself observed in his travels, save for the obstinate few in the remotest islands—a variation of an old cliché. On further objection by Colman, Wilfrid entered on a long discourse explaining John's pardonable error, identifying Peter's practice with the contemporary Roman, and rhetorically charging that Colman was out of accord with John and Peter as well as the Law and the Gospel. Unfortunately for Colman, he countered Wilfrid's argument by citing an alleged statement by Anatolius of Laodicea (ca. 270), really a forgery. Wilfrid was ready with his own version of Anatolius' teaching. An adroit debater, Wilfrid now turned to a vein of patronizing appreciation for Columba and his followers, beloved of God in their "rustic simplicity." Columba is not to be preferred to Peter, to whom Christ said "on this rock I will build my church" and gave the keys of the Kingdom of Heaven. Colman, on the king's questioning, admitted that Columba had been given no such authority. Thus Wilfrid's argument had been carefully directed to win an immediate and unequivocal decision from King Oswy, and the result was obtained. "I will not gainsay the doorkeeper," the king declared, "lest perchance when I come to the gates there be none to open them."[24] It was a momentous decision for the course of English history.

Oswy made all haste to conform to Rome. St. Hilda seems to have yielded for the sake of peace, as did also Bishop Cedd, whose death soon followed. Cuthbert, a monk of Melrose, a small branch of the Iona community, was another to accept the change, but only after some years. He was later to be made bishop of Lindisfarne against his will; but he did not regard the episcopate as an administrative task, and a passion for the life of a recluse caused him to relinquish his episcopal duties and retire to Farne, a tiny island to which Aidan on occasion withdrew for private devotion. There Cuthbert lived out his days "content with the society of angels."[25] Like King Oswald, Cuthbert was an Englishman thoroughly Celtic in his piety.

Colman's function at Lindisfarne was ended. Taking with him his Irish monks and thirty like-minded Englishmen of the brethren, and carrying away some of St. Aidan's relics, he led the defeated company to Iona and thence to Ireland's farther shore. On the island of Innisbofin he established a new monastery. Strife followed when in summer days the Irish members deserted the farm duties to go about among the people, leaving the Englishmen to do the work. Finally Colman found a spot for the English to have a monastery of their own at Mayo, which in Bede's time was a flourishing institution still recruited from England.[26] We have no need here to follow the long and stormy career of Wilfrid, who amid many changes and conflicts remained constant in his allegiance to Rome and did his utmost to promote the Romanization of the English church. The process was more ably promoted, however, by Archbishop Theodore, who distrusted and opposed him.

Although Bede says there was "no small disputation" about the tonsure at Whitby, he does not report its nature; and here, as in other instances where the reform of the Easter calculation was adopted, the Roman tonsure followed. The Celtic "ear to ear" frontal tonsure, which some suppose to have left a fringe above the forehead, may have been derived from the druids, who were called *magi* in Latin texts. It was repeatedly referred to in Romanizing circles as derived from Simon Magus. It was replaced by the shaven circle on the crown of the head, the hair fringe being thought of as symbolic of the Crown of Thorns, a style that had then a sanction of about two centuries' use.

It should not be assumed that the Celtic character firmly implanted in Lindisfarne was suddenly altered, or that the Celtic cultural features of the Northumbrian Church were promptly obliterated. Abundant evidence contrary to such assumptions is presented by J. L. Gough Meissner, who shows that the ascendancy of a Celtic party in Northumbria lasted well into the eighth century and finds Celtic survivals to a much later period not only there but in Mercia and Wessex as well.[27]

At Lindisfarne Colman was soon followed by Tuda, a southern Irishman who had learned Roman usages in Ireland, and though he shortly died of the plague, there was no return to Celtic ways. Yet the art of the Celtic church continued to be influential in Northumbria. Bede informs us that in the late seventh century young Englishmen thronged the Irish monasteries in quest of learning and were received with kindness. The abbot Eadfrid, scribe of the Lindisfarne Gospels, spent some of his youthful years as one of these (below, pp. 126–27). Numerous English missionaries to continental German tribes were among those who got their higher education, and probably their missionary purpose, from a sojourn in Ireland. Among these was the eminent St. Willibrord, a supporter of Wilfrid who was forced into banishment and spent twelve years in Irish monasteries. In 690 he went to Frisia with eleven companions. His work was soon crowned with such success that at Pepin's nomination he was made archbishop of Utrecht (695). The flourishing monastery of Echternach in Luxemburg was his foundation, and there he died in 739.[28] From its scriptorium came the celebrated Echternach Gospels, a companion manuscript to the Lindisfarne book. Willibrord supported the early work of St. Boniface, who was to leave a record of even greater achievement.

Bede has a memorable story of two English martyr missionaries who were namesakes and were known as Black Hewald and Red Hewald, both of whom had spent many years in the Irish schools. Both went to preach to the Old Saxons (in Schleswig-Holstein) and, having offended pagans by their psalm-singing, were savagely slain by local authorities.[29] Two other Englishmen of note among Bede's worthies were in their youth companions in Irish study: Chad, brother of Cedd and like him a former disciple of Aidan, and Egbert, who became an important agent in bringing about the adoption of the Roman Easter. Chad, a Northumbrian thoroughly trained in the Irish discipline, was for some years Bishop of York and then, at the insistence of Archbishop Theodore, was made bishop of Lichfield in Lincolnshire (669), submitting to the reconsecration required by Theodore because his earlier consecration had been at the hands of British bishops. During the two-and-one-half years left before his death (672), Chad labored in the manner of a Celtic missionary bishop. Like Aidan, he preferred to make his pastoral journeys on foot, but Theodore commanded him to use a horse and on one occasion is said to have lifted him physically into the saddle. His friend Egbert, instead of returning to England, lingered in Ireland, preparing himself in ardent expectation for a mission to the still pagan ancestral home of his people in Germany. But in the end he felt himself redirected and commissioned to win northern Ireland and Iona to the Roman usages. Having seen this accomplished, partly through his efforts, he died at Iona in 729.[30]

The movement to adopt the Roman Easter was by this time making its appearance in the Cornish Peninsula. In 705 Aldhelm of Malmesbury became bishop of Sherborne, a see newly formed under the pious king Ine of the West Saxons in close cooperation with Berhtwald, archbishop of Canterbury. Aldhelm had been teacher, correspondent, and friend of Aldfrith, whom we met as a young prince at Whitby. It is noteworthy that both these gifted Englishmen owed much to Irish teachers. Aldfrith had spent years in Ireland and was able to write verses in Irish, while Aldhelm had been trained under Maildulf at Glastonbury. Yet they had both become admirers of Wilfrid and strong contenders for the Roman usages. From 685 to his death in 704, Aldfrith was sole king of Northumbria, where by moderate measures he promoted the Romanizing changes begun at Whitby. Aldhelm's scholarship and influence had been recognized at Rome, where he paid a visit on the invitation of Pope Sergius I (687–701). The Sherborne diocese extended into Devon, where Celtic usages prevailed. From the standpoint of Canterbury and of Rome, Aldhelm was an excellent appointee to this frontier post. Nobody could have been more eager to promote the change from Celtic to Roman practices. Promptly on becoming bishop, he addressed to the Devon prince Gerontius a sharp letter of reproof for sanctioning in his domain numerous deviations from the "evangelical [Roman] tradition." These included the erroneous Easter date and the "tonsure of Simon Magus." The Britons, obstinate in error, are likened to Nestorians and Pharisees.[31] No response to this message of censure is on record, but Bede regarded it as effective. It may have played a significant part, along with Bede's own account of the Synod of Whitby, in introducing the Roman usages in the peninsula, and even in directing the minds of those Welsh churchmen who were later to bring about the authorization of these changes in Wales (see below, pp. 196–97). The Saxon pressure on Devon and Cornwall ("West Wales") was increased under King Egbert who between 813 and 835 repeatedly overran the whole peninsula, without annexing it permanently to Wessex. He devoted a portion of the spoils to churches, which thereby came increasingly under Saxon influence.

Before the time of Egbert's stay at Iona the abbot Adomnan, through contacts with the Northumbrian church, had become a convert to the Roman dating of Easter. As we have seen, Adomnan had occasion to visit Northumbria in 686 (see chapter 6). He was warmly received by King Aldfrith, who had himself studied in Irish monasteries, and he became a friend of Coelfrid, abbot of Jarrow and later of Wearmouth. Coelfrid had introduced the Benedictine Rule and was a strong advocate of the Romanizing changes that followed Whitby. In the congenial atmosphere of Northumbria Adomnan became convinced of the Roman positions, and was prepared to advocate the Roman Easter in Irish circles. Some ten years later his leadership bore fruit in the adoption of the Roman usages by the Synod of Birr (696). Evidence is lacking, but we may suppose that this decision was not reached without a good deal of effort on the part of both Egbert and Adomnan. In the meanwhile, Adomnan had been disappointed in Iona itself, where the monks simply refused to follow his wishes in this matter, a remarkable instance of the resistance of monks to their abbot. He now lived most of the time in absence from his beloved Iona; he returned there however shortly before his death, which took place in 704.[32]

Iona now remained the last outpost of Irish resistance to the Romanizing reforms. It seems to have been largely through the zeal of the now aged Egbert, together with the political pressure exerted by the Pictish king, Nechtan IV, that Iona was finally led to yield. Nechtan, seeking improved relations with Northumbria, sent a delegation to ask instruction of Coelfrid (710 or soon after). He received in reply a long letter filled with learned argument based largely on patristic citations and ingeniously interpreted Old Testament texts, with the alleged example of St. Peter, bearer of the Keys of Heaven. Coelfrid also deals, though more briefly, with the tonsure. Quoting his own conversation with Adomnan many years earlier, he condemns the frontal tonsure as derived from Simon Magus.[33] The letter satisfied Nechtan and confirmed his intention to order the changed system throughout his kingdom. Priests were supplied with the new Easter tables and all clerics received the coronal tonsure. But Nechtan found the Iona monks still recalcitrant. At this stage Egbert went to reside at Iona (716) and his gentle persuasion proved finally effective. About 718 Nechtan decreed the expulsion from his realm of all remaining nonconformists.[34] If there was a die-hard remnant subjected to this treatment, they cannot have found harborage in neighboring Strathclyde, for the Strathclyde Britons had adopted the Roman usages in about 688. But they may have betaken themselves to Wales, where (to Bede's exasperation) the Celtic Easter was still retained. At Iona itself a few resisters, in schism from their brethren, were permitted to remain.

The Christianization of the English kingdoms in the seventh century was mainly the work of Irish monks and their English pupils. By comparison the Roman mission in England was carried on less extensively and with less local continuity. It is noteworthy that the Britons, whether among the conquering Anglo-Saxons or in Wales and Strathclyde, where they were still independent, evidently took only a minor if not a negligible part in the conversion of the invaders. The original and continued aggression of the English at the expense of the Welsh caused a deep-seated alienation so strong as to exclude any positive religious concern, and to render only slight and occasional any fellowship between the Welsh churches and those being formed in the English kingdoms. The unresolved Easter question remained long after the time of Aldhelm a symbol of a deeper cleavage between the Welsh and the English. Such deeds as the slaughter of a host of praying monks by a pagan Northumbrian king (chapter 4) were not erased from Welsh memory by the English adoption of Christianity; Saxon churchmen were loyal and grateful to those of their kings who supported and enriched the churches in their domains, while Welshmen saw those same monarchs in the light of menacing neighbors or despoilers. Thus it was that the Celtic influence in early English Christianity and Christian culture was almost exclusively Irish.

But whereas in Ireland the saints tended to exercise an influence superior to that of kings, in the English scene it was otherwise. The events here surveyed show typical instances of the fact that the attitudes and decisions of kings largely controlled the course of development for the church.[35] Thereby a precedent was being established for much that would happen in the later history of England.

Eight | Learning, Art, and Worship

IN THE FRAMEWORK of an exacting routine that involved continual self-abnegation, the monks of Britain and Ireland lived a life that was intellectually and devotionally rich and rewarding. The comprehensive learning attributed to Illtud, fifth-century abbot of Llantwit Major, has already been noted (see chapter 3). We are told that "very many scholars flowed to him" and that among these were Samson, Paulinus, Gildas, and David. The *Life of Samson*, from which Illtud's reputation for learning is derived, was written well within a century after his time and can be taken as an authentic report of Illtud's fame as a scholar while living. It would appear that he gave personal instruction to the young men of talent in his monastery, and that it was for his learning that he was most admired. As the chief teacher in the monastery he was fulfilling an office which was fully recognized as distinctive and highly honorable. In Ireland this functionary came to be called the *fer léginn*, the man of reading, and we may think of him as the senior professor and director of studies. The pagan Celts had revered their druids for their store of traditional learning. This knowledge, however, was passed from one generation to another in oral instruction. The expert was not a "man of reading," since there was nothing written to be read. Yet, as we saw in chapter 1, the course of study in the druidic schools was exacting and protracted. It was natural that something no less demanding would characterize monastic learning. In Ireland, however, with all its store of learning, only traces of writing appear in pre-Christian times. If some Latin teachers preceded Patrick, this was in his time a recent beginning. It was essentially within Christianity that the Irish learned to read and write.[1] In the monasteries Irishmen moved with surprising promptness into the front rank among the Latin writers and teachers of the age. In Britain Latin schools had arisen with the Roman conquest, and Latin writing was revived in the Welsh and other British monasteries.

It was in Ireland that Celtic monastic learning chiefly flourished; and Irish learning was to exert a vast influence on the European continent. From an early date the Irish monks show an acquaintance with various Church Fathers, with notable continental monastic authors including John Cassian, and with Vergil, Horace, and various Latin poets of antiquity. A seventh-century Irish commentary on Vergil's *Eclogues* and *Georgics* containing references to a number of early Latin authors is attributed in the manuscripts to "Adannanus," in which form many scholars recognize "Adamnan" (now from his own practice commonly spelled "Adomnan"). This would seem an attempt to make it a work of the celebrated abbot of Iona. St. Columban must have acquired in Ireland that familiarity with Horace, Vergil, Juvenal, and other classical authors which is revealed in his writings (see below, pp. 157, 259). The fame of Irish monasteries as seminaries of learning drew many scholars from the Continent as well as from England. As early as 536 no fewer than fifty continental students at once are said to have been seen by St. Senan of Iniscathy on their way to Lismore, and we are told that seven shiploads of foreign scholars came up the Shannon to pursue their studies at Clonfert in Brendan's time.[2] We may be wary of exaggeration in such statements; but a few names of eminent Franks who spent years in the Irish schools are known to us (pp. 104, 108, 171). In a revealing passage Bede states that in the plague year 664 many English nobles and commoners were in Ireland, having gone there either for sacred learning or for a stricter monastic discipline. Some of these joined Irish monasteries, while others went about as students, visiting noted teachers for instruction and reading eagerly. "The Scots," he adds, "most willingly received them and provided them with food and books free of charge."[3]

There is much to show that the study of Scripture was central in Irish and other Celtic monastic schools. But the visiting scholars may sometimes have been disquieted by the liberal strain of Irish education with its uninhibited attention to the literature of classical paganism. Even an able English pupil could sense in this study a danger from familiarity with the pagan stories of the gods. St. Aldhelm (d. 709), who had doubtless been introduced to classical literature by his Irish teacher Mael-Dubh (Maildulf), founder of the school at Malmesbury (Maildulfs-bury), warned his younger friend Eahfrid, who was about to depart for a second period of study in Ireland, against the perils of pagan philosophy and mythology. He complains, too, that boatloads of young Englishmen go to Ireland to study grammar, physical science, and the interpretation of Scripture.[4] Aldhelm points to the excellence of the school at Canterbury then recently developed under Archbishop Theodore and the scholar Hadrian. But the letter is an exercise in rhetoric and may have been understood by its receiver in a humorous sense. Aldhelm himself spent a fruitful period of study in the Canterbury school and returned, well versed both in classical literature and in theology, to enrich the Malmesbury curriculum. Eahfrid is probably to be identified with Eadfrith, later the scholarly abbot of Lindisfarne and the skillful penman of the Lindisfarne Gospels (which will be discussed later in this chapter).

Aldhelm's letter to Eahfrid exemplifies the affected style of writing known as "Hisperica Famina" (literally, "Western Sayings"), from the title of a tract in which it is exemplified and explained. This literary aberration, marked by a startlingly unfamiliar vocabulary and a distorted phraseology, had its chief vogue in the ninth and tenth centuries; but it is a playful or perverse invention of Irish or British writers of a somewhat earlier time. Its beginnings have been associated by some with the "rhetors" encountered by Patrick (see chapter 4), whom Zimmer regarded as refugee scholars from Gaul; but its first appearance is in writings of monks and clergy. Some passages in Gildas are held to be in the Hisperic style, and elements of the same learned trifling appear in various Irish and Irish-trained English writers. Many of Aldhelm's letters have passages in this style, and it is not unlikely that he acquired the knack of it in Maildulf's circle. At any rate, the Hisperic style was almost certainly invented by insular scholars amusing themselves amid Latin studies, and probability points to Ireland.[5] Even saints of undoubted austerity were addicted to lapses into showy frivolity in their verses in Latin or Irish. In this connection Brendan Lehane refers to "the Irish pleasure in exotic words" and notes the assigned number and imposing names of the Magi as an Irish elaboration of the Matthean nativity narrative.[6]

That Greek was known and taught in the Irish schools is a not unreasonable inference from the fact that Irish scholars in the Frankish Empire were found to be acquainted with Greek, in a few cases to the point of expertness. So far is this the case that Nora Chadwick can speak of a knowledge of Greek under the

Franks as "an Irish monopoly."[7] Bede gave some attention to Greek in his youth, and M. L. W. Laistner infers from his silence about Roman teachers that he had "a teacher trained by the Irish."[8] This is only what might be expected in Northumbria during the late seventh century.

Among the simple structures of each Celtic monastery stood a hut that was used as a scriptorium,[9] a busy place where manuscripts were written and made into codices. Before the era of monasticism the codex had replaced the more clumsy roll in Christian book-making; the more conservative pagans, to their own disadvantage, kept the old style longer. The writing surface was a laboriously prepared vellum, the skins for which came from flocks and herds owned by the monastery or otherwise available. Quill pens were made by the monks from the feathers of large birds such as geese, swans, and crows. The conception of writing as an art and not merely a utility for preserving valued compositions seems to have been dominant. The earliest extant writings by Irishmen are in a majuscule script with some elementary decoration of selected initial letters, or other illumination, a style apparently imitated from Gallic or Italian models. Many books now lost must have been used—and many written—by Patrick and his contemporaries, and their influence on later calligraphy must be assumed. But Irish monastic scribes soon went on to develop their artistic manuscript styles independently and with amazing skill. The Ogham script found on about 350 memorial stones in Ireland and Wales, using an alphabet of straight lines at right angles or in diagonal juncture with a basic line, is an ingeniously contrived device suitable for short inscriptions in a narrow vocabulary. But Ogham has nothing to do with books. Most of the Latin manuscripts painstakingly written and embellished were portions of the Scriptures, and no effort was spared in making the revered text a thing of beauty to the eye. Brilliant and durable colors were obtained by the use of seashells and plant juices, and patterns of great complexity were introduced. These were in many instances geometrically designed for a space, or a page, and made use of crosses, medallions, trumpet shapes, symbolic animal forms, and human figures, with much interlacing of flowing ribbons and elongated reptilian creatures. Appropriation, with variations, of elements from Syrian, Coptic, and other Eastern Christian art has been recognized in certain details, and this, together with the constant use of authentic Christian symbolism, indicates that scholarly and theologically sophisticated minds controlled the illuminator's hand.

As the scriptoria multiplied and became veritable factories for the reproduction of books, no doubt the need of economy in the use of vellum asserted itself, and was a factor in the adoption of the Irish half-uncial or reduced majuscule script, as well as the still more economical minuscule which more directly contributed to what became the dominant continental cursive, a practical script for speed of writing and economy of space. In Ireland countless manuscripts were doomed to destruction in the violence and pillage often inflicted on monasteries in local wars; and from about 800, ruthless Norsemen in their incursions burned or otherwise destroyed monastic libraries, first ripping off the rich metal ornamentation of the finest volumes. We have evidence enough that the precious codices left, by which Irish calligraphy and illumination must be judged, form only a minute portion of the actual production; and the known fortunes of some of the extant manuscripts read like adventure fiction.

Sulpicius Severus, the biographer of St. Martin, praises that saint's constancy in praying and reading. Adomnan adds to these two a third employment, writing, when in his second preface to the *Life of Columba* he describes the activities of Columba and his companions. Close studies of the "Cathach" of St. Columba have left us with the possibility that it is a genuine product of the saint's pen. It has been preserved in a damaged condition, more than half of its original 9-by-6-inch leaves having been lost. Already thus mutilated, in the eleventh century it was encased in a wooden box, which was much later enclosed within a silver case. When it was opened up in 1813, its leaves were stuck together; but it was made legible and deposited in the Royal Irish Academy, Dublin. The name "Cathach," meaning Battler, has reference to its use as protective talisman by the O'Donnell chiefs in their battles. It now consists of 58 pages of the Psalter in majuscule script, with a few illuminated large initial letters featuring such themes as the Cross (*crux quadrata*) and the open-mouthed heads of beasts.[10] Tradition makes Columba the scribe of many manuscripts of which no trace is left, and we can hardly doubt that this is true of other scholarly monastic leaders of his generation. Manuscripts written in the monastery of Columban in Bobbio a few decades later than Columba's time bear a recognized resemblance to the Cathach. But within Ireland the next important illuminated manuscript is the *Book of Durrow*, the date of which lies between 650 and 700.

Whatever its origin, this famous manuscript found lodgement in the abbey of Durrow at the site of an early foundation of Columba in County Offaly. After the dissolution of this monastery it did duty as a magic cure for sick cattle, but found its way to Trinity College in 1661. It contains the four Gospels in the Vulgate version with a free admixture of the Old Latin. The pages measure 9½ by 6½ inches. The manuscript is in a smoothly executed majuscule, and the decoration is elaborate, with the use of four colors—red, green, yellow, and brown—on a background of deep black. Most pages are bordered on all sides by an elaborate band of interlaced ribbon work. This feature has parallels in Syriac and Coptic manuscripts. Very impressive too are the "carpet pages," the entire page occupied with a rich pattern of exquisitely wrought intricate detail. On one such page we have closely wound spirals gathered within six circular rims which on observation prove to be themselves spirals and connected in an unbroken sequence, the whole surrounded at top and sides by an interlaced border. Another carpet page has a central medallion with broad friezes of interlaced, elongated animal forms having beaklike grasping jaws. It has been suggested that the designers of these carpet pages owed something to the patterns of early oriental carpets which they may have seen.[11] The place of origin of the Book of Durrow has not been determined. Some writers have argued, chiefly from the scripture texts used, that it originated in Northumbria. Françoise Henry, our best authority on Irish art, sees no reason, in text or ornamentation, to look for a source outside of Ireland, and points to Derry—another of Columba's foundations—or Durrow itself, of whose art and learning little is known.[12]

A still more fascinating product of Irish manuscript skill is found in the *Book of Kells*, which was completed probably shortly after 800. Following a destructive Viking raid on Iona in 802, many of the Iona monks escaped to Kells in Meath, and it is thought that they brought with them this manuscript of the Gospels and that the decoration was completed in their new home. E. A. Lowe has called the calligraphy "the most eminent example" of the Irish half-uncial.[13] With a larger page than the book of Durrow, about 12 by 9 inches, it affords more generous space for ornamentation. Medieval misadventures robbed it of five folios, but it is otherwise well preserved, despite a narrow escape recorded in the Annals of Ulster for 1006. The annalist describes the book as "the chief treasure of the Western world" because of its ornate cover, and he records that marauders took it from the stone church at Kells, stripped the gold ornamentation from its binding, and buried it under a sod. It was soon recovered, and was to become in later times the highly prized treasure of Trinity College, Dublin. Doubtless the precious cover ornament would delight us if it had been preserved, but the manuscript is a far greater "treasure of the Western world."

The ornamentation of this matchless book is profuse, and is the work of several hands. One full-page pattern has a cross with double arms embracing eight minutely worked medallions. The decorated initials of each paragraph are of imposing size. That of Matthew 1:18, beginning the word Christus with the Chi-Rho symbol, fills a page, spaces within and around being intricately adorned in whorls, spirals, and other forms in a variety of colors. Imaginative portraits of the Gospel writers, along with their conventional symbols, are brilliantly presented. A page is devoted to the Virgin Mary with a most unrealistic child Jesus, and with attendant holy persons appearing at the four corners of the page. Several letters following the initial usually appear somewhat enlarged (this is done also in the Book of Durrow), as if to secure continuity in the reader's mind. Both letters in the ornamented "LI" of *Liber* are equally enlarged, and they are interlocked as if to form a monogram. The symbols of the four evangelists are treated with impressive boldness, dividing a page among them. Faces and figures are rigorously stylized and symbolic, except in a few instances where a minor human or angelic figure may be given a naturalistic pose or expression. The multiple variety, endless inventiveness, firmness of line, and mastery of color exemplified throughout give to the *Book of Kells* a distinctive rank among the priceless achievements of human hands.[14]

Another work of great distinction is this class is the *Lindisfarne Gospels*, which though written and decorated by an Englishman, bears the marks of Irish models. The writer and illuminator was Eadfrith, who later became bishop and abbot of the Irish foundation of Lindisfarne. He is usually identified with the "Eahfrid" to whom Aldhelm addressed the letter referred to above in this chapter. Eadfrith had from his youth been instructed by Irish teachers at

Lindisfarne, and later continued his studies for six years in Irish monasteries. He wrote a beautiful half-uncial script, and his ornamental pages, expertly drawn and colored, use interlaced curvilinear patterns that have been set with the aid of mathematical instruments applied on the reverse side of the membrane.[15] This one-man production of an art manuscript is probably unusual, and it is unusual also that we should know the artist's name. The ornamentation has affinities with numerous metal and stone treatments of its themes found in Ireland, as well as with those which occur in other Northumbrian manuscripts, including the Echternach Gospels associated with St. Willibrord (chapter 7). The latter, a product of the Irish-Northumbrian art school, is less prodigal of ornamentation than the Lindisfarne book, but a work of exquisite beauty. Some works that belong in the field of worship were similarly embellished. Among these are the seventh-century *Antiphonary of Bangor* and the ninth-century *Stowe Missal.*

Françoise Henry, in her authoritative two-volume work on Irish art, shows the detailed continuity between the themes and patterns in metal and stone work and those which appear in the decoration of manuscripts. She has high praise for the inventiveness and resourcefulness displayed in the shaping and ornamentation of metal, and for the "incredible delicacy" often attained, especially in gold filigree. We come to realize that Irish art, whether it is studied on stone slabs and crosses, on altar furniture, or on vellum manuscripts, has a remarkable unity, and is predominantly associated with religion. The ornamented metal objects, such as bells and the shrines made to cover them, decorated croziers, reliquaries, clasps, and vessels for church use, have their counterparts in stone and in books.[16] Filigree and enamel work represent ancient Celtic skills that were never lost and came to be vigorously revived in Christian Ireland.

Among treasures of metalwork, the most highly prized object is the Ardach Chalice. It has attracted the admiration of beholders in a degree comparable to that bestowed on the *Book of Kells.* It may have been a possession of the monastery of Clonmacnois at a time before the Norse invasions, when it was either stolen or buried for safety by responsible persons who did not live to retrieve it. But it became known to us only because a lad digging potatoes unearthed it from a hillside near Ardach, County Limerick, in 1868. This wide silver cup with flanged base finished in green and gold bands of minute filigree and adorned with resplendent beads of crimson and blue glass, cannot be seen without calling forth astonishment and superlative praise. Miss Henry finds in it "a regal feeling for balance served by a technical virtuosity which is such as to cause stupefaction." The creation of some unnamed genius of the eighth century, it marks the culmination of more than a millennium of Celtic metal ornamentation, now put to the service of Christian worship.

Every visitor to Ireland has his attention drawn to the standing stone crosses that despite the perils of war and weather have kept their stations through the centuries. More than thirty of these are left, ranging in height from ten to twenty-two feet, usually rising from a massive plinth which bears a studied proportion to the towering shaft and arms. Although the typical Celtic cross has a circle or wheel around the junction of its members, this feature is far from universal, and the structures vary freely. These crosses are, of course, not crucifixes; rather, the crucifixion is usually found portrayed in carved panels, and more often on grave slabs than on upright crosses. In one notable instance, at Kells, the figure of the Crucified is central and the arms are extended partly over the arms of the cross itself; but the structure was left unfinished. The circle at the head of the cross may have been developed from the Chi-Rho monogram of Christ popularized by Constantine and familiar in Gaul and Britain from his time. But it added structural security, and it acquired its own symbolism. The circle has neither beginning nor end, a reminder of the divine nature and of the Alpha-Omega declaration in Rev. 22:12.

The broad surfaces of the larger crosses offered spaces which busy artists filled with representations of biblical and other religious scenes carved or engraved in great variety and often with a mastery of execution. The finest as well as the largest Irish crosses are the later ones, erected after the Viking invasions, in places and times of relative peace. Celebrated among these are the so-called Cross of the Scriptures at Clonmacnois, Muiredach's Cross at Monastirboice, and the High Cross of Durrow. The first two of these are dated about 900, the third a little later. Comparable to these in quality are a few of the same era in Scotland and England. Perhaps best worth attention among these is the Ruthwell (Dumfriesshire) Cross, dated by Baldwin Brown and by Meyer Schapiro[17] in the late seventh century but now thought to be a century later. The sculptures of the Muiredach Cross, first closely studied by R. A. S. Macalister in 1914,[18] treat pivotal incidents in the Old and New Testaments. On the east side are panels presenting Adam and Eve, Cain and Abel, David and Goliath, Saul and Jonathan, Moses at the rock, the Adoration of the Magi, and, spread across the arms, the Last Judgment, with thirty-six human figures in suitable parts. The west side has the arrest of Christ, Doubting Thomas, Christ giving the Keys to Peter and the Scriptures to Paul, and, at the center, the Crucifixion with the spear-bearer and the sponge-bearer (traditionally named respectively Longinus and Stephaton), a common feature in Crucifixion scenes. The Ruthwell Cross portrays Mary Magdalene at Jesus' feet, John the Baptist carrying the symbolic lamb, Christ and the beasts in the wilderness, the Annunciation, and, at the base, the Crucifixion. In tribute to the Egyptian hermits, Paul of Thebes and Anthony share their loaf brought by the raven, pulling it apart as in the well-known tale. In the many human figures which appear on the panels of the Celtic crosses there is no striving for naturalistic effect and no hesitation in admitting physical disproportion. As in the older Celtic art, faces tend to be unnaturally broad above and narrow below. Yet some of them register emotion, and the postures sometimes give an appropriate impression of effort or strain. Most of the themes here noted, and many others drawn from Scripture and the beginnings of Christianity, appear with independent detail on crosses not here described, exhibiting much thoughtful labor and study, and dedicated skill.

Of Irish Christian art in general it may be said that it testifies both to a persistent memory of ancient Celtic art features and to an eager readiness to utilize Christian continental and Eastern elements. Pagan predecessors had decorated vessels, swords, shields, scabbards, personal ornaments, and horse trappings with curvilinear patterns, fanciful and monstrous beasts, fishes, and other zoomorphic forms, all of which became traditional and acceptable as accompaniment of the Christian and biblical message which the devout artist of the new era attempted to convey. It is the work of well-taught and disciplined minds, of men who could adopt without prejudice a legacy from more primitive ages. Even strange creatures are embraced within the artist's love, and they lend the fascination of a world of unreality and symbolism, the world of the Physiologus and the Bestiaries, without the sacrifice of unity and composure.

We saw in chapter 2 some evidence of a tendency to pagan-Christian syncretism in the late decades of Roman Britain. The sculptured stones of early Scotland provide interesting evidence of a mingling of pagan and Christian motifs in the course of a transitional era. Numerous examples are found in the museum collections at Meigle in Perthshire and in St. Vigean's near Arbroath, once Pictish territory. Pictish horsemen parade on prancing horses and, along with fabulous animals and elongated, interlaced reptiles, keep company on some cross slabs with biblical figures such as Daniel among the lions.[19]

In architecture, Ireland remained a backward nation until the Anglo-Norman invasion. Bede notes that at Lindisfarne the monk Finan built a church "after the manner of the Irish not of stone but entirely of hewn oak, and covered it with reeds."[20] Commonly in Ireland the monastery was protected by a *cashel* or *vallum*, a wall of unmortared stone, in some instances more than twelve feet thick. The buildings were chiefly wooden structures with roofs of wattle and daub. Adomnan uses the word *tugurium*, hut, for the abbot's house at Iona. At Glendalough, the earliest church now found is built of shaped granite stones; the plan is modest in size (26 by 14 feet), and the structure plain, low, and oblong. Reference was made in chapter 5 to the many ruins of beehive huts in west Ireland in which the occupant was protected from rain by a skillfully corbelled stone roof. The Celtic apprehension of monastic holiness embraces the principle of simplicity with respect to material surroundings. Perhaps in setting up high crosses rich with ornament, the monastic builders felt something of the appeal of grandeur; but they did not seek to glorify God or immortalize themselves in magnificent edifices such as were in their age arising in Constantinople and Rome. There appears to be only one notable exception to this, and not a true exception, since the church we are concerned with was built in all probability for utility rather than as an admirable work of architecture. During the century or more between St. Brigid and her biographer, Cogitosus, the original church at Kildare was replaced by another which Cogitosus describes with admiration. Built to accommodate an increased number of worshippers, it was spacious and lofty, with three large oratories divided from each other by walls of timber but under one roof. In the western section men and women worshipped, separated by a partition. In the eastern part the bishop and clergy administered the rites. To receive communion the priests and men entered this area by one door, the women by another. A church building so spacious and imposing must have been rare indeed in seventh-century Ireland or anywhere in the Celtic realms.[21]

Labor, study, writing and ornamentation were not allowed to invade the schedule for the corporate devotional life in which we recognize the core of the monastic experience. The Celtic monasteries took their rise in an era of less controlled uniformity in Christian worship than later prevailed. In all probability the liturgy and canonical hours showed a good deal of local variation in practice. The Latin liturgy used by the British church from which St. Patrick came, and presumably in the Irish churches founded by him, cannot be recovered. It probably resembled closely the Gallican rite which took shape in southern Gaul under "Ephesine" influence. The Catalogue of Irish Saints states that the saints of the Second Order, 543–99, received a Mass from the Britons Gildas and Cadoc.[22] As we noted in chapter 6, this eighth-century document is untrustworthy; but we have other evidence that Gildas did exercise an influence in Ireland and it is not unlikely that he had to do with some reform of worship. On the other hand, it seems improbable that in any formal act, by a synod or otherwise, the whole Irish church at once adopted a new form of the Mass.

Worship in the Celtic churches was, so far as known, never in the vernacular but always in Latin. The source documents for its history belong to the era subsequent to the adoption of Roman usages on the disputed points of Easter and the tonsure (see above, chapter 7); yet they indicate that the worship practices continued for centuries to be widely at variance from the Roman. The evidence furnished by the *Antiphonary of Bangor* and the *Bobbio Missal*, both of the seventh century, and by the *Stowe Missal* and the *Book of Deer* of the early ninth century, indicates an affiliation with the Gallican Rite, but with some additional elements from Eastern sources, and from the Mozarabic Liturgy. An increasing contribution from the Roman canon of the Mass marks the ninth-century documents. There are traces of this in the *Book of Deer*, and the trend becomes pronounced in the *Stowe Missal*, which is thought to represent seventh-century usage of Tallaght. The missal contains within the canon of the Mass a commemoration of many saints, the names being taken from the Old Testament and from Irish lives of saints.[23]

It is evident that monastic worship was dutifully and reverently practiced. Its verbal content may have been somewhat variant and experimental. As with monasticism everywhere, it made large use of psalmody. This reached the limit possible in the *laus perennis*, the uninterrupted chanting of psalms which became a feature of some of the continental Irish monasteries. Since psalm-singing on an extensive scale was assigned to monks as a penance even for minor infringements of the rules, this happily chosen penalty may sometimes have assumed the aspect of "perpetual praise."[24] In his edition of the *Antiphonary of Bangor*, Warren treats the eight canonical hours of Irish monastic worship. These occur at three-hour periods, at 6 A.M., 9 A.M., noon, 3 P.M., 6 P.M., 9 P.M., midnight, and 3 A.M. At each of the first four of them—Prime, Tierce, Sext, and None—three psalms were sung; at the next three—Vespers and First and Second Nocturn—twelve psalms each; and at the last service, Third Nocturne with Lauds and Matins, from twenty-four to thirty-six psalms were sung Monday to Friday, and on Saturday and Sunday thirty-six to seventy-five.[25] Glass chalices were in early use, and we read of chalices of glass and wood, and of one golden chalice that was anciently used at Iona but suffered destruction in modern times. The use of glass for chalices was forbidden in the *Leabhar Breac* (Speckled Book) in 1397.

The original texts used by the monks were largely Latin antiphons, hymns and prayers, a number of which are in the *Antiphonary of Bangor*.[26] It contains the much admired communion hymn *Sancte venite* to be sung when priests communicate. Some of the verses show an experimental use of rhyme, and this was to become a characteristic of later Irish poetry. One of the earliest and finest Christian poems by Irishmen is the celebrated *Altus prosator*, attributed to Columba and, at any rate, not much later than his time. It is a long alphabetical rhymed Latin poem describing with Miltonic grandeur the creation, fall of man, hell and paradise, the return of Christ, and the Judgment Day when "we shall soar to meet Our Lord." According to legend, Gregory the Great criticized Columba for a lack of emphasis on the theme of redemption in the *Altus*, and in response Columba wrote *Te Christi credentium*; but the latter, though of Irish origin, is of later date and hardly worthy of the same author. There is an evening hymn beginning *"In pace Christi dormiam"* (I shall sleep in Christ's peace), in which numerous saintly persons are invoked, including Patrick.

Many of the so-called hymns are really panegyrics and invocations addressed to early Irish saints. Such is the *Amhra Colum Cille*, extolling Columba in alliterative, unrhymed Irish verse, which has already come to our attention in chapter 6. Columba, it is said, having seen it, declined to allow its circulation while he lived. If this is true he may have judged it as does "Frank O'Connor" (Michael O'Donovan) to be "dull, tortuous, and obscure." But the poem as we have it is an elegy, assuming that the saint has died. Columba however, did not lack a finer poetic tribute. O'Connor translates from a text edited by Myles Dillon an anonymous rhymed Gaelic poem for which he has high praise. It gives a lively image of the saint as a devout missionary fearlessly traversing the perilous island seas.[27] Very different is the warmly devotional hymn of uncertain date made familiar in Eleanor Hull's versification of Mary Byrne's translation from the Gaelic, "Be thou my vision." Many of the Irish monks had a facility in verse-making and practiced it freely. Sometimes it was conjoined with the true charisma of hymnody.[28]

It is impossible to describe with confidence the curricula and class routines in a typical Celtic monastery. We read of outdoor classes at Clonard, and this may have been typical in favorable weather. The range of instruction must have depended on the talents and preferences of the teachers and on the direction given by the supervising master, the *fer léginn.* But there is much to indicate that in addition to Bible study the Irish schools with some consistency featured the "seven liberal arts" as these were understood from the exposition by Martianus Capella and Boethius. The writing scholars show familiarity with these fields of study at a time when they were being widely neglected in non-Celtic Europe. The seven included music; and in the monasteries this most popularly cherished art among the Celts had academic standing and importance. Something comparable to this appears in pre-Christian Ireland.

Engene O'Curry, in his *Lectures on the Manuscript Materials of Ancient Ireland* (1872), reciting the story of an ancient Irish harper, referred to the "ollamhs of music," who, to qualify for admission to this order, had to prove their ability to induce in their spellbound hearers slumber, tears, or laughter at will.[29] The successors of the "ollamhs of music" were the monastic professors who taught music as one of the liberal arts, such as Moengall of St. Gall (see below, p. 188). Within the churches it was the human voice rather than any instrumental skill that was chiefly cultivated, though it is alleged that during the Norse invasions organs were destroyed in many churches. It seems possible that the extraordinarily protracted psalmody of Celtic monastic practice was especially congenial to a race steeped in music. Outstanding ability to sing is admiringly attributed to numerous saints.

The features of Celtic and especially of Irish monastic culture that have been discussed here were of varying importance in relation to the Europe-wide influence of Celtic Christianity. Manuscript illumination was little imitated in Frankish Europe, stone monument designs hardly at all, while the distinctive handwriting style was reproduced by the pupils of Irishmen, with progressive changes. It was the breadth and richness of Irish monastic learning derived from classical and patristic authors that gave to Irish monks abroad a unique role in the history of Western culture.

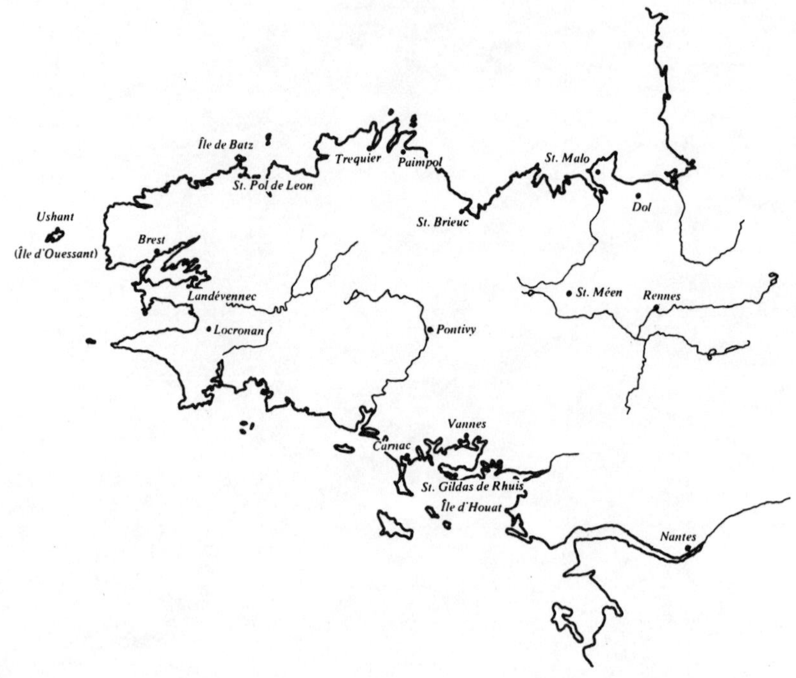

Early Christian Brittany

Nine | Founders of Christian Brittany

It is an arresting fact that in Brittany today more than a million people use as their household speech an ancestral Celtic language. This language is derived, however, not from the Gaulois spoken by the Celtic inhabitants in pre-Roman times, but from that of the Christianized Britons who overran the peninsula during the two centuries following the Anglo-Saxon conquests in what had been Roman Britain.

Archaeology takes the human story in Brittany back to far millennia, possibly to a date as early as 8000 B.C.[1] Geographical factors have caused it to be from early times differentiated from the rest of France in its culture. This appears even in the megalithic monuments erected by a skilled people who came by sea probably from the Mediterranean during the fourth millennium B.C. The most impressive of these monuments are found at Carnac in the department of Morbihan: a series of long avenues of standing stones set in planned order with incredible labor nearly 5000 years ago. In many other locations there are numerous lone-standing stones (menhirs), constructions of four or more of these with a capstone (dolmens), formations of menhirs in circles (cromlechs), and elaborate chamber tombs. The Gauls, who entered Brittany after 3000 B.C., left little visible evidence of their culture. The Hallstatt type of iron implements reached Brittany late, and relatively few of the La Tène Celtic patterns have been found. There was probably some mingling of the dominant Celts with the sparse earlier population.

An outstanding characteristic of the pre-Roman Celts of Brittany was a natural consequence of their maritime situation. The name of the Roman province Armorica is made up of two Celtic words, *ar*, meaning "on," and *mor*, "sea." From earliest times the peninsula nursed a sea-going people, to whom the coasts of Britain and Ireland were easily accessible. In modern times the French navy has been largely manned by Breton men. When Caesar invaded Britain he had learned that British supplies were reaching the Veneti who were leading the Armorican resistance to the Romans. Their capital, Vannes, was the largest population center in the land and an active port of trade. Having built a fleet of galleys to overmatch the 220 high-masted vessels of their navy, Caesar annihilated the latter in a day-long battle on Quiberon Bay, 56 B.C.[2] The victory was followed by vindictive severities; but resistance was renewed in a futile revolt five years later. It does not appear, however, that the Roman occupation of Armorica was ever so intensive as that of Britain and of most parts of Gaul; and we have no evidence of a thriving Latin culture such as appeared in the regions of Bordeaux and Autun. Much of the rough and forested interior apparently went unoccupied.

There exists no reliable early record of the first entrance of Christianity into Armorica. There, as elsewhere in Gaul, apostolic missions were legendary in the Middle Ages. It was believed that one Maximin preached the Gospel at Rennes in the days of the Apostles, and the name of St. Clair (Clarus) appears as a missionary sent by Linus, alleged successor of Peter at Rome. These are fallacious traditions; but there is a possibility that Clair was the name of a third-century missionary.[3] We have, however, good reason to believe that Christianity had been a minority religion in the province for a considerable period before the legions were finally withdrawn. The martyrdom of the brothers Donatianus and Rogatianus at Nantes is attested in a circumstantial account, though the date given, 288, has been questioned.[4] At dates now unknown but not later than the early fifth century, bishoprics were established in at least three centers in eastern Armorica, namely Nantes, Rennes, and Vannes. Christianity may have been largely confined to Roman centers of administration, the scattered rural population being left in its Celtic paganism.

As we consider the invasion, settlement, and mastery of the Britons that took place in Armorica, it is well to remember that at the time of their first arrival the peninsula had suffered a long period of disorder and devastation. The failure of Maximus Magnus in his attempt to gain the imperial power by an invasion from Britain through Armorica (387) helped to bring on the collapse of the Roman control of the province, and after much disorder the last of the Romans were thrust out about 410. Thereafter there was no authority capable of organizing resistance to the Saxon and other Germanic raiders who came by sea to ravage the land, spreading death, disorder, and dismay.[5] These marauding strangers did not settle in the province; but they left it in a state of disarray that made it inviting to new invaders. The Britons seem to have been able usually to land without resistance and to deploy their companies almost at will. If, as Joseph Loth observed, they showed an addiction to war and plunder,[6] that was exercised chiefly against encroaching Franks and Visigoths. We read of 12,000 of them in an expedition under their "king" Riothemi, advancing from Brittany into Berry, only to be defeated by the Visigoth Euric (470).[7] Such numbers of available soldiery were probably sufficient to overawe any possible resistance within the occupied districts of Armorica.

The flow of British migration to Armorica began soon after the Saxon treasonous alienation from British allies that we noted in chapter 2 in connection with the visit of Germanus of Auxerre in 429. It was supposed by Ferdinand Lot[8] that the real beginning was earlier, following the displacement of some of the inhabitants of South Wales by Irish invaders in the fourth century. Some British followers of Maximus Magnus may also have settled in Armorica. But the major occasion of the migration was undoubtedly the unrelenting pressure of the Anglo-Saxons which rendered many Britons homeless. After about 450 this condition became more intense, and the volume of migration increased. It may be that the hard-earned victories attributed to King Arthur eased the pressure for a time, but the tide of the movement was high again at the middle of the sixth century, and the migration did not cease until well into the seventh. The statement of J. Loth in 1883 that the coming of the Britons was "not a slow infiltration but an inundation" is quoted with approval by recent scholars. It proved so overwhelming as to begin an entirely new era for the Province. Armorica was called Britannia by its new masters and, by their relatives in Britain, Britannia Minor.[9]

The entering Britons came with their weapons but appear to have had little occasion to use them against the Armoricans. One reason for this was that they chose to settle in sparsely occupied areas, avoiding the towns. Landing first on the north coasts, they soon gave their attention to the western parts where little resistance could be offered by the few inhabitants. The latter were assimilated to the invaders, who were soon numerically dominant. Gradually they gained control of the eastern parts of the peninsula, where they came in as "colonies" amid a larger population.[10] In the interior, wooded areas settlements were to gather about religious pioneers who had all the Celtic monastic genius for finding habitable spots in the wilderness.

There is reason to think that the incomers were mostly from the Cornish peninsula, but it is well known that with few exceptions the spiritual leaders among them were natives of Wales. Moreover, the latter, so far as dates can be assigned, belong to generations later than the first British migrants. This being so, it seems necessary to modify Nora Chadwick's view that "the so-called missionaries were the educated men who negotiated the settlements and organized the colonists" and that the migration was set afoot by "Welsh princely families" served by "literate clerics."[11] Nor is Arthur le Moyne de la Borderie's neat conception of a clan-by-clan migration supported by reliable evidence. No doubt the incomers arrived often in companies of considerable numbers, and some persons of princely rank and commanding authority were among them; but that there was any overall pattern in the movement has not been shown.

A word may be said here of the trend of historical interpretation in this field. De la Borderie's voluminous *History of Brittany* began to appear in 1885, and his first volume, with which we are here concerned, reached its definitive edition in 1896.[12] This volume is still required reading for our present topic. But a more critical approach was instituted by the celebrated historian Louis Duchesne (like Borderie, of Breton birth), whose studies on the episcopate in ancient Gaul appeared between 1890 and 1915. Duchesne was critical of Borderie's too incautious use of materials from saints' lives, documents often late and tendentious.[13] This large body of material has since been sifted with due care by competent scholars, with the result that, notwithstanding many remaining uncertainties, new lines of interpretation have gained credence. Particularly significant is the elaborate dissertation of René Largillière published in 1925, which placed in a new light the relation of the "saints" to the Christian communities formed by the home-seeking immigrants.[14] The Breton term *plou*, parish, has special significance in this study. Largillière abandons de la Borderie's concept that the *plou* is "le clan modifié," and represents it as normally taking its origin through the grouping of newcomers around a pioneer monk in priestly orders who, to pursue his devotional life in seclusion, had taken up his abode in an uninhabited but fertile spot. His fellow countrymen from Britain, being at least nominal Christians, formed a community to avail themselves of his priestly and pastoral services. This in church terms was a *plou* or parish, in Latin, *plebs*; and the place name became that of the saint with *plou* prefixed. In typical cases the settlers reached Brittany unguided and unaccompanied by clerics and came under their leadership afterward. Largillière points to a comparable sequence in the origins of French Canada, where some priests came with purpose to serve already existing settlements. In Brittany, however, the missionary or pastoral role was often undertaken because the new settlers felt the need of the services of a qualified priest who lived where he was available to them. They had arrived in the country in unorganized companies and were dispersed in small cultivable areas.

The beginning of church organization was not something projected in the original migration but rather was the natural upgrowth of the conditions faced by the home-seekers. No episcopal authority was exercised. In Britain the bishops had already largely yielded leadership to monks and were not charged with episcopal jurisdiction as it was practiced in Gaul. The numerous clerics in episcopal orders among the migrants assumed no administrative duties in Brittany. The new pastors knew nothing of any previous parish organization where they labored. Thus the church of the Britons in Brittany was a new creation, but reflecting the pattern of the mother church of Cornwall and Wales. The bounds of the parishes were not set by superior ecclesiastical planners, but emerged with relation to topography and population. Probably many of the parishes arose in previously unpopulated or unchristianized areas where no parish organization had preceded. There are, of course, well-known instances of the coming to Brittany of famous saints with twelve or more companions, an arrangement with many Irish parallels. For Brittany such groups are of sixth-century date, and there appears no coordination of their members in missionary action. Clearly the rise of the Breton church was marked by the greatest individualism.

The Briton who served as a monastic priest and parish founder in early Brittany had to meet conditions new and strange to him. Formerly under the discipline of monastic residence, he was now the master of a local community of lay folk, without obligation to abbot or bishop and with little contact with the outside world of religion and culture. As a class these founders deserve praise for their adaptability and for their steadfastness. Many of them lived out their lives as country pastors in the communities which they had helped to create. As a consequence their names were only locally celebrated and are not duplicated in dedications elsewhere. But some others traversed the land freely, founding churches which they soon left to successors and spreading their renown widely.

Continued migration and expansion brought ultimately the imposition of the language of the Britons in most areas; and from it the Breton speech of today, with its dialect variations, is derived. Celticists find it closely linked with Cornish and less intimately with Welsh. In recent years this derivation has been challenged by F. Falc'hun who insistently argues that its origin is in ancient Gaulois. His view, vigorously rejected by Kenneth H. Jackson,[15] has gained little acceptance.

The *plou-* prefix in place names is most common in those areas in which the Breton language is still spoken, the departments of Finistère, Côtes du Nord, and Morbihan. Another prefix, *tre-*, originally an oratory in a remote location, came into similar use where people gathered to worship with one who had begun as a solitary. As monasteries were founded and became numerous, a good many place names were applied beginning with the prefix *lan-*, equivalent to Welsh *llan*, a monastery. The process of spreading a network of Christian organized communities through Brittany occupied most of two centuries. Although writers on Brittany point to the many fragmentary remains of ancient paganism that survived through later centuries, these were retained as accompaniment rather than as challenge to an accepted Christian establishment, and the process of Christianization was carried forward to essential completion.[16]

Scholars who attempt to indicate the role played by prominent individuals in this constructive work encounter great difficulties. The "lives" are nearly all late, and their writers were not biographers in any acceptable sense of that term. They frequently borrow incidents written by other hagiographers about other saints. They abound in incredible anecdotes, and for what is credible they omit dates. Nevertheless, it is possible to sketch in broken outline a few careers of notables in this company, and to name others whose location in Brittany is known.

The signatures of those present at the Council of Tours held under Archbishop Perpetuus in 461 include the entry. "Mansuetus, Episcopus Britannorum." Since the archdiocese of Tours laid claim to jurisdiction over Brittany, Mansuetus is to be regarded as coming from some location in Brittany already occupied by Britons. Haddan and Stubbs speak of him as "a regionary bishop,"[17] which leaves much to conjecture. In our lack of specific facts it has been suggested that he may have come into the council incidentally while on pilgrimage at Tours.[18] It may be that in styling himself "a bishop of Britons," he merely wished to have it understood that he had episcopal orders in the British Church, something that many a monk or abbot might have claimed. In any case we are at a loss to account for his presence in the council and the entry of his name as that of a qualified and participating member. We know nothing of his background or of his credentials. If his signature implies subjection to the Archbishop of Tours, this is a concession far from typical of Breton churchmen. The document at least attests an ecclesiastical existence of Breton Christianity in 461.

An elusive figure is Riocatus, to whom Sidonius Apollinaris refers in a letter of about 478 as "bishop and monk," and who is thought to have been at that time in Brittany, possibly at Aleth on the Rance.[19] A generation later some early pathfinders of the Irish peregrini lingered about the Rance estuary before going to Reims. Flodoard's *History of the Church of Reims* lists the names of seven brethren, "peregrini for the love of Christ," and three sisters of this unusual party. J. L. Gough Meissner shows possible identifications of some of their names with place names of the region.[20] In Cornwall the same group had been led by St. Breaca, a nun of Kildare, and had included Ronan, who is represented as a son of two converts of St. Patrick. St. Ronan, it seems, returned to Ireland but was soon back in Cornwall whence he passed to Brittany in about 500. After a stay in the Pays de Léon he finally moved to a remote location on a wooded slope above the western Bay of Douarnenez, where he ministered to a primitive pagan tribe that had been left unaffected by Roman civilization. The place, Locronan, is one of the many Breton places of pilgrimage.[21]

St. Budoc, the hero of fantastic wanderings, is sometimes given a fifth-century date. The child of parents who had already settled in Brittany, born in a sealed cask in which his mother had been put to sea, released with her at Waterford, Ireland, he grows to manhood there, then crosses the sea to Brest floating on a stone coffin. It is possible that Budoc actually restored the ruins of a church built in Roman times on the tiny island of Lavret off Plaimpol and founded a monastery there. The little archipelago in which Lavret belongs may have been frequented by monks and the scene of a number of typical Celtic monastic island foundations.[22] Legend associates St. Budoc with St. Mawes, thought to have been an Irishman, who settled on the island of Modez off the Léon coast. He was remembered as a teacher who held his classes in the open air. There remains on the Isle Modez a low, squat tower of granite topped by a cone with a knob (*calotte*), to mark the location of the abbot's house, which was central to numerous monks' cells, as in the arrangement at Iona.[23] Somewhat more ample are the data on St. Brieuc. The son of Cardiganshire parents and descended from Maximus Magnus, he was known in Wales as Tyfriog. Having labored in Cornwall and made a beginning in Brittany at Tréguier in the Léon area of Côtes du Nord, he revisited his Welsh home, but returned to found the notable monastery that passed on his name to the town of St. Brieuc. He died there at a great age, probably in the early sixth century, but dates elude us. St. Tudwal, said to have been Brieuc's nephew, and the cousin of a ruler of Damnonia in north central Brittany, succeeded Brieuc at Tréguier. A nearby foundation by Tudwal was called Lan Pabu, Tudwal being affectionately known at Pabu, Father. The word in Latin was "papa," and a wild legend identified him with one of the historic popes.[24]

St. Samson of Dol has already come to our attention as a Welsh saint of wide activity and renown (see chapter 3). He was probably well over sixty when he reached Brittany, but he retained his vigor until his death at eighty, in about 565. The fact that he had episcopal orders while in Wales made it natural that when in the ninth century his monastery of Dol gave rise to an episcopal see he should come to be referred to as "Bishop of Dol." The anonymous writer of the early *Life of Samson* makes no such statement but treats him constantly as an abbot.[25] The book was written about 610 at the behest of a later abbot of Dol, Tigernomalus, who was also of episcopal rank. With a troupe of fellow clerics Samson landed at the mouth of the Gouioult which flows into the Bay of St. Michel, and moving to higher ground instituted the monastery of Dol. From that center, we read, he "founded many monasteries through almost the entire province." The "province" here is probably Domnonia (the name is identical with the Latin name of Devon), which extended through a great area of northeastern Brittany and was ruled by princes of British race. An internal enemy of the ruler had brought about the latter's death through intrigues with the Franks, and the rightful heir, Judwal, was imprisoned by King Childebert at Paris. Samson took upon himself the task of effecting Judwal's release, visited Childebert's court, and, according to the *Life*, through the use of miracles and a conditional malediction, succeeded in the undertaking. He won the warm favor of Childebert, and attended the Third Council of Paris (between 555 and 563), subscribing its decisions as "Samson peccator Episcopus," a style used by the other signatories. Thereafter, with Childebert's encouragement, he founded a monastery at Pentale on the Seine. Judwal was set free, to crush his opponents in Domnonia, while Samson returned to Dol.[26] He was next to set out with untiring energy on a mission of some duration in the Channel Islands of Jersey and Guernsey, possibly extending his mission to some of the Scilly Isles, where his name is also remembered. He ended his days at Dol. His biographer does not give us the locations of the "many monasteries" Samson founded in Brittany; but since he wrote conscientiously amid the scenes of Samson's activity less than half a century after his death, the statement is not to be lightly dismissed. On the other hand, it would be a mistake to regard Samson, an unusually powerful personality and a man of high birth and lordly ways, as typical of the missionary founders. Many, as we have seen, were content in some narrow environment to serve in modest faithfulness, doing their necessary part in the inception of the Breton Church.

A capricious fame visited some of these saints who would have been happy in obscurity. A typical instance is that of St. Méen, or Mehan, a Welshman from Gwent of slightly later date than Samson, who, accompanied by his godson Austel, plunged into the great forest of Brocéliande. This vast upland tract of northern Brittany was a realm of nature full of perils, sparsely inhabited by half-pagan tribesmen, with none of its later Arthurian romance or pleasant palaces of Breton kinglets.[27] He founded a monastery near Gael toward the northeast edge of the forest. Here was to flourish the medieval Abbey of St. Méen, and a healing fountain created by his touch would draw throngs of pilgrims for centuries.

But his life story has yielded place to legendary marvels. Equally regrettable is the lack of clear historical material on St. Winwaloe or Winnoc, commonly called Guénolé in Brittany, who founded the influential monastery of Landévennec (Lan-to-Winnoc in Finistère. Of the four medieval attempts to write his life, that by Wrdisten (or Gourdisten), one of his ninth-century successors in the office of abbot, may preserve some facts, though it has been regarded by more than one scholar as fictional and almost valueless.[28] Wrdisten makes him the son of a Welsh prince named Fracan. With his wife Gwen, Fracan migrates to Brittany shortly before the saint's birth, lands at Ploufragan, and settles on an island at the mouth of the Aulne. Fracan has to defend the spot from pirates, which he does with the aid of the boy's prayers. From the spoils taken in this victory a monastery is built. Guénolé is put to school with St. Budoc of Lavret, where he is trained as a monk. While still young he leads a band of twelve to form a community on an island shore, but the exposed situation proves too forbidding and he goes with his companions to a more hospitable location. The monastery of Landévennec was planted in a sheltered valley south of the estuary of the Aulne near the harbor of Brest. Conjectures of his death-date have been 504 and 532. The certain fact is that Landévennec rose to distinction among Breton monasteries. Nowhere else in Brittany was the Irish monastic element so prominent. Wrdisten's statement that Guénolé at one time wished to join St. Patrick in Ireland (a remark made with free disregard of the century between the lives of the two) no doubt reflects awareness of the relation with Irish monasticism. The discipline bore a resemblance to that of Iona, and may have been based upon the rule of Columban of Luxeuil.[29] How Landévennec took on this Irish character is not made known. It was probably in the forefront as a teaching center during most of its early history. The era of its glory ended with a Norman raid in 914. After many vicissitudes it has been restored as a Benedictine abbey.

St. Paul Aurelian seems to have been a younger contemporary of Guénolé, and his career is hardly less elusive. A *Life* written by Wromonoc of Landévennec in the ninth century which is largely a package of extravagant miracles makes him the son of a South Welsh chief. King Mark, alias Cunomorus, who briefly held power in Cornwall and Brittany, patronizes his early efforts as a monastic founder in Wales and Cornwall till, warned by an angel to go beyond the sea, the saint crosses to Brittany. It is thought that he landed on Brittany's western island of Ushant but founded a monastery on Batz, an island off Roscoft, which marks the northernmost part of the Finistère coast. There he is said to have died at a great age in about 573. A late document records his alleged appointment, on an appeal from the local people, as Bishop of Léon by King Childebert in 512, and his consecration by the Frankish court bishops without reference to the jurisdiction of Tours.[30] But the existence of such a bishopric in the sixth century is open to question. He probably planted a center for his mission on the mainland at the spot where later bishops had their see, north of Morlaix and a mile from the Channel shore. There his name remains in the form St. Pol de Léon.

The seaport and town of St. Malo had an illustrious history in later times, but the saint himself is a comparatively minor figure among Breton founders. He is the St. Maclovius who came from Llancarfan in Gwent and founded a monastic settlement at Aleth on the Rance. He was a contemporary of St. Samson; both died about 565. Aleth later became an episcopal see, but lost this distinction to the town of St. Malo in the ninth century. Jacques Cartier was born in that town, and sailed from its harbor on his momentous voyages to the St. Lawrence in 1534 and 1535.

Contemporary with these Welsh founders in Brittany was St. Gildas, whose migration to Brittany cannot be regarded as a certainty although it was confidently affirmed by a Breton author of the eleventh century (see chapter 3). It is in Brittany and not in Wales that he was celebrated in place names. "St. Gildas de Rhuis" to the east of the Bay of Quiberon stands by the site of the monastery of Rhuis which he is alleged to have founded. Southward from the bay lies the rectangular island of Houat, supposed place of his final retreat and death.

Though our information is inadequate to provide a clear narrative of the planting of the Church of Brittany, it is sufficient to show that this was achieved by missionaries who became religious guides to the British settlers, chiefly at points on or near the coast. The maritime situation of the new foundations together with their occurrence in remote places was pointed out early in the course of modern research. Haddan and Stubbs, referring to some early studies by de la Borderie, remarked in 1873: "The Gallo-Roman missionaries from Tours evidently could not penetrate the forest of

Brékelien, and their Christianizing efforts were practically confined to the dioceses of Rennes and Nantes and probably the south of Vannes. The British immigrants came by sea, planted the whole coast—Ruys, Landévenech, St. Matthew's abbey, Léon, Tréguier, St. Brieuc, Aleth, Dol—and penetrated to the heart of the forest mentioned above at St. Méen."[31]

Through the period of the development of Breton parishes and monasteries the claims of the Archbishop of Tours to ecclesiastical control of Brittany were repeatedly asserted but little regarded. About 486 Tours itself came within the Frankish domain through the western conquests of Clovis. Whatever intercourse may have occasionally taken place between Tours and Breton leaders was now severed, and at times Bretons and Franks were at open war. Within Brittany a succession of bishops was maintained, their consecration by previously consecrated nonterritorial bishops being conducted in the Celtic manner, regardless of the prohibition of this by the Second Council of Tours.[32] Brittany also maintained the Celtic Easter and tonsure. The Breton founders, it will be remembered, had left Britain before the reforms instituted by Wilfrid, Adomnan, Cummian, and Elfodd. Their successors in Brittany apparently remained unresponsive to the changes in Britain and Ireland which these names recall. The Fourth Council of Orléans, in 541, whose decisions were subscribed by the Archbishop of Tours, adopted the *laterculum*, or book of directions, of Victorius of Aquitaine (see chapter 7), but this action did not prevent subsequent disagreement on the dating of Easter. Gregory of Tours, who in his *History of the Franks* largely neglects Brittany, indicates that about 590 the Easter reckoning followed by him at Tours was not that used in many other places. He regards this as a consequence of a variation in the text of the Victorian tables, some observing and others rejecting the inserted phrase: "not to celebrate on the same day as the Jews."[33] It is not apparent, however, that this created any crisis of controversy at the time, nor does it appear that Gregory had in mind the Celtic practice in Brittany. It may be that in sixth-century Gaul some variety of usage with respect to Easter was tolerated with relatively little annoyance and that in view of other divergences no special attention was given to the Breton Celtic variation.

Brittany succeeded in holding off the Frankish aggression to a remarkable degree until it was renewed under Pepin and Charlemagne. But these monarchs never were so free from other affairs as to undertake a conquest of the peninsula. Essentially they sought arrangements with cooperative Breton chiefs and clergy by which a certain suzerainty was implied, and some tribute was collected. The important cities of Vannes and Rennes were at this period held by the Franks. Louis the Pious (814–40), finding himself strongly resisted by a Breton movement led by the chief Morvan, attempted the subjugation of Brittany. From temporary headquarters at Priziac near Quimper, Louis took measures to alter the Breton church customs (817). For this purpose he summoned to his presence Matmonoc, Abbot of Landévennec, and, inquiring of him about the way of life (*conversatio*) in the monastery and the tonsure of the monks, he was told that in these matters they followed the Irish system. We have noted the strong Irish influence at Landévennec; whether Matmonoc was an Irishman or not, he appears to have thought of the monastery as originally Irish, an assumption contrary to fact. An early comment on this document describes unfavorably the severity of the discipline at this monastery, comparing it with that of the Egyptian monks.[34] It is possible that a similar austerity characterized Breton monasticism elsewhere. No doubt with previous intention, Louis commanded the adoption of the Roman tonsure and of the Benedictine Rule. In selecting one monastic center of prime importance and influence for the promulgation of this command, Louis was following the precedent set by his father, Charlemagne, who in 787 had inaugurated a general educational reform by his celebrated letter to Baugulf, Abbot of Fulda.

Throughout this period Brittany had no one ruler over all its parts. Its major divisions were governed by hereditary or usurping chiefs, called "counts" in Frankish documents from about 500. From time to time some of these showed ambition to make themselves kings of the whole territory. As early as 470 the war thief Riothemi (see above, p. 139) styled himself king of the Bretons. Judicaël, son of Howell III and count of Cornuailles, on his father's death in 612 assumed the title of king. He was, however, thrust into the monastery of St. Méen. In 632, through the mediation of St. Eloi (see below, p. 171), Judicaël came to terms with Dagobert I and resumed the exercise of the kingship. But in 638 he was obliged to return to the monastery[35] and until his death in 658 he was a model monk, earning the designation "saint." It was not until the ninth century that Brittany produced a ruler of kingly stature; and his reign was brief and troubled. This was Nominoë, son of one Ravillon, who enters history as a politically motivated war chief. By 824 he had attained such prominence that Louis the Pious felt it necessary to treat with him. Louis saw the possibility of gaining control of Brittany through an agent who was a native of the country and a man of competence and courage. The negotiation proved fruitful. Louis acknowledged Nominoë as his ally, with the title of Duke of Brittany. During the reign of Louis Nominoë fulfilled his function well, bringing about internal pacification by prompt action where necessary. But soon after the succession of Charles the Bald (840) he broke from the Frankish alliance. In 842 he proclaimed himself King of the Bretons. He subdued Nantes, which had sided with Charles; but this historic city was presently captured by the Normans, who held it for nearly a century. Unable to retake Nantes, Nominoë attempted to enlarge his domain by a deep invasion of Anjou and Marne. Trading these gains for one more valued, he wrung from Charles a recognition of independence for Brittany (846).

In ecclesiastical matters, Nominoë adopted a high-handed policy, by which the structure of the Church of Brittany was transformed. He promoted a form of episcopacy similar to that which prevailed in continental lands generally, but closely related to the kingship and self-contained within the country. Where bishops had held some importance and were under Frankish influence, he abruptly replaced them by his own nominees. This occurred, for example, at Vannes, Quimper, Léon and Aleth. He favored for orderly church administration the metropolitanate as it had developed in Charlemagne's empire. But he would have nothing to do with Tours and firmly rejected the metropolitan authority in Brittany traditionally claimed by that see. Instead he declared the bishop of Dol to be the archbishop of Brittany, and strove to make this a reality. The Breton political hero thus became the agent of an ecclesiastical revolution in which the church was externally remade on the continental model. But the assumption of metropolitan rank by the bishops of Dol was to be disputed through more than three centuries, with eminent popes rendering opposite decisions.[36]

As for Nominoë himself, he was again on the warpath against the Franks when, amid new victories, death overtook him in March 851.[37] His son Erispoë gained recognition from Charles the Bald as King of Brittany; but, designing a marriage of his daughter with Charles's son Louis, Erispoë was slain in 857 by his uncle Salomon, younger brother of Nominoë. Salomon's policy toward the church was a continuation of that of his brother, and he was able to reign in relative peace until intrigues with young Louis against Charles occasioned his deposition. He spent his late years in penance for the assassination of his nephew, planned but could not perform a penitential journey to Rome, and died in a monastery (874).

By this time the church of Brittany had shed some of its peculiarly Celtic characteristics. It had come to adopt the Roman festival of Easter; its monasteries were under the Rule of St. Benedict, and an episcopal system, with an archbishop resident within the realm, was exercising an increasing authority. But in Celtic Brittany the church never bore great marks of distinction in learning, art, and heroic devotion such as we find in the church of Ireland and Britain. After the first age of brave initiative, the note of high achievement is missing. The Breton church of that era was not the matrix either of many missionary leaders or of eminent scholars. The monasteries remained important for the internal life of the church, but never acquired the reputation of internationally recognized schools of learning. Two factors may be cited to account for the relative mediocrity of the Breton Celtic church. One is the local "particularism" and individualism, partly incidental to the predominantly rural condition of the people, that prevailed in its life and spirit. The second and more obvious limitation placed upon its health and expansion is the almost constant violence and menace of war amid which it could do little more than survive. Most of the dangers came from outside forces, and the whole people had to be occupied with political and military struggles. The contribution of Breton Christianity to Europe may have been greatest in the humble labors of monks in the busy scriptoria. It is true that the many "lives" of saints there produced have their defects; for the most part they leave the personalities they treat buried under an accumulation of contrived miracles. But no estimate can be placed on the value of the numerous writings saved for posterity by Breton copyists.

The successors of Nominoë, Erispoë and Salomon, had to contend against Norse invaders. Alain the Great defeated them in 890, and his grandson Alain of the Twisted Beard (Alain IV) came from refuge at Athelstan's court in England, on the appeal of the abbot of Landévennec, and, with the approval of the French king Louis IV, restored Breton independence (ca. 937). During the tenth century the Breton clergy were reduced in number by a substantial exodus caused by ravages of war.[38] In the vicissitudes of the eleventh century many Bretons joined William the Conqueror's invasion of England, fought at Hastings, and settled in Cornwall, instituting a slow migration from Brittany to the Cornish peninsula whence their ancestors had come. This movement continued through the Middle Ages.[39] The losing struggle to maintain an autonomous Breton state under "dukes of Brittany" ended only in 1491 with the marriage of the duchess Anne of Brittany to Charles VIII of France. Meanwhile the independence from Tours of the "archbishop" of Dol and the church of Brittany had been surrendered when, under Pope Innocent III, a bishop of Dol made his obedience to the Archbishop of Tours (1200).

Although integration of the Breton church with that of France was structurally completed at that time, Celtic elements remained, especially in popular festivals, to differentiate the church life in Brittany from that elsewhere. Brittany has been called "the land of the Pardons" with reference to the annual celebrations of early saints at the churches they founded. These festivals, called "pardons" from pious belief in the efficacy of the saint's intercession, are marked by many traditional features and serve to renew an awareness of the early Christian Breton traditions. The Breton language, still in household use by a large percentage of the people, is the only Celtic language still spoken on the Continent. Apart from these obvious survivals, some writers would attribute to such eminent writers as twelfth-century Abailard and nineteenth-century Châteaubriand and Renan a Celtic quality of mind to be associated with their Breton heritage.

A note may be appended here on a fragment of British Christianity that turns up in sixth-century Spain. An episcopal see named Britona, also referred to as *sedes Britonorum* (or *Brittonorum*), finds mention in connection with the synod held at Lugo in 569. To it belong "the churches that are among the Britons" together with "the monastery of Maximus." We learn that "*Mailoc, Britonensis ecclesiae episcopus*" was a signatory of the Acts of the Second Council of Braga, 572. Pierre David would identify this Mailoc with one Maliosus who was at the earlier Council of Braga, 561. The see of the Britons was situated in the province of Galicia, a Celtic area of ancient times, and was quite near to the northwest corner of the peninsula between Lugo and the Bay of Biscay. The exact location of the monastery and episcopal residence cannot be certainly indicated, but it has been with some probability identified with the site where later stood the Church of Santa Maria de Britona, "two leagues from Mondonhedo." The district had been since the early fifth century under the control of the Germanic Suevi, who were converted from Arianism to Catholic orthodoxy through the efforts of St. Martin of Braga (d.580).

We know nothing of the circumstances in which the colony of Britons was planted; but it is presumed that, like those who migrated to Brittany, they had been menaced or dislodged in Britain by Anglo-Saxon aggressors. They must have entered Spain in such numerical strength as to be able to shoulder aside, or bring to terms, the Suevi around them and to plant a stable settlement. With the enterprise that characterized their brethren in Brittany, they had formed an organized church. Whether this had existed for some time in detachment from the diocesan organization of the province or not, when first mentioned in documents it is found in full association with the wider organization. The mention of "the monastery of Maximus" in 569 strongly suggests, in view of analogies in Britain, that this monastic community had formed the nucleus of what by that time had become a bishopric; and it seems not improbable that Mailoc was at once bishop and abbot of the monastery, the latter having been founded by one Maximus. The Britons of Britona were represented in councils held in 646 and 653, perhaps also in 683 and 693; but the bishopric seems to have become inactive with the Arab conquest of 711. In 850 it came under the jurisdiction of the bishop of Oviedo, and it ultimately became a part of the diocese of Mondonhedo.[40] It would be misleading to associate the Britona church with the action of the Fourth Council of Toledo (633) requiring the coronal tonsure of all clerics, since the practice there condemned, an abuse customary "in parts of Galicia," is not the Celtic frontal tonsure but shaving a small circle at the top of the head.

It is of interest here to recall the curious statement of Paulus Orosius where, in his *Seven Books of History*, he introduces a description of some localities in Spain: "There in Galaetia is situated the city of Brigantia which raises its towering lighthouse, one of the few notable structures of the world, toward the watchtower of Britain."[41] Orosius was probably a native of Braga, the ancient Bracara, some distance southward from the later British church foundation. His words, written about 418, testify to a traditional awareness in Galicia of Britain as a neighbor over the water. The seaways connecting Britain, Ireland and Spain had been frequented from primitive times and a migration to Spain of Britons in distress need not surprise us.

Ten | St. Columban and Other Missionary Peregrini

IT IS NO negligible phase of European history that now claims our attention, as we survey the widespread activities of Celtic missionaries and scholars among continental peoples during the formative era of Western Christendom. The attention of historians had been drawn to the colorful story of warrior tribes moving westward to form a patchwork of kingdoms where unity had been imposed by Rome, rather than to the religious and cultural invasion that moved eastward from islands once thought of as beyond the frontiers of civilization. The new invaders were unarmed white-robed monks with books in their satchels and psalms on their lips, seeking no wealth or comfort but only the opportunity to teach and to pray.

For more than half a millennium a stream of educated and dedicated men poured from the monasteries of Ireland to "go on pilgrimage for Christ" wherever they might feel themselves divinely led. A lesser number from Wales and Cornwall participated in the migration; but the distinguished names are nearly all Irish. Most of them entered this foreign service wholly on their own initiative. They were not conscripted or appointed by their superiors. In typical instances they were men of more than youthful years who found themselves aware of a divine call to be up and away. They would obtain the consent of their abbots and start out eagerly, often taking with them companions they had enlisted. We do not read of inner crises of decision; rather we get the impression of prompt and unhesitating response to a divine imperative. They were fond of citing the example of Abraham who obeyed the command: "Get thee out of thy country and from thy kindred, and from thy father's house, to a land that I will shew thee" (Gen. 12:1); and this pattern they followed literally. It was typical too that in the circumstances they broke off communication with their home monasteries. They were not directed by committees or expected to make periodic reports to a home base. The home base for them was only a prized memory. With a strange eagerness they sentenced themselves to perpetual banishment and went forth never to return. They began the new career without specific plans other than the intention to teach a foreign people. They found their way over rough seas and perilous roads and among strange tribes until they came to a spot that seemed by some circumstance divinely indicated as their place of labor.

Of course it is incredible that in all cases the only motive in these personally momentous decisions was obedience to a divine call. The Celt has, perhaps more than men of most other races, felt the drive of wanderlust. In the later era of our present interest terror spread by the Vikings on Irish, Hebridean, and British shores must have swollen the ranks of migrating saints. But our sources offer little that reveals a consciousness of these matters as background for a saint's peregrination, and certainly nothing that can justify a broad judgment to account for the phenomenon along these lines. In some instances, as in that of Columba cited above (chapter 6), the pilgrimage for Christ is enjoined or undertaken as a penance for confessed sin. And the true peregrinus is aware that by his setting forth his life course is broken in two. His life is thereafter lived with enhanced vividness and with a resolute commitment that makes him a person to be reckoned with wherever he goes.

The words *peregrinus* and *peregrinatio*, which they adopted gladly in self-description, should not mislead anyone into the supposition that these men were wandering and unstable persons. It is not to be denied that such characters existed, forerunners of the "wandering scholars" of the later university era.[1] The Italian poet Fortunatus lived a life of this sort before settling down as bishop of Poitiers in 599; but he was not a Celt. There were also men and women who made fleeting visits to holy places with as much curiosity as piety and with no life-purpose involved. But our missionary peregrini were men of a totally different type. They went promptly and diligently to work where they first settled, and if they subsequently changed location it was usually after a good many toilsome years and under force of adverse circumstances. They bore no resemblance to religious tourists like the celebrated Aetheria (ca. 390) nor yet to the monastic hoboes excoriated by St. Benedict as "gyrovagi." Nor are they to be classed with the late medieval pilgrims who went in throngs to visit saints' shrines for spiritual benefit or merit, or for the travel experience, and returned to their homelands. The peregrini went abroad not to receive benefits but to impart them. They were prepared to accept the hardships of pioneering, asking for themselves only the fellowship of a dedicated community and, in many cases, a private hideaway where they might read their books and commune with God. If we could inquire of them what they were hoping for in life, many of them might reply in the words of Columban, the greatest of them all, "multorum salutem et secretum mihimetipsi"—"the salvation of many, and solitary spot of my own."[2] Often at the inception of their missions they sought favorable relations with a prince or local ruler, and they were disposed to cooperate where possible with the secular powers. But this was not allowed to compromise their freedom of speech and criticism. They were men who knew their own minds and did not fear to rebuke the mighty.

The impact of the missionary peregrini was first strongly felt in Frankish Gaul through the work of Columban of Luxeuil and Bobbio. He wrote his name as "Columba" and liked to remember that it meant "dove" like the biblical "John" and "Jonah." Some German scholars have called him "Columba the Younger," but in Latin texts he usually appears as "Columbanus." There is no mention in his writings of his namesake of Iona, who was about twenty years his senior. Like Columba he was tall and vigorous of body, austere in his asceticism, a masterful and competent leader, an eloquent preacher, and a gifted poet. While he probably surpassed Columba in the range of his learning, he lacked the diplomatic discretion which the latter seems to have possessed. Both these great Irishmen were in active career to their life's end and died spent with labor well past three-score and ten. We are at an advantage in dealing with Columban, as compared with Columba, in two respects. First, his biographer, Jonas, came to Bobbio about 618, three years after Columban's death, and wrote the *Life of Columban* about 630, having first traveled to the localities where he had worked, and interviewed persons who knew him intimately. Moreover, Jonas, unlike Adomnan, who neglects narrative to make way for miracles, shows a genuine interest in biographical facts.[3] Secondly, we possess a considerable body of Columban's authentic writings: a monastic rule and penitential, letters, sermons, and Latin verses playful and grave. In these the learning, versatility, and ardor of the man are revealed with a clearness rarely paralleled among medieval personages.

While preeminent among the peregrini, Columban is in many ways typical of them. His birth took place somewhere in Leinster, between 540 and 543. With parental encouragement he began early the study of grammar, rhetoric, geometry, and Holy Scripture. A time came in his youth when his good looks attracted the attention of "lascivious maidens." He asked counsel of a godly woman who, warning him by reference to the ills associated with Eve, Delilah, and Bathsheba, urged him to take flight from his homeland. This he did with such firm resolution that Jonas, in reporting it, uses language supplied by an exhortation of Jerome: Columban in departing steps over the prostrate body of his pleading mother. Leaving his "homeland" did not imply leaving Ireland; but within Ireland he went from the southeast to the northwest, to the monastery at Gleenish on Lough Erne in County Fermanagh. There the abbot was Sinell, a former disciple both of Finnian of Clonard and of Comgall of Bangor, and like these masters a scholar and a stern disciplinarian. Columban remained with Sinell, engaged in the study of the Bible, long enough to write a commentary on the Psalms, now lost,[4] and some hymns. He then went to Bangor, where Colman was in full career. Here, for nearly twenty-five years under Comgall's direction, his studies proceeded with intensity, he had experience in teaching, and his monastic personality ripened. Columban was in his middle forties when he applied to Abbot Comgall for permission to go on pilgrimage. The petition was granted, and a band of twelve was recruited to go with him. The date is uncertain but not far from 590.

Their journey lay through "Britannia," and good scholars differ on whether by this Jonas meant Britain or Britannia Minor, Brittany. They may indeed have passed through Cornwall and landed in Brittany at a northern port such as St. Malo. But they passed on into the heart of Frankish Gaul. At this time the political and social conditions in Frankland were altogether deplorable. The debased descendants of the conqueror Clovis were engaged in almost continuous strife featuring assassinations. Jonas has some inexact references to these rulers; what he says of their behavior corresponds to the portrayal found in the pages of Gregory of Tours. Amid these royal ruffians Gregory finds one "good king" in Guntram of Burgundy (561–92), crediting him with many benevolent acts toward churches and with popular recognition as a saint.[5] Columban and his brothers engaged in some itinerant preaching before approaching the king and then procured, either from Guntram or from his successor (593) Childebert II, permission to establish a settlement of monks. The location chosen by Columban was remote from the royal court at the abandoned fort of Anagrates (Annegray) in the foothills of the Vosges, near Burgundy's northern border with Austrasia. The people round about were Suevi, a fragment left behind by that tribe in its westward migration.

The little community was, as described by Jonas, an exemplary one, living together in ideal brotherliness and in strictest discipline. Already inured to hunger, they were at the outset on the verge of starvation, until a farmer brought them horse-loads of food and asked for prayers for his sick wife. Soon an abbot, Caramtog, whose name suggests that he may have been a Briton, sent his cellarer with a supply of food. Friendly contacts with the people widened. "Crowds," we read, came to the monks' lodgment at the old fort seeking health, and the sick were healed through Columban's prayers. But the urge to cultivate his soul in secret devotions led him to spend certain holy days in the hollow of a rock whence he had by gentle persuasion expelled a bear, and where his sustenance was wild apples, herbs, and water. While there he was served by a boy named Domoal as secretary and messenger to and from his brethren.

The penalty of holiness was popularity. Men thronged in to join the devoted band or came, repenting of their sins, to receive the remedies (*medicamenta*) of penance. Soon sheer numbers and the need of productive land required the creation of a new center. Luxeuil, eight miles away, where the warm springs had attracted many in Roman times, was founded and rapidly became a community of thousands. With this surprising expansion, a third foundation followed three miles northward, at Fontaines. Jonas has a vivid anecdote of harvest time at Fontaines. The monks feared the loss of their crops from threatening rain. Columban stationed "four men full of religion," three Scots and a Briton, at the four corners of the field to pray while the rest labored to cut and save the grain. He himself was a stout workman with a sickle or an axe. In other incidents Jonas has the monks fishing, at the somewhat arbitrary direction of their abbot, in the mountain streams that flow into the Moselle. Columban moved freely from one to another of his foundations, using provosts to govern in his absence.

For perhaps ten years all went well, and the region had been in that time deeply and permanently affected by the mission. Then Columban found himself in serious trouble. He had failed to obtain the approval of the bishops who nominally controlled, but had hitherto neglected, the area of his work; and he had failed to keep on safe terms of acceptance with the rulers who had followed Guntram. He was now to realize that he had alienated both these powers, and that his very success had undermined his security. Neither a worldly episcopate nor a depraved court could continue to tolerate his presence. The bishops had indeed what from their point of view was a legitimate grievance. Columban had left Ireland long before the adoption of the Roman Easter date there, and he had followed the Celtic practice in this and had imparted it to his converts. Besides, his now numerous adherents were in no way under episcopal sway. In Ireland bishops were often functionaries of monasteries under obedience to abbots, and he had not reckoned with a system in which abbots and monasteries were answerable to bishops. There was no charge that he and his followers were doctrinally heretical, but to the bishops they were schismatic and to be brought under obedience.

Sensing the approach of trouble on the Easter question, Columban wrote to Pope Gregory the Great (ca. 600) stoutly defending the Irish Easter. The letter is worded with incautious freedom and does not lack that clever playfulness which its writer could seldom repress. Less than fortunate is his allusion to an earlier pope, Leo the Great, with the wry use of the scripture quotation, "a living dog is better than a dead Leo." Not even his warm praise of Gregory as an author is sufficient to accredit a distant stranger to the pope. No reply to the letter is on record. If it reached Gregory, he may have thought it an impertinence,[6] and considering the gravity of the situation, it still seems strangely trivial.

Three years later Columban was summoned to appear before a synod of bishops meeting at Chalons sur Saône (603) to answer for his irregularities. His reply was by letter only. While the spirit of his response is friendly and fraternal, it is not that of compliance. He prefers the tradition of his own country on the Easter matter, for which he claims the support of Eusebius and Jerome; but let them decide whom they will follow, on the principle, "Prove all things, hold what is good" (I Thess. 5:21). The letter bears strong, if somewhat indirect, suggestions that the bishops should rather be attending to needed reforms of discipline: "he who shuns the toil of opposing sinful men is a hireling." If we choose to cast off pride and to be "humble and poor for Christ's sake" all God's people may "enjoy a true peace." The inference is clear that Columban had a low opinion of the bishops and felt no obligation to them. He only asks that he may be allowed to live as a stranger in their midst, beside the bones of seventeen dead of his community, and he hopes that they and he may love and pray for one another. "I am not the author of this difference, and it is for the sake of Christ the Savior . . . that I have entered these lands as a pilgrim [*in has terras peregrinus processerim*]."[7] It is not required here that we should reach a judgment about the bishops he was addressing. The view of Jonas was that through their negligence the Christian faith had almost disappeared from Burgundy before Columban came.

But for Columban a crisis was mounting through the enmity of Brunhilda, the Visigothic princess who had gained ascendancy in Burgundy after the assassination (575) of her husband Sigebert who ruled at Metz. After the death in 597 of both Childeric II and her rival in wickedness and ambition, Fredegondis of Neustria, her influence was paramount. She directed the policy of her grandson Theuderic II, a profligate young prince. The decisive confrontation came when she called upon Columban to bless the illegitimate sons of Theuderic. He came before the court in high anger, cursed the boys as the offspring of harlotry, and foretold their fate never to come to royal power. Theuderic had him seized and taken to Besançon, where he found opportunity to preach to a numerous band of condemned prisoners. He soon found his way back to Luxeuil.

Theuderic as a boy had visited Luxeuil, and admired Columban. He now shrank from putting to death a celebrated saintly monk, whom he perhaps personally revered. Instead he thought to secure Columban's deportation back to Ireland. But this Columban, peregrinus for life, was resolved to avoid. Deeply loyal as he was to Ireland and its people, it would have been for him a crushing defeat to return, abandoning the "pilgrimage for Christ." The king's soldiers came to expel him once more, this time taking along those of his monks who were Irish (610). One of these, the aged Deicola, unable to keep pace with the others, bade Columban farewell and built for himself a hut in the wilds. Overcoming the hostility of a local priest, he became the founder of the notable monastery of Lure.[8]

A military guard escorted the Irishmen to Auxerre, on to Nevers, and down the Loire, halting at cities on the way. At Orleans Jonas has the saint cure a blind man in response to the plea of his wife, a Syrian woman. At Tours he prays all night at the tomb of St. Martin and is entertained at breakfast by the bishop. It was at Nantes that his guards were to place him on shipboard for the voyage to Ireland. He was with his companions duly put on a ship that was about to sail; but soon after starting the vessel ran aground on the river bank and with the captain's collusion Columban and four companions made their escape.

During the trying days of his expulsion and detainment by order of Theuderic, Columban had his monks at Luxeuil much in mind. From Nantes he wrote to his "sweet sons and dear disciples" a letter of deep concern and affection. He has nothing here to say about his hardships except to refer to the possibility of escape, in language that, considering the outcome, it not surprising: "Now as I write a messenger has reached me, saying that the ship is ready for me, in which I shall be borne unwillingly to my country; but if I escape there is no guard to prevent it; for they seem to desire this, that I should escape."[9] His concern is really lest discord in the community, some evidence of which had already troubled him, should become dangerously intensified in his absence. The letter reveals that monastic ideal in which are combined firmness of discipline and unity of spirit.

Though cast out of Burgundy, Columban had good reason to hope that other Frankish realms would welcome him. Neustria and Austrasia were now increasingly alienated from Burgundy. Soon Columban was in conference with Clothaire II of Neustria in Soissons. Though received most kindly by Clothaire, he chose not to remain in his kingdom. He went on to Metz on the Moselle, to visit the court of King Theudebert II of Austrasia, whom he also found friendly to his projects. With Theudebert's consent the region of the northern lake country of Switzerland was designated for a new missionary enterprise. Columban and his little company were soon on their way up the Rhine in a river barge with oars and sail. They reached Tuggen, a place on the Timmat, a Rhine tributary now in the Swiss canton of Zug. Here they excited pagan anger by destroying idols and spilling quantities of wine that had been consecrated to Woden. But they made some converts by their preaching. What interpreters they had we do not know; but at least one of their number, St. Gall, had acquired the ability to preach and converse in Germanic speech. Largely, perhaps, as a result of an inconsiderate approach, the response here was on balance disappointing, and the monks were unwelcome to the local authorities. On the advice of Willimar, a priest at Arbon, they departed to Bregenz at the eastern end of Lake Constance. Some months were spent here in organizing a monastic home, but it proved only temporary.

Soon after his final expulsion from Luxeuil, Columban had conceived a project for a mission to the Lombards of Italy, and he may have regarded Bregenz as a mere step on the way to Lombardy. But St. Gall, who had been with him and had been a staunch supporter from the beginning in Bangor, decided to remain in the area. It is not from Jonas, who had interviewed St. Gall, but from a later writer, Walahfrid Strabo (d. 849), that we have the story of an altercation between Columban and Gall, the latter refusing to go further on a plea of illness that was not convincing to his stern superior. In a less than friendly parting, Columban forbids Gall to say mass while he, Columban, is alive.[10] At any rate, the year 612 sees Columban, with a reduced band of followers, making his way by some Alpine pass into the smiling plain of Lombardy. Pausing first at Milan, they soon went on to Pavia, capital of this Lombard Kingdom.

The Lombards had come into Italy in 568 as Arian Christians, but their king Agilulf had married a Bavarian princess, Theudelinda, who was an orthodox Catholic and popular with his subjects. He permitted the propagation of orthodoxy and had good relations with the popes. At his court in Pavia, Columban and his travel-weary monks were hospitably received. They were assigned a portion of ground on which to build a monastery at Bobbio on the Trebbia, a southern tributary of the Po. Situated about thirty miles southwestward from Piacenza and a like distance from Genoa on the Mediterranean, the spot was sufficiently withdrawn from the activities of trade and politics to be adapted for the site of a religious community. When Columban took possession of the place it had a decayed church, traditionally founded by St. Peter. This was rebuilt, and other necessary structures soon surrounded it. Columban, entering his seventies with well-preserved strength, shouldered sticks of lumber and otherwise did his part in the work of construction.

The Burgundy nobles, long discontented under Brunhilda, with the willing help of Clothaire II of Neustria, now overthrew her, and she suffered death in one of the most brutal public executions in history (613). Clothaire, who was now in a dominant position among the Franks, aided the Bobbio enterprise with money, and afterward sent a deputation to invite Columban back to Luxeuil. This was declined with thanks, and Columban went on with his task in Bobbio, finding time to participate in the theological controversies that were then rife in Italy. He had already at Milan written a treatise, which is not extant, against Arianism. From Bobbio he addressed a long letter to Pope Boniface IV (608–15) on the already old issue of the Three Chapters on which fresh strife had been raised in Italy.

The Fifth Ecumenical Council, held at Constantinople in 553 had, under pressure from the Emperor Justinian, condemned Theodore of Mopsuestia for his allegedly Nestorian writings and therewith certain treatises of Theodoret of Cyrrus and of Ibas of Edessa. The language of the council's threefold decree came to be known as the Three Chapters. The council's action was at the time opposed by Pope Vigilius (538–55), but after much mistreatment he yielded to the Emperor. Columban held Vigilius at fault for his submission, and responsible for the perpetuation of the controversy. But his letter is strangely inexplicit theologically and so cumbered with superfluous rhetoric as to be exasperating to the reader. It is clear enough, however, that he is deeply agitated by the current partisan discussions and is pressing for a settlement by a conference or council, which he asks the pope to convoke. He indicates that the letter is written at the bidding of King Agilulf and Queen Theudelinda, who were deeply concerned because their realm was disturbed by a harsh conflict among Catholics. King, queen, and all others are, he says, asking that the pope take action to bring peace: "Let the king follow the King, do you follow Peter, and let the whole Church follow you."[11]

Columban's freedom of utterance in addressing popes has been variously interpreted. He has been accused of insolence, commended for independence, and more objectively examined phrase by phrase for tokens of his attitude to the papacy. On this topic the letter to Boniface is revealing but hardly decisive. Certainly it lacks the note of submissive obedience due to an infallible judge and ruler. Even some of the complimentary phrases freely sprinkled through it seem framed to suggest the limitations rather than the universality of papal sway. Boniface is "the fairest head of all the churches of Europe," and, again, "head of the churches of the world saving the singular prerogative of the place of Our Lord's resurrection." Columban is shocked by a widespread suspicion that heresy is countenanced by the papacy, and laments the ill repute (*infamia*) of the Chair of Peter. "One must grieve and mourn if in the Apostolic See the Catholic faith is not maintained." This sentence is perhaps the best key to his basic attitude. It is because he expects much from the successor of Peter and is jealous for his honor that he feels obliged to protest against what seems to him negligence on the part of Boniface. By contrast, he notes, "we Irish" have been constant in the faith since it was first received from Rome. He fears that Boniface is following Vigilius in this lack of responsibility, and the thought affords him the irresistible occasion for a barbed pun: *"Vigila, atque quaeso, papa, vigila, et iterum dico, vigila; quia forte non bene vigilavit Vigilius* [Be watchful then, I beseech you, pope, and again I say, be watchful; since perchance he who was called the Watchman did not watch well]."[12] Again he has the expression, "I strive to stir thee up as the Prince of Leaders [*tanquam ducum principem*]." Leadership (and his *ducum* may bear a military metaphor) is the function of the pope, and it is he who should "defend the faith in a synod."

It should be remembered that at the time Columban was writing, the Celtic churches had not been concerned with the issue of papal authority. It was still half a century before the Synod of Whitby. Columban was one of the earliest spokesmen of Celtic Christianity to glimpse the problem of defining the papal position, and what he says does not indicate mature and consistent thinking about the matter. But his initiative in writing the letter to Boniface implies a claim that a concerned Christian may become a monitor of a pope who seems remiss: and some of his language seems to link him with the late medieval Conciliarists. But this springs not so much from systematic thinking as from an Irish habit of mind. He reminds Boniface of "the freedom of discussion characteristic of my native land."

Reference was made in chapter 5 to the monastic rule (*Regula coenobialis*) of Columban, which is thought to reflect the rule of

Bangor under Comgall and is taken as the key to Comgall's discipline, otherwide undocumented. Columban's *Penitential*, similarly severe, shows a good deal of verbal dependence on that of Finnian of Clonard,[13] but its references to a Frankish environment show that it was probably written at Luxeuil. Since these documents are readily available in English, it is not necessary to enlarge upon them here. They represent a rigid type of discipline expressed in exact legal terms with brief paragraphs of interpretation. The *Penitential* deals separately with the offenses of monks and laymen. The "cure by contraries" derived from Soranus of Ephesus and the early Methodist School of physicians, is affirmed by both Finnian and Columban. Thus in the latter we read: "The talkative person is to be sentenced to silence, the disturber to gentleness, the sleepy fellow to watchfulness."[14] The inner motive of the offender is constantly brought to attention. Before going to Mass one should diligently make confession, "chiefly regarding the motions of the mind." In both documents there are many provisions requiring physical punishment, with a distinction in severity between blows (*plagae*) and strokes (*percussiones*).[15]

The Rule of Columban requires about twice as much psalm-singing as that of Benedict, and apparently permits about half as much food. "The food of monks shall be coarse, consisting of cabbage, vegetables, flour mixed with water, and a biscuit, and taken towards evening." The meagerness of the diet and the harshness of the penances, even for minor offenses and lapses in liturgical services, would be thought inhuman in any modern context. Amid these forbidding regulations we do find a few expressions of considerateness and compassion. A monk who "breaks into the noise of laughter" during the services must perform a specially imposed fast "unless it has happened pardonably." But whatever there was of such mitigation in practice, the sternness of Columban's discipline is extreme. We might have supposed that it was such as to alienate young men, thus stifling the growth of the institutions he fathered. But it is an arresting fact that for at least a century the houses founded by him and his immediate disciples multiplied and drew numerous recruits. By the end of the seventh century there were approximately sixty of these monasteries in Frankish territory.[16]

Columban left some record of his diligent preaching in thirteen sermons (*instructiones*). G. S. M. Walker believes that these were preached in a series while he paused at Milan in 612.[17] They offer a limited sample of what must have been a large body of sermon material. Jonas repeatedly reminds us that "wherever he went, he declared the Gospel Word." Those sermons we have are hortatory, designed to win decisions; but they are artfully constructed and abound in exclamatory apostrophes, arresting contrasts and rhetorical questions. The insistent emphasis is the disparagement of earthly in comparison with heavenly concerns. He does not shrink from references to hell-fire (*ignis aeternus*) that may remind us of frontier preachers of the early 1800s; but he has the elegance of a cultivated mind. In some passages a certain sublimity is attained, coupled with spiritual fervor, chiefly where the theme is the greatness of God as Creator and Redeemer. In these skillfully wrought addresses Columban is the earnest proclaimer of the Christian message from the standpoint of monastic ideals and with accent on the contrast between this fleeting and insecure existence and that which is to come. Human life is vain except as a pilgrimage toward the heavenly regions.

Columban is also the author of a number of poems (*Carmina*) of such distinction as to mark a point in the history of late Latin poetry. The themes and meters alike range fairly widely. Again, as in the sermons, there is a preacher's emphasis on the world's impermanence and the joy of heaven. One poem, addressed to a friend, Setus, contains a touching description of the distresses of old age as evidence of the folly of seeking wealth. Another piece, addressed to his "brother" Fidolius, is an experiment in Adonic (two foot) meter. At the close are six hexameter lines in which he deplores his own frail old age. Better known is his happy Boat-song, which may have been composed when going up the Rhine. The flowing hexameters are punctuated by the refrain: *"Heia viri! nostrum reboans echo sonet Heia!* [Ho, fellows, and let answering echo sound our Ho!]." This striking feature of the poem seems to capture the experience of singing loudly while rowing between resounding river banks. But here, as in all the *Carmina*, a religious element enters, and the refrain becomes a tribute to Christ.[18]

There is something difficult for twentieth-century minds to grasp in this seventh-century Irishman who by choice lived below our poverty level; who founded a series of monasteries among foreign peoples; who made friends of bears and squirrels in a forest retreat; who wrote and enforced the severest ascetic rules; who took it upon himself to give advice to popes and dared to rebuke rulers with power to put him to death; who preached diligently from a fund of biblical knowledge; who was unsurpassed in classical learning among his contemporaries, loving and in a free way imitating the Latin poets; and who in his late years wrote a versified letter in a rare meter which, he explains, was practiced by Sappho.

When Columban was dying, he sent his abbatial staff to St. Gall, who had been ill with a fever when Columban left him. At Arbon on Lake Constance east of Bregenz Gall was befriended by the priest Willimar and nursed back to health by two kind clerics. One wonders whether he was thinking of Deicola, supposedly his elder brother, who had made a home on the woods near Lure (see above, p. 161). Like him he would seek a remote place in the woods and make it the center of a monastic mission to a Germanic people. For Gall this would be the Alemanni, a once widely successful federation that had been pushed south-eastward by the Franks. A deacon named Hiltebold, who had some knowledge of the woodlands southward from Bregenz and Arbon, became Gall's guide and companion among the bears and wolves. Gall stumbled on some underbrush as they reached a sheltered and inviting spot by the little stream Steinach. Taking this as a divine intimation, and regardless of the wild beasts, he determined to remain there. Like many other Celtic saints, he made friends with beasts in the woods. He is said to have brought to obedience a bear that on command picked up a heavy stick of firewood, laid it on Gall's fire, and was rewarded with a loaf of bread. With a handful of his original Irish companions a modest beginning was made in this solitude. Workmen sent by the count of Arbon helped in the construction of an oratory, and huts for the monks' dwellings were soon made ready.[19]

St. Gall had been a zealot against paganism and had been the leader in the violent destruction of pagan shrines and idols when Columban's company first reached the neighborhood of Lake Zurich. But his mission to the Alemanni was conducted with patient persuasion. In Roman times some Christianizing effort had been made in this region, and there were a few clergy rather feebly maintaining places of worship. Gall made friends among these, and won also the favor of Duke Gunze and other local rulers. Yet he was, like Patrick of Ireland, essentially a pioneer, and he is rightly regarded as the chief agent of the conversion of the Alemanni and the greatest figure in the founding of the Swiss church.

According to Walahfrid Strabo's *Life of St. Gall,* he had, while at Bregenz, a supernatural reminder of the conflict of religions in which he was to play a notable part. While fishing on Lake Constance, he overhears a distressed conversation between the demons of the mountain and of the lake. These are startled and indignant at the intrusion of a servant of Christ.[20] This story dramatizes the sense of combat with demonic powers common among Celtic saints and may well reflect Gall's own consciousness of the crucial importance of his work. But he gained the wisdom that made him less aggressive and more persuasive, a model missionary, not unlike his much admired contemporary St. Aidan of Lindisfarne (see chapter 7). Like Aidan, he went about among the people, carrying his message to their homes. When he died in 645 the whole territory of the Alemanni had adopted Christianity.

The number of his helpers may have remained quite small. No doubt the busy preacher little dreamed that a great abbey bearing his name would one day arise at the scene of his labors. He refused opportunities that would have taken him from his chosen task. In 627, on the death of St. Eustace, second successor of Columban at Luxeuil, he declined an invitation to become abbot of that growing monastery. He had already, about 616, been offered an appointment to the bishopric of Constance. Instead he secured the election of his trusted pupil John, the deacon who had shared his studies and his teaching, a native German. It was Gall who preached at John's consecration, using a Latin text which the new bishop interpreted to the large assembly of clergy and people. This sermon is the only extant writing from St. Gall's pen. It reads like a summary of his popular preaching message. He briefly recites the Bible story from the creation and fall of man to the death and resurrection of Christ, the bestowal of the Spirit and the mission of the Apostles. The style is clear and unpretentious, and evidently the discourse is intended for lay converts, although the high occasion demanded that it be presented first in Latin. At the close we have an earnest exhortation to the people to maintain the faith and works of their Christian profession.[21]

We now turn again to St. Fursa, whose foundation at Burghcastle in East Anglia came to our attention in chapter 7. Anticipating a destructive attack by the pagan prince Penda of Mercia, Fursa left the new monastery to the direction of his brother Foillan and made his journey to Gaul. When Penda's blow had been struck, Foillan—with a third brother, Ultan, who had been an anchorite—followed Fursa to the Continent. Two other Irishmen, Caidoc and Fricor, had already independently begun work in Picardy and were located at St. Riquier, the place so called from the name of their first convert of noble rank. They were soon followed in that area by St. Valery, who had been a monk and a gardener at Luxeuil.

Fursa entered Gaul through Brittany and was implored to remain at Mayoc near Pontivy but pressed on to Neustria. There, after some perils, he was warmly received by Erchinwald, Mayor of the Palace and, King Clovis II being a minor, the real ruler in that Frankish kingdom. Fursa was given a site for a monastery at Lagny on the Marne, east of Paris. The monastery was founded about 644, and was maintained for nearly a century under Irish abbots, Fursa's brother Foillan being his immediate successor. We find Fursa in contact with a number of less distinguished Irish missionary saints, including Caidoc and Fricor just mentioned; and he gained such eminence that Kathleen Hughes can speak of his "paruchia" in northeastern Gaul in the generation after him. It was not at Lagny but at Péronne that his name was chiefly remembered, where with Erchinwald's patronage a monastery was founded about the time of his death, with his brother Ultan as succeeding abbot. When his strength failed, Fursa was seized with a desire to return to England, but when he had started on the way he died at Mézerolle (ca. 649). A month later his body was taken by Erchinwald to Péronne and splendidly entombed in a collegiate church built in his honor.[22] This important city on the Somme became so greatly frequented by Irish monks and pilgrims that it was known as *Perrona Scottorum* and in the *Annals of the Four Masters* as "the city of Fursey." In the Frankish lands no less than in England Fursa's ecstatic visions (see above, p. 105) were long remembered. His description of heaven and hell captivated the medieval mind as if it were an authentic revelation. The cult of St. Patrick on the Continent is thought to have been introduced by Fursa, and the monastic centers under his influence kept in contact with Ireland and apparently with Irish foundations in Germany.[23] The Péronne monastery suffered destruction by Norse invaders in 880.

The reign of the last powerful Merovingian, Dagobert I of Austrasia, a prince highly favorable to Irish and other monastics, ended in 639. His young grandson, Dagobert II, son of Sigebert III, was on his father's death (656) exiled and conveyed to Ireland, where he was educated by monks. He was brought back to Austrasia—with the intervention of St. Wilfrid, according to Eddius Stephanus—and held the kingship for three years. His death by treachery while hunting (679) was regarded as martyrdom and he was called a saint.[24]

Generally speaking, in this era royal and politically influential personages took a favorable attitude to the monks, and some queens and princesses were particularly active on their behalf. Thus Itta, wife of the mayor Pepin of Landen bestowed a property on Foillan, Fursa's brother, to found a monastery at Fosses, having herself already founded a nunnery at Nivelles and made her daughter, St. Gertrude, abbess. After a mission in Brabant, Foillan was murdered by highwaymen while on journey between Nivelles and Fosses (655?). Ultan, the other brother of Fursa, remained at Péronne until his death in 686.[25] St. Bathildis, an English girl taken to the Continent by pirates and purchased by Erchinwald to be a slave, became the queen of Clovis II and the mother of three kings, each of whom held the rule of all the Franks for a few years. She was extremely generous to monastic foundations, and was responsible for the origin of the nunnery at Chelles and of several monasteries, including that of Corbie, which she placed under an abbot brought from Luxeuil. She was closely associated with the earnest reforming bishops St. Eloi (Eligius) of Noyon and St. Ouen (Audoenus) of Rouen. Both of these, together with St. Faro of Meaux and St. Didier of Cahors, encouraged Irish peregrini who located within their jurisdiction. St. Eloi's admiration for Columban is indicated by his foundation at Salignac under an abbot who was responsible to the abbot of Luxeuil.[26] British girls are said to have been recruited for the inception of the nunnery of Hohenburg in the Vosges founded by St. Odilia, whose brother, Adalbert, gave the island of Hanau in the Danube (Hanaugia Scottorum) to the peregrinus Benedict. Here a monastery flourished until 1290, when the island was flooded and the community was removed to Reinau. Another island foundation was that of St. Fridolin at Sekingen in the upper Rhine; but it has been questioned whether Fridolin was an Irishman, as stated in his twelfth-century "life." Trudpert, who penetrated southeastern Germany and founded a monastery in the southern Black Forest in the district of Breisgau in Baden, is thought to have been Irish.[27]

There is no uncertainty about the nationality of St. Kilian who spent many years in eastern Franconia. He came there from Ireland in 643 with twelve companions and preached at Würzburg and neighboring places and in Thuringia. Having rebuked Duke Gosbert of Thuringia for marrying his deceased brother's wife, Kilian was at her instigation murdered in 689, together with two of his helpers, the priest Coloman and the deacon Totnan. Their relics were enshrined in the cathedral at Würzburg in the eighth century, and the martyrs were long celebrated in Germany.[28]

It was left to the great English missionary and administrator, St. Boniface (d. 754), to effect the Christian organization of the entire region and to build a structure of ecclesiastical government in which Celtic peculiarities had no place. Boniface had no direct and personal debt to Irish teachers, and he was much more an administrator than a preaching missionary. Early in his missionary activity he took a solemn oath to Pope Gregory II that he would maintain the unity of the Catholic Church against leaders (*antistites*) who violate "the ancient institutions of the holy fathers" and to resist and hinder those who labor outside the Roman obedience. Although he was instrumental in the appointment of an Irishman named Abel to the important See of Rheims, and although another of his appointees, Burchard, enshrined the bones of Kilian at Würzburg, his general policy toward the Celtic peregrini, who remained aloof from the tightly organized hierarchical church system he earnestly fostered, was one of suspicion and even hostility.[29] The "wandering bishops" (*episcopi vagantes*) condemned in various eighth- and ninth-century councils were undoubtedly Celtic monks who had obtained the episcopal office in connection with the nondiocesan Irish or British church and felt authorized to ordain and consecrate others where they went in Europe. They were regarded by Boniface, and by the territorial bishops in the developing hierarchical structure, as a serious menace to unity and order. Quite in the spirit of Boniface, the council of Mainz held in 813 denounced these intruders as monstrous creatures, *"acephali . . . hippocentauris similes, nec equi nec homines."*[30] Although the jurisdiction of Boniface was greatly enhanced by Gregory III in

732 when he was made Metropolitan of Germany east of the Rhine, he was not very successful in dealing with the intransigent Celts. Yet his policy bore fruit after his lifetime. The peregrini of the later ninth century, with all their distinctiveness, were rarely under censure as ecclesiastical outlaws. In a real sense, Boniface was the successor, as he was the censor, of the Celtic pioneers. The Celts had already awakened to a Christian culture most of those Germans whom he brought under hierarchical control. There is truth in the remark of Philip Schaff: "He reaped the fruit of their labors and destroyed their further usefulness, which he might have secured by a liberal Christian policy."[31]

Columban was not the earliest of the Irish peregrini to reach Italy. St. Ursus (French, Ours; Italian, Orso), on leaving Ireland, spent some years in the area of Digne in southern France before going across the Alps to Aosto. This was not later than the latter half of the sixth century, but dates cannot be made explicit. What is known of him indicates that he was a bishop of Aosto and that his labors were rendered difficult by Arian opposition emanating from the Lombards which he resisted with great energy by a preaching and teaching campaign in the region. In the same period St. Fridian (Frediano)—reputed son of an Ulster king—who has been needlessly confused with St. Finnian of Moville (see chapter 5), established a monastery at Lucca and, about 560, became bishop there. "A man of wondrous power," Fridian had a hard struggle against "barbarians," probably Arian Lombards, in his diocese.[32] Among numerous other Irish monks and churchmen in Italy the most famous names are those of two ninth-century scholars; these will receive mention in our next chapter.

The participation of British monks in the missions to continental peoples occasionally comes to notice. We read of some Britons who were members of monasteries under Irish founders, and of British bishops operating independently of the church structure who were regarded as schismatics or heretics in parts of Germany. In 739 Pope Gregory III felt it necessary to warn the bishops of Bavaria and Allemania who were under the direction of St. Boniface against false and heretical British bishops coming into these principalities. Apparently in these areas Britons constituted a large percentage of the troublesome *episcopi vagantes*; but the charge of heresy can probably be discounted in this condemnatory utterance. The activities of these intruders have not been made clear. There may have been more actual missionary contribution by Britons in Germanic areas than can now be documented.

In recent years scholars have become aware that Celtic monks played a pioneer role as missionaries in Slavic lands. Nearly a century before the supposed planting of Christianity in Moravia by Methodius and Cyril (ca. 863) unnamed Irish and British missionaries penetrated in some numbers into that kingdom. The excavation of a stone church of Irish type built about 800 at Modrá in the heart of old Moravia was completed in 1954. It was 9 by 7 meters in size with an additional rectangular presbytery and resembled one at Glendalough of similar date. Such a building would naturally have been preceded by a good many years of missionary work. The scholars Josef Cibulka and Zdenek Dittrich both confidently attribute the origins of this mission to the activities and influence of Vergil of Salzburg (d. 784) and the monastery of St. Peter of which he was abbot. Here too a British element from Bavaria was associated with the Irish mission. These Celts were the earliest missionaries to operate in Moravia with lasting success.[33]

There is probably some historic fact behind the strange legend of St. Sunniva, who is alleged to have led a company of her adherents from Ireland to the island of Selje near the western coast of Norway. The incident is dated within the tenth century. The legend makes Sunniva an Irish king's daughter who was left to rule his little kingdom when he was slain by Norse invaders of Ireland. Intent on a religious life, Sunniva resisted the advances of an enemy of her father who would have married her and ruled her people. She asked those of her subjects who would go with her to take ship and trust themselves to the seas. Three ships carried the devoted band eastward until they landed, in hunger and exhaustion, on this lonely island. Sheltering themselves in caves beside a mountain, they prayerfully awaited death. Their sufferings ended when rocks from the mountainside fell upon them. Some time afterward the body of Sunniva was found in a state of complete preservation. King Olaf Trygvason (995–1000) is said to have built a fine church on the island in her honor, and other churches were later built on Selje where one "little white ruined chapel" remains.[34]

This chapter has in a limited way brought to attention some leading missionary personalities and phases of their work. It is sometimes said that the peregrini were not basically missionaries, since we find in many of them a primary search for a place of solitude as an opportunity for the cultivation of personal devotion. In such instances, however, they characteristically responded to the interest created among their new neighbors, entering on the role of missionary teachers with the greatest alacrity. Many of them, indeed, manifestly reached the Continent eager for the missionary role. One may guess that some of them were reacting energetically from an experience of anchorite life with its rigid self-training and experience of solitude. Complete freedom from superiors beyond their own communities in the mission field made them adaptable to local needs and opportunities. They rapidly enlisted Frankish and other German youth who, working harmoniously with them, made Christianity indigenous and self-perpetuating.

Only a few have here been mentioned of an uncounted army of monks on pilgrimage for Christ from the late sixth to the early eighth century. The creative era of this strange invasion was to continue for three centuries more. That one small island should have contributed so rich a legacy to a populous continent remains one of the most arresting facts of European history. "The weight of the Irish influence on the continent," wrote James Westfall Thompson, "is incalculable. It penetrated the still unchristianized regions of central Europe . . . . For three hundred years the light of Ireland flamed, shedding its rays upon Scotland, England and the Continent, until diminished in the darkness of the Norse invasions."[35] We shall concern ourselves with some later manifestations of the Irish influence in Europe, which attains a new dimension in the Carolingian era.

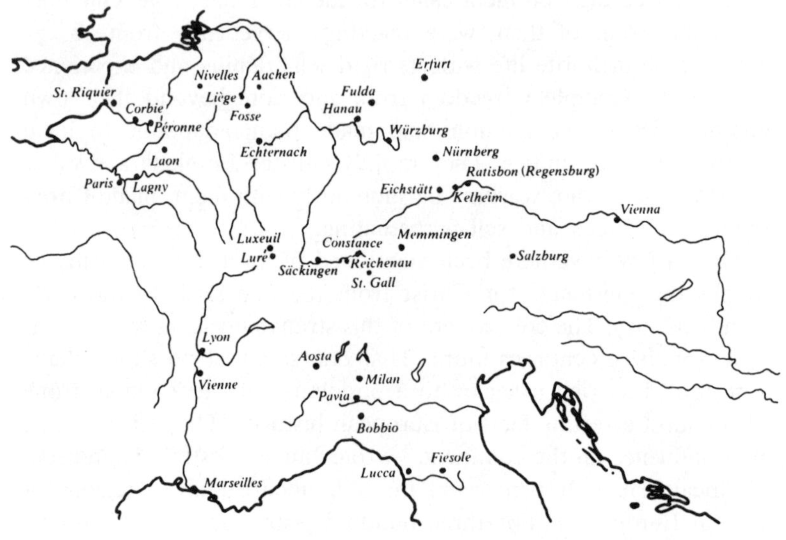

Principal Irish Monastic Foundations in Continental Europe, with Some Other Ecclesiastical Centers

Eleven | Irish Scholars in European Lands

THE FLOW OF Irish clerical migration across Europe continued through the eighth, ninth, and tenth centuries. But about the middle of the eighth century a change in motivation and approach is discernible. The earlier apostles of the movement with their kerygma of salvation give place in large degree to a troupe of professors whose qualifications and interests lay more largely in sacred and profane learning and the liberal arts. Reinforcing the educational activities were those of a considerable number of persons who, though natives of continental countries, were trained in the Irish schools. Aldhelm's reference to English students crowding to Ireland "in fleets," and the similar testimony of Bede (see above, pp. 115, 122) can in some degree be paralleled with reference to visitors from the Frankish kingdoms. We have evidence of the attendance of large numbers of Frankish and other Continental students in Irish monasteries. Although this fact drew the attention of Heinrich Zimmer as early as 1891,[1] no adequate study of the topic has yet appeared. The so-called Dark Age was in fact characterized by deep craving for scholarly knowledge, and the monastic schools of Ireland were everywhere esteemed as offering the best opportunity of acquiring it.

But the main traffic in scholarship was the migration of Irish teachers to the Frankish domains and, in fewer numbers, beyond these both southward and eastward. It was inevitable that their independent behavior and opinions would engender some hostility among the hierarchy, who under the leadership of St. Boniface were building a pyramided system of church order informed with undeviating Nicene orthodoxy. Boniface in his day was troubled by Irishmen who expressed unfamiliar speculative opinions. In 745 he asked Pope Zachary to deal severely with a Scot named Clement who held disquieting views not only on Christ's descent into hell but also on the marriage of bishops. Clement was condemned, but not, as Boniface wished, committed to prison for life. Another Irishman, Vergil (Feargall) "the Geometer," was also a trial to

Boniface. Vergil was abbot of a monastery in Salzburg and was appointed bishop of that place (ca. 745). But he chose to continue his abbatial duties and made use of a substitute to perform his episcopal functions, an Irish bishop named Dobdegrecus. The last part of this name suggests the man's qualifications in Greek. When Vergil refused to hold invalid a baptism administered by an uneducated priest in foolishly erroneous Latin, the pope upheld him in this against the judgment of Boniface. Vergil also caused alarm by his belief that "there is below the earth another world." This was apparently a version of the ancient doctrine of the Antipodes, but novel and shocking to both Boniface and Pope Zachary as challenging the biblical assumption of the unity of mankind in Adam. Vergil, however, was able to avoid deposition or other penalty and remained in office until his death in 784. Ludwig Bieler, following the findings of Heinz Löwe, regards Vergil as the author of the *Cosmographia* attributed to the imaginary "Aethicus Ister," a book of mock geographical exploration, full of absurdities backed by pompous alleged citations of authorities. It was probably intended as a satire on pretentious writing, but it was written with such learned unintelligibility as to bewilder rather than amuse.[2]

During the Carolingian era the number of Irish peregrini in various parts of the Frankish world was such as to impress contemporary writers. Walahfrid Strabo (d. 849), abbot of Reichenau and voluminous author, writing his *Life of St. Gall* (see chapter 10) with Irishmen about him and aware of both Gall's time and his own, remarks that the Irish have a *consuetudo peregrinandi*, a custom of living abroad, that is "almost a second nature."[3] Heiric of Auxerre, dedicating his versified *Life of St. Germanus* to Charles the Bald about 870, exclaims: "Almost all Ireland, despising the sea is migrating to our shores with a herd of philosophers [*cum grege philosophorum*]." Heiric had been trained at Soissons under Marcus, who is described as a bishop and a Briton who had studied in Ireland, though some suppose that he was himself Irish. Heiric at any rate admires the insular scholars. By philosophers he means simply men of sound learning. We have hints that the pervasive presence and needy condition of the Irish caused some impatience in Frankish circles. One of the incomers, Dungal, acknowledges that their thronging numbers and "noisy importunity" may be disagreeable to the Franks.[4]

Decade after decade the stream of learned immigrants flowed. They brought with them what in Ireland was sometimes called "divine and human wisdom," a comprehensive knowledge of the Bible and its chief patristic interpreters supplemented by a familiar acquaintance with the Latin classical poets and to a lesser extent the prose writers. The Greek fathers they read chiefly in Latin translations, but some of the Irish had made a beginning of the study of Greek, and in a few cases expertness in that language can be affirmed. It is held by Louis Gougaud and others that their primary study being in the Scriptures, all other learning was for them ancillary to this. But a real enjoyment of the pagan poets for themselves was not absent, corresponding with the traditional Irish Christian attitude to their own bardic literature and hero tales. The already formalized scheme of studies known as the Seven Liberal Arts had entered the Irish schools and was employed in their teaching. This classification of studies had been derived primarily from Greek educators and worked over by Varro, Augustine, Martianus Capella, and Boethius. Capella's elaborate *Marriage of Philology and Mercury* (ca. 420), written partly in verse, expounded at length the Seven Liberal Arts and was read and commented on by Irish writers, including John Scotus Eriugena. The Seven were divided by Capella and by Boethius (d. 525) into the Trivium (Grammar, Rhetoric, and Dialectic) and the Quadrivium (Arithmetic, Astronomy, Geometry, and Music). On the basis of Capella's treatise, a number of Irish scholars wrote textbooks on one or another of the seven.[5]

Most of the migrant scholars seem to have reached the Continent without any predetermined destination. Irishmen might turn up anywhere, and many of them were penniless and needy. But within the seventh century, provision began to be made for the shelter of Irish wayfarers. About 650 St. Fiacra, a peregrinus settled near Meaux, set up a hospice for their use beside his monastery, and thereafter many such resting-places arose under Irish auspices and with royal approval to serve the needs primarily of Irish scholars on journey. Some nunneries provided guesthouses for women. Later the Irish hospices, being favored by rulers, became numerous and deteriorated through interference. Whatever the motive, an attempt was made to suppress them; but in 846 Charles the Bald, at the prompting of Archbishop Hinkmar of Reims, renewed their authorization, with suitable regulations for their discipline.[6]

Charlemagne's biographer Einhard tells us that Charlemagne "loved the peregrini [*amabat peregrinos*],"[7] and this is equally true of his father, Pepin the Short, and of his successors in the ninth century. No longer making their homes in the forests, the incomers now frequented the courts of kings and emperors who appreciated the help they could render in raising their people to a higher level of Christian culture. It was, however, an English and not an Irish scholar whom Charlemagne made the first head of his Palace School at Aachen (Aix-la-Chapelle). From 781 to 796 Alcuin of York reigned over a realm of culture associated with the court circle. Alcuin had profited by the instruction of Irish scholars at York. The Irishman Colchu, to whom Alcuin wrote in 790 with the deference due to an eminent teacher, has sometimes been identified with the celebrated abbot of Clonmacnois of that name who was perhaps still living. Such an identification would bring the inference that Alcuin had studied in that monastery. But the letter contains no suggestion that it is being sent to Ireland and is naturally read as chiefly a report on continental events to a master in York. Colchu is an Irish name that appears frequently, and Alcuin's correspondent is an otherwise unknown but evidently at the time highly esteemed Irish scholar at York, one of countless others of his class. Through Alcuin, he had a part in the revival of learning promoted by Charlemagne.[8]

But there were many of these who reached some fame in Charlemagne's educational circle. In 790 Alcuin paid a visit to York. On his return to Aachen he brought with him a Scot named Joseph who had been a pupil of Colchu. Joseph wrote Latin poems and treatises on Jerome; he died shortly after 800.[9] When Alcuin retired to become abbot of the monastery at Tours in 796, his place was taken by (a second) Clement the Scot. At Tours Alcuin put to advantage the writing skill he had acquired from the Irish at York to develop the much admired "Carolingian minuscule," which would be a standard script for centuries. From the Monk of St. Gall—presumably Notker Balbulus, who wrote the *Gesta Karoli Magni* (the Deeds of Charlemagne)—we learn that Clement came to Frankland with another Scot, here called Albinus, in the company of some Britons who had wares to sell (ca. 791). These two introduced themselves as merchants of "wisdom" by calling out to groups of people: "If anyone desires wisdom we have it to sell." They were brought into the presence of Charlemagne who inquired the price of their wisdom. Their answer was, "suitable places and ready students, and food and clothing without which our peregrination cannot be carried on." They are described as "incomparably erudite both in secular matters and in Holy Scripture." Albinus was sent by Charlemagne on an errand to Pope Hadrian I and remained in Italy. He may have been identical with the scholar Dungal who spent his later days in Pavia. Clement joined the court scholars and was soon to succeed Alcuin; but he remains little known for one in high office at the court. Theodulf of Orleans, in witty verses addressed to Charlemagne satirizing the Scots and other scholars at the court, appears to regard Clement as a man too arrogantly sure of himself. (Theodulf had also a disagreement with Alcuin, but he probably shared with Alcuin some disquiet about the number of Irishmen maintained by the king. In allusion to this, Alcuin wrote to Charlemagne that the "Egyptians" had replaced the Latins at the court.) Nothing from the pen of Clement is extant except a Latin grammar, his authorship of which is only a probability. It contains an interesting reference to "the Greeks whom we make use of in all our teaching [*in omni doctrina*]." He is thought to have died while on a visit to Würzburg.[10]

The Monk of St. Gall liked a good anecdote, and he may have neglected to test fully his source of information about Clement and his companion. But a comparable incident dated a century later and recorded in the Anglo-Saxon Chronicle is more certainly historical. Here we learn that in the year 891 three Irishmen, "wishing for the love of God to be in foreign lands, they cared not where," crossed the sea to Cornwall in a coracle without oars and found their way to the court of King Alfred. The Anglo-Saxon Chronicle gives their names but fails to inform us of their later service to Alfred in his revival of learning or in the conversion of the Danes in England. It was later alleged that the Irish visitors went on to Rome.

A scholar of some renown was Dungal, who came from Ireland about 784 and became famous while living as a recluse at St. Denis. Following a discussion about an eclipse of the sun (810), he was invited to explain it, and this he attempted in a letter to Charlemagne in 811. Here he relies on the Ptolemaic system, but shows a tendency to speculate independently on the motions of the stars. Later he defended the use of images in worship in *A Reply to the Perverse Opinions of Claudius, Bishop of Turin* (827). He may have known Claudius personally when the Spanish puritan was a chaplain of Louis the Pious, who sent him to Turin in 814. But we know so little of Dungal's course of life that it remains doubtful whether he is to be identified with the Dungal who flourished in Pavia in the 820s. This Dungal was made supervisor of education for northern Italy under Lothair II, who required the scholars of other schools to resort to him for fresh instruction. The latter was in all probability the Dungal who ended his days in Bobbio and left his library to the monastery there. The fact that the *Antiphonary of Bangor* was among his books had led some to surmise that in Ireland he had been a Bangor monk. That Columbanus the founder of Bobbio was himself a Bangor alumnus may add to the probability of this.[11]

One of the most original scholars of the era was Dicuil, an Irishman who appeared in Frankland about 814, when he wrote a treatise on astronomy. In this he made use of earlier studies he had made in calculating dates of the Christian Year. In 825 he presented his celebrated *Liber de mensura orbis terrae*, the first medieval treatise on geography. Dicuil, of course, does not call it geography; that science was subsumed under "geometry" in his time. He incorporates in this short work material provided by classical writers, treating his authors selectively and not uncritically, and employs a book of similar title to his own, prepared for Theodosius II about 425. And he has made inquiries of contemporary travelers on whose observations he can rely. He has especially profited from information furnished by one "Brother Fidelis," probably an Irish monk, who had visited Egypt and Palestine. From Fidelis he obtained remarkably accurate information on the pyramids (the "barns of Joseph") and the "Sweet-water canal" (later disused until modern times) that led off from the Nile Delta eastward to Ismalia. His references to the islands off Scotland, including the Faroes, have the authority of personal knowledge. He had "lived in some of them, visited others, and seen some only from the sea." He tells us that the (Celtic) anchorites who had settled in the islands had been annihilated by Viking pirates. It is quite possible that Dicuil had himself been a monk of Iona who escaped at the time of the Viking raid of 806. On Iceland (Thule) he quotes a third-century author, Julius Solinus, and recounts information that he himself had obtained from some Irish monks who had lived there from 1 February to 1 August 795. At the summer solstice they were able, they said, to see clearly enough by natural light at midnight to delouse their shirts. Moreover he learned that the sea about Iceland is not frozen over in winter; this condition would be found only a day's sail farther north. He has a creditable desire to present only tested facts. In this spirit he leaves blanks for the length of some great rivers, thinking the estimates given him exaggerated. In a reference to the famous elephant (Abulabat) presented by Haroun-al-Rachid to Charlemagne in 802, Dicuil notes that, contrary to hoary popular belief in the West about elephants, he had been observed to rest lying down instead of leaning against a tree. Very little information about Dicuil himself emerges from any of his writings. He is likely to have written most of a poetic tribute to Charlemagne formerly attributed to Dungal which is extant under the pseudonym "Hibernicus exul."[12]

The middle of the ninth century marks the floruit of Sedulius Scottus, who had then become a resident of Liège, where Charles the Bald (840–77) held his court and played host to many Irishmen. A group of these came in 848 bearing a message from the Irish king Máel Seclain announcing a victory of the latter over the Vikings. Some of them asked also for the protection of Charles through his domains on their way to Rome. According to Nora Chadwick, the route then commonly followed by Irishmen on their way to the Continent lay through Gwynedd in Wales, where King Mervyn's court was frequented by learned men, and she believes that Sedulius had paused there for some time on his way to Frankland; but James Carney holds that without any such interruption he came to the Continent "a fully competent versifier in a large range of classical metres."[13] In Liège he had an assigned place of residence with grounds for a pasture. He was joined by a few Irish companions, one of whom was a priest. It was a little community of celibates, but the discipline was not monastic. At Liège Sedulius quickly became a literary celebrity; some of his verses were reproduced in silken needlework by the Empress Ermingarde. The poems that are certainly his are all in Latin. Those of recognized excellence include a triumphal ode on the "slaughter of the Northmen," but it is uncertain what victory it was that he was celebrating. He makes frequent use of symbolism and allegory, and in one piece that is not without humor he rather offensively likens a ram that has been torn by dogs to the Lamb of God in agony. One of the better-known verse pieces doubtfully ascribed to him, *The Scholar and His Cat*, which is written in Irish, whimsically compares Pangur the Cat with the author: both are keen hunters, the one for mice, the other for book knowledge. In another poem he anticipates the Romantic poets as he celebrates the gladness of Easter and springtime: a time of gay flowers, when birds soften the air with their songs, the heavens rejoice, the earth is glad, voicing a hundred Alleluias. M. L. W. Laistner refers to Sedulius as "the most versatile metrical artist since Prudentius."[14]

His poetry has, perhaps unfairly, received more attention than his prose writings. He was a scholarly student of Scripture and wrote long commentaries on some Bible books. He also wrote treatises on grammar. It may have been as a teacher of elementary Latin that he wrote a poem in eight lines, six of which ended with the name of his friend Robertus with its six case endings as a Latin noun—a very suitable item for a beginner's Latin book. He added his signature in Greek script to a Psalter which he copied, and he probably had a fair knowledge of Greek. His book *On Christian Rulers* was primarily designed to give guidance to the king, Charles the Bald (840–77; crowned Emperor 875), amid the problems of sectionalism and invasion with which he was plagued. But it was written in such general terms and with such wide learning as to be of use to any Christian ruler of a professedly Christian state. It was a notable contribution to the "mirror of princes" literary genre that was to culminate in Erasmus' *Christian Prince*. Sedulius recognizes the king's right to appoint bishops, but he would reserve to the Church some measure of autonomy. He urges, on the example of Constantine, the calling of Church councils and respect for their decisions. His prose style profited by a surprising familiarity with Cicero, of whom, like his contemporary Lupus of Ferrières, he was one of the early medieval admirers.

Sedulius differs greatly from the ascetic peregrinus of Columban's type. Though probably a celibate of exemplary character, he was quite frankly fond of good food and good wine, and he appears as one who shines in the relaxed company of intellectuals, "wearing all that weight of learning lightly like a flower."[15]

Chronologically much earlier (ca. 650), but related in theme to Sedulius' treatise *On Rulers*, is an anonymous work by an Irishman abroad entitled *The Twelve Abuses of the Secular World*. This is an ingeniously contrived description of "what's wrong with the world," an exposure of the sicknesses of society as they appear in all ages. Beginning with "the teacher who is not a doer" this Scotus Anonymus discusses at some length each of the twelve abuses he has observed among rulers, prelates, and people. He freely quotes both classical moralists and Christian fathers, and the book is a noteworthy contribution to the literature of Christian social ethics. Its ideas proved stimulating to a number of ninth-century writers, including Sedulius and Hinkmar of Reims. The numerous extant manuscripts of this work indicate a wide circulation; this was probably enhanced by the fact that it was attributed in turn to Cyprian and Augustine.[16]

The Irish attention to poetry is illustrated also in a contemporary of Sedulius who made his mark in Italy: Donatus, bishop of Fiesole from 829 to 876. The story is that having paid a visit to Rome and other holy places, he reached Fiesole at a time when the people there were exercised over the election of a bishop and had assembled for prayer. The appearance among them of an Irish pilgrim led to his being abruptly chosen for the office. He is credited with vigorous attention to his episcopal duties marked by faithfulness in promoting both piety and learning. Like others of the peregrini, he never forgot his Irish heritage. He placed under the rule of Bobbio a nunnery of St. Brigid that had been established at Piacenza. One of his extant poems is eloquent with praise of Ireland, a land of wealth and health, of milk and honey, free from savage beasts and venomous serpents, where only the Scottic race deserves to dwell. He is said to have died with a quotation from Vergil on his lips. His epitaph, written by himself, states that he was of Irish stock (*Scottorum sanguine creatus*).[17]

The most illustrious Irishman named in these pages is John Scotus Eriugena (ca. 810–77). His early life is unrecorded; but the form he chose in which to write his name was such as to make it clear that he was a native Scot—born in Eriu, that is, Erin. He turns up, as one already known in the learned world, about 845. Soon after that date Hinkmar, bishop of Laon, nephew of Archbishop Hinkmar of Reims, asked him to write in confutation of Gottschalk, the Augustinian theologian who affirmed the doctrine of predestination in its double application to the elect and the reprobate. Eriugena was then probably at Laon, one of Charles the Bald's places of residence. In response he wrote *On Divine Predestination*, a treatise as unwelcome as Gottschalk's teaching had been, since it denied not only the predestination of evil men but the real existence of evil itself. He had already broken from the Western tradition and independently adopted a Neoplatonic philosophy. His work on predestination was condemned in two councils, but he remained in royal favor. Charles commissioned him to translate from the Greek the famous treatise known to us as the *Pseudo-Dionysius* but then believed to be the work of Dionysius the Areopagite (Acts 17:34), of which a manuscript lay at Paris, the gift of an Eastern emperor. This labor he achieved to the satisfaction of medieval scholars, who welcomed a Latin version of what they regarded as a document of early Christianity. But since it led into the mazes of Neoplatonic mysticism, it gave to Western thought a new dimension, and played a notable part in later controversies. A Roman critic, Anastasius, admitted his surprise that a barbarian from the ends of the earth should have become such a master of Greek as to be able to comprehend and translate it. Eriugena made other translations from Greek of minor importance and, with a knowledge of Greek unmatched in the West for centuries, read his way into the thought of antiquity, pagan and Christian. No Christian father later than Origen can be thought of as his forerunner in this range of scholarship. Eriugena's piety was deep, but it had an intellectual accent. "O Lord Jesus," he prays, "no other reward, no other blessing I ask of Thee save that purely and without any error or false theory I may understand Thy words, which have been inspired by thy Holy Spirit!"

For Eriugena, ecclesiastical authority has no dominion in matters of the mind; rather reason reigns. Man can attain for himself the knowledge of God in which religion and philosophy find their unity. In his greatest original work, *On the Division of Nature* (ca. 867), philosophy embraces and transforms theology. The work takes the form of a dialogue between master and pupil and follows the course of the latter's questions. The word "nature" is used for all that exists. The discussion is presented in four divisions: nature creating and uncreated; creating and created; created, not creating; and finally, neither created nor creating. The uncreated creator is God, as is also in another sense the last category, since all created things through the agency of the Word return to God. The things we know had eternal existence in the mind of God, and this is true of every man and of all nature.

The pantheistic trend of such thinking is obvious. Creation of finite beings is a self-limitation of God, who yet remains within what He has created. Man has a God-given knowledge of all things: this has been concealed by sin and the Fall, but it may be recovered so far as we turn to God. Eriugena's numerous minor works include a commentary on the Prologue to John's Gospel.

William of Malmesbury's well-known story that on the death of Charles the Bald (877) Eriugena went to serve Alfred's educational projects in Wessex and taught at Malmesbury, may or may not be a late invention. At that time Alfred's educational reforms were already begun, and the Welshman Asser was at his court. Glastonbury had been for centuries a haunt of Irishmen. But the decorative detail that Eriugena was stabbed to death by the pens of his infuriated students is almost certainly drawn from the sometimes macabre humor of college residence. Anyway the substance of the incident is found in the *Peristephenon* of Prudentius, where the schoolmaster Cassian suffers the same fate. It is hardly surprising that such a yarn should light on Eriugena's memory; he must have been a trial to elementary students. Malmesbury's more pleasant anecdote of Eriugena at Charles the Bald's table contains what has been called "the best *bon mot* of the Middle Ages." Charles, to tease him, asks what is the difference (*Quid distat*) between a Scot and a sot (*sottum*, a fool)? Facing the king across the board, Eriugena rejoins: *"Mensa tantum"* ("Only the table"). Already a hoary jest, no doubt, but we thank Malmesbury for associating it with one well qualified to have originated it, and reminding us that the profoundest philosophers can *desipere in loco*.[18]

Eriugena left behind him a strange legacy. Of his writings it was the translation of the pseudonymous Dionysian treatise that awakened the most approving response. It may be said to have fixed in the medieval consciousness the image of the Heavenly Hierarchy with its earthly counterpart. His profound original work was inadequately understood, and its influence was rather indirect. It was not directly wrestled with by the great scholastics, but its ideas tended to crop up among mystics and to be appropriated by sectaries. In our century the *De Divisione* is beginning to receive the attention it deserves as a daring and profound exploration in search of ultimate truth.[19]

The monk Andelm who taught at Laon in Eriugena's time was, despite his name, an Irishman, and was reputed to be a brother of Eriugena. He was the writer of a copy of Paul's Epistles, swollen by extensive commentary material compiled from earlier writers.[20] In the same generation St. Gall Abbey school flourished under

Irish leadership. Eminent among the teachers there was Moengall, an Ulster man, who died about 871, having been for some years both choir master of the monastery and chief professor in the school. The chronicler Ekkehard IV, writing in about 1030 his colorful continuation of the Chronicle of St. Gall (begun by Radpert), narrates the story of the arrival of Moengall with his uncle, Marcus, returning from Rome with a numerous company of pilgrims. While the others went on their way toward Ireland, these two chose to remain. Moengall was called by the brethren Marcellus, the diminutive of his uncle's name. He was, says Ekkehard, equally well equipped "in divine and human learning" and in his teaching treated the Seven Liberal Arts, especially Music. He may have become acquainted with musical practice while at Rome; but his stay in Rome had been brief, and he must have been a gifted and accomplished musician already. The proof of Moengall's success as a teacher lies in the distinction of a number of his German students, especially in the fields of music and hymnody. Notker Balbulus, Radpert, and Tutilo, designated by G. G. Coulton "the three inseparables," became prominent in their time, and Coulton provides a translation of two revealing and amusing passages from Ekkehard about incidents of their earlier days. Notker the Stammerer (ca. 840–912), we are told, stammered with his lips but not in his mind. He is famed for his "sequences," based on the repetition of melodic phrases to which hymn compositions were fitted, a primary contribution to the development of church music.[21]

The Irish brain-drain to European nations culminated in Sedulius, Eriugena, and Moengall. The age of the great Irish scholars who ate at the tables of kings ended with the late Carolingians. But Irish monks still came in teeming numbers. Many of them had been dislodged by the invading Northmen and were refugees from conditions in which they could not survive as monks. Some of them had responded to the stern asceticism which, as we saw, was revived at Tallaght and elsewhere. The old craving for solitariness asserted itself anew in some of these newcomers. Radpert, in that part of the St. Gall Chronicle which he wrote, tells of an Irishman named Eusebius who having entered that monastery became a hermit and lived on Mount St. Victor nearby for thirty years. Before his death in 884 he induced Charles the Fat to grant to the monastery the title to his hermitage.[22] Such men were by no means misanthropic, nor did they wish to sever contact with others. As in earlier asceticism, the solitary life was rendered busy by writing tasks and advisory consultations in addition to devotional exercises.

Nor were the enclosed anchorites (*inclusi*) out of intercourse with the monastic life around them. It was one of these at Ratisbon who persuaded Marianus Scottus to settle there. This Marianus (d. 1088) was one of two Irish monks of the time who wrote under that name. His Irish name was Muirdach mac Robartsaig, and he came of a Donegal family. Having started on a pilgrimage to Rome, he was halted in Germany and about 1076 built the monastery of St. Peter's at Ratisbon. He won a reputation for speed and skill as a scribe and was credited with writing "innumerable" copies of the Old and New Testaments. At the same time he was a practical adviser to many peregrini and promoted the beginnings of a number of foundations in Bavaria and in France.[23] Still more famous was the other Marianus—in Irish, Máel Brigte—(1028–82), a former monk of Clonmacnois under abbot Tighernach, who for reasons unknown had been sentenced to exile by the abbot of Moville. In 1059 he adopted the life of an inclusus at Fulda, whence ten years later he removed to Mainz to resume his enclosed condition. With thirteen years still to live, he there dictated and corrected a chronicle in three parts, the last of which extends from the Ascension to 1082 and contains useful data on the Irish in German lands.[24]

In this later era there were many earnestly religious Irish immigrant ascetics, whether solitary or in ordinary monastic communities, but they can hardly be compared, either for enterprise or for influence, with the apostolic peregrini of the seventh century. The challenge of paganism was less clamant than of old. Yet when the call came for heroic witness, Irishmen were ready to respond. In the eleventh century the peregrinus known as John of Ireland, called "Maccabeus" by his friend Adam of Bremen, was missionary bishop of Mecklenberg with a wide field of endeavor in north Germany. During his years of labor and of hardships suffered from pagan hostility, he planted Christianity among the Wends—a Slavic people very tenacious of their pagan customs. Angry devotees of their god Radigost finally took his life, after ingeniously savage tortures, at Rothre about 1066.[25]

The later phase of Irish monk migration is associated with the appearance of a group of monasteries in Germany known as the Schottenklöster, which spread almost entirely from a daughter house of the monastery of St. Peter at Ratisbon. A long series of Irish abbots followed Marianus here, though the discipline soon became Benedictine. With a continued influx of monks from Ireland, expansion became necessary, and the large monastery of St. James was established at Ratisbon about 1089. This flourishing house mothered most of the other Schottenklöster, including, in order of their dates of origin as given by Joseph P. Fuhrmann, those of Würzburg, Erfurt, Nürnberg, Constance, Vienna, Memmingen, Eichstätt, and Kelheim.[26] It does not appear that the era after Marianus the Chronicler was remarkable for notable Irish personalities on the Continent. There is some doubt about the nationality of "David the Scot," who was a prominent teacher in the Schottenklöster at Würzburg, became chaplain and chronicler to the Emperor Henry V, accompanied Henry to Italy in 1111, and wrote a history of his Italian expedition. His name being Welsh, some have supposed that he is to be identified with the David who was bishop of Bangor in Wales 1120–39, presumably a Welshman, though tagged "Scotus" from his association with the Irish.[27]

In an early adventure the monks of St. James of Ratisbon found their way to Russia. They first wrote to Vratislav II (d. 1092), Christian ruler of Bohemia, asking escort through his territory to Poland. This being obtained, they dispatched a band of monks led by one Mauritius to traverse Bohemian and Polish areas into Russia. They reached Kiev (ca. 1089) and apparently made a lasting impression there. On their return they brought some carriage-loads of Russian furs, the gift of the prince of Kiev. These were not used to warm the brethren but rather were sold to obtain funds for the rebuilding of their church. (See below, pp. 220–21.)

The Schottenklöster were all under the Benedictine Rule almost from their beginnings; but they continued to be recruited largely from Ireland and constituted a recognizable family of monasteries. They were, however, no longer charged with the vigor of earlier times but, like much other monasticism of the twelfth century, were showing signs of decay. The administrative genius of Innocent III was directed to their improvement. In 1215 he drew the Irish houses in Germany into what was called the Congregation of the Schottenklöster, under the authority of the abbot of St. James of Ratisbon. This attempt to reinvigorate the life of these institutions apparently met with quite limited success; but we leave the outcome to our next chapter.[28]

Wherever they went, the Irish brought with them, and continued to produce, manuscripts with the characteristic insular features. Their style of writing and illumination was copied with variations by their continental pupils. The Irish scribes and illuminators themselves felt the influence of Italian and French styles, and they readily adopted novel features. There is thus no uniformity or stabilization over long periods in Irish continental handwriting. But experts find a variety of telltale Irish elements both in their work and in that of their non-Irish students and imitators. In Ireland itself the wanton destruction of books and libraries by pagan invaders nearly extinguished the written page. King Brian Boru (1002–14) is credited with having sent emissaries to the Continent to recover copies of the lost books.[29] It must also be remembered that Western Europe generally suffered great loss in manuscripts from similar violence. The preservation of precious books was a constant care. In 925 the whole library of St. Gall abbey was removed temporarily for safety to Reichenau. The sheer task of maintaining a literary basis for education against this more or less constant menace remained a great one for European scholars down to the age of printing. During the early Middle Ages it could hardly have been even meagerly performed without the dedicated industry of Irish, Welsh, and Breton scribes. With a happy abandon, sometimes punctuated by a half-humorous complaint, they plied their pens in uncomfortable cells and scriptoria, lighting up their pages with brightly colored ornamentation. The Irish who came to the Continent carried in their satchels copies of ancient works, some of which no other than Irish eyes had seen for centuries; and where opportunity was given, they resumed their writing habits and taught their skills to others. In some cases their application to this task resulted in what we might call quantity production. But manuscripts were worn out or heedlessly destroyed or scattered beyond recovery. What remains to us of their work is a meager fraction of the whole. Their books came to be distributed widely among continental monastic libraries, with large deposits in a few of these such as Bobbio, St. Gall, and Reichenau. In modern times, in various ways and by a long process, the precious residue has been placed in a chain of European libraries from Paris to Leningrad.[30]

We see that the homelands of Celtic Christianity bred a vast expansive movement that reached out with conquering energy into many regions of Europe. For this reason they have been likened to first-century Palestine. The Celtic mission planted a form of Christianity unimpeachably orthodox but singularly lacking in preoccupation with doctrinal issues. It was well equipped with the intellectual riches of antiquity but employed its learning primarily in the understanding and interpretation of the Scriptures. With respect to asceticism, the gulf between Celtic Christianity and Protestantism is very wide. Nineteenth-century Protestants sometimes tried to identify the Celtic church polity with their own. A kinship might be claimed far more plausibly on the basis of the acceptance of scriptural authority. The Bible was read with orthodox presuppositions but with personal directness, with no meticulous attention to the language of the Ecumenical Councils of the fourth and fifth centuries, and with little regard for the authority of any ecclesiastical hierarchy. The message of Celtic Christianity was borne through many lands by an army of heroic, ascetic adventurers, in dispersed bands whose only head was Christ, implanting a culture in which a primary reverence for Holy Scripture was harmoniously matched with a delight in classical literature.

Ireland—a green spot in the Western ocean, 32,500 square miles in extent—with some cooperation from Celtic Britain and from Irish-trained Englishmen, exerted for six centuries a pervasive, life-giving influence upon the major part of Europe. It is to the limited area that has been disparagingly called "the Celtic fringe," and most of all to Ireland, that Western civilization owes in large measure its early medieval recovery from a crude barbarism that might otherwise have prevailed for centuries longer. No wonder that by some of the beneficiaries, Ireland came to be looked upon as a kind of second Holy Land. In 860 Ermenrich, Benedictine abbot of Reichenau, exclaimed in a letter to Grimald, abbot of St. Gall: "How can we forget Ireland, the island where the sun of faith arose for us, and whence the brilliant rays of so great a light have reached us? Bestowing philosophy on small and great, she fills the Church with her science and her teaching."[31]

Twelve | The Celtic Churches Incorporated in the Western Hierarchical Church

IN RELIGIOUS and cultural life the Celtic churches experienced a large measure of unity, but they never sought a mutual coordination in structure and control that could have made of their various parts one externally visible church. The upgrowth of Celtic Christianity took place in the same era as that of the rise of the Roman see as the organizing center of the Christian West. Popes of high talent—Innocent I, Gregory I, Nicholas I, and many others—were instrumental in the enlargement and intensification of the papal sway. It was inevitable that the strongly organized Roman system with its universal claims would sooner or later absorb the relatively uncoordinated, dispersedly directed Celtic communities. With every encounter there would naturally come a loss of autonomy for the Celtic party. Thus the issues of Easter and the tonsure were settled in each Celtic area by the adoption of Roman usage. The firm principles of Gregory the Great, Augustine of Canterbury, and Boniface of Crediton were to prevail. The Benedictine order, having early found acceptance in the English kingdoms, finally gave its rule to the scores of monastic houses of Irish origin in France, Germany and Italy. By the time of Pope Innocent III (1198–1216) little remained of the former Irish spontaneity and self-direction in continental lands. We need not think of this administrative absorption as complete assimilation. No doubt something very Celtic was retained in the psychology of many who not unwillingly accommodated themselves to the more efficient polity of the hierarchical church. It was the way of progress, and there was no alternative. Nevertheless, the abounding energy and apostolic impetuosity of an earlier day were no longer characteristic. In terms of great leadership and bold endeavor we enter on a descending slope.

WALES AND CORNWALL

Here our attention turns back to the home churches of the Celtic world, and first to those of Britain. South of the Tweed the Anglo-

Saxon conquest left Wales and Cornwall in ecclesiastical independence. The Welsh Church, alienated by Augustine's inept initiative in 602, long remained unresponsive to the advances of his successors. But the claim of Canterbury to exercise authority in Wales was at no time modified. Archbishop Theodore in the acts of the Synod of Heathfield (680) styles himself "Archbishop of the Island of Britain."[1] On the other hand, Welsh writers of the period regularly apply the name "Britannia" to the unconquered portion of the former province which they inhabited.

Only in a few incidents did the separating barriers seem to break down. According to Welsh sources King Cadfan of Gwynedd gave asylum to the refugee boy-prince who was to become King Edwin of Northumbria. We noted in chapter 7 the evidence tending to the view that the baptism of Edwin was at the hands of Rhun, son of King Urien of Rheged, a British warrior turned priest, a view which, though in conflict with Bede's statement of the matter, has been seriously entertained by twentieth-century scholars. The almost forgotten first wife of King Oswy of Northumbria was a granddaughter of Rhun. At the consecration of Chad as bishop of the Northumbrians in 665 during a vacancy in the see of Canterbury, the bishops who officiated were Wini of Wessex and "two bishops of the British nation." Later, however, Archbishop Theodore, disallowing this irregularity, required Chad's reconsecration, and this was enacted.[2] Theodore's unqualified rejection of orders conferred by Celtic bishops is clearly documented in his Penitential: "Those who have been ordained by Irish or British bishops who are not Catholic with respect to Easter and the tonsure are not united to the Church, but they shall be confirmed again by a Catholic bishop with the imposition of hands. Churches they have consecrated must be reconsecrated, and persons from these nations must profess their wish to be with us in the unity of the Church [in order to qualify for admission to baptism or the Eucharist]."[3] It may perhaps be conjectured that the last of these regulations was applied chiefly to those British Christians who remained within the conquered areas and were seeking connection with the churches of the English. There may also have occurred occasional migrations of British laymen across the borders to Anglo-Saxon territory for whose admission to the sacraments such directives were to be invoked. Clearly for English churchmen responsible to Theodore, Celtic lay Christians, whether Welsh or Irish, whose priests had not received the ordination of Roman clerics, were to be held alien and un-Catholic and excluded from the sacraments until they should apply for admission to membership with the faithful under the accepted ministers. There is good evidence, however, that spokesmen for the rising English church felt no such antagonism toward the Irish, most of whom by Theodore's time had accepted the Roman Easter, as they showed toward the Welsh. The protracted adherence of the Welsh to the Celtic Easter and tonsure continued to disqualify them for the approval of Canterbury and of Rome. Bede has many disparaging blanket statements about the Britons. In describing their rejection of Augustine's requirements (chapter 3) he speaks of them as "that perfidious race."

Although Welsh churchmen were under peculiar displeasure in Rome and Canterbury, it has sometimes been supposed that the Welsh and Cornish church polity was all the while a step nearer than that of Ireland to the hierarchical system nurtured from Rome. The British Church, it has been believed, always held bishops in such authority that they were not subjected to abbots. In this view, even in the era of monastic expansion, the bishop stood at the head of the monastery at his see, and exercised something of territorial jurisdiction. Six Welsh bishoprics, corresponding to the larger principalities of Wales, constituted stable administrative units, and meetings of the bishops with abbots and other clerical officials gave general direction to the Church. But this construction of the early Welsh ecclesiastical pattern is largely abandoned by contemporary scholars. A study by Christopher Brooke has well presented the revised interpretation.[4] He notes that the eleventh-century *Life of St. Cadoc* by Lifris (see chapter 3), and the lives of St. David and St Finnian of nearly the same date, bear evidence of a rise of diocesan consciousness in the period of their compilation rather than earlier. The rivalry between Cadoc and David, and Finnian's award of the primacy to David, expresses a late rivalry between Cadoc's foundation of Llancarfan and the see of St. David's at a time when the latter had taken leadership in the Norman era. Actually diocesan boundaries corresponding to principalities are not attested before Norman times. Professor Brooke finds the approach to diocesan episcopacy directly related to Norman pressure on Welsh districts. As A. W. Wade-Evans had earlier shown, the monastic church of Llanelwy, founded not, as long believed, by Kentigern, but by his earlier relative St. Asaph, had no bishop before the Norman Gilbert in 1143. Bishop Elfodd is called "Archbishop" in the *Welsh Annals* (*Annales Cambriae*), and Asser so designates his cousin Nobis, bishop of St. David's. Professor Brooke's comment on such instances is: "It is possible that the position of chief bishop in a great kingdom was one firmly recognized in the ninth century; but it is equally possible that these titles represent the personal eminence of a leading bishop." There appears no real evidence that the title was more than honorific, or that it was claimed by any prelate in Wales before the twelfth century.

The term *clas* had some prominence in the church polity of Wales. It was applied to a monastic community with a scriptorium and a body of scholars. The bishop had his residence in the clas, and functioned within the area served by the monastery. Thus we are led to regard the early medieval Welsh Church as in large measure similar in its polity to that of Ireland and lacking anything like typical diocesan episcopacy. The sixth-century Welsh church, says Brooke, "was organized like the Irish, on a monastic basis."[5]

The adoption of the Roman Easter in Wales came about in circumstances that cannot be fully described. According to the *Annales Cambriae* the date of the change was 768 and the agent of it was Elfodd (Elbodogus, with variations), a bishop in Gwynedd. But Gwynedd is a region and not an episcopal seat, and his actual place of residence is not known. Though Elfodd's life story cannot be reconstructed, he was evidently a forceful and devout churchman, highly esteemed in his time. In the texts in which he finds mention, he is "a man of God" and "the most holy of bishops." The latter expression is used by Nennius, his loyal disciple, who drew from him some statements made in the *Historia Brittonum*, including the incident of Edwin's baptism by Rhun (see chapter 7). Evidently still young in 768, Elfodd lived to a ripe age, for we read again in the *Welsh Annals* under date 809: "Elbodug, archbishop of the region of Gwynedd, migrated to the Lord."[6] It is impossible to think of him as an archbishop in any administrative sense. The word is an encomium on a bishop of outstanding achievement. One who was able to lead the Welsh clergy to break the long-defended customs of their national church must have been as able as he was reputed to be holy. Wade-Evans supposed that Bede's *History* had been read in Wales, notably by Elfodd himself, and had a part in persuading the Welsh leaders to fall in line with Rome.[7] But Bede's language about the Britons is more condemnatory than inviting. In contrast with the Irish, they remain in his time (ca. 730) inveterately hostile, showing their heads without the coronal tonsure, and, though practicing a kind of Christian worship, they are without fellowship in Christ's Church.[8] Before Bede there was Aldhelm's reproachful letter to Gerontius (chapter 7), which Bede himself held to have been effective among those Britons who were under Saxon rule.[9] If Bede is right in this, it is also possible that Aldhelm's letter was effectively circulated in Wales. But is it not equally possible that the Irish example of the previous century obtained a slow response among the Welsh in the decision of Elfodd and his contemporaries? A friendly intercourse between Welsh and Irish leaders was maintained, and Welsh churchmen were more likely to accept suggestions from an Irish than from an English source.

Apparently some opposition to the reform remained when it was adopted in 768; but only at the time of Elfodd's death did this become an active movement. The chronicle known as the *Brat-y-Tywysog* states that at that time (809) there arose a great tumult over the Easter issue, and that the bishops of Llandaff and Menevia, "themselves archbishops of older privilege," repudiated Elfodd's policy.[10] This language gives the impression of a serious reaction, but its effects must have been impermanent. In subsequent history the Welsh Church observed the Roman Easter and Elfodd was held in honor. The change did not at the time affect the relation of the Welsh bishops to Canterbury, and did not imply any intention by Elfodd and his supporters to move in the direction of integration with the Church of England.

But the course of history was to lead inevitably to this result. Under the pressure of Saxon and Norman rulers Wales was to be increasingly brought into the orbit of England, while making in return a contribution to English culture. Despite frequent strife we begin to detect some evidence of a more tolerant attitude toward the Welsh on the part of their neighbors, and to note some incidents in which there was fruitful intercourse affecting politics and religion. We have noted above that King Alfred the Great received in 891 three Irish monks who had crossed the sea in a curragh and were "on pilgrimage for the love of God." At that time the Welsh scholar, Asser, formerly a monk of St. David's, was Alfred's counselor, actively cooperating in the educational reform which had already begun. Other leaders in this effort had come to Alfred from Mercia, into which kingdom the brothers Cedd and Chad had brought from Lindisfarne something of the Irish learning. The wide kingdom of Mercia, reaching from Northumbria to Wessex, flanked the entire eastern border of Wales. Conflicts had caused a shifting of this border, but did not prevent acquaintance on the English side with the poetry of Welsh Christian bards. An influence from this Welsh poetry, abundant in the region of Powis, which then embraced much of North Wales and a part of modern Shropshire, has been found in early English poetry of Mercian origin.[11] These Celtic elements entered into the background of Alfred's renaissance, and he was aware of their value. Confronted as he was by the dire peril of the Danish invasion, he could not have afforded to deal harshly with the Welsh or the Irish even if he had been so disposed; and he had no such inclination. Instead he was prepared to make use of their religious and cultural contribution.

Moreover, political strife within Wales led an important segment of Welsh leaders to look to Alfred for help. Certain South Welsh chieftains menaced by the aggression of Rhodri Mawr of Gwynedd and his sons, asked Alfred to assume their protection. Thereby an unprecedented bond was formed between elements of the hitherto hostile races.

The reputation of the scholarly cleric Asser of St. David's came to the king's notice, and Asser was invited to join him in his educational reforms. Asser had much at heart the interests of St. David's, where he seems to have held some administrative office. At the time of Alfred's approach to him St. David's was endangered by the hostility of Hemeid, a local ruler. In 886 Alfred and Asser met and had a long conversation. It was arranged that, with the consent of his colleagues at St. David's, Asser would serve there for half of each year and spend the other half with Alfred. This plan was entered upon and, the distance between his posts being short, Asser followed this divided schedule for some years. But the plan must have been modified in favor of Wessex when Asser undertook the episcopate of Sherborne and other ecclesiastical offices in the gift of Alfred. During the last twelve years of Alfred's life (887–99) their cooperation was close and fruitful. Asser aided the king's own studies, and wrote textbooks for general use. He outlived the king by about ten years. He left a *Life of Alfred*, far from complete, but the chief source of knowledge of his career and battles, laying stress upon his wisdom and acts of piety.[12] There is historic significance in this unprecedented association of a learned Welsh churchman with an English king. Not since the age of Aidan and Oswald had any Celt held a position of similar influence in the counsels of a powerful English ruler. The adoption of the Roman Easter and tonsure in Wales was now a century in the past, a fact which removed one of the chief occasions of the earlier hostility and made it easier for a Welshman to become an English bishop.

The authority of Canterbury was soon to be recognized throughout the Cornish peninsula. In 909 Archbishop Plegmund divided the diocese of Sherborne, creating the bishopric of Crediton for Devon and a small area of Cornwall, and making a separate bishopric for most of Cornwall and another for Somerset. "Bishop of the Church of Cornwall" is the designation of a number of persons whose names appear in records of manumissions at St. Petrock's during the tenth and eleventh centuries. The Cornwall see was apparently at St. German's on the south coast; its bishop, Conan, signed documents in the 930s as an attendant on King Athelstan. But in 1040 Cornwall was again placed under the see of Crediton. This place was, however, exposed to sea attack, and about 1050 bishop Leofric removed to Exeter. The Leofric Missal, which he presented to Exeter cathedral, is believed to have originated at Glastonbury in Somerset about 970, in circumstances conducive to the mingling of Welsh, Irish, and Roman features of worship, all of which are reflected in its contents. It testifies to the cult of St. David; but the dominant strain is Roman rather than Celtic, bearing evidence of the tenth-century Romanizing process that was to prevail. At the time of Leofric's death (1072, about a century after the compiling of the Missal), that process must have been far advanced.[13]

The approach of Wales to Saxon England was continued, with interruptions, during the tenth century, when both countries enjoyed more internal unity than before. A grandson of Rhodri Mawr, of more pacific disposition than his grandfather, obtained the mastery of most of Wales. He was Hywel Dda, Howel the Good, whose long and prosperous reign (915–50) is best remembered for the legal code which he promulgated and which remains a revealing source for Welsh social history of the time. The story is that in 926 he went to Rome with three Welsh bishops and the Llandaff scholar Bleggwyrd to inquire about the laws of Roman Britain. Howel undoubtedly held the papacy in high regard, and his visit to Rome is probably authentic, but the laws which he framed and which Bleggwyrd wrote down are not the product of any such research. They deal with contemporary conditions and reflect Welsh medieval legal concepts. When the preparation of the laws was completed, he is said to have revisited Rome with a company of clerics to obtain the pope's approval, which was duly given. He then submitted the code to the *cantrevs* and *commetes* (the hundreds and manors, voting districts) and to "the verdict of the people," by which process it was finally adopted. Actually, its promulgation may have been delayed until Howel's kingdom reached its full extent about 943, and experts find evidence of still later insertions. It is extant in three somewhat divergent texts, as circulated in Gwynedd, Dimetia (Dyfed), and Gwent.[14] In these laws we cannot fail to see that Wales presented the features of a stabilized society in which all classes are protected and the clergy have the secure and special public recognition that goes with an established church. We learn from them something of the duties and privileges of clerical officials about the court; but they are disappointingly uninforming about the life of priests and monks and their functions among the people. It is significant that Howel the Good did homage to the Saxon kings Edgar the Elder and Athelstan. A pervading influence from the English church system was preparing Wales for the inception of a regular territorial episcopate. Concern for the delimitation of boundaries of episcopal jurisdiction is evident in various contentions over the diocesan limits. This interest is illustrated in a charter ascribed to King Edgar in which he is said to have set the limits of the diocese of Llandaff. The twelfth-century *Book of Llandaff* records consecrations of bishops of Llandaff and St. David's by archbishops of Canterbury between 972 and 995.[15]

The Norman era brought increased control of the Welsh Church by the rulers of Church and state in England. In 1081 William the Conqueror visited Wales and dispensed gifts to some of the clergy. In this connection the much-admired Sulien of St. David's was replaced by a more pliable Welshman, Gryffydd, or Wilfred, who later subjected himself to Anselm of Canterbury. Sulien was a married bishop who had been trained under Irish teachers and was regarded as an eminent scholar. His son Rhygyvarch (d. 1098), unequaled except by his father in reputation for learning and piety, is viewed by the annalists as the last of a line of great teachers at St. David's. The process of replacing Welsh bishops by men in the king's favor went steadily on. During a vacancy between Lanfranc and Anselm, Thomas of York consecrated a Breton, Hervé, bishop of Bangor. Two years later he was violently ejected by the "barbarous" populace that he had tried to discipline.[16] It was under Norman influence that the bishopric of St. Asaph was created at the former Llanelwy in North Wales, although it became in twelfth-century legend a foundation of St. Kentigern.[17] In 1107, by appointment of Henry I, Urban became bishop of Llandaff and was consecrated by Anselm, promising obedience to Canterbury. In 1115 Henry, without consulting Welsh interests, appointed Bernard, the first Norman bishop of St. David's; Bernard promptly professed obedience to Archbishop Ralph of Canterbury. In 1127 a suit brought against Bernard by Urban of Llandaff was adjudicated at Westminster. But the suit was carried to Rome and two popes were involved in the protracted litigation that followed. Bernard was so encouraged by the outcome that, repudiating his obligation to Canterbury, he applied to Innocent II in 1135 for recognition as a metropolitan bishop; one chronicler mistakenly says that he obtained the pallium for that office.

The effort of St. David's to obtain metropolitan status, and therewith independence of Canterbury, is a feature of twelfth-century history. But in retrospect we see that it had little chance of success. Too many bishops in Welsh sees had already pledged submission to Canterbury and to the English kings. Moreover, despite its preeminence, St. David's had never been looked to as having authority over other Welsh sees. Bernard kept up his agitation without result until his death (1148); but his successor, David Fitzgerald, made at Canterbury an act of submission to Archbishop Theobald. In 1152 that wayward and romantic historian, Geoffrey of Monmouth, was consecrated bishop of St. Asaph by Theobald at Lambeth, promising subjection and obedience.

The David Fitzgerald just mentioned was an uncle of the brilliant and self-assertive Giraldus Cambrensis (Gerald de Barri, 1146–1220), whose writings fascinatingly depict many aspects of his age. Giraldus was one-quarter Welsh, born in Wales at the Norman castle of Manorbier near Pembroke. While we find him criticizing the Welsh clergy, he seems to have had a genuine desire to serve the interests of the Welsh Church. A child of privilege, he early became a scholar of distinction, and later gave ample proof of unusual ability and versatility as a writer. His election by the chapter of St. David's (1176) to the bishopric of that see was disallowed by Archbishop Hubert Walter and King Richard I because of his Welsh connections. Another candidate was appointed, but Giraldus pressed his claim at Rome, and in doing so became a vigorous advocate of the autonomy of St. David's and its recognition as a metropolitan see for Wales against the claims of Canterbury. Through the patience or indecision of the popes the case was prolonged to the days of King John and Pope Innocent III. Meanwhile Giraldus was engaged in many activities. He added to his reputation by giving lectures at the University of Paris. When King Richard decided to go on crusade, he induced Archbishop Baldwin to preach the crusade through Wales. On this mission (1188) Giraldus was Baldwin's companion, and in his *Itinerary of Wales* Giraldus, with his usual self-approval, rates highly his own part in the preaching. Baldwin was to die in a crusader camp; but Giraldus was given tasks in the service of Prince John that kept him busy for some years in Wales and Ireland. A new vacancy in the see of St. David's occurring 1198, Giraldus was once more elected by the chapter there; but he had numerous opponents, and John, who would be king a year later, knowing Giraldus' pro-Welsh leanings, was now afraid that he might in office prove a dangerous opponent of the royal policies in Wales. A new election was ordered by Innocent, and a new bishop took office in 1203. Thus, very significantly, Rome in the end voted for Canterbury and the English king. Giraldus, who had pursued for long years his desire to "wear a horned mitre," making numerous visits to Rome and Canterbury, accepted his defeat with resignation. He was treated with respect by the winning party and retired on an annuity "to enjoy his books and repent his sins" until his death (ca. 1220). His treatise *On the Right of the Church of Menevia*, written at the height of the struggle, his autobiographical *De rebus a se gestis* (an apologia composed engagingly in the third person), with other writings and documents concerned, supply rather ample source material on this critical chapter in Welsh church history.[18] His failure to obtain St. David's was not merely the defeat of an ambitious churchman. It was a final blow to the cause of Welsh church autonomy.

A fundamental change was coming over the monastic life in Wales. During Norman and Angevin times, a great many abbeys of foreign connection were founded in Wales, many of them under the control of ecclesiastics in England. Between 1121 and 1226 no less than thirteen Cistercian abbeys were planted in locations well distributed throughout the Welsh shires—Pembrokeshire, where St. David's stood, being excepted.[19] Other monastic orders, and both Franciscan and Dominican friars, had also entered. While all the changes in church and government seemed calculated to overwhelm Welsh nationality, this trend was in part countered by an upsurge of the national bardic literature of hero tales and romantic poetry. A national spirit sometimes found expression within the new monasticism itself. But at no time were internal political discords overcome so as to make united action toward independence possible.

In the later thirteenth century a courageous contender for Welsh autonomy, Llewelyn ap Gruffyd, made an impressive effort to rally the nation against the powerful Edward I of England (1272–1307). But his policy of close control over the bishops, even those of his own appointment, led in his later years to disastrous strife between him and the bishops of St. Asaph and Bangor, who both, as it happened, bore the name of Anian. Llewelyn's adventurous career was ended, possibly by treachery, in 1282; but probably a longer life would not have brought him success. He lacked political sagacity to match his patriotism and courage. Many of his opponents were Welshmen; for some years these included his younger brother David. Many churches were plundered by the English; but Edward later adopted a policy of generosity to the clergy while still treating ruthlessly the patriots in arms. Thus a favorable response to Edward was cultivated in clerical and other influential circles, helping him to bring the discordant nation under his control.[20]

With Llewelyn's death and Edward's triumph, there was nothing to prevent the full incorporation of the Welsh Church into that of England. Subjection to Canterbury would be only slightly modified by access to Rome. The changed situation is dramatized by the visitation of the Welsh dioceses by Archbishop John Peckham in

1284. This was something quite different from Baldwin's tour of Wales to preach the crusade a century earlier. Peckham, a Paris-educated Franciscan, treated Wales as a part of his ecclesiastical field of authority, a section of the province of Canterbury. He gave authoritative directions for changes and reforms as he had been doing in his visitations in England. He obtained the acceptance, though not the enforcement, of canon law principles condemning clerical marriage. Peckham had earlier concerned himself with Wales and had conferred with Llewelyn but found him intractable. He is thought to have prompted Edward's later policy of conciliating the Welsh clergy. But he did not become a subservient instrument of the King. In Wales he called to account Thomas Bek, who had been made bishop of St. David's at Edward's behest but tried to revive the now obsolete claim of metropolitan status for his see. Peckham's character was that of a sincere and active reformer.[21] His presence for six weeks touring the country, searching out conditions and conferring with clergy and laity, left with them the lasting impression that Canterbury was henceforth to be regarded as no distant and negligible shadow power but the reforming and controlling religious capital with which they must make terms. With Peckham's visitation, the Celtic Church of Wales leaves behind its independent existence and becomes, in organization and worship, a part of the Church of England.

Scotland

Meanwhile a rather different course was taken in the history of the Church in Scotland, and to this we may now turn. Here it is necessary to check with the reader a change in the application of the name "Scotia." In the times of Columba and of Bede, Scotia was the name used, interchangeably with Hibernia, for Ireland, the homeland of the Scots. The name applied to most of modern Scotland was Alban, and somewhat earlier, Caledonia. But Scots had already occupied a part of Alban, having formed the kingdom called Dalriada in the southeast, and these Scots in Britain were sometimes included in the application of the name Scotia. In 844, Kenneth Mac Alpin, the Scotic king of Dalriada, who had a Pictish mother, was able to gain control of Pictland, the eastern and northern part of what is now Scotland. He thus became the ruler of most of the mainland of Scotland and the adjacent islands, the Orkneys and Shetlands being then under Norse control.[22] The Angles of

Northumbria were still trying to extend their kingdom to include southern Scotland. Since Ireland was still Scotia in most Latin texts, the application of the name Scotia to Scotland came slowly and not without some ambiguity and misunderstanding.

Kilrymont, later St. Andrew's, allegedly founded by St. Kenneth, friend of Columba, was beginning to acquire importance through the belief that St. Regulus had brought the Apostle Andrew's relics from Greece and deposited them there in 747. Already, about 730, the Pictish king Angus won a victory over Nechtan IV after invoking St. Andrew, so that the coming of the relics was well timed. King Kenneth, however, adopted Dunkeld as his capital, and brought there the relics of St. Columba (ca. 850). The term *ecclesia Scoticana* first appears in a document of the late ninth century in which King Giric (Grig) (ca. 878–900) granted "liberty" to that church. Neither the liberty granted nor the area called *Scoticana* can be certainly defined. But the action of Giric seems to lie behind the compact made between King Constantine II and Bishop Cellach of St. Andrew's in 906, assuring equality between Pictish and Scottic elements in the church, and presumably implying some measure of unification. During the tenth century the idea of one Church of Scotland was becoming a reality. The nation itself was also becoming a stable entity. The Pictish victory in 685 at Nechtansmere (Dunnichen, Forfarshire) ended the northward pressure of the English: but it was not until the battle of Carham in 1018 that a Scottish king obtained secure sway as far south as the Tweed.[23]

Both parties to the conflict with the English were Christian, or so regarded themselves. It was otherwise with the Vikings, or Northmen, who when they sailed out of the fiords of Norway or left the shores of Denmark were totally untouched by Christian influences, save insofar as they had reacted adversely to the militant proselytism of the Christian Franks. In their "long ships," staunch vessels swiftly propelled by sails and many oarsmen, these strong warriors traversed the northern seas, ravaging coastal settlements and plundering the treasures of civilization. They were aware that monasteries and churches were the unarmed custodians of gold and silver altar furnishings and of books in cases overlaid with metalwork. These were tempting prizes, for the precious metals could be reforged to any requirement. Not less desirable were the rich vestments and tapestries which the adverturers might proudly present to their home folk on return from a foray. Some of them, believing in their own gods, had, no doubt, a special animus against Christianity. It is not surprising that Christian institutions and clergy were often the objects of their attacks. We have seen that in Ireland monasteries of old renown suffered repeated violence, with heavy loss of life, accompanied by massive destruction of irreplaceable treasures. In the Scottish coastlands and islands, uncounted hermitages and small communities were extinguished.

The massacre of the monks of Eigg in 617 (see chapter 6) marks one of the early incursions of the sea-rovers in the Hebrides. Late in the seventh century they were molesting Irish monastic groups in the Shetlands. But it was a century later still that their raids began to reach the chief Christian centers. Under date of 793 we read in the Anglo-Saxon Chronicle the ominous sentence: "On the sixth of the Ides of June the ravaging of the heathen men lamentably destroyed God's church at Lindisfarne."[24] Some of the Lindisfarne monks were stripped and tortured. In 801 the raiders came again, this time to destroy the buildings with fire. In 806, finding tenacious monks still on the site, the visitors slew as many as 80 of them. The abbey was rebuilt but in 867 was again burned by Danish pirates. In 870 the nuns of Coldingham in Berwickshire, formerly but no longer a "double monastery," mutilated their own faces in order to escape outrage by the invaders; but they were mercilessly put to death by fire. While the nearby coasts were becoming the haunts of freely roving Vikings, on Lindisfarne the remaining monks maintained a menaced existence until 875. In that year, expecting an immediate attack, they dug up and carried off St. Cuthbert's and some of St. Aidan's bones; then, with some lay fugitives, and driving their cattle before them, they crossed at low tide to the mainland and slipped away to safer ground. Cuthbert's bones went to Chester-le-Street and later to Durham; they were returned to Lindisfarne in 1082, when Durham was threatened, but soon brought back to Durham, where they were with some probability identified in 1827. The island was left to the seabirds for more than two centuries; only when Benedictines came to establish a priory in 1082 did it become again a habitation of men.[25]

Not less tragic was the fate of Iona. There the last remnant of the Roman-Celtic schism had ended only in 767. By 794 the long ships were wreaking havoc in the Hebrides, and in that year the buildings at Iona were looted. In 801 they were burned down, but the brethren struggled on. In 806, in a new onslaught, 68 of the monks were put to the sword, probably at Martyr's Bay just south of the present village. Enfeebled and cut off from its dependent churches in Scotland, the remnant transferred its headquarters to Kells in Ireland in 814 (see chapter 8) and carried with them Columba's relics in a gold and silver shrine. Monks who still remained at Iona undertook to rebuild the monastery, and the casket with the founder's relics was later returned and hidden. The final blow came on 19 January 825, when raiders demanded the precious shrine. The abbot being absent, the monks were rallied to passive resistance by Blaithmac, who knew but refused to disclose where it was concealed. First permitted to celebrate their customary Mass, they were all slain on the spot. The historic community of Iona was all but extinguished. We know little of its story in the subsequent era; but in 986 there were enough monks there to attract pirates and to suffer yet another massacre.

Iona lived on now chiefly in the minds and spirits of men. It was a place of hallowed memory, not only for its early achievement but now also for its holy martyrs. Kings and chieftains desired that their bones should rest in its sacred precincts. A long line of Scottish kings, including Kenneth Mac Alpin (860), Duncan (as Shakespeare knew) (1040), and Macbeth (1057) lie buried in the Ridge of Kings at Reilig Oran with the kings of Dalriada of earlier times. According to the statements in old chronicles no less than 60 royal personages had their last resting-place there. Even rulers who were of Viking race, when once they came under Christian influence, felt the spell of Iona. One of these, Anlaf (Olaf the Red), whose consort was a daughter of Constantine III of Scotland, ruled for twelve years over Northumbria; later, when thrust out of England and defeated in Ireland, he retired to Iona to live a religious life, died there, and was given royal burial (980). In 1549 a visitor to Iona, Donald Munro, found three mounds (*tumuli*) with inscriptions to identify them as containing respectively the remains of kings of Scotland, of Ireland, and of Norway. It is believed from the evidence of the chronicles that, of the 60, the crowned kings of Scotland numbered 48, while 4 were Irish and 8 were Norwegian. No distinguishing tombstones were erected for them. It was sufficient that their bodies should rest in that sacred ground. Iona, being relatively difficult of access even in times of peace, did not become, like Compostella or Rome or Canterbury, a place of pilgrimage. Men did not often go to visit it; rather, it visited them in memory and imagination.[26]

The entrance of Roman influence, apart from the adoption of the usages in dispute, progressed slowly, and this trend was apparently halted in a reaction toward monastic features of the churches of Columba. Essentially the church remained Celtic to the late eleventh century. As in Bede's time, the Bible was used in Latin by both Picts and Scots, but preaching was in the vernacular. Learning was still prized, and each monastery had its *fer leginn*, or supervisor of education. The most important literary treasure of the Scottish Celtic Church is the *Book of Deer*, which dates from the ninth century. It indicates that whatever the original role of St. Drostan (see chapter 6) in northeastern Scotland, he and St. Columba were alike revered there three centuries later. The book contains in Latin, chiefly in the Vulgate version, portions of the three synoptic Gospels and the whole of the Gospel of John, together with later extraneous marginal notes in Gaelic recording transactions in Church property. Its decorative features, such as colored figures, interlaced designs, and minute tracery, are similar, if somewhat inferior in quality, to those of the great Irish manuscripts to which attention was called in chapter 8.[27]

Between the ninth and the twelfth centuries there are frequent references to the Culdees (in Scottish documents, "Keledei") as the typical monastic clergy of the kingdom. Until the present century the difficult problem of the Culdees was rendered more confused by the ecclesiastically motivated solutions that were proposed. But even with the most unprejudiced approach, the topic remains somewhat enigmatic. The Irish Culdees (Céli Dé, bondservants of God) sprang from the stern disciplinary reform of Máel-rúain (d. 792) at Tallaght, which constituted a revival and codification of the earlier rigorous anchorite life (above, pp. 81–82). At an early stage the Scottish Culdees seem to have lived as anchorites, subject to the direction of an abbot and sometimes undertaking the cure of souls. Like most Celtic anchorites, they were in no way unapproachable or irresponsible. They appear, in the role of clerics with appointed duties, at Lochleven, Monymusk, Abernethy, Dunkeld, St. Andrews, Brechin, and elsewhere. When King Brude—probably Brude Mac Ferdach, the Pictish predecessor of Kenneth Mac Alpin—presented the island of Lochleven to St. Serf and the Keledei hermits (as stated in the Registry of St.

Andrew's priory), it was evidently recognized that the Culdees there thought of themselves as spiritual descendants of that sixth-century saint (see above, p. 46). The Scottish Keledei may have had some justification in believing that they drew their origin from that early time, but it seems likely that their order was expanded and invigorated from the Irish Culdee movement instituted by Máel-rúain. It is believed that some of these fled from Ireland at the time of the Danish ascendancy there to find a welcome in Scotland. Actually we have the name of "Maenach the Culdee" alleged in the chronicles to have come over in 920 "to establish the ordinances of Erinn" which, says W. F. Skene, "may have been the rule of St. Maelruain." Contemporary with Maenach was St. Cadroe, who having studied long at Armagh is said to have joined his uncle, Bean, at Strathearn.[28]

Such a word as "Culdee," servant of God, is manifestly capable of wide application, and it was apparently used somewhat indiscriminately. Some of the Scottish Culdees were among those who were appointed to be diocesan bishops in the twelfth century. Some of them too, in sharp contrast with Máel-rúain's principles, were married men. A family succession (*successio carnalis*) in church offices was sometimes practiced and appears to have gone largely unblamed. The coarb system of abbatial succession within the founder's family lent itself to a direct father-son transmission of office. It should be remembered that clerical marriage was common at that time in all the West: the reforms of Hildebrand were still in the future. The designation "Culdee" seems to have become virtually equivalent to "cleric" in medieval Scotland.[29]

The inevitable infiltration of non-Celtic influences into Scottish Christianity was promoted by the beneficent presence of the gifted queen and saint, Margaret, who in 1059 became the consort of King Malcolm Canmore (1058–93). The descendant of a line of English princes but born of a Bavarian mother, Margaret spent her early years in Hungary while her parents were exiled from England; but she was later tutored, at Lanfranc's advice, by the Benedictine Turgot, who came with her to Scotland. Margaret outclassed her poorly educated husband in ability, and with his admiring consent took much responsibility in public affairs. By her genuine goodness and piety she won the love of the people and was in a position to press for reforms that would change the ecclesiastical life of Scotland. In this she had the help of Turgot and of monks sent at her request by Archbishop Lanfranc. Her method involved no direct English interference but was that of persuasion. Conferences of Celtic clergy were held in which her proposals were presented. Although he could not write, Malcolm could speak English as well as Gaelic, having spent some time in exile at the court of Edward the Confessor, and he served as interpreter between Margaret and the Scots. Margaret had clear views of ecclesiastical usages, even where these involved theological issues, and her arguments prevailed. The irregularities corrected in the reforms she introduced were in large degree symptoms of a prevailing negligence rather than matters of prized Celtic tradition. But the requirement that what was called a "barbarous ritual" of the Mass should be abandoned apparently meant the suppression in certain localities of a liturgy that came ultimately from the old Gallican rite (see above, p. 131). The days from Ash Wednesday to the following Monday were added to the older and shorter Lent which till then had been practiced in Scotland. Margaret took a strong stand against the (strangely persistent) Scottish abstention from the Eucharist through fear of Paul's warning to him who, partaking unworthily, "eats and drinks judgment to himself" (I Cor. 11:29). Her reforms were broadly wholesome for the life of the church, while at the same time conducive to its coordination with English and continental practice.[30]

In 1093, four days after her husband's death in battle, St. Margaret herself died, at the age of forty-eight, leaving six children who had been nurtured in her piety. A brief bid for power by Duncan II, Malcolm's son by his earlier marriage with Ingeborg of Denmark, disturbed the course of affairs, but order was restored under Margaret's sons Edgar and Alexander in turn. It was Margaret's third son, David I, who during his long reign (1124–53) best perpetuated her policy toward the church.

While lacking his mother's religious sensitivity, David constantly promoted the foundation of monasteries and the establishment of bishoprics. Before his time the bishoprics of St. Andrew's, Glasgow, Moray, and Dunkeld had reached a more or less advanced stage of organization. During his reign Ross, Caithness, Aberdeen, Brechin, Dunblane, and Galloway were added. He bestowed church endowments with great liberality. For this reason one of his successors is said to have remarked that "David was a sair saint for the crown." For the first time Scotland had a nation-wide diocesan episcopate. David, and his brothers before him, however, strongly resisted the claims of York to ecclesiastical jurisdiction in Scotland. When in 1107 Turgot was made bishop of St. Andrew's, he was consecrated by the Archbishop of York, but with the explicit proviso demanded by King Alexander that no subjection to York was implied by this. Both Alexander and David repeatedly opposed papal decisions that would have subordinated the Scottish to the English church. Glasgow as well as St Andrew's was involved in resistance to the claims of York. The alert and determined leadership of the kings in this matter was supported by clergy and people. David ruled in alienation from Rome during the thirties while he was at war with England, but made peace with a papal legate in 1139. This was followed by a more friendly agreement with a legate of Pope Eugenius III in 1151; and thereafter until his death in 1153 David maintained good relations with the pope.[31] Thus the Scottish Church, unlike the Welsh, was to remain independent of the English metropolitans while becoming an integral part of the Roman system.

With David I the Celtic era of Scottish church history comes to an end. St. Andrew's was not to be designated an Archbishopric until 1492; but by the twelfth century it exercised an undefined primacy among the bishoprics. The numerous clergy at St. Andrew's had been Keledei with a semi-monastic discipline, and there the Culdee organization remained longest. Elsewhere the order was largely replaced—not without some exercise of compulsion—by Augustinian canons. The very name "Keledei" went out of use in most places; but in St. Andrew's a dwindling company of Keledei fought a long battle for survival. A corporation of ten prebendaries with a provost survived to the Reformation.[32] A pathetic and inglorious company, they had long lost any pretense of representing the once effective ministry of the ancient Church of Scotland.

Ireland

In the centuries of Roman expansion Ireland escaped armed invasion. When the Roman power receded, significant migrations in force were made by Irishmen into areas of Wales and Caledonia. But Christian Ireland at the high period of its monastic expansion was repeatedly and destructively invaded by pagan Northmen and Danes. The pattern of attack was similar to that on the British coasts already noted. In 795 the devastating raids began on islands off both the east and the west coasts of Ireland. Becoming bolder, the destroyers went up the rivers in strength to plunder and lay waste much that was cherished in Irish civilization. A third stage was that of actual conquest and colonization. At the direction, it is supposed, of their designing leader, Turgesius (Turgeis), a shadowy figure in the background, the foreigners began to build forts for permanent occupation as convenient bases of operation, and to maintain fleets in coastal waters. The spoils were rich, the prospects encouraging, and large numbers of both Norwegians and Danes were involved. Contention between these two races, called respectively in Ireland the White and the Black Strangers, arose over the possession of Dublin, which had its beginning as a Norwegian settlement and stronghold. The Norwegians were the winners of this contest (851) and made Dublin the center of their activities for half a century. In 902 it came into Irish hands, only to be lost and retrieved several times thereafter.

Politically the most disastrous feature for Ireland was the failure of her own clans to unite their not inconsiderable forces against the ravagers of their country. In many instances ambitious Irish chiefs took opportunity from the disturbance of their neighbors to enlarge their own borders and power. If Danes fought Norwegians, Irishmen fought Irishmen as willingly as they resisted the intruders. Yet some defeats were inflicted on the latter, who also lacked coordination. Against them Maelsechlain II of the Hy-Neill won a notable victory in 980, releasing Ireland, as the-sixteenth century annalists, the Four Masters, said, from its Babylonish captivity which was "next to the captivity of hell." But the victor was himself defeated and reduced to vassalage by Brian Borumba of Munster, whose Irish army won from the foreigners the battle of Clontarf in 1014.[33] There was at that time no thought of driving away from Ireland the invading peoples and their descendants. Many of them had married into Irish families, and all were to be gradually integrated into the Irish Christian community. But when Brian was slain at the moment of victory, Ireland was still far from national unity. It continued to be plagued by strife led by the chieftains of proud clans for whom national patriotism was hardly a virtue.

In 1155 Henry II of England, wishing to expand his sway to Ireland, sent an embassy to the English pope, Hadrian IV, to obtain sanction for this. The scholar John of Salisbury was one of those sent, and in his *Metalogicus* (1159) John tells us that it was he who induced the pope to grant the petition. Adrian's Bull *Laudabiliter*, as recorded by Giraldus Cambrensis in his *Conquest of Ireland*, authorizes Henry's invasion of the island, commending his pious and laudable desire to enlarge the bounds of the Church and amend the deplorable state of the Irish people. At the time Henry took no action, whether because of the pope's reminder that by the Donation of Constantine all outlying islands had been bestowed on the see of Peter or because his mother, Matilda, dissuaded him from the enterprise. It was fourteen years later that an irresponsible chieftain gave the Normans an opportunity in Ireland.

Dermot MacMurrough, descendant of kings of Leinster, when worsted by the king of Connaught, fled to Bristol and then crossed to France, where he conferred with Henry and helped Henry's Anglo-Norman vassals to plan the invasion of Ireland. Richard of Pembroke, known as Strongbow, was the chief commander of the invasion. Wexford was captured in 1169, and soon afterward Strongbow took Waterford and joined MacMurrough in the capture of Dublin. Most of their defeated opponents were of Danish stock, since Danes now constituted the main population of these sea-port towns. Henry himself took no direct part at first in the adventure, being distrustful of its headstrong leader; but he was persuaded to countenance it and in 1171–72 spent half a year in Ireland, chiefly in Dublin. Henry received the submission of many Irish princes, and tried to lay the foundations of orderly government on the feudal model.[34] But the outcome of the invasion was far from decisive. The Norman barons, like the Viking jarls, were unable to agree among themselves, or to subjugate the Irish throughout the island. Indeed, from the earliest Viking raids through the time of the Anglo-Norman invasion, Ireland endured a long era of indeterminate strife and futile suffering, in which churches and clerics were often the victims of violence.

It was naturally the monasteries and churches with their treasures of artistically wrought vestments and metalwork that chiefly invited the attention of the Viking rovers. Early in the ninth century they laid waste such venerable monastic communities as Comgall's Bangor, Finnian's Moville, Brendan's Clonfert, Brigid's Kildare, and Ciaran's Clonmacnois. Armagh's substantial buildings were repeatedly looted and in 840 were burned to their foundations. Later generations saw many acts of violence in which the monks were sufferers, and some in which they participated as fighting men. Irish religious zeal, intense as it was, failed to create a peaceable temper in political life. Irish chiefs themselves on occasion raided and looted monasteries. Felim MacCriffan of Munster, who was both a king and a churchman in office, rivaled the Northmen in his atrocities.[35] During four centuries there were at best only intervals of peaceful existence for monasteries and churches. The tenth century saw the rise of the round towers that still mark the Irish landscape. Most of them stand like sentinels close beside monastic churches, whose treasures they housed in times of danger. Built skillfully of shaped stones, they rise to a lofty height. They were used as belfries, and as watchtowers to give warning of the approach of assailants. They were impressive but not very effective bastions against anarchy. Refugees in them were sometimes burned to death. What was to become of the Irish tradition of learning and devotion in such an environment?[36]

The long era of conflict was costly beyond estimate in the lives of good and learned men, in church treasures and books, and by the flight of thousands of displaced monks to foreign lands. In chapter 8 we referred to the few choice illuminated manuscripts that remain to our time. In manuscript art, it appears, the peak was reached about the time of the beginning of the Viking raids. The scribe of the Stowe Missal lived till 846, but his work was done under an abbot, Torbach, who ruled only to 808. After that period Irish illumination was produced in continental scriptoria by Irishmen or their non-Irish pupils. In a few instances ornamented manuscripts of Irish origin reached the Continent in some monk's travel bag. One of the finest of these was the Turin Gospel book, long kept at Bobbio but no longer extant. There is, of course, the unsolved problem of the book of "angelic" beauty that made Giraldus gasp on his visit to Kildare in 1185. His ecstatic description of it has led some to suppose that it was the *Book of Kells*; but this work was kept at Kells in Meath and can hardly have been temporarily at Kildare. Giraldus alludes to the intricate, delicate and subtle patterns of the Kildare book, and its fresh and vivid colors. His close and prolonged examination of it left him "lost in ever fresh amazement." At Kildare they told him it was written in the age of St. Brigid.[37] If this was the case, it is remarkable that no early writer on St. Brigid mentions it. If it was a genuine work of earlier centuries it must have been more than once concealed from plunderers. Giraldus alone refers to it; it evidently became a war casualty of the Anglo-Norman era, perhaps of the brutal "War of Kildare" of 1234.

Amid the tumults of Ireland's dark age one branch of Christian art flourished surprisingly. The tenth century was the time of the erection of some of the finest of the sculptured stone crosses. They testify to well-trained skill of hand, and they show an impressive variety of design, and an alert receptiveness to foreign influences. The themes in many instances reflect patristic learning and the legends of early Christian saints. Happily the great crosses were too heavy to be moveable as booty. Many of them, ignored by the invaders, stand today unharmed where they originally stood, a reminder of the undiscouraged faith and devotion of anonymous artists and scholars in an adverse world.

With respect to Christian learning and religious writing, the troubled centuries were not entirely unproductive. Monasticism, though harrassed and enfeebled, maintained some semblance of its earlier character. Gradually its houses were superseded by those connected with orders of foreign origin. The first Cistercian monastery was instituted at Mellifont, near Drogheda, County Louth, in 1142, under the influence of St. Malachy, to whom we shall presently return. Later many Cistercian abbeys were established under Anglo-Norman patronage, and a number were endowed by Irish kings. According to Giraldus, Cistercians obtained the lands of Irish churches and sometimes obliterated all trace of the former buildings. He tells of a priest who, returning to the site of his church after a short absence, was so startled to find there only empty ground that he thought the world had ended.[38] Nevertheless, at this period the Cistercians, of all foreign orders, best answered to the spirit of the "reform movement" that had already taken rise in Ireland.

This movement appeared first in areas controlled by the now Christianized Danes. It acknowledged papal authority, craved a new structural organization, and looked abroad for leadership. In the eleventh century monastic authority was giving place to episcopal authority, which accorded better with Cistercian and other continental orders than with the Irish monastic system. Sitric, Danish king of Dublin (d. 1042), having visited Rome to receive baptism, donated the ground for a church which was to become Dublin's Cathedral of the Holy Trinity. The first bishop, Donatus (Dunan), an Irishman, died in 1074, and his successor, Patrick by name, was, on action of the clergy and people of Dublin, sent to Canterbury for consecration. But this was not a fully accepted pattern of procedure. Bishop Samuel O'Hanley (1095–1121), who had been a monk in England, conceived a plan to make Dublin an archiepiscopal see independent of both Canterbury and Armagh. Dublin, with its population of Danish extraction, was ecclesiastically a troublesome newcomer, all the more because its aspirations for independence from Armagh were encouraged by the Canterbury primates Lanfranc and Anselm. Canterbury recognized Armagh, associated as it was with the prevailing name of St. Patrick, as its natural rival for the primacy of Ireland. The abbot-bishops of Armagh, as coarbs of St. Patrick, exerted a wide if not well-defined authority, each making a circuit of visitation and receiving tribute even in far-off areas of the island.

Amid these counter-claims and uncertainties, an important contribution to the structural reform of the Church was made by Gilbert, bishop of Limerick, who became papal legate in Ireland some time before 1110. Gilbert was a correspondent of Anselm, but no partisan of Canterbury in Irish matters. He was the author of the influential treatise *De statu ecclesiae*, proposing an Irish church polity similar to the English system but independent of it, within the Roman obedience. His plan provided for a number of archbishops, each with not more than twenty bishops in his archdiocese, all subject to one primate of all Ireland and all, like the primate himself, commissioned by the pope. He refers many times to this structure as a series of "pyramids." The plan gave no ecclesiastical role to the abbots, who had already lost to the bishops much of their autonmy and influence. Local churches and monasteries would come under the jurisdiction of the bishops.[39]

This treatise was in part reflected in the action taken in the Synod of Rathbreasil, near Cashel, in 1110, which was presided over by Gilbert as papal legate. Provision was made in the synod for twenty-four bishoprics, twelve in North and twelve in South Ireland, with Armagh in the north as the primatial see. We have earlier observed separate action on the Easter date in the northern and southern parts of Ireland. The north-south division in the Rathbreasil decision actually revives a very ancient but unforgotten tradition of Ireland's separation into "Conn's Half" and "Mogh's Half."[40]

But Armagh's final victory was not yet won. The plan of Rathbreasil was unacceptable to the advocates of Dublin's ascendancy. It was the synod of Kells in 1152 that determined the final structure of the Irish medieval Church within the Roman obedience. Leading up to this settlement were synods of 1134 and 1148, and extended negotiations with several popes. Cardinal John Paparo, legate of Pope Eugenius III, presided in the synod of Kells. He presented the pallium of the archiepiscopal office to each of four bishops, respectively those of Armagh, Dublin, Cashel, and Tuam. The primacy of Armagh, which since 1074 had been under a series of five prelates who had pledged obedience to Canterbury, was fully confirmed and was accepted by Dublin as by the other two. The new metropolitan sees were advantageously located. Cashel, in County Tipperary, boasted St. Patrick as its founder and had no quarrel with far-off Armagh. For long centuries it had been the seat, with its rock-fortress, of the kings of Munster but in 1101 had been deeded to the bishop by King Murtagh O'Brian. Tuam, in County Galway, Connaught, emerged from relative obscurity when it became a bishopric in 1110. In the period preceding the Kells synod the ambitious King Turlough O'Connor of Connaught had put forward its metropolitan claim.[41]

Thus, amid much rivalry and controversy, and with the guidance of able papal legates, the Irish Church obtained a typical medieval provincial structure and orientation. The constant interplay of politics and special church interests in the twelfth century tends to obscure evidences of religion itself. But two persons of undoubted saintliness challenge attention as actors in the changing scene. The earlier and more impressive of these is St. Malachy, born, it is thought, about 1094 at Armagh, the son of a married cleric whom the Four Masters describe as "*lector primarius*," a first-rank scholar, "in all western Europe." An anchorite fostered young Malachy's piety, leading him to love ascetic retirement and study. But he was drawn into ecclesiastical affairs and served as bishop of Down and later of Connor. He was next induced by the papal legate Gilbert to accept the archbishopric of Armagh. This was a significant break in the line of hereditary coarbs long dominant there. During his short term of office (1134–37) he showed himself an active reformer of liturgy and discipline. But with a not uncommon Celtic dislike for administrative routine, he left the office and retired to a monastery. He later performed other services to the Church and visited Rome (1139–40) to seek archiepiscopal status for Armagh and possibly Cashel. His visit to Clairvaux on the way resulted in a deep personal friendship with St. Bernard and in the establishment of the first Irish Cistercian house at Mellifont, as we have noted. Later another visit to Rome was required, and this time Malachy fell ill at Clairvaux and died in Bernard's arms (1148). The great Cistercian, in his informing *Life and Acts of St. Malachy*, invites our admiration for this able, zealous, and humble bishop. Malachy's qualities remind us of the early Irish saints, but he saw the path of reform as that of harmony with the papacy and the adoption of vital elements of continental piety.[42]

The second of these saints of the Romanizing era is St. Laurence O'Toole (1130–80). He was the son of a Leinster chief and was born at Kildare. In childhood he suffered harsh treatment as a hostage of Dermot MacMurrough, but was later allowed to pursue his training at Glendalough where he became abbot. The Primate Gelasius of Armagh selected him to be archbishop of Dublin in 1162. He had the delicate task of representing Irish interests in audiences with Henry II in 1173, and he attended the Fourth Lateran Council held under Alexander III in 1179. He was appointed papal legate for Ireland but had to interview Henry in Normandy before being permitted to return home. Obtaining this permission, he set out for Dublin, but died suddenly at Eu near Rouen. There is much that is pathetic in the career of this honest and patriotic prelate.[43]

In these two blameless and gifted men we recognize qualities that remind us of Ireland's famous sons of earlier times. But their lives and acts may be said to mark the end of the Celtic era of Irish Christianity. Nation and church were henceforth to be increasingly subjected to English and continental influences. Certain enrichments would ensue from these pressures, but along with them would come the virtual extinction of those Celtic peculiarities that had once been precious. A detailed account of the long continuing process would lead beyond the province of this book, and the facts are available in scholarly volumes of recent years.[44] Only a few observations reaching into the later medieval centuries may be permitted here.

The churches and monasteries of Ireland were constantly involved in the harsh political realities of the age. Their constant interaction with the local rulers tended to bring church and society to a common level in which Christianity had a real but limited influence.[45] Popular literature contained visionary elements colored by biblical apocalypticism, and such religiously motivated imaginary tales as the Voyage of Brendan (see chapter 5); but this type of fiction might shade off into the mockery of the Vision of MacCongline, whose quest ends happily in "a fort made of delicious edibles with a well of wine."[46] In poetry sincere religious aspiration is sometimes associated with admission of the perilous appeal of worldliness and sensuality. Lay religion tended to find expression in relic cults and pilgrimages to shrines. The cave known as St. Patrick's Purgatory in Lough Derg, Donegal, became famous abroad and drew curious pilgrims and sincere penitents from continental lands—a practice maintained even after the papal suppression of the shrine in 1497.[47] Serious efforts at reform were never very successful, and religious life was of a mediocre sort.

In the early thirteenth century the Cistercians, who had earlier contributed much to Irish religious and cultural life, fell into gross abuses and disorders. The visitation in 1228 by Stephen of Lexington, later an abbot of Clairvaux, arrested, at least temporarily, this deterioration. Stephen insisted on the ability of postulants to read Latin and French and encouraged monks to seek higher learning at Oxford or Paris. He set up a system of visitation, issued a schedule of strict disciplinary instructions, and enlisted secular authorities in the suppression of disobedience and schism.[48] But in Ireland as elsewhere the pristine vigor of the Cistercian movement was already largely spent. It was now the turn of the mendicant and teaching friars to expand in Ireland. Dominicans, Franciscans, and, in fewer numbers, Carmelites and Augustinians, formed scores of houses from which their work expanded through most of the island. It was primarily on English initiative that the friars came. This, according to Watt, is true even of the Franciscans, who were formerly supposed to have come from Spain in the days of St. Francis. But there remains some uncertainty about the actual achievement of the friar missions. Surprisingly, they left no evidence of establishing schools of learning in Ireland during this era.[49] Whatever they achieved in education then, it was not till the eve of the Reformation that notable writing scholars begin to appear among the friars. All the four orders of friars seem to have become increasingly active in the fifteenth century, spreading their influence to neglected western sections of the island.[50]

The theme that predominates in the history of the medieval Irish church is that of Anglicization, and therewith Romanization, since all was done with papal support. There were incidents of strong Irish resistance, with expressions of hatred, indignation, and desperation; but the process was little interrupted by such protests. When Edward Bruce fought for the kingship of Ireland against Edward II in the years 1313–18, he had the open support of many churchmen and friars of Irish race. The struggle occasioned an impassioned Remonstrance from these people to Pope John XXII in 1318, denouncing English—rulers, people, and clergy—in Ireland as heartless oppressors. The papal response was in favor of the English. It was papal policy to support consistently the authority of the English kings in Ireland, on the basis not of the bull *Laudabiliter* but of King John's submission to Innocent III in 1213, in which Ireland as well as England by act of an English king became a papal fief.[51]

During the eleventh and twelfth centuries, while this transformation was taking place, the migration of Irish monks to the Continent ceased to have its former significance. From the ninth century we see evidence of an increasing flow of uncommitted pilgrims to Rome and other holy places of Italy and to the Bible lands. These travelers were not the peregrini of former times, who left Ireland for life in resolute commitment to the service of Christ among foreign peoples. They traveled abroad with the intention of returning to their old way of life at home, and their coming and going had no traceable effect on the course of history. Exceptions occured when a transitory pilgrim, captured by an opportunity that presented itself, halted on his way, to live out his life in distinguished service abroad. This is illustrated in the ninth-century instances of Fridian, Donatus, and Moengall that we noted earlier (pp. 173, 185, and 188); but in later times, with the stabilization of clerical organization, such opportunities were not to be expected.

Mention was made earlier of an eighth-century Irish and British mission to the Slavic kingdom of Moravia. About three centuries later Irish monks undertook a somewhat different mission to Kiev, then Russia's most active center of the trade. This enterprise was undertaken by the monastery of St. James, Ratisbon, at the very time of its inception (see p. 190). Father John Hennig has briefly called attention to this little-known venture, which Professor Mikhael Shaitan earlier investigated in some detail. Shaitan regards Mauritius, leader of the first Irish monastic visit to Kiev (ca. 1089), as an emissary of the emperor Henry IV (1084–1106), who intended to establish mercantile intercourse between the empire and the Russians. Shaitan calls special attention to the role apparently played by the devout and capable Polish princess known as St. Gertrude, sister of Casimir II of Poland and wife of the Russian prince Izaslav of Kiev. She is represented as a patroness of the Irish and seems to have been on friendly terms with the emperor. When the monastery church at Ratisbon was completed in 1090 with the aid of funds obtained from Russian furs brought back by Mauritius, it was dedicated both to St. James and to St. Gertrude. Shaitan shows evidence for the continuing presence of an Irish monastic community in Kiev from the late eleventh century to 1242.[52]

The general adoption of the Benedictine Rule, with its variant customs as developed by Cluniacs and Cistercians, foreclosed the possibility of reproducing the traditional Celtic type of monasticism on the Continent as in the days of Columban. Reference was made above to the origin of the Schottenklöster. In 1215 there were nine of these monasteries, eight of them stemming from St. James, Ratisbon, and they were still being recruited largely from Ireland. After the Fourth Lateran Council of that year, Pope Innocent III issued a special bull exempting them from the council's legislation for other monasteries and creating the Congregation of the Schottenklöster. They had already been placed under the Benedictine Rule, but irregularities had crept in and they were deteriorating. Innocent's plan was to provide for the correction of disorders while recognizing a traditional fraternal relation among them. Certain of the abbots of St. James had already made some efforts to improve the discipline in other houses, but with no permanent results. In Innocent's plan the abbot of St. James and his successors were given full disciplinary authority as "Visitor and Corrector of all Monks and Brothers of the Irish Nation" in Germany. A series of St. James abbots did what they could to reform the houses, but conditions were unfavorable. On their visitations they often met with resentment and disobedience. The Irish houses shared the general downward trend of monasticism in the later middle ages, the increasingly difficult problem of recruitment, and the losses from the Black Death (1348–49). Their numbers shrank to a mere handful in most houses. Of the remaining monks, very few were Irish by 1500, and some of them were, fairly or unfairly, accused of disorderly behavior. The locally recruited Germans were more numerous; and there had been a limited influx from Scotland.

It is sometimes implied that the Schottenklöster ended their corporate existence in the fog of a historical blunder. When they had their beginnings Scotia was Ireland, whence came their founding fathers. But in the sixteenth century Scotia was Scotland and the Scots were Scotsmen in the modern sense. In 1515 the enterprising Benedictines of Dunfermline were able to obtain from Pope Leo X, as representing the Church of Scotland, possession of what was left of the properties of the Schottenklöster. But this is an oversimplification. The Irish element in the various houses had then almost died out; a few recruits were coming from Scotland, and several of the abbots were from that province. However, the declining communities were in some cases incapable of managing their affairs, and local town authorities became the administrators of the properties.

Leo X's action was not intended to suppress the houses; rather it was taken in the hope of their restoration. But they showed little capacity to recover from their low state. Some real effort in this direction was made under Ninian Winyet (Winzet, Wingate), abbot of St. James, Ratisbon, 1577–92. Winyet comes to attention as a schoolmaster of Linlithgow at the time of the Reformation in Scotland. He became a doughty opponent of John Knox, and was forced into exile in 1562. After fifteen years in France, chiefly at Paris and Douai, he succeeded another Scottish abbot at St. James. Conditions were most unpromising as a result of controversy between the two Ratisbon houses, and of a dearth of recruits. He succeeded in restoring a small monastic group and in making St. James once more a place of good learning. He also attempted to promote reforms in other monasteries of the Congregation. But his diligent efforts had only limited and fleeting success.[53] With new misfortunes and losses the time came when all that was left of the Schottenklöster was a small remnant of the St. James community of Ratisbon. In 1862 this last fragment of medieval Irish monasticism was suppressed by Pope Pius IX. This was the delayed euthanasia of a body long moribund. Only a few of the buildings that had served the monks, "Schottenkirchen" in the guide-books, remain, as in Ratisbon and Vienna, to remind the modern visitor of their prosperous days.

Retrospect

THROUGHOUT these twelve chapters narration and evaluation have been mingled, and in parting from the patient reader the author will spare him any recital of the detailed judgments that have been expressed. But in retrospect certain quite simple generalizations seem to call for mention. One is that the history of Celtic Christianity is a story of persons far more than of institutions. It revolves around the achievements of leaders known as "saints." Their personalities come before us in robes of miracle, the tribute of imaginative writers of later times to their single-minded and fruitful devotion. It was once possible to suppose that St. Brigid hung her rain-drenched cloak on a sunbeam to dry; that St. Dubnata kept a cage full of pet bees that were on occasion set loose to rout cattle reavers; and that St. Mocholmoc, as supervisor of St. David's apiary, so charmed the bees that they all accompanied his boat to Ireland, introducing there an industry whose modern product many of us have relished. Who would want to deny that birds fluttered and sang about St. Kevin as he prayed, or that St. Brynach's trained wolf faithfully herded his great white cow? But we with our insistent search for historic fact cannot express in this way our admiration and wonder at the deeds and motives of the saints. The emergence of the new attitude appears as early as Giraldus Cambrensis who once confessed: "I know that I have written some things which will appear to the reader absurd or impossible, nor am I desirous that a hasty credit should be given to all that I have asserted, nor do I believe it myself."

But the ascertained facts themselves give us cause enough for wonder. The austere and unrelaxed devotion of the Celtic saints is so alien to the modern spirit as to be now almost incomprehensible. We are not familiar with men who choose to subsist on one meal a day, who sleep on hard floors with their heads on pillows of stone, who spend many hours of the day and night singing psalms and hymns, and yet with unfailing energy exercise creative leadership, changing the society in which they move and schooling barbarous peoples. Few of these strange characters can be thought of as men of genius; rather they were remarkable for moral stature and rectitude, and for sound learning. With very few exceptions they cannot be classed as theologians if by that term is meant persons primarily concerned with theological problems and definitions. While their studies were centered in the Bible they were at the same time lovers of poetry and the *litterae humaniores*; conscious followers of the first Christian apostles, they were also admirers and imitators of the pagan poets. In art as in literature these starveling monks exhibit an instinctive response to the things that are excellent. In their carved ornamentation of stone crosses, inimitable metalwork, and manuscript illumination, they brought to supreme expression these forms of art. Wherever they went, in their homelands or in far-off provinces of Europe, they planted active colonies of religion and culture, with lasting ameliorative effects that cannot be measured. It is wholesome for us to reflect on the debt of the modern world to these dedicated islanders.

Not less strange to us is the fact that nothing of all this was planned with consultation and forethought by master minds at any head office. Caesar discerned in the ancient Celts a certain political ineptitude, a lack of coordination that made them vulnerable. So it was with the Celtic Church. Its leaders were never concerned to create an overall authoritative church polity that could have channeled and directed their spiritual energy and missionary expansion. While they recognized, in qualified terms, the authority of Rome, their work was done on their own initiative and without consulting the popes. When their religious influence became paramount in wide areas of Europe, they made no attempt to give it an enduring structure. Caesar might have said; "I told you so." Meanwhile the organizing genius of the now fallen Roman Empire had been reborn in the Roman Church. Local churches originated by Celtic missionaries were readily absorbed into the hierarchical system centered in the Papacy, and the monastic sons of Columban, Gall, and Fursa bore the easier yoke of Benedict.

To complain of this would be to quarrel aimlessly with the inevitable course of history. But it is an arresting fact, in this age of complicated organization and too little unity of spirit, that in the era of their free enterprise the Irish saints largely evangelized, and tutored in Latin culture, the Germanic world. Coming to pagan tribes almost as squatters in their midst and without ecclesiastical credentials, but in unquestioning obedience to "the heavenly vision" that filled their consciousness, they found a way of approach to the minds and spirits of their hearers. Without question, inherent vitality is what is essential to a church: organization is secondary and too easily becomes a hindrance to initiative. Yet the lack of concern for widespread organization may have tended to limit the impact, great as it was, of Celtic monastic culture in Europe.

It is fair to add that the Celts had no monopoly of vital religion, or of scholarly interest, in their day of service. It was not within the compass of this book to estimate the work of such eminent teachers as Cassiodorus, Isidore of Seville, Paul the Deacon, Peter of Pisa, Theodulf of Orleans, Rabanus Maurus, Hinkmar of Reims, and other writers who owed little or nothing to the Celtic teachers and who like them helped to recover the earlier culture. Not to underestimate these celebrities, it may be questioned whether in this momentous enterprise any of them had the peculiar zest and *abandon* that characterized their Irish coworkers. The people who have been our companions through these pages constitute a rare and choice company, and they have left us a heritage to be cherished.

Abbreviations

CCL: Corpus Christianorum, Series Latina (Turnhout, Belgium 1953–)

CSEL: Corpus Scriptorum Ecclesiasticorum Latinorum (Vienna, 1886–)

Bede: *Baedae Historia ecclesiastica gentis Anglorum*

Haddan and Stubbs: Arthur West Haddan and William Stubbs, *Councils and Ecclesiastical Documents relating to Great Britain and Ireland*, 3 vols. (Oxford, 1869–73)

IER: Irish Ecclesiastical Record, 5th Series

Kenney: James F. Kenney, *Sources for the Early History of Ireland, I, Ecclesiastical* [Columbia University Records of Civilization, XI] (New York: Columbia University Press, 1929; with a new preface and "addenda, 1966" by Ludwig Bieler, New York: 1966)

MGH: Monumenta Germaniae Historica, ed. G. H. Pertz *et al.* (Hanover and Berlin, 1826–)

MGH, SRM: Scriptores Rerum Merovingicarum within the *Monumenta* series

MHP: Medieval Handbooks of Penance, a Translation of the principal Libri Poenitentiales and Selections from Related Documents, by John T. McNeill and Helena M. Gamer. Columbia University Records of Civilization, XXIX (New York: 1938; New York, 1965)

MPG: Jacques Paul Migne, *Patrologiae cursus completus, Series Graeca*, 161 vols. (Paris, 1857–66)

MPL: Migne, *Patrologiae cursus completus, Series Latina*, 221 vols. (Paris, 1879–90)

Notes

Chapter One

1. The more important passages in ancient Greek and Latin authors that have been consulted for this chapter are: Herodotus, *History* I, vii–xiii; ibid. II, xxiii; Xenophon, *Hellenica* VII i, 20, 31; Polybius, *Histories* I, vi, xiii, xvii, lxxvii, lxxx; ibid. II xiii–xxxv; ibid. III, xl, xli, xlvii, lxvii, lxviii, cxv, cxviii; ibid. XVIII, lxi; Caesar, *Gallic War* I, xxx; ibid. III, ix, x, xix; ibid. VI, xi–xvii; ibid. VII, xxxii, lxiii; Diodorus Siculus, *Historical Library* IV, lvi, 3; ibid., XXII, ix, xi; ibid. XXV, xii, xiii; Strabo, *Geography* III, iv, 16, 17; ibid. IV, i, 13, 14; ibid. IV, iv, 2, 4; Livy, *History* V, xxxiv–xlviii; Pomponius Mela, *De situ orbis* III, ix; Ammianus Marcellinus, *Rerum gestarum libri* XV, xii.

2. *MPL* 26:357, and *Letters of St. Jerome*, tr. Thomas Crawford Lawler, Ancient Christian Writers, vol. 33 (London and Westminster, Maryland, 1962), letter 3, p. 31.

3. *The Celts* (New York, 1958), p. 17.

4. Henri Hubert, in a posthumous work edited by Marcel Mauss *et al., Les Celtes et l'expansion celtique jusqu'à l'époque de La Tène* (Paris, 1932), gave a new scientific direction to the study of Celtic origins. The book appeared in English, translated by M. R. Dobie, as *The Rise of the Celts* (London, 1934). The field has continued to be explored in numerous books and articles, among which the following will be found useful: Jacques Moreau, *Die Welt der Kelten* (Stuttgart, 1958); Allan Rees and Brinley Rees, *Celtic Heritage* (London, 1961); Jan Filip, *Celtic Civilization and its Heritage*, tr. Roberta Finlayson Samsour from the 1960 Czech edition (Prague, 1962); G. E. Elton, *The Earliest Relations between Celts and Germans* (London, 1934); Myles Dillon and Nora K. Chadwick, *The Celtic Realms* (London, 1967); Powell, *The Celts;* Nora K. Chadwick, *The Celts* (Harmondsworth, Eng., 1970); Anne Ross, *Everyday Life of the Pagan Celts* (London and New York, 1970). Of these the volume by Dillon and Chadwick serves as an authorative general guide. Filip helpfully locates areas of early Celtic activity in central and eastern Europe. Good use is made of archaeological materials by Powell and by Miss Ross. Among the numerous studies in this field by R. A. S. Macalister are his *Ancient Ireland, a Study of the Lessons of Archaeology and History* (London,

1955), and "The Language and Inscriptions of the Picts," in *Essays and Studies Presented to Prof. Eoin MacNeill*, ed. John Ryan (Dublin, 1940), pp. 184–226. H. M. Chadwick, in *Early Scotland: The Picts, the Scots and the Welsh of Southern Scotland*, ed. N. K. Chadwick (Cambridge, 1949), seeks out these early population elements through a study of language, place names and legends. Albert Grenier in *Les Gaulois* (Paris, 1945), sheds light not only on the ancient Celts of various parts of France but on those of the Danube Valley, Bohemia ("a Celtic land"), Galatia, Spain, and Italy. In Emrys Estyn Evans' *Prehistoric and Early Christian Ireland* (New York, 1966) fresh attention is given to archaeological evidence. In *The Celts*, ed. Joseph Rafferty (Cork, 1964, 1967), amid six competent essays by other contributors, the editor treats "The Archaeology of the Celts of Ireland," and Otto Hermann Frey discusses "The Archaeology of the Continental Celts." This volume has also J. J. Tierney's essay, "The Celts in Classical Authors," which is to be linked with his illuminating study, "The Celtic Ethnography of Posidonius," in *Proceedings of the Royal Irish Academy* 60 (1960), sec. C, pp. 189–275. The Rafferty volume also has T. G. E. Powell's study, "The Celtic Settlement of Ireland." Still suggestive for early Ireland is Eoin MacNeill's *Phases of Irish History* (Dublin, 1919). Francis John Byrne in "Tribes and Tribalism in Early Ireland," *Eriu* 22 (1971); 128–66, counters Eoin MacNeill's negative view of this subject. Calvin Kephart, in *Races of Mankind, Their Origins and Migrations* (New York, 1960), argues for an Asian origin of the Celts. Michael Rostovtzeff's *Iranians and Greeks in Southern Russia* (New York, 1922), calls attention to Celtic contacts with Scythians and Sarmatians. P. Jacobsthal's *Early Celtic Art* (Oxford, 1944) has been followed, but not superseded, by innumerable studies in that field; here N. K. Sandars in *Prehistoric Art in Europe* (Baltimore, 1965) and in his article "Orient and Orientalizing in Early Celtic Art," *Antiquity* 45 (1971): 103–12, presents some results of later research.

5. The Celts were ingenious and inventive not only in war equipment but in their farm implements. Pliny, in his *Natural History* XVIII,72, describes a reaping machine used by the Celts in Gaul, consisting of a capacious cart on two wheels with iron teeth along the edge in front. It was pushed by an ox harnessed in the rear, and its motion cut off the ears of grain, which fell back into the cart. This implement was in use for some centuries and helped to prompt the modern invention of farm reapers. The fourth-century writer Rutilius Palladius, in his *De re rustica* VII,2, gives a more intimate description of the "Gallic reaper" than we have from Pliny. The cart, of adjustable height from the ground, has a series of lance-like teeth in front, slanted upward, by which all the ears are severed, to be lodged in the cart. (I am

indebted for copies of these texts to Professor Blanche Boyer of the Department of Classics, University of Chicago.) For further explanation see "A Virginia Farmer," *Roman Farm Management* (New York, 1913), pp. 158 ff.; Jack Lindsay, *Our Celtic Heritage* (London, 1962), pp. 82 f., with a modern representation of the machine. On early Celtic technology see Stuart Piggott, *Ancient Europe* (Chicago, 1965), pp. 215–56.

6. Pliny, *Natural History* XVI, 92–95; XXIV, 6.

7. Nora K. Chadwick, *The Druids* (Cardiff, 1966), has an informing appendix on Divitiacus and Dumnorix, pp. 103–11.

8. *Irische Texte*, ed. Ernst W. O. Windisch and Whitley Stokes (Berlin, 1897), 3: 393. Cf. J. T. McNeill, *The Celtic Penitentials and Their Influence on Continental Christianity* (Paris, 1923), p. 101.

9. On Celtic paganism and the Druids the following are among the outstanding and relatively recent books and studies: N. K. Chadwick, *The Druids*; Francois della Roux, *Les Druides* (Paris, 1964); Stuart Piggott, *The Druids* (London, 1968); Gerard Sorbanesco, *Les Celtes et les Druides* (Paris, 1968); Myles Dillon, "Celtic Religion and Mythology" in Rafferty, *The Celts*, pp. 59–72, and his "Celtic Religion and the Literature of the Underworld" in Dillon and Chadwick, *Celtic Realms*, pp. 134–58; Marie MacNeill, *The Festival of Lughnasa* (Oxford, 1962); Marie Louise Sqoestedt, *Gods and Heroes of the Celts*, tr. Myles Dillon (London, 1949). A. L. Owen, *The Famous Druids* (Oxford, 1962), treats English interpretations of the Druids since Holinshed, 1571. The books by Jan Filip, Jacques Moreau, and Anne Ross cited in note 4 above, and Thomas F. O'Rahilly's *Early Irish History and Mythology* (Dublin, 1964), give considerable space to Celtic paganism. The older scholarship is well represented by J. A. McCollough, *The Religion of the Ancient Celts* (Edinburgh, 1911); Thomas D. Kendrick, *The Druids, a Study in Keltic Pre-history* (London, 1927); Alexander Macbain, *Celtic Mythology and Religion* (Stirling, 1917); and Joseph Vendryes and others, *La religion des Celtes* (Paris, 1948). Survivals of Celtic pagan beliefs and ideas are abundantly illustrated in the legends of saints and in practices penalized in the Penitential Books: cf. J. T. McNeill, "Folk-Paganism in the Penitentials," *Journal of Religion* 13 (1933): 450–66.

10. See Fred Gealy's note on Crescens in *The Interpreter's Bible*, 12 vols. (New York and Nashville, 1955), 11: 514; Elie Griffe, *La Gaule Chrétienne à l'époque Romaine*, new ed. (Paris, 1964), p. 17.

11. *Ecclesiastical History* V, i, 3–63; also in J. Stevenson, trans., *A New Eusebius: Documents Illustrative of the History of the Church to A.D. 337* (London, 1957, reprinted 1963), pp. 31–41. The names of the martyrs of Lyons are in Gregory of Tours *De gloria martyrum* xlix, in *MPL* 71:751 and *MGH, SRM*, vol. 1 (1885), pt. 3.

12. For Symphorian see Gilbert H. Doble, *The Life of St. Symphorian,* (Truro, Eng., 1931); Alban Butler, *Lives of the Saints,* ed. Herbert Thurston and Donald Atwater, 4 vols. (New York, 1943), 3:380–81; Hugh Williams, *Christianity in Early Britain* (Oxford, 1912), p. 109.

13. *Historia Francorum* [ed. Wilhelm Arndt] I,xxviii, *MGH, SRM,* 1:47. This work appears in a translation by O. M. Dalton, *The History of the Franks by Gregory of Tours,* 2 vols. (Oxford, 1927), 2:20–21.

14. *Dictionnaire d'archéologie chrétienne et de liturgie,* ed. Fernand Cabrol and Henri Leclerq, 37 vols. (Paris, 1907–53), 6:1781–88, 11:2680.

15. Prudentius, *Peristephanon* [ed. Mauricius F. Cunningham] IV,34, *CCL* 126:287; *MPL* 60:363.

16. Cyprian to Pope Stephen, letter lxvii, in *CCL,* vol. 3, pt. 2, p. 63; see also the translation by Sister Rose Bernard Donna, *St. Cyprian's Letters,* Fathers of the Church vol. 51 (Washington, D.C., 1964), 1:239–43 (from the edition by Wilhelm Hartel, *CSEL,* vol. 7 [Vienna, 1871], pp. 744–49).

17. For the beginnings of Christianity among the Celts of Gaul, T. Scott Holmes, *The Origin and Development of the Christian Church in Gaul* (London, 1911), is still usable but has to be checked by later studies. Robert Latouche's critical studies are well represented by his *Caesar to Charlemagne: The Beginnings of France,* tr. Jennifer Nicholson (London and New York, 1968). This work and the earlier volume by Emile Mâle, *La fin du paganisme en Gaule et les plus anciennes basiliques Chrétiennes* (Paris, 1950), both use fresh archaeological data. The critical work of the Breton scholar Louis Duchesne, author of *Mémoire sur l'origine des diocèses épiscopeaux dans l'ancienne Gaule* (Paris, 1890) and *Fastes épiscopeaux de l'ancienne Gaule,* 3 vols. (Paris, 1894–1915), encouraged the rise of a mounting body of French research. Other recent treatments of the church history of Gaul include *A History of France,* by Lucien Romier and A. L. Rouse (London, 1964), and Elie Griffe, *La Gaule Chretienne,* cited in note 10 above.

Chapter Two

1. *Annales Ecclesiastici* (with critical notes by P. Antonius Pagius) (Lucca, 1788), 1:508. A. W. Morgan has presented the case for St. Paul in *St. Paul in Britain,* 5th ed. ([1861]; Oxford, 1925). The book was pronounced "ludicrously worthless" by Arthur West Haddan in *Remains of the Late Arthur West Haddan* (Oxford and London, 1876) p. 212. On Aulus Plautius and other Roman commanders in Britain see Donald R. Dudley and Graham Webster, *The Roman Conquest of Britain* (London, 1965), esp. pp. 89–127.

2. William of Malmesbury's *De antiquitate Glastoniensis ecclesiae* was edited by Thomas Hearne within his edition of Adam of Domeran's *Historia de rebus gestis Glastoniensibus*, 2 vols. (London, 1727), tr. H. F. Scott Stokes, *Glastonbury Abbey before the Conquest* (Glastonbury, 1932). Parker's claim is stated in Matthaei Parker, *De antiquitate Britanniae Ecclesiae* [1572], ed. Samuel Drake (London, 1729), pp. 4 ff. According to Parker, Joseph died A.D. 76 and was buried at Glastonbury, "*in Glasconia in Avaloniae solitudine*" (p. 5). The literature of Glastonbury is abundant. The development of the legend is treated by Reginald Francis Treharne in *Glastonbury Legends: Joseph of Arimathea, the Holy Grail and King Arthur* (London, 1967). For a thoughtful judgment of the importance of Glastonbury in early British Christianity see Margaret Deanesly, *The Pre-Conquest Church of England* (London and New York, 1961), pp. 12 ff.

3. Bede I, iv. Bede's *History* in the Latin text with translation is available in the Penguin Classics edition by Leo Shirley-Price, revised by R. E. Latham (Harmondsworth, Eng., 1968), and in the annotated edition by Bertram Colgrave and R. A. B. Mynors (Oxford, 1969).

4. *Adversus Judaeos* vii, in *MPL* 2:850. Hugh Williams, on other grounds than those here presented, makes Tertullian's oft-discounted statement seem acceptable; see his *Christianity in Early Britain* (Oxford, 1912), pp. 73–77. Even if, as suggested by W. H. C. Frend, the report reached Carthage "from some returning merchant" it need not for that reason be dismissed; see Frend, "The Christianization of Roman Britain," in *Christianity in Britain, 300–700*, ed. M. W. Barley and R. P. C. Hanson (Leicester, 1968), pp. 37–49, esp. p. 37.

5. *Fourth Homily on Ezekiel* (ca 340), in *MPG* 23:203.

6. *Evangelical Demonstrations* III, v, in *MPG* 22:203.

7. Bede I, vii, xviii. In I, vii Bede quotes Venantius Fortunatus, *In laude virginum* VIII, 6; see *MPL* 88:270.

8. Professor Jocelyn M. Toynbee's studies, "The New Roman Mosaic Found in Dorset," *Journal of the Royal Society* 54 (1964): 1–14, and "Pagan Motifs and Practices in Christian Art and Literature in Early Britain," in Barley and Hanson, *Christianity in Britain*, pp. 177–92, illustrate this syncretism. Miss Toynbee's "Christianity in Early Britain," *Journal of the British Archaeological Association*, 3d. ser., 16 (1953): 1–24, is a comprehensive summary of the archaeological evidence as it was known twenty years ago. Later studies include: George C. Boon's monograph *Roman Silchester: The Archaeology of a Romano-British Town* (London, 1957), pp. 128–131, in which the evidence for Christian worship is cautiously evaluated; John Wall's "Christian Evidences in the Roman Period: The Northers Counties" [within modern Scotland], *Archaeologia Aeliana* 43 (1965): 201–25 and 44 (1966):

147–64; and, among other essays in the Barley and Hanson volume, that by A. C. Thomas, "The Evidence from North Britain," pp. 93–121. More than a century ago the industrious and competent antiquarian John Stuart examined the principal early Christian monuments of Scotland in his *The Sculptured Stones of Scotland*, 2 vols. (Aberdeen, 1856 and 1867). The silver hoard found in 1919 on a hillside at Traprain Law near Haddington in East Lothian has received much attention. Alexander Ormiston Curle, in his meticulous and amply illustrated monograph *The Treasure of Traprain, a Scottish Hoard of Silver Plate* (Glasgow, 1923), brought to notice the numerous biblical scenes and Christian symbols represented on a large tankard, a wine sieve, bowls, vases, spoons, and other objects in this treasure, which is roughly dated by some coins of the emperors from 363 to 423 contained in it. Curle conjectured that it may have come from Gaul in the hands of pillaging Saxons. In Wall's second article (in *Archaeologia Aeliana*, vol. 44) some more recent findings, especially at Mildenhall, make it seem possible that the Traprain hoard is of British provenance. The damaged condition of most of the articles evidently resulted from violence, whatever the circumstances. It appears to have been hastily buried, as might have happened in the case of stolen valuables when thieves encountered a crisis in which, as it turned out, their operations had to be ended. Wall's description of the hoard as "possibly part of the tableware of a wealthy Roman or philo-Roman, a traveling official who was also a Christian" is an allowable guess; and the owner may have had his home not many leagues away. We have no means of dating the beginnings of Christianity in that area. In his first article, Wall studies the "Latinus" tombstone at Whithorn and the memorial stones naming three "praecipui sacerdotes" at Kirkmadrine on the Rhinns peninsula some twenty miles west of Whithorn. Cf. Stuart, *Sculptured Stones of Scotland*, 2:35ff. A. R. MacEwen noted that one of these highly placed clerics, Mavorius, seems to bear "a Romanized British name"; he held that the phrase used indicates that they were bishops—a view held also by Wall. The date of these monuments is within the fifth century and the honoring of three deceased bishops in that place would imply an early extensive development of Christianity is southern Scotland. See Alexander Robertson MacEwen, *A History of the Church in Scotland*, 2d ed., 2 vols. (London and New York, 1915), 1:14.

9. Haddan and Stubbs, 1:7 *CCL* 147 (1863): 15. From Hadrian's time (117–38) the three strongly garrisoned towns in Britain were York, Chester, and Caerleon; but London was much the most populous city. See Archibald R. Lewis, *The Northern Seas* (Princeton, 1958), p. 14; H. E. Mellersh, *The Roman Soldier* (New York, 1965),

p. 145; R. G. Collingwood and Ian Richmond, *The Archaeology of Roman Britain*, rev. ed. (London, 1969), pp. 16–25.

10. Haddan and Stubbs, 1:9.

11. Nora Chadwick, "St. Ninian: A Preliminary Study of the Sources," in *Transactions and Journal of Proceedings of the Dumfriesshire and Galloway Natural History and Antiquarian Society* [hereafter cited as *Transactions*], 3d ser. 27 (1950): 9–53. The *Miracula Nynie Episcopi*, ed. Karl Stecker, in *MGH*, vol. 4, *Poetae Latini Aevi Carolini* (Berlin, 1923), pp. 943–62, has been republished with introduction and translation by Winifred W. Macqueen in *Transactions*, 3d ser. 37 (1961): 21–51. On the archaeology of Whithorn see C. A. Raleigh Radford, "Excavations at Whithorn, 1949," in *Transactions*, 3d ser. 27 (1950): 85–126. See also P. A. Wilson's article "St. Ninian of Candida Casa: Literary Evidence from Ireland" in *Transactions*, 3d ser. 41 (1964): 156–85, and Alan Orr Anderson, "Ninian and the Southern Picts," *Scottish Historical Review* 27 (1948): 25–47. Anderson points to Bede's seeming uncertainties and rejects the Martin dedication in 397.

12. Alexander Penrose Forbes, *Lives of St. Ninian and St. Kentigern Compiled in the Twelfth Century* (Edinburgh, 1874); Aelred's *Life of Ninian* occupies pp. 6–26 (English) and pp. 137–57 (Latin).

13. Paul Grosjean, in "Less Pictes apostats dans l'Epitre de Saint Patrice," *Analecta Bollandiana* 76 (1958): 347–78, examines the Ninian question as it is related to St. Patrick's two references to "apostate Picts" in his *Letter to Coroticus* (below, p. 65). In this and other studies in the Bollandist *Analecta* the Jesuit scholar has presented a modified judgment of Ninian's work as compared with that of W. Douglas Simpson. Dr. Simpson's thesis runs through his books: *The Historical St. Columba* (Aberdeen, 1927); *The Celtic Church in Scotland* (Aberdeen, 1935); *St. Ninian and the Origins of the Christian Church in Scotland* (Edinburgh, 1940) (with a number of supporting articles). John A. Duke's *The Columban Church* (Edinburgh, 1932, rpt. 1957), with its spirited vindication of Columba's pioneer role, drew Simpson's caustic criticism, especially for its lack of archaeological evidence. John MacQueen, in *St. Nynia, a Study based on Literary and Linguistic Evidence* (Edinburgh, 1961), would set forward past the year 400 the inception of Ninian's mission and from Welsh sources would give Ninian a diocese of such extent as to include Carlisle. For the *Poem of Ninian* referred to, see Karl Stecker, *Miracula Nynie Episcopi*, pp. 960–62, and W. Levison, "An Eighth Century Poem on Ninian," *Antiquity* 14 (1940): 281–91. In criticism of Simpson's position see especially A. C. Thomas in Barley and Hanson, *Christianity in Britain*, pp. 94–97. Mosa Anderson's *St. Ninian, Light of the Celtic*

North (Westminster, 1964), based confidently on Aelred, is an example of modern hagiography. G. A. Frank Knight's *Archaeological Light on the Early Christianizing of Scotland*, 2 vols. (London, 1933), uses much valuable information to support perilous conclusions.

14. On Victricius of Rouen is this connection see Frend, "Christianization of Roman Britain," pp. 43, 49; Simpson, *St. Ninian*, pp. 63 ff.

15. Another site has been proposed for Rosnat by Charles Thomas who, following P. A. Wilson's denial that it was Whithorn, argues that it was Tintagel on the northern coast of Cornwall: "Rosnat, Rostat, and the Early Irish Church," *Eriu* 22 (1971): 100–106.

16. In his chapter, "The Literary Evidence," in Barley and Hanson, *Christianity in Britain*, pp. 55–73. Arthur himself remains a shadowy figure. For some probabilities concerning his career which have been brought to light, see Beram Saklatvala, *Arthur, Roman Britain's Last Champion* (New York, 1947); Jack Lindsay, *Arthur and His Times* (London, 1958; New York, 1966); Richard L. Pringle, *Arthur, King of Britain* (New York, 1964); and Geoffrey Ashe, *King Arthur's Avalon, the Story of Glastonbury* (London, 1957). Another dimension is given to the Arthurian legend by Roger Sherman Loomis and Laura Hibbard Loomis in *Arthurian Legend and Medieval Art* (London and New York, 1938). A work of ample research is Leslie Alcock's *Arthur's Britain: History and Archaeology, A.D. 367–634* (London, 1971).

17. Fresh light on Pelagius is furnished by John Ferguson in *Pelagius, A Historical and Theological Study* (Cambridge, 1956), and by Robert E. Evans in *Pelagius, Inquiries and Appraisals* (New York, 1968). Both give attention to Jerome's hostile comments. See also J. N. L. Myers, "Pelagius and the End of Roman Rule in Britain," *Journal of Roman Studies* 50 (1960): 21–96.

18. Bede 1.20, based on Constantius, *Life of Germanus*, bk. 18.

19. Prosper, *Chronicle, anno* 429, *MPL* 51:594. Father Paul Grosjean accepts Germanus' second visit as historical and favors for it the date 444: "Le seconde visite de S. Germaine d'Auxerre en Grande Bretagne" and "Le dernier voyage de S. Germaine," nos.28 and 29 of his "Notes d'hagiographie Celtique," *Analecta Bollandiana* 75 (1957): 174–85. Nora K. Chadwick discusses "St. Germanus of Auxerre and the Growth of Ecclesiastical Biography" in her *Poetry and Letters in Early Christian Gaul* (London, 1953), pp. 240–74. The *Life of Germanus* by Constantius of Lyons was apparently written as early as 480. It is translated in F. R. Hoare, *The Western Fathers* (New York, 1954), pp. 284–320. See esp. sections 12–18 and 25–27.

20. R. P. C. Hanson, *St. Patrick, His Origins and Career* (Oxford, 1968), p. 52. For what can be known about Vortigern see H. M. Jack-

son, "Vortigern," in Nora K. Chadwick, ed., *Studies in Early British History* (Cambridge, 1954), pp. 21–46. Jackson is more favorable to Nennius than is the French editor of the *Historia Brittonum*, Ferdinand Lot. This work had been edited by Theodor Mommsen in *Historia Brittonum cum additamenta, MGH* 3.1, *Chronica Minora Saec. IV–VII* (Berlin, 1894), pp. 111–222, and by Lot in *Nennius et l'Historia Brittonum* (Paris, 1934). Lot, in his introduction, supplies some useful tabulated material, but his edition has been unfavorably compared with Mommsen's. On Fastidius and Faustus see *The Works of Fastidius*, ed. and tr. S. T. Haslehurst (London, 1938); see also the works cited in note 17 above; and the numerous references to both in Hanson's *St. Patrick* and in the monograph by G. Weigel, *Faustus of Riez* (Philadelphia, 1938).

Chapter Three

1. Many monks like Martin of Tours abandoned a military career for the spiritual warfare of the devotional life, and the idea that the monk was a soldier of Christ entered deeply into the monastic consciousness and is reflected in many lives of saints. See Jacques Fontaine, ed., *Sulpice Sévère, Vie de Saint Martin* (Paris, 1967), 1:143–60; John T. McNeill, "Asceticism versus Militarism in the Middle Ages," *Church History* 5 (1936): 3–23.

2. Arthur W. Wade-Evans, *Welsh Christian Origins* (Oxford, 1934), pp. 132 ff. This author and other specialists note that our most reliable information on Illtud is derived from the seventh-century *Life of St. Samson* (see n. 4, below) rather than from the fanciful twelfth-century *Life of St. Illtud*. In *Welsh Christian Origins*, pp. 57 ff., 121 ff., Wade-Evans gives some elements of the legend of St. Dubricius. For fuller information on these saints see Gilbert H. Doble's *St. Dubricius* (Guildford, 1943) and *St. Iltut* (Cardiff, 1944).

3. Wade-Evans, *Welsh Christian Origins*, pp. 142 ff., 155–60.

4. Ibid., pp. 138 ff., 205–33. The earliest life of Samson, written shortly after 600, was translated by Thomas Taylor, *The Life of St. Samson of Dol* (London, 1925). See the section on Samson in Kenney, pp. 135 f. The legendary lore of British saints in Ireland, Irish saints in Britain, and both in Brittany is abundant and will find further illustration in later chapters. Some examples are cited in Kenney, pp. 180 ff. See also Charles Plummer, *Vitae Sanctorum Hiberniae*, 2 vols. (Oxford, 1910), 1:cxxiv ff. On the family of Brychan see Gilbert H. Doble, *S. Nectan, S. Keyne and the Children of Brychan in Cornwall* (Exeter, 1930), pp. 1–20.

5. William Jenkins Rees, *Lives of the Cambro-British Saints* (Llandovery and London, 1853), pp. 402–88 (Welsh and Latin); J. W. James,

ed., *Rhigyfarch's Life of David: The Basic Mid-Twelfth Century Latin Text with Introduction, Critical Apparatus and Translation* (Cardiff, 1967); A. W. Wade-Evans, *Life of St. David* (London, 1923), and his *Welsh Christian Origins*, pp. 146 ff., and *Vitae Sanctorum Britanniae et Genealogiae* (Cardiff, 1944), pp. 150–70; *MHP*, pp. 169–74, with translation of the *Excerpta quaedam.*

6. J. R. Morris in M. W. Barley and R. P. C. Hanson, eds., *Christianity in Britain*, p. 71.

7. Wade-Evans, *Vitae Sanctorum Britanniae et Genealogiae*, pp. 47–95; idem, *Welsh Christian Origins*, pp. 126–32. For *The Wisdom of Cadoc* see the translation by Owen Jones in his *Myvyrian Archaiology of Wales*, 2 ed. (Denbigh, 1870), pp. 754–72. On Welsh gnomic poetry see Thomas Parry, *A History of Welsh Literature*, tr. H. Idris Bell (Oxford, 1955), pp. 37–40.

8. In his *Welsh Christian Origins*, ch. 17, "Auctor Badonicus and the Perversion of Welsh History," pp. 289–312.

9. The *De Excidio et Conquestu Britannaie* of Gildas has often been edited. The edition by Hugh Williams, *Gildas: The Ruin of Britain*, Cymmrodorion Record Series III (London, 1899–1901), is accompanied by a translation which replaces earlier ones; the *Prefatio Gildae de penitentia* is edited and translated by Williams in the volume referred to, pp. 272–85. A translation mainly from the text in Haddan and Stubbs 1:113–15 is in *MHP*, pp. 174–78. Among Gildas studies, the reader may find especially useful C. S. Stevens, "Gildas Sapiens," *English Historical Review* 56 (1941): 353–73, and F. Kerlouégan, "Le Latin du 'De Excidio Britanniae' de Gildas," in Barley and Hanson, *Christianity in Britain* pp. 151–76.

10. Gilbert H. Doble, *The Saints of Cornwall* (Chatham, 1960) (in three parts separately paged). Many saints locally celebrated in Cornwall had a more prominent later role in Brittany. Valuable here too is Thomas Taylor, *The Celtic Christianity of Cornwall* (London, 1961). Taylor explores the relations of Brittany and Cornwall through later times.

11. J. L. Gough Meissner, in Walter Alison Phillips, ed., *History of the Church of Ireland from the Earliest Times to the Present Day*, 3 vols. (Oxford, 1934), 1:228 ff. For particulars see p. 243 in chapter 9 below.

12. W. F. Skene, ed., *Chronicles of the Picts and Scots* (Edinburgh, 1867), p. 6; A. O. Anderson, *Early Sources of Scottish History, A.D. 500–1280*, 2vols. (Edinburgh and London, 1922), 1:cxx ff.; Meissner in Phillips, *History of the Church in Ireland*, 1:223 ff.; The *Life of St. Boite* is in Plummer, *Vitae Sanctorum Hiberniae*, 1:87–97; see the comment in Plummer's introduction, pp. 34 ff.

13. Alexander Penrose Forbes, *Lives of St. Ninian and St. Kentigern* (Edinburgh, 1874); English text for Kentigern, pp. 33–119; Latin, pp. 161–312. On the unreliability of Jocelyn see Alexander R. MacEwen, *A History of the Church of Scotland* (London, 1913, 1915), 1:25 ff.

14. The *Vita Sancti Servani* found in W. M. Metcalfe's edition of Pinkerton's *Lives of the Scottish Saints* (Paisley, 1889), 2:119–28, is too fantastic to serve any historical purpose.

15. W. Douglas Simpson, *Saint Ninian and Christian Origins in Scotland* (Edinburgh, 1940), p. 98; A. C. Thomas, "The Evidence from North Britain," in Barley and Hanson, *Christianity in Britain*, p. 110.

16. Meissner in Phillips, *History of the Church in Ireland*, 1:362.

17. Jocelyn, *Life of Kentigern*, chap. 40.

18. Dorothy N. Marshall, *History of Bute*, 4th ed. (Kingarth, 1967), p. 29.

19. Cockburn, *The Celtic Church in Dunblane* (Dunblane, 1954), pp. 49–85; 137–54.

20. Bede 1.23–38.

21. Bede 2.2; see also John Godfrey, *The Church in Anglo-Saxon England* (Cambridge, 1962), pp. 84–92, and Margaret Deanesly, *Augustine of Canterbury* (London, 1964), pp. 83–88. The importance of this incident in the emotion of the Welsh and their poetry is shown by Nora K. Chadwick in her chapter on "The Battle of Chester," *Celt and Saxon: Studies in the Early British Border* (Cambridge, 1963), pp. 167–85.

22. Among other books and studies that have been found useful for this chapter are: Sir John Edward Lloyd, *A History of Wales . . . to the Edwardian Conquest*, 3d ed. (London, 1954); Sir Frank Stenton, *Anglo-Saxon England* (Oxford, 1948); Nora K. Chadwick, ed., *Studies in the Early British Church* (Cambridge, 1958); W. H. Davies, "The Church in Wales" in Barley and Hanson, *Christianity in Britain*, pp. 131–50; E. G. Bowen, *The Settlement of the Celtic Saints in Wales* (Cardiff, 1954); Margaret Deanesly, *Sidelights on the Anglo-Saxon Church* (London, 1962). Davies, in the amply informing study mentioned, makes numerous references to archaeological evidence, citing special studies by V. E. Nash-Williams, whose *Early Christian Monuments of Wales* (Cardiff, 1950) offers general guidance in that field. The maritime orientation and seafaring habits of the British and Irish monks have been impressively illustrated by E. G. Bowen in "The Irish Sea in the Age of the Saints," *Studia Celtica* 4 (1969): 56–71, and in *Britain and the Western Seaways*, Ancient Peoples and Places series (London, 1972), esp. pp. 70–91.

Chapter Four

1. George T. Stokes, *Ireland and the Celtic Church*, 3d ed. (London, 1892), p. 19. Stokes held it remotely possible that an Irish soldier with the Romans was in Jerusalem. If such was the case, he would have been enlisted in Gaul: Britain was not yet Roman, but there was constant intercourse between Ireland and Gaul. The tale of Altus, however, bears the marks of a late invention.

2. Stokes, *Ireland and the Celtic Church*, pp. 66 ff.

3. Heinrich Zimmer, "Die Keltische Kirche," in *Realencyclopedie für Protestantische Theologie und Kirche*, vol. 1, (1901), trans. by A. Meyer, *The Celtic Church in Britain and Ireland* (London, 1902). Zimmer's treatment of Patrick was first closely criticized in J. B. Bury's *Life of St. Patrick* (London, 1905), Appendix 21, pp. 384–91.

4. Walter Alison Phillips, ed., *History of the Church of Ireland from the Earliest Times to the Present Day*, 3 vols. (Oxford, 1934), vol. 1, appendix D (by J. L. Gough Meissner), pp. 376–80.

5. Prosper, *Chronicle, anno 431*, in *MPL* 51:595; *Contra Collatorem* xxi, 2, in *MPL* 51:271. The latter work of Prosper is directed against the semi-Pelagian John Cassian, author of the *Collationes*, conferences with Egyptian monastic fathers.

6. Zimmer's *Pelagius in Iraland* (Berlin, 1901), proves only that Irish monastic scholars were well acquainted with the thought of Pelagius.

7. *Sancti Columbani Opera*, ed. G. S. M. Walker (Dublin, 1957), pp. 38 ff.

8. Ludwig Bieler, *St. Patrick and the Coming of Christianity*, History of Irish Catholicism, vol. 1 (Dublin, 1967), p. 7. This study shows some modification of views stated in Bieler's chapter "The Chronology of St. Patrick" in *Old Ireland*, ed. Robert McNally (New York, 1965), an essay "written three years earlier" (p. 1).

9. T. F. O'Rahilly, *The Two Patricks* (Dublin, 1942); James Carney, *The Problem of St. Patrick* (Dublin, 1961); D. A. Binchy, "Patrick and His Biographers," *Studia Hibernica* 2 (1962): 7–173; Ludwig Bieler, "The Mission of Palladius," *Traditio* 6 (1948): 1–32; R. P. C. Hanson, *St. Patrick, His Origins and Career* (Oxford, 1968). For an acute refutation of O'Rahilly's thesis, see Francis Shaw, "The Myth of the Second Patrick," *Studies* 50 (1961): 5–27, and "Postmortem on the Second Patrick," *Studies* 51 (1962): 237–67. The course of modern research on Patrick to 1961 is recited by Robert E. McNally in "St. Patrick, 461–1961" in *Catholic Historical Review* 47 (1961): 305–24.

10. Ludwig Bieler, *The Life and Legend of St. Patrick* (Dublin, 1949), pp. 42 ff.

11. John Morris, "The Dates of the Celtic Saints," *Journal of Theological Studies*, n.s. 17 (1966): 342–91, esp. pp. 365 ff.; R. P. C. Hanson, *Saint Patrick*, pp. 376–80.

12. Muirchú's *Life* was translated by Albert Barry, 2d ed. (Dublin, 1902). The *Tripartite Life* was elaborately edited with a translation by Whitley Stokes, *The Tripartite Life of St. Patrick*, 2 vols. (London, 1887). Stokes himself anticipated some improvements on his work, and it was criticized in detail: see Kenney, p. 342. Eoin MacNeill regarded Tírechán (ca. 700) as its author; see "The Tripartite Life of St. Patrick," *Eriu* 40 (1932): 1–41. The supposition of so early an origin gave weight to its representation of Patrick's itinerary over Ireland: cf. Eoin MacNeill, "The Topographical Importance of the Tripartite Life," in *St. Patrick*, ed. John Ryan, with a memoir by Michael Tierney (Dublin, 1964), pp. 191–220. In a painstaking examination of the texts, Kathleen Mulchrone brought the edition of Stokes under detailed criticism, "Die Abfassungszeit and Überlieferung der Tripartita," *Zeitschrift für Celtische Philologie* 16 (1927): 1–94. Here she dates the now lost original between 895 and 901. Her new edition with translation followed: *Betha Phátraic: The Tripartite Life of St. Patrick*, 2 vols. (Dublin, 1939). Vol. 1 has the critical text; vol. 2 introduction and translation. The accumulation of legendary marvels in later centuries becomes evident in the *Life of Patrick* by Jocelyn of Furness (ca. 1185), which contains the story of the "Staff of Jesus" received by Patrick, the huge giant resurrected from a mound and baptized (lxxi), the expulsion of reptiles from Ireland (clxx), and like fantasies; James O'Leary, *The Most famous Ancient Lives of St. Patrick, Including the Life of Jocelyn*, 3d ed. (New York, 1877).

13. For a translation of this text by Kathleen Hughes, see *The Church in Early Irish Society* (London and Ithaca, 1966), appendix, "Liber Angeli," pp. 276–81.

14. Newport J. D. White, ed., *Libri Sancti Patricii* (London, 1918), tr. *St. Patrick, His Life and Writings, with a Commentary* (London, 1920); idem., *The Writings of St. Patrick* (London, 1932; reprinted 1954); Ludwig Bieler, ed., *Libri Epistolarum Sancti Patricii Episcopi* (London, 1961), tr. *The Works of St. Patrick*, Ancient Christian Writers, vol. 17 (London and Westminster, Maryland, 1953); Arnold Marsh, *St. Patrick and His Writings, a Modern Translation* (Dundalk, 1966). Marsh uses homely language with a Welsh coloring as accordant with Patrick's style.

15. D.C. Marsh-Edwards, "Was St. Patrick Irish?" *Downside Review* 88 (1969): 285–90.

16. Paul Grosjean would identify the Victorinus (or "Victor," as in Muirchú) of Patrick's vision with Victricius of Rouen, who may have

been to Patrick a model missionary as Martin probably was to Ninian; see Grosjean, "Notes hagiographiques celtiques," "Saint Patrice et Saint Victrice," *Acta Bollandiana* 63 (1945): 94–99. Cf. p. 58, above. Eoin MacNeill in "Silva Focluti," *Proceedings of the Royal Irish Academy* 36 C (1923): 249–55, would read "Silva Uluti" and locate this as Ulaid in Antrim County east of Lough Neagh. This view is accepted by Kenney, p. 168, and favored by Bieler in "The Problem of Silva Focluti," *Irish Historical Studies* 3 (1943): 351–64. But it has been cogently rejected by O'Rahilly, *The Two Patricks*, pp. 34–35, who accepts Tírechán's Tirawley location.

17. *The Church of Ireland* (London, 1892), appendix B, p. 420.

18. Carney, *The Problem of St. Patrick*, pp. 20–30, 66–67.

19. *The Life and Legend of St. Patrick*, pp. 60 f.; "Interpretationes Patricianae," *Irish Ecclesiastical Record* 107 (1967): 5–7. The reader should note that "grex porcorum" is straight from the Vulgate of Luke 8:32.

20. Hanson, *St. Patrick, His Origins and Career*, pp. 121–22.

21. Both sets of canons were edited with valuable notes in Haddan and Stubbs, vol 2, appendix A, 328–31, 333–38. Annotated translation in *MHP*, pp. 78–85.

22. Arnold Marsh, impressed by Patrick's oft-reiterated claim of divine authorization and his silence about any ecclesiastical consecration, thinks he may have been irregularly consecrated in Gaul and having later learned that the act was invalid continued to labor as bishop in the assurance that God had consecrated him (*St. Patrick and His Writings*, p. 15).

23. *The Latin of St. Patrick* (Dublin, 1961). Beiler in a perceptive description of Patrick's writings, thinks of these as forming "a mosaic of reminiscences of his reading," his Latin being "rusty" as well as "rustic" (*Life and Legend*, pp. 36–37).

24. Hanson, *St. Patrick, His Origins and Career*, pp. 158–70.

25. Kuno Meyer, "Aus dem Nachlass Heinrich Zimmers," *Zeitschrift für Celtische Philologie* 9 (1913): 117–18.

26. Hanson, *St. Patrick, His Origins and Career*, pp. 111–12.

Chapter Five

1. John Ryan, *Irish Monasticism: Its Origins and Early Development* (London and New York, 1931), pp. 100–101, 168–69. This work is still the most informing general treatment of its subject; it has been reprinted (1972) with modernized bibliography. An indispensable companion volume offering a wealth of factual detail for the entire medieval period is *Religious Houses in Ireland, with an Appendix on Early Sites* by Aubrey Gwynn and R. Neville Handcock (London, 1970); A guide to the early Irish monasteries, founders and dates

occupies pp. 20–46. See also Francis Carty, *Two and Fifty Irish Saints*, with a foreword by John Ryan (Dublin, 1941).

2. Kathleen Hughes, *The Church in Early Irish Society* (London and Ithaca, N.Y., 1966), pp. 123, 130–33.

3. Ryan, Irish Monasticism, pp. 114 ff.; John T. McNeill, *The Celtic Penitentials and Their Influence on Continental Christianity* (Paris, 1923), pp. 32–34. (Chapters 1–4 of this University of Chicago dissertation were reprinted from articles in *Revue Celtique* 31 [1922]: 257–300; ibid. 40 [1923]: 51–103, 320–41.) For references to related literature see Kenney, pp. 235 ff. Thomas P. Oakley, in "Celtic Penance: Its Sources, Affiliation and Influence," *Irish Ecclesiastical Review* 52 (1938): 198–264, 589–601, tends to minimize the distinctiveness of Celtic penance, largely on the ground that the authors of the Penitentials were familiar with Cassian and continental writers on the deadly sins.

4. Cf. chapter 3, note 3.

5. Haddan and Stubbs, vol. 2, pt. 2 (1878), pp. 292–94.

6. Kenney, p. 3.

7. Charles Forbes René, Comte de Montalembert, *Les moines d'Occident depuis Saint Benoît jusqu'à Saint Bernard*, 7 vols. (Paris, 1860–77), 3:88.

8. H. C. Lawler, *The Monastery of St. Mochaoi of Nendrum* (Belfast, 1925); Edwin S. Towill, "St. Mochaoi of Nendrum," *Ulster Journal of Archaeology*, 3d ser. 27 (1964): 103–20. Towill explores the possibility of Ninian's influence in the founding of Nendrum. Cf. E. G. Bowen, *Britain and the Western Seaways* (London, 1972), p. 87.

9. *Navigatio Sancti Brendani Abbatis*, ed. Carl Selmer (Notre Dame, Indiana, 1959). This is a critical edition with ample textual and historical notes, lists of manuscripts, and so forth. In many instances Selmer traces the motifs in the fanciful incidents to earlier Eastern and Western sources. J. Webb's translation is in the Penguin Classics series: *Lives of the Saints: The Voyage of St. Brendan; Bede's Life of St. Cuthbert; Eddius Stephanus' Life of St. Wilfred* (Harmondsworth and Baltimore, 1965), pp. 31–68. W. W. Heist has re-edited *Vitae Sanctorum Hiberniae ex codice olim Salmanticense nunc Bruxellense* (Brussels, 1965), which contains *Vita Prior et navigatio Sancti Brendani* (not the ninth century *Navigatio*) and *Vita altera Sancti Brendani*, pp. 324–34. For a readable summary of Brendan's voyage, see Brendan Lehane, *The Quest of Three Abbots* (New York, 1968), pp. 70–99. The Brendan story has attracted wide attention as a possible clue to the history of early Atlantic navigation. Geoffrey Ashe, in *Land of the West: St. Brendan's Voyage to America* (New York and London, 1962), infers from some intriguing but hardly convincing evidence of an Irish presence in America during the Middle Ages, not

necessarily that of St. Brendan. George A. Little, in *Brendan the Navigator: An Interpretation* (Dublin, 1945), pp. 147–48, 170–71, tells of Irish-speaking Indians in Florida and Panama! The material evidence is discounted by Samuel Eliot Morison in *The European Discovery of America: The Northern Voyages* (New York, 1970), pp. 13–31, although he thinks some Irishmen located in Iceland, in flight after a Norse landing there in 870, may have sailed westward and missing Greenland reached an American coast.

10. Sir J. Y. Simpson, "On the Stone-Roofed Cell or Oratory on the Island of Inchcolme," in *Archaeological Essays*, ed. John Stuart (Edinburgh, 1872), pp. 66–136 (illustrated). For the Gallerus structure see the illustrated description in Harold Graham Leask, *Irish Churches and Monastic Buildings*, 3 vols. (Dundalk, 1955–60), 1:21–26. This work is a valuable supplementary volume to those mentioned in note 1, above.

11. Françoise Henry, "Early Monasteries, Beehive Huts and Drystone Houses in the Neighborhood of Caherciveen and Waterville (Co. Kerry)," *Proceedings of the Royal Irish Academy* 58 C (1957) (with numerous plates); Daphne Desirée Charlotte Pochin Mould, *Irish Pilgrimage* (New York, 1957), pp. 1–50.

12. Ryan, *Essays and Studies*, p. 124.

13. The numerous "lives" of St. Kevin are all late and so fanciful that scholars cannot reconstruct his life story with any fullness. See Kenney, pp. 403 f.; C. Plummer, *Vitae Sanctorum Hiberniae*, 2 vols. (Oxford, 1910), 1:234–57; Mrs. Liam Price, "Glendalough, St. Kevin's Road," in *Essays and Studies Presented to Professor E. MacNeill*, ed. J. Ryan, Dublin, 1940, pp. 244–71; Maire and Liam de Paor, *Early Christian Ireland*, (London, 1958), pp. 61 ff., 155. Many Irish saints are reputed to have fraternized with wild animals and birds. Sister M. Donatus has discussed the references in *Beasts and Birds in the Lives of the Irish Saints* (Philadelphia, 1934). Cf. Plummer, *Vitae Sanctorum Hiberniae*, introduction, 1:cxlvi. The resemblance between the Celtic saints and St. Francis of Assisi in this respect has not escaped notice. See Anselmo M. Tommasini's extended treatment, "The Irish Religious and the Franciscan Movement," *Irish Saints in Italy*, trans. J. F. Scanlon (London, 1937), pp. 442–92. Louis Gougaud has remarked: "From the materials furnished by these [Celtic saints'] lives it would be easy to compile a collection of anecdotes, a forerunner of the *Fioretti*" (*Christianity in Celtic Lands*, trans. Maud Joynt [London, 1932], p. 56).

14. Alice Courtayne, *St. Brigid of Ireland* rev. ed. (Dublin, 1955); Phelim Briain, *St. Brigid, Her Legend, History and Cult* (Dublin, 1938); Sabine Baring-Gould and John Fisher, *The Lives of the British Saints* (London, 1907), 1:254–68; for the Scottish phases of the

legend, see James Wilkie, *St. Bride, the Greatest Woman of the Celtic Church* (Edinburgh, 1913). The *Sanctae Brigidae Virginis Vita* by Cogitosus is in *MPL* 62:775–90. For the seventh-century church at Kildare, see below, p. 130. Kildare is considered with numerous similarly organized monasteries by Mary Bateson, whose study "The Origin and History of the Double Monasteries," in *Transactions of the Royal Historical Society* 13 (1899): 137–98, has not been superseded.

15. Kenney, pp. 174–75; Hughes, *Church in Early Irish Society*, pp. 186 ff. For Maél-rúain and the Irish Célé-Dé, see E. J. Gwynn, "The teaching of Maél-rúain" and "The Rule of the Céli Dé," *Hermathena*, second supplemental volume (Dublin, 1922), pp. 1–63 and pp. 64–87.

16. Alexander R. MacEwen, *A History of the Church in Scotland*, 2d ed., 2 vols. (1915), 1:131.

17. Haddan and Stubbs, 2:119–21.

18. Annotated text and translation in Ludwig Bieler, *The Irish Penitentials* (Dublin, 1963), pp. 74–95; it is also translated, with introduction and notes, in *MHP*, pp. 86–97. E. J. Gwynn edited "An Irish Penitential," in *Eriu* 7 (1914): 121–95, a typical document of the series, in Old Irish.

19. McNeill, *The Celtic Penitentials and Their Influence on Continental Christianity* (Paris, 1923), For other features of the Penitentials see *MHP*, pp. 24–50.

20. *Ireland and the Celtic Church*, 2d ed. (London, 1888), pp. 178–79. Similarly Nora K. Chadwick remarks: "Anchorites are an integral part of the earliest Irish Church" (*The Age of the Saints in the Celtic Church* [Oxford, 1961], p. 117). It is generally recognized that both Welsh and Irish monastic founders and legislators drew their principles in some degree from the Egyptian desert fathers. Stokes shows some evidence that Syrian elements in southern Gaul mediated the austere forms of monasticism to the West and to the Celtic churches (*Ireland and the Celtic Church*, pp. 166–182). For Egyptian or Coptic influence on Celtic monasticism, see Clinton Albertson, *Anglo-Saxon Saints and Heroes* (New York, 1967), appendix D ("Celtic Christianity and Egypt") of "Life of St. Cuthbert," pp. 82–84, and passages indexed under "Coptic" and "Egyptian." Familiarity on the part of Celtic monks with the literature of Egyptian monasticism was by no means confined to the writings of Cassian.

Chapter Six

1. Adomnan's second preface to the *Vita Sancti Columbanae* in Allan Orr Anderson and Marjorie Ogilvie Anderson, *Adomnan's Life of St. Columba*" (London and New York, 1961), p. 87. On the reasons for Columba's departure from Ireland see the Introduction to

this edition, pp. 71–74, see also the old compendious edition by William Reeves, *"The Life of St. Columba, Founder of Hy," Written by Adamnan* . . . (Dublin, 1857), pp. 247 ff. Cf. Charles Plummer, *Vitae Sanctorum Hiberniae* (Oxford, 1910), 2:139. See also J. T. Fowler, *Adamnani "Vita S. Columbae" edited from Dr. Reeves' Text with an Introduction*, rev. ed. (Oxford, 1920). Especially valuable to the scholarly reader are: Ludwig Bieler, "The Celtic Hagiographer," *Studia Patristica* 5 (1962): 243–65; and D. A. Bullough, "Columba, Adomnan, and the Achievement of Iona," *Scottish Historical Review* 43 (1964): 111–30, and 44 (1965): 17–24. Both offer acute textual examination of the *Vita Columbae* and bring comparisons with the *Vita Brigidae* by Cogitosus.

2. Six other foundations in Ireland—Kilmore, Boyle, Swords, Rechra, Raphoe, and Drumcliff—are confidently credited to Columba by W. G. Hanson, *The Early Monastic Schools of Ireland* (Cambridge, 1927, 1971), p. 15. Several of these places are affectionately mentioned in a poem doubtfully attributed to Columba: see Lucy Menzies, *St. Columba of Iona*, 4th ed. (Glasgow, 1964), p. 11.

3. Kenney, p. 135. The story is given in detail by numerous writers on Columba and often incautiously taken as assured history. It has been vividly elaborated in historical fiction by Jane Oliver in *Isles of Glory* (London, 1947), pp. 133–52. Another variant of the tale is that one Curnan, who had caused the death of a competitor in the games at Tara and fled for sanctuary to Columba, had been snatched away and slain by Diarmit, thus arousing Columba's righteous wrath.

4. W. F. Skene, *Celtic Scotland*, 2d ed., 2 vols. (Edinburgh, 1886–87), 2:84; George T. Stokes, *Ireland and the Celtic Church* (London, 1888), pp. 112 ff.; Isabel Henderson, *The Picts* (New York, 1967), pp. 44–45. Some uncertainty may arise from the similarity of the names of Dalaradia and Dalriada. Dalaradia was from great antiquity inhabited by Picts, whose coming to Ireland cannot be dated. It lay to the east from Lough Neagh in Ulster. Dalriada was northward from Dalaradia and was, like the rest of Ireland, inhabited by Scots. When the Scots of Dalriada in Ulster invaded southern Alban, the modern Scotland, they extended the name Dalriada to designate their new kingdom formed in what is now Argyllshire.

5. Henderson, *The Picts*. Malgwyn's favorable attitude to monasteries is referred to by D. W. Davis; "The Church in Wales," in M. W. Barley and R. P. C. Hanson, eds., *Christianity in Britain 300–700* (Leicester, 1968), p. 141.

6. W. Douglas Simpson, *The Historical St. Columba* (Aberdeen, 1927), pp. 18–21, 63–72. E. C. Trenholme tried to trace the missionary journeys of Columba and his aides in *The Story of Iona* (Edinburgh, 1909), pp. 44–48. Reeves gives a total of 58 foundations in

Scotland (*Life of St. Columba*, p. xlix). D. A. Bullough has presented a searching treatment of Columba's missionary work in "Columba, Adamnan, and the Achievement of Iona," *Scottish Historical Review* 43 (1969): 111–50, and 44:17–33.

7. A version of Dallán Forgaill's *Amhra Colum Cille* (Eulogy of Columba) is given in John Henry Bernard and R. Atkinson, *The Irish Liber Hymnorum*, 2 vols. Henry Bradshaw Society Volumes 13, 14 (London, 1897, 1898), 1:62–83. Kenney (p. 426) prefers Whitley Stokes, "The Bodleian Amra Choluimb Chille," a series of five articles in *Revue Celtique* 20 (1899) and 21 (1900).

8. Anderson and Anderson, *Adomnan's "Life of St. Columba,"* p. 547. Baithene, Columba's cousin, foster son, and chosen successor, is the first in the list of the twelve pioneer companions of Columba at Iona and is often mentioned with commendation by Adomnan.

9. Text in *MPL* 101:694–722. Clinton Albertson omits from his translation of this work virtually all the miracle sections; see *Anglo-Saxon Saints and Heroes* (New York, 1967), pp. 217–93.

10. Bede V, xv–xviii. Bede calls it "a book very useful to many" and quotes its descriptions of Bethlehem, Jerusalem, Mount Olivet, and Hebron. Cf. James P. B. Bulloch, "Iona and the Outer World," *Records if the Scottish Church History Society* 7 (1958): 1–14. Denis Meehan has provided an excellent edition of the *De locis sanctis*, with introduction, topographical analysis, and translation: *Adamnan's "De Locis Sanctis"* (Dublin, 1958).

11. Ed. and tr. Kuno Meyer, *Cáin Adamnáin: An Old Irish Treatise on the Law of Adamnan*, in *Anecdota Oxoniensia*, Medieval Series 12 (Oxford, 1905). Selections, including the opening "speech of the angel" in *MHP*, pp. 135–39.

12. Text in Haddan and Stubbs 2:111–14; tr. in *MHP*, pp. 130–34.

13. C. S. Boswell, in *An Irish Precursor of Dante* (London, 1908), includes an account of Adomnan's life, pp. 1–26, and a translation of the *Fis Adamnáin*, pp. 28-47. Cf. Kenney, pp. 444–45.

14. Bede V, xv; cf. V, xxi. A. O. Kelleher and G. Schepperle edited and translated the Irish text of the *Life of Columba* compiled by Magnus O'Donnell in 1532: *Betha Colaim Chille* (Urbana, Ill., 1918). It contains fascinating anecdotes, a number of which are found in legends of other saints. Columba founds 300 churches and writes 300 books (p. 435). In the *Annals of Clonmacnois*, ed. Dennis Murphy (Dublin, 1896), the 300 books are all copies of the New Testament. (p. 95).

Chapter Seven

1. Adomnan, *Vita Columae* III, 10, 22. For editions see chapter 6, note 1.

2. C. J. Godfrey, *The Church in Anglo-Saxon England* (Cambridge, 1962), p. 65.

3. Bede II, ix.

4. Bede II, xiii.

5. Kenneth Jackson, "On the Northern British Section in Nennius," in Nora K. Chadwick, ed., *Celt and Saxon: Studies in the Early British Border* (Cambridge, 1963), pp. 20–62, esp. pp. 32–33; see also Nora K. Chadwick, "The Conversion of Northumbria, a Comparison of Sources" ibid., 138–67, and "The Celtic Background of Anglo-Saxon England," ibid., pp. 323–52.

6. Bede II, xx.

7. Bede III, i. According to Bede, Oswald had his soldiers kneel with him about a wooden cross at dawn before the battle.

8. *"Ad maiores natu Scottorum,"* Bede III, iii.

9. Bede III, xix; J. L. Gough Meissner in W. A. Phillips, *History of the Church of Ireland* (Oxford, 1933), 1:271 ff.

10. Bede III, v.

11. Bede III, xiv, xvii. C. J. Godfrey's perceptive treatment of Aidan's work should not be overlooked; see *The Church in Anglo-Saxon England*, pp. 104–11.

12. Bede III, xxi–xxiv.

13. Nennius and other Welsh sources indicate that Oswy contracted an early marriage (ca. 665) with a British princess, Rieinmelth, a granddaughter of Rhun. By this alliance, it would appear, Oswy was enabled to extend his sway over the British Christian kingdom of Rheged. See Kenneth Jackson in *Celt and Saxon* (note 5 above), pp. 41 ff., and Mrs. Chadwick's essay, "The Conversion of Northumbria," ibid., pp. 158–59, 164; see also Peter Hunter Blair, *An Introduction to Anglo-Saxon England* (Cambridge, 1962), p. 45.

14. Joseph Barbour Lightfoot, *Leaders of the Northern Church* (London, 1890), p. 9. Cf. James Bulloch, *The Life of the Celtic Church* (Edinburgh, 1968), p. 72: "All England north of the Thames was indebted to the Celtic mission for its conversion." A helpful account of the Lindisfarne mission is given by Gareth Dunleavy in *Colum's Other Island* (Madison, 1960). Dunleavy's chapter, "The Irish Scribe and the Insular Hand," pp. 45–65, has useful illustrations.

15. Bede III, vii. J. L. Gough Meissner has shown the fragmentary and unsatisfactory character of Bede's reference to Birinus, and suggests that Birinus was an Irishman. Bede makes him an appointee of Pope Honorius but settling at a place of his own choice, like a typical Irish peregrinus, and having nothing to do with Canterbury. Oswald's presence at the baptism of Cynegils is significant. Oswald, pupil and patron of Irish saints, was about to become the son-in-law of Cynegils

and probably had a part in bringing about his conversion; see Meissner in Phillips, *History of the Church of Ireland*, 1:276 ff., and in his *The Celtic Church of England after the Synod of Whitby* (London, 1929), p. 172 Cf. Godfrey, *The Church in Anglo-Saxon England*, p. 100.

16. Bede, III, viii.

17. Bede (IV, xiii) describes Dicul's community as a *"monasteriolum"* with only "five or six brethren serving God" in a spot between forest and sea. As we have seen, such tiny and remote monastic settlements were abundant in Ireland (see chapter 5).

18. Andrew Lang, *History of Scotland*, vol. 1 (Edinburgh, 1890), p. 34.

19. The older dating of the Synod of Whitby, 664, has been revised, to the satisfaction of many scholars, by Sir Frank Stenton in his *Anglo-Saxon England* (Oxford, 1947), p. 129. The argument rests on Bede's alleged dating of the new year. There remains some uncertainty, and such recognized authorities as Wilhelm Levison and Paul Grosjean have rejected the change. Cf. Clinton Albertson, *Anglo-Saxon Saints and Heroes* (New York, 1967), p. 103.

20. For the Quartodecimans and the second-century Easter controversy see Eusebius, *Ecclesiastical History* V, xxiii–xxv, in J. Stevenson, *The New Eusebius* (London, 1963), pp. 147 ff.. with Stevenson's note pp. 150 ff. Like the Celts, the Quartodecimans claimed the authority of St. John.

21. Blair, *Introduction to Anglo-Saxon England*, p. 130. Many historians have presented, with varying degrees of clarification, their interpretations of the competing Easter cycles and of the documents of the controversy. Kenney supplies useful references (to 1929) and explains the development of the Easter cycles and tables, pp. 210–17. There is a clear account in Nora K. Chadwick's *The Age of the Saints in the Early Celtic Church* (London, 1961), pp. 117–38. For a full treatment see Paul Grosjean, "La controverse pascale chez les Celtes," *Analecta Bollandiana* 64 (1946): 200–243.

22. Kenney, pp. 220–21, arrives at the date 631 by inference from Cummian's reference to a month's difference between the two Easter dates. Cummian's letter is in *MPL* 87:969–78. See also the informing article by J. E. L. Oulton, "The Epistle of Cummian, *De Controversia Paschalis*," *Studia Patristica* (Dublin, 1957), vol. 1, pt. 1, pp. 128–33.

23. Bede III, xxv.

24. Bede, ibid. The *Life of St. Wilfrid*, by Eddius Stephanus, a contemporary, while written in admiration of Wilfrid, is respectful to Colman and the Celts. Like Bede, Eddius features the king's deciding voice in the outcome. He notes that Oswy's question on the relative

authority of Columba and Peter was spoken "with a smile" (*subridens*); it would seem that he had already made up his mind. The text of Eddius is translated with valuable notes by Clinton Anderson in *Anglo-Saxon Saints and Heroes* (New York, 1967), pp. 89–162. See esp. pp. 103 ff. and, in the same work, the anonymous *Life of St. Cuthbert*, pp. 53–54, note 24.

25. Anonymous *Life of St. Cuthbert* IV, xi, tr. Clinton Albertson in *Anglo-Saxon Saints and Heroes*, p. 73.

26. Bede IV, iv. "Mayo of the Saxons" remained a notable monastery until late in the Middle Ages.

27. Meissner, *Celtic Church of England*, pp. 134–81.

28. Wilhelm Levison, *England and the Continent in the Eighth Century* (Oxford, 1946), pp. 54–71. Levison is the editor of the *Vita Willibrordi Archiepiscopi Trajectensis* in *MGH, SRM*, vol. 7 (1920), pp. 81–141.

29. Bede V. x.

30. Bede V, xxii.

31. Aldhelm's *Epistula ad Gerontium* is in P. Jaffé, *Bibliotheca rerum Germanicarum*, vol. 3 (Berlin, 1866), pp. 21–31, and in *MPL* 89:90. An excerpt is found in Haddan and Stubbs 3: 258–59.

32. Nora K. Chadwick, in Myles Dillon and Nora K. Chadwick, *The Celtic Realms* (London, 1967), p. 185.

33. The Letter of Coelfrid on Easter is given in Bede V, xxi. Alexander R. MacEwen holds that Bede here ascribes his own ideas to Coelfrid; see *History of the Church in Scotland* (London, 1915), 1:99.

34. John H. S. Burleigh, *The Church History of Scotland* (London, 1960), pp. 34 f. MacEwen, in *History of the Church in Scotland*, 1:99, implies that Nechtan's declaration was partly ineffective.

35. William A. Cheney has shown the continuity in Christian times of the sacral kingship of the pagan Anglo-Saxons. He examines the complex relationships in law of kings and churchmen. As in the Old Testament, the king was the Anointed of the Lord (*Christus Domini*) but obligated to heed the reminders and warnings of the Church's spokesmen; see *The Cult of Kingship in Anglo-Saxon England* (Berkeley and Los Angeles, 1970), pp. 195–96, 247–59.

Chapter Eight

1. The argument of P. W. Joyce for a pre-Christian use of writing hardly gets beyond Ogham and falls short of proof; see *A Social History of Ireland* (Dublin, 1913), 1:400–407.

2. Texts cited by Benedict Fitzgerald, *Ireland and the Making of Britain* (New York and London, 1922), pp. 53 ff. Cf. Chapter 11, note 2 below. Continental references to learning in Ireland from the sixth to the ninth century are usually couched in superlative terms.

From a distance, at least, Ireland seemed to seekers of learning one dispersed university. Alcuin, writing between 792 and 800 to Irish monks, recognizes a long tradition of Irish scholarly excellence: "In ancient times very learned teachers used to come from Ireland to Britain, Gaul and Italy" (Kenney, p. 535; *MPL* 100:500). Ireland's preeminence in learning was no doubt made possible by its long immunity for invasion as well as the constant activity of its schools. The basis for the study of classical literature in Ireland may have been laid by the coming of scholars in flight from the Continent during the sweep westward of the Germanic tribes in the early fifth century, as Heinrich Zimmer and Kuno Meyer believed. Cf. chapter 4, note 3, above, and Meyer's *Learning in Ireland in the Fifth Century* (Dublin, 1913). W. G. Hanson treats the subject at large in *The Early Monastic Schools of Ireland* (Cambridge, 1927). See also John O'Healy, *Insula Sanctorum et Doctorum: Ireland's Ancient Schools and Scholars*, 3 ed. (Dublin, 1897). George P. Fedotov saw a parallel between the eagerness of Irish and English scholars such as Columban and Bede to acquire Latin classical learning and that of the first generations of Russian Christians to acquire the culture of the Greeks; see *The Russian Religious Mind* (Cambridge, 1946), p. 381. Further treatment of Irish learning will be found in chapter 11, below.

3. Bede I, xxvii.

4. *Adhelmi Opera*, ed. R. Ehwald, *MGH, Auctores Antiquissimi* vol. 15 (Berlin, 1919), pp. 486–87. M. L. W. Laistner seeks to distinguish between Aldhelm's studies under Maildulf and under Hadrian at Canterbury: see *Thought and Learning in Western Europe A. D. 500–900* (New York, 1931), pp. 118 ff.

5. Francis Jenkinson, ed., *Hisperica Famina* (Cambridge, 1908) (on Gildas see the Introduction, pp. xix–xxii); Nora K. Chadwick, ed., *Studies in the Early British Church* (Cambridge, 1932), chapter 8, "Intellectual Contacts between Britain and Gaul in the Fifth Century."

6. *The Quest of Three Abbots* (New York, 1958), pp. 64, 104, 194. The earliest known mention of the Three Holy Kings by name is in the *Kollectaneum Bedae* found in *MPL* 94:539–60. Formerly ascribed to Bede, this miscellany is now attributed to some eighth-century Irish writer (see Kenney, p. 680). The theme of the kings was elaborated, if allegorically, by numerous Irish writers on the Continent. See the illuminating essay "The Three Holy Kings in Early Irish Writing," by Robert E. McNally, in *Kryiakon, Festschrift Johannes Quasten* (Münster, 1970), 2:667.

7. Myles Dillon and Nora K. Chadwick, *The Celtic Realms* (London, 1967), p. 195. A similar opinion has been expressed by many scholars. Cf. chapter 11, note 31 below.

8. Laistner, *Thought and Learning in Western Europe*, p. 125.

9. For the principal monastic scriptoria in Ireland see Kathleen Hughes, "The Distribution of Irish Scriptoria and Centres of Learning from 730 to 1111," in Nora K. Chadwick et al., *Studies in the Early British Church* (Cambridge, 1958), pp. 243–72.

10. On the Cathach and its history see Françoise Henry, *Irish Art in the Early Christian Period* (*to 800 A.D.*) (Ithaca, 1965), 1.58–59; Duncan Maclennan, "The Cathach of Colum Cille," *Gaelic Society of Inverness* 15 (1929): 2–25; and Douglas Chretien, *The Battle Book of the O'Donnells* (Berkeley and Cambridge, 1935), the material of which is largely drawn from the *Life* by Manus O'Donnell referred to in chapter 6, note 14, above.

11. Nora K. Chadwick, in Dillon and Chadwick, *Celtic Realms*, p. 309.

12. Henry, *Irish Art*, p. 173. The Book of Durrow has been handsomely reproduced by the Urs Graf Verlag: *Codex Durmachensis*, 2 vols. (Olten, Lausanne and Freiburg im Br., 1960). Volume 2, *Prolegomena*, contains valuable essays by the editors, Arthur Anton Luce, George Otto Simms, Peter Meyer, and Ludwig Bieler; very helpful in the present context is Meyer's detailed treatment of "The Art of the Book of Durrow," in ibid., 2:101–74. See also Kathleen Hughes, *The Church in Early Irish Society*, (Ithaca, N.Y., 1965), pp. 100–101.

13. In his essay "Handwriting," in G. C. Crump and E. F. Jacobs, eds., *The Legacy of the Middle Ages* (Oxford, 1926), p. 309.

14. Henry, *Irish Art*, 2:68–94. The *Book of Kells* may be consulted in the Urs Graf reproduction, *Evangeliorum quattuor Codex Cenannensis*, 3 vols. (Bern, 1950–51); volume 3 consists of "Preliminary Essays;" Peter Meyer, in "Notes on the Art and Ornament," has a section comparing Irish and Coptic ornament. The resemblances indicate some undocumented intercourse between Egypt and Ireland, "not mediated, it would seem, through Rome or Gaul" (ibid., 3:48–51). A detailed description of the *Book of Kells* is furnished by Sir Edward Sullivan, *The Book of Kells*, 5th ed. (London and New York, 1955).

15. Henry, *Irish Art*, 1:223. *The Codex Lindisfarnensis*, ed. T. D. Kendrick et al. has been reproduced by the Urs Graf Verlag (Olten and Lausanne, 1956). The Latin text has been edited by Joseph Stevenson and George Waring for the Surtees Society, *The Lindisfarne and Rushworth Gospels*, 4 vols. (1854–65).

16. Henry, *Irish Art*, 1:92–158.

17. "The Religious Meaning of the Ruthwell Cross," *Art Bulletin* 26 (1940): 229–45. Schapiro concludes his study with the sentence: "The cross is Anglian and classic in its forms, mainly Celtic in its re-

ligious content." Stuart Cruden, in *The Early Christian and Pictish Monuments of Scotland: . . . Descriptive of the Meigle and St. Vigeans Collections* (Edinburgh, 1964), p. 10, calls it "a pure Northumbrian work." But the terms like "Anglian" and "Northumbrian" may be misleading to those unaware of the primary debt of Northumbrian Christian art to the Irish mission operating from Lindisfarne. Cf. Henry, Irish Art, 1:160.

18. H. A. S. Macalister, *Muiredach, Abbot of Monasterboise, 850–925: His Life and Surroundings* (Dublin, 1914; rpt. 1941).

19. For illustration see Stuart Cruden, *Early Christian and Pictish Monuments*, pp. 18–21 and plates 10, 12, 13, 19.

20. Bede III, 25.

21. The description of the church is in the *Vita Sanctae Brigidae* by Cogitosus, *MLP* 72:788–89.

22. F. E. Warren, *The Liturgy and Ritual of the Celtic Church* (Oxford, 1881), p. 63. This indispensable work should now be supplemented by more recent studies. Among these may be recommended John Henning, "Old Ireland and Her Worship," in Robert E. McNally, *Old Ireland* (New York, 1965), pp. 60–89.

23. George F. Warner, ed., *The Stowe Missal*, 2 vols. (London, 1906, rpt. 1915).

24. John T. McNeill, *The Celtic Penitentials and Their Influence on Continental Christianity* (Paris, 1923), p. 140; "The Celtic Penitential Discipline and the Rise of the Confessional," in idem, *History of the Cure of Souls* (New York, 1951), pp. 112–35; John Ryan, *Irish Monasticism: Origins and Early Development*, (Dublin, 1931; Ithaca, N.Y., 1972), pp. 333–45.

25. Warren, *Liturgy and Ritual*, pp. 42–43, and the treatment of the *Cursus Psalmorum* by J. L. Gough Meissner in Walter Alison Phillips, ed., *A History of the Church of Ireland* (Oxford, 1933), 1:364–68.

26. *Antiphonarium Benchorense*, ed. F. E. Warren, 2 vols. (London, 1893–1895); Warren, *Liturgy and Ritual*, pp. 143–44, 187–94; Fernand Cabrol and Henri Leclercq, *Dictionnaire d'Archéologie chrétienne et de Liturgie* vol. 2, 1, pp. 183–91.

27. Frank O'Connor, *A Short History of Irish Literature* (New York, 1967), pp. 25–28.

28. On early Irish poetry, secular and religious, in Latin and Gaelic, the following titles may be recommended: Kuno Meyer, *Selections from Ancient Irish Poetry* (London, 1911, rpt. 1959); Eleanor Hull, *The Poem-Book of the Gael: Translations from Irish Gaelic Poetry* (London, 1912), esp. pp. 119 ff. and note on p. 354; Robin Flower, *The Irish Tradition* (Oxford, 1947); David Green and Frank O'Connor, eds., *A Golden Treasury of Irish Poetry,* A.D. *600–1200* (London,

1967); Gerald Murphy, *Early Irish Metrics* (Dublin, 1961); Eoin Neesen, *Poems from the Irish* (Cork, 1967). The literature of Welsh bardic poetry and heroic tales that has survived, represented by the collections known as the *Mabinogion* and the *Goddodin*, contains little that in its extant form is earlier than the eleventh century. This does not imply that the celebrated sixth-cenury bards Taleissen and Aneirin never lived. They were probably court poets and composers of heroic verses like those preserved in the later compilations named. See T. Parry, *A History of Welsh Literature*, tr. H. I. Bell (Oxford, 1955); Sir Ifor Williams, *Lectures on Early Welsh Poetry* (Dublin, 1944).

29. O'Curry's *Lectures on the Manuscript Materials* (Dublin, 1872) consisted of lectures delivered in 1856; my reference is to page 254. The work is a rich treasury of Irish lore. On musical instruments see also O'Curry, *Manners and Customs of the Ancient Irish*, ed. W. K. Sullivan (London and Dublin, 1873), pp. clxxxiii–ccxxxvi.

Chapter Nine

1. Jean Delumeau et al., *Histoire de Bretagne* (Paris, 1969), Introduction.

2. Caesar, *Gallic War* III, vii–xvi.

3. The tradtion that a certain third-century St. Clair was the first bishop of Nantes may have led to his being turned into a first-century missionary in a legend somewhat analogous to that of St. Dionysius of Paris; see E. Durtelle de Saint-Sauveur, *Histoire de Bretagne des origines à nos jours* (Rennes, 1935), 1:26.

4. Arthur le Moyne la Borderie, *Histoire de Bretagne*, rev. ed., vol. 1 (Rennes, 1896), pp. 187–94, gives the substance of the martyr legend of Donationus and Rogationus from Theodore Ruinart, *Acta primorum martyrum sincera et selecta* (Paris, 1689), 1:96–97.

5. For the chief incidents and wide range of the Saxon attacks in Armorica see Ferdinand Lot, "Les migrations saxonnes en Gaule et en Grande-Bretagne," *Revue Historique* 119 (1915): 1–40; Nora K. Chadwick, *Early Brittany* (Cardiff, 1969), pp. 124–33.

6. Ferdinand Lot, in *Bibliothèque de l'école des Chartes* 61 (1900): 547–49.

7. Nora K. Chadwick, "The Colonization of Brittany from Celtic Britain," *Proceedings of the British Academy* 51 (1965): 235–99; see esp. pp. 257 ff., with citations of Nennius and Geoffrey of Monmouth.

8. Joseph Loth, *L'Emigration bretonne en Armorique du V*e *au VII*e *siècle de notre ère* (Paris, 1883), p. 93; Haddan and Stubbs, 2, pt. 1, pp. 69 ff.; Ludwig Schmidt, in *Cambridge Medieval History* (Cambridge, 1911), 1:283.

9. Cf. Chadwick, *Early Brittany*, p. 193. It has been alleged that in the fifth century large numbers of Irish from Ossory and Wexford entered western Brittany: Sabine Baring-Gould, *Brittany*, 3d ed. (London, 1921), p. 13.

10. Armand Rébillon, *Histoire de Bretagne* (Paris, 1957), p. 22.

11. Myles Dillon and Nora K. Chadwick, *The Celtic Realms* (London, 1967), p. 89.

12. De la Borderie, *Histoire de Bretagne*, vol. 1.

13. See his severely critical review of De la Borderie's volume 1 in *Revue Historique* 66 (1898): 182–91.

14. René Largillière, *Les saints et l'organisation chrétienne primitive dans l'Armorique Bretonne* (Rennes, 1925).

15. F. Falc'hun, *Histoire de la langue Bretonne* (Rennes, 1951); idem., "Les langues pre-Bretonnes en Armorique," *Mémoires de la Société d'Histoire et d'Archéologie de Bretagne* 43 (1963): 5–17; Kenneth H. Jackson, "The Linguistic Geography of the Breton Language," *Zeitschrift für classische Philologie* 28 (1961): 272–93; Chadwick, *Early Brittany*, pp. 200–205.

16. The above paragraphs on Breton Christian origins reflect the view taken by Largillière, *Les saints et l'organisation chrétienne primitive*; see esp. his pp. 2–40, 197 ff., 207–27. There is some useful documentary material in Haddan and Stubbs 2, pt. 1, pp. 86–96, 139 ff. Chadwick, *Early Brittany*, pp. 272–90, should also be consulted. To the works, above cited, by Loth, Delumeau, and Rebillon should be added Henri Waquet, *Histoire de la Bretagne* (Paris, 1948); see esp. p. 20.

17. Haddan and Stubbs, vol. 2, pt. 1, p. 73.

18. Delumeau, *Histoire de Bretagne*, p. 118.

19. Haddan and Stubbs, vol. 2, pt. 1, p. 73.

20. Meissner, in Walter Alison Phillips, ed., *History of the Church of Ireland* (Oxford, 1934), 1:227–28.

21. Sabine Baring-Gould and John Fisher, *Lives of the British Saints, the Saints of Wales and Cornwall, and Such Irish Saints as Have Dedications in Britain*, 4 vols. (London, 1907–13), 54:120 ff.; Meissner, in Phillips, *History of the Church of Ireland*, pp. 229–30.

22. For Budoc see Baring-Gould and Fisher, *Lives of British Saints*, 1:529–37. Mrs. Chadwick has provided a useful map of the "archipelago;" see *Early Brittany*, facing p. 1.

23. Illustration in Fernand Cabrol and Henri Leclercq, *Dictionnaire d'archéologie Chrétienne et de liturgie*, 11:1261. On St. Mawes see Baring-Gould and Fisher, *Lives of British Saints*, 3:441–49. A map showing no less than seventy-six dedications to St. Mawes (Modez) in Brittany is given by E. G. Bowen in *Britain and the Western Seaways*

(London, 1972), p. 85. The sixteenth-century antiquarian and traveler John Leland made notes on parishes near Pendennis and Falmouth in western Cornwall that had been dedicated to St. Mawes (Mawa or Mausa); see *The Itinerary of John Leland*, ed. Lucy Toulmin Smith (Carbondale, Ill., 1964), 1:200; 322.

24. Albert Le Grand, *Les vies des saintes de la Bretagne Armorique* (1636), ed. A. M. Thomas et al. (Quimper, 1901), pp. 667–79, recites the legend of Tudwall. The election to the papacy will be found on p. 668: "in papam eligitur."

25. *The Life of St. Samson*, one of the few early and relatively reliable lives of Celtic saints, has been translated, with a valuable introduction, by Thomas Taylor, in *The Life of Samson of Dol* (London, 1925). The Latin text, *Vita antiqua Sancti Samsonis Dolensis episcopi*, was edited by Dom François Plaine in *Analecta Bollandiana* 6 (1887): 77–150.

26. *Life of St. Samson* liii–lix; Haddan and Stubbs vol. 2, pt. 1, pp. 75–76; A. W. Wade-Evans, *Welsh Christian Origins* (Oxford, 1934), pp. 228–31. Cf. Le Grand *Les vies des saints*, pp. 314–36.

27. See Nora K. Chadwick, *Early Brittany*, pp. 292–354, and her reference to St. Meen in Dillon and Chadwick, *Celtic Realms*, pp. 87–88. Cf. Le Grand, *Les vies des saintes*, pp. 251–62.

28. The two studies by Robert Latouche, "Les origines d'une province celtique en France (Bretagne) pendant le haut moyen âge" and "L'Abbaye de Landévennec et la Carnouaille," in his *Études Médiévales* (Paris, 1966), pp. 91–114, are of value here. Professor Latouche derived from his early studies under Ferdinand Lot the view that the *Life of Guénolé* "belongs to the realm of fable" and is unusable for history. In the second of these studies he examines the circumstances of the ninth century in which it was written and the motivation of its author, Gourdisten.

29. Haddan and Stubbs (Vol. 2, pt. 1, p. 79) regard it as the Rule of St. Columban, but this is not proved.

30. Haddan and Stubbs, vol. 2, pt. 1, p. 74.

31. Haddan and Stubbs, vol. 2, pt. 1, p. 87.

32. Haddan and Stubbs, vol. 2, pt. 1, p. 75.

33. *History of the Franks* V, xvii, and esp. X, xxiii.

34. Document in Haddan and Stubbs, vol. 2, pt. 1, p. 79.

35. *Biographie Universelle*, s.v. "Judicael."

36. Haddan and Stubbs, vol. 2, pt. 1, pp. 91–96.

37. Rébillon, *Histoire de Bretagne*, pp. 30–33.

38. *Biographie Universelle*, s.v. "Erispoé" and "Salomon."

39. For some details consult Thomas Taylor, *The Celtic Christianity of Cornwall* (London and New York, 1918).

40. Haddan and Stubbs, vol. 2, pt. 1, pp. 99–101; Pierre David, *Etudes historiques sur la Gallice et le Portugal* (Lisbon and Paris, 1947), pp. 57–69; Chadwick, *Early Brittany*, pp. 267–68; E. A. Thompson, "Britona," in M. W. Barley and R. P. C. Hanson, eds., *Christianity in Britain 300–700* (Leicester, 1968), pp. 201–5. J. N. Hilgarth's essay, "Old Ireland and Visigothic Spain" in Robert McNally, ed., *Old Ireland* (New York, 1965), pp. 200–227, has references to "Britona" and some material on ancient Gallicia. Two centuries ago the see of Britona (Britonia) was treated at some length by Henrique Florez in *España Sagrada*, 51 vols. (Madrid, 1754–1789), 18: (1764): 1–21.

41. Orosius, *Seven Books of History against the Pagans* I, 2, tr. Irwin Woodworth Raymond, Records of Civilization, vol. 26 (New York, 1936), p. 42. J. H. Todd, in *The Irish Version of Nennius* (Dublin, 1948), pp. 238 ff., attempted an interpretation of this passage.

Chapter Ten

1. Cf. Helen Waddell, *The Wandering Scholars* (London, 1907). Eleanor Shipley Duckett, in *The Wandering Saints* (London, 1927), admirably describes numerous personalities of firm stability. On the word "peregrinus" as applied in this chapter, see Joseph P. Fuhrmann, *Irish Medieval Monasteries on the Continent* (Washington, D.C., 1927), pp. 2 ff. Walter Delius, *Geschichte der irischen Kirche* (Munich and Basel, 1954), pp. 100–124.

2. *Sancti Columbani Opera*, ed. and tr. G. S. M. Walker (Dublin, 1957), p. 28. We may recall here the saying attributed to St. Samson: "Ah, to win souls I am ready for anything" (A. W. Wade-Evans, *Welsh Christian Origins* [Oxford, 1934], p. 217).

3. The *Vita Sancti Columbani* by Jonas was edited by Bruno Krusch *MGH,SRM* 4 (1902: 1–52. It was translated from the Migne edition (*MPL* 87:1011–84) by Dana C. Munro, Pennsylvania Translations and Reprints II,7 (Philadelphia, 1899). Jonas was born at Susa in Piedmont. He spent some of his later years as a missionary in the Netherlands and was last heard of in 665; see George Metlake (pseudonym for J. J. Laux), *The Life and Writings of St. Columban, 542?–615* (Philadelphia, 1914), pp. 15 ff.

4. A commentary on the Psalms by Columban was listed in early catalogues of St. Gall and Bobbio libraries, but it is not extant. Attempts to identify it with a work commonly attributed to Theodore of Mopsuestia have been unsuccessful. See Walker, *Sancti Columbani Opera*, pp. lxiv–lxv; R. I. Best, ed., *Commentary on the Pslams with Glosses in Old Irish, preserved in the Ambrosian Library* (Ms C 301

inf.), Facsimile with Introduction (Dublin and London, 1936); and Robert Deveresse, *La Commentaire de Théodore de Mopsueste sur les Psaumes* (Vatican City, 1939), pp. xx–xxviii.

5. *History of the Franks* VII, vii, xii, xiii, xxiv.

6. The letter to Gregory occupies pp. 2–13 in Walker edition of *Sancti Columbani Opera.*

7. Walker, *Sancti Columbani Opera*, pp. 13–22.

8. John Colgan, *Acta Sanctorum veteris et maioris Scotiae seu Hiberniae, sanctorum insulae* (Louvain, 1645), has a *Life of Deicola*, pp. 115–177. It was written about 965 by a monk of Lure.

9. The letter to the Monks of Luxeuil is in Walker, *Sancti Columbani Opera*, pp. 26–36.

10. Walahfrid Strabo, *Vita Sancti Galli* I, ix, in *MPL* 114:985; and in B. Krusch's edition, *MGH, SRM* 4:291. The words ascribed to Columban are: *"Ne me vivente in corpore missam celebrare presumas."* Fritz Blanke accepts this incident as historical; see *Columban und Gallus, Urgeschichte des schweitzerischen Christentums* (Zurich, 1946), pp. 100, 161. The *Vita Sancti Columbani* by Wettin, ca. 820, reports that Columban's harsh injunction was uttered as a pleasantry, and Ludwig Hertling says that the words were spoken *"cum hilaritate animae"* (*Irish Monks of the Golden Age*, ed. John Ryan [Dublin, 1963], p. 96). But we may well question whether Columban's sense of humor extended to so grave a matter. Cf. Georges and Bernadette Cerbelaud Salagnac, *Irlande, Ile des Saints* (Paris, 1961), p. 136. In the Ryan volume, Marguerite-Marie Dubois, observing Columban's ardor in seeking the peace of the Church, sees him in the light of "a zealous apostle of the ecumenical movement." She notes that Pope John XXIII honored the saint on a visit to Bobbio in 1950, and that a Columban chapel has been placed in the crypt of St. Peter's (Ryan, *Irish Monks*, pp. 58–59).

11. Walker, *Sancti Columbani Opera*, p. 57.

12. Walker, ibid., pp. 40–41.

13. *MHP*, pp. 86–97 (Finnian) and 249–56 (Columban); Jean Laporte, *Le Pénitential de Saint Columban* (Tournai, 1956).

14. *MHP*, p. 265, and Introduction, p. 44. Numerous other instances of the application of this principle in the Penitentials may be readily found from the index of this book under "Contraries, medical principle of."

15. This translation is based on the explanation by Raban Maur, "Plaga est percussio dura" (*MPL* 112:1019). Cf. *MHP*, p. 265, note 46. G. S. M. Walker has reversed this in his translation of the Rule of Columban. The *Regula coenobialis* is in Walker, *Sancti Columbani Opera*, pp. 128–43.

16. Walker conservatively numbers the abbeys, nunneries, and hermitages originating from Columban's work during the seventh century as "no less that fifty-three" *Sancti Columbani Opera*, p. xxxiii. Most earlier estimates are much higher. Margaret Stokes, in *Three Months in the Forests of France in Search of Vestiges of Irish Saints* (London, 1895), p. 79, lists sixty-three founders who were Columban's disciples and holds the total of daughter institutions to have been 105. The weight of Columban's influence can be further measured by the list of twenty-one canonized saints drawn from his monastic followers during twenty years. These are listed (from Montalembert) by Oscar D. Watkins, who gives also the oft-quoted tribute by Adso of Montier-en-Der, ca. 968: "And now what place, what city, does not rejoice in having for its ruler a bishop or an abbot trained in the discipline of that holy man [Columban]? For it is certain that by virtue of his authority, almost the whole land of the Franks has been for the first time properly furnished with regular institutions" (*A History of Penance*, 2 vols. [London, 1920], 2:626).

17. Walker, *Sancti Columbani Opera*, p. xliii. Henry Davignon has shown the predominance of Columban's influence in monasteries founded in Belgium following his mission in Burgundy: see "The Irish in Belgium," in Daneil-Rops, ed., *The Miracle of Ireland*, tr. Earl of Wicklow (Dublin, 1959), pp. 92–95.

18. In Walker's text the *Carmina* occupy pp. 182–97. Ludwig Bieler finds in them evidence of Columban's extensive reading of ancient poetry; see *"Versus Sancti Columbani," Irish Ecclesiastical Record*, 5th ser. 76 (1951): 376–82. Bieler is, however, somewhat critical of Columban's Latin style in his study "The Humanism of St. Columban," contributed to the twelfth centennial memorial volume, *Mélanges Colombaniens* (Paris, 1950), pp. 95–102. The high probability of Columban's authorship of the *Carmina* is strongly argued by Walker, but one critic, Johannes Wilhelmus Smit, has learnedly assailed his arguments; *Studies in the Language and Style of Columba the Younger* (Amsterdam, 1971). Smit disparages Columban's scholarship, while denying his authorship of the poems, and holds a rather low view of Irish learning. Whether this argumentative dissertation will convince the experts remains to be seen. At present it seems best to follow the favorable estimate of Columban's scholarship arrived at by Walker and others. Walker credits him with being "well read in Horace," able to "quote Vergil readily," and familiar also with Ovid, Juvenal, Martial, and Sallust" as well as with numerous poets of Christian times. He had a mastery of "a wide tract of classical mythology," and in his mind "classical Latin joined forces with the Gospel." *Sancti Columbani Opera*, pp. lxvi–lxvii.

19. Walahfrid, *Vita Sancti Galli*, I, ix–xi. Walahfrid's *Life*, written about 833, as edited by Jean Mabillon, is in *MPL* 114:975–1030; the critical edition by Bruno Krusch is in *MGH, SRM* 4 (1902): 280–337. Walahfrid used two earlier and quite inferior *vitae*, one of which was by his teacher Wettinus. The work has been translated with a historical introduction by Maud Joynt, *The Life of St. Gall* (London, 1927). The passage cited offers a revealing instance of a peregrinus finding a location for his life work. Walahfrid (I, x) gives the legendary incident of the obedient bear that carried a log and laid it on St. Gall's fire. Cf. Blanke, *Columban und Gallus*, p. 195.

20. Walahfrid *Vita Sancti Galli*, I, xii.

21. For the Sermon here outlined see *Thesaurus Monumentorum Ecclesiasticorum, sive Henrici Canisii Lectiones Antiquae*, ed. Jacobus Basnage, vol. 1 (Amsterdam, 1725), pp. 785–92.

22. Kenney, pp. 501 ff.; *Vita et miracula S. Fursei*, in W. W. Heist, *Vitae Sanctorum Hiberniae ex codice olim Salmanticensi nunc Bruxellensi* (Brussels, 1965), pp. 37–50; "St. Fursa and the Peregrini minores," in Louis Gougaud, *Gaelic Pioneers of Christianity*, tr. Victor Collins (Dublin 1925), pp. 17–23. Bede used one of the early Latin *lives* of Fursa. An Irish *Life* was edited and translated by Whitley Stokes, *Revue Celtique* 25 (1904): 385–404.

23. Ludwig Traube, *Perrona Scottorum: Ein Beitrag zur Ueberlieferungsgeschichte und zur Palaeographie des Mittelalters* [in *Sitzungsberichte*, Munich Academy] (Munich, 1900); Kathleen Hughes, *The Church in Early Irish Society* (Ithaca, 1966), pp. 92 ff. Margaret Stokes in *Three Months in the Forest of France*, vividly records, with historical interpretation, visits made to the sites of monasteries of Columban, Fursa, Foillan, and Ultan.

24. Louis Grougaud, *Christianity in Celtic Lands*, tr. Maud Joynt (London, 1932), p. 153; Wilhelm Levison, *England and the Continent in the Eighth Century* (Oxford, 1946), pp. 49–51; Kenney, pp. 496–97. It is supposed that Dagobert spent his boyhood in the monastery of Slane, Cavan County; see John O'Healey, *Insula Sanctorum et Doctorum: Ireland's Ancient Schools and Scholars*, 3d ed. (Dublin, 1897), pp. 489–90.

25. Gougaud, *Christianity in Celtic Lands*, pp. 128–31. A short contemporary account of the death and burial of Foillan is edited by Bruno Krusch in *MGH, SRM* 4 (1902): 449–51.

26. On Bathild see Levison, *England and the Continent*, pp. 9–10, and Eleanor Duckett, *The Wandering Saints* (London, 1959), pp. 146 ff. St. Eligius, a zealous promoter of monasticism, was St. Bathild's counsellor in her benefactions. The charter of his foundation of Solignac is

quoted by Oscar D. Watkins in his *History of Penance* (London, 1920), 2:527–28, from *MGH, SRM* 4 (1902): 747. It strangely acknowledges jointly the Rule of Benedict with that of Columban and solemnly enjoins Rimalcus, the appointed abbot, to submit himself and his house to correction by the abbot of Luxeuil. Eligius had in early life been a skilled goldsmith, and some of his reliquaries may have been among those works of church art preserved from that era. He was probably of Celtic extraction. For editions of his *Life* written by St. Ouen of Rouen, see Kenney's note, pp. 293–94.

27. Fuhrmann, *Irish Medieval Monasteries on the Continent* (Washington, D.C., 1927), pp. 34–52.

28. Kenney, pp. 512–13; John O'Hanlon, *Lives of the Irish Saints*, 10 vols. (Dublin, 1875–1905), 8:432. The *Passio prima Sancti Kiliani* was edited by Wilhelm Levison, *MGH, SRM* 5 (1910): 711–28. Cf. Aubrey Gwynn, "New Light on St. Kilian," *Irish Ecclesiastical Record* 82 (1957): 1–16.

29. The pledge of Boniface to Gregory II, in 723, with its clause "if I can hinder them I will hinder them," implied an undertaking to suppress all Celtic or other nonconformists. He had to confront a still vigorous paganism in some areas, and he felt strongly the need of obedience and unity of command in the Church. It does not appear that in his dealings with the rulers he advocated prosecuting policies other than repudiation and excommunication toward the recalcitrant Celts. Delius *Geschichte der irischen Kirche*, p. 134, holds that Boniface was not in direct opposition to Irish Christianity.

30. Council of Mainz (813), canon 22; J. D. Mansi et al *Sacrorum Conciliorum nova et amplissima collectio*, 31 vols. (Florence and Venice, 1759–1798), 14:71. On the *episcopi vagantes* see the survey of the use of this term from the fourth to the nineteenth century by A. J. Macdonald, "*Episcopi vagantes* in Church History," *Church Quarterly Review* 127 (1940): 246–57. Apropos here are his pp. 234–39. Macdonald thinks some of the Irish wandering bishops tried to form small independent dioceses. He recites numerous synodical acts directed against them.

31. Philip Schaff, *History of the Christian Church*, vol. 4 (New York, 1910), p. 98.

32. Anselmo M. Tommasini, *Irish Saints in Italy*, tr. J. F. Scanlan (London, 1937), pp. 360–77.

33. Josef Cibulka, *Velkomoravsky Kostel u Modré u Velehradu a zacátky Krestanstvi na Morav* (Prague, 1958), has (facing p. 296) a full-page photographic illustration of the excavated base of the Modrá church. A German summary of the text occupies pp. 297–343. The work

by Zdenek Dittrich, *Christianity in Greater Moravia* (Gronigen, 1962), supplies essential information in English; see esp. pp. 3, 41–43, 52.

34. The Sunniva legend bears some resemblance to that of St. Ursula and her maidens in that Ursula, a British girl, and her company are also fleeing from suitors; but the outcome is different in that Sunniva is slain not by barbarians but by a convulsion of nature. The fact of Olaf Tryvason's church-building soon after the alleged even points to some historic reality behind the story. See Alban Butler, *Lives of the Saints*, ed. Herbert Thurston and Donald Atwater (London, 1956), 3:42–43. The story of St. Sunniva has been charmingly told by Sigrid Undset in *Saga of Saints*, tr. E. C. Ramsden (London, 1934; rpt. 1968), "St. Sunniva and the Selje-men," pp. 68–86.

35. James Westfall Thompson and Edgar Nathaniel Johnson, *An Introduction to Medieval Europe, 300–1500* (New York, 1937), p. 216.

Chapter Eleven

1. Heinrich Zimmer, *The Irish Element in Medieval Culture*, tr. Jane Loring Edmands (London, 1891); cf. ch. 8, note 2, above. Benedict Fitzpatrick, *Ireland and the Making of Britain* (New York and London, 1952), supplies numerous references, pp. 52–61. See also Nora K. Chadwick, *The Age of the Saints* (London, 1961), pp. 112–13.

2. *Ireland, Harbinger of the Middle Ages* (London and New York, 1963), p. 104. On Vergil see Francis S. Betten, *St. Boniface and St. Virgil: A Study from Original Sources of Two Supposed Conflicts* (Washington, 1927); Paul Grosjean, "Virgil of Salzburg," in John Ryan, ed., *Irish Monks that Moved the World* (Dublin, 1963), pp. 73–85.

3. Walahfrid's *Vita Sancti Galli* II, xvii, in *MGH, SRM* 4:236, and *MPL* 114:1029. In Maud Joynt's translation, *The Life of St. Gall* (London, 1927), p. 151.

4. Heiric's *Vita Sancti Germani*, in *MPL* 124:1131–1208, esp. 1133. See note in Kenney, p. 593. Dungal's letters are in *MPL* 105:447–58. In letter 4, asking for a horse to visit Charlemagne, he admits: "We poor pilgrims, it may well be, appear a disagreeable burden to you because of our numbers and our noisy importunity" (Kenney, p. 540). See also Benedict Fitzpatrick, *Ireland and the Foundations of Europe* (New York and London, 1927), pp. 166 ff.; and Louis Gougaud, *Gaelic Pioneers of Christianity*, tr. Victor Collins (New York, 1923), p. 75.

5. Andrew Fleming West, *Alcuin and the Rise of the Christian Schools* (New York, 1912), pp. 5–27; William Harris Stahl, with contributions from B. Johnson and E. L. Borge, *Martianus Capella and*

the Seven Liberal Arts, vol. 1, Records of Civilization, no. 84 (New York and London, 1971). In this connection see esp. pp. 202–224, on Harmony.

6. Joseph P. Fuhrmann, *Irish Medieval Monasteries on the Continent* (Washington, 1927), pp. 54–65, supplies information on numerous hospices.

7. *Vita Caroli Magni* [ed. G. Pertz] in xxi, *MGH, SRM* 2:459. This work was republished by G. Waitz (Hanover, 1880), and is translated by A. J. Grant, *Early Lives of Charlemagne* (London, 1907; rpt. 1922); see pp. 27–28. See also Kenney's reference, p. 536, to Theodulph of Orleans, who in verse satirizes "Scotellus," an Irishman of the court circle. (Theodulph [d. 821] is well known as an earnest churchman and reforming bishop; he also played an interesting role as court scholar and poet.)

8. The question whether the Colchu addressed by Alcuin was the distinguished abbot of Clonmacnois in the role of visiting professor at York is raised incidentally by Kenney, p. 534. The date would make this possible. But the name is of rather frequent occurrence. For Colchu see also Eleanor Shipley Duckett, *Alcuin, Friend of Charlemagne: His World and Work* (New York, 1956), pp. 29, 130, 134, 160. Miss Duckett thinks Alcuin may have been "a little appalled" by the Irish "Egyptianizers" (admirers of secular literature) (ibid., pp. 288–89).

9. Joseph may have been a nephew of Colchu. Two letters to him from Alcuin are extant (Kenney, pp. 534, 536).

10. Kenney (p. 533) rejects as "pure fiction" the anecdote of the merchants of wisdom; for Clement, see Kenney, pp. 537–38.

11. Anselmo M. Tommasini, *Irish Saints in Italy*, tr. J. F. Scanlan (London, 1937), pp. 120–24; Louis Gougaud, *Gaelic Pioneers*, p. 82.

12. James J. Tierney, ed., *Dicuili liber de mensura orbis terrae* [with contributions by Ludwig Bieler] (Dublin, 1967). This excellent edition contains an adequate introduction, text and translation, and extensive historical notes. Bieler had earlier contributed "The Text Tradition of Dicuil's Liber de mensura," *Proceedings of the Royal Irish Academy* 64, sec. C (1960): 1–29. Dicuil is inclined to be incredulous of his authorities, such as Caius Julius Solinus whose *Polyhistor* he has frequently consulted, where seemingly improbabilities are presented. In quoting Pliny, where he finds unacceptable estimates of distance, he leaves a blank space for his readers to fill in more accurately. See esp. Tierney's edition, pp. 28–29, 43 ff., 62–63, 72 ff., 82–83, 112. Dicuil's earlier writings included his Computus, a treatise on astronomy presented to Louis the Pious in 819.

13. From Carney's essay, "Sedulius Scottus," in Robert McNally, ed., *Old Ireland* (New York, 1965), p. 229.

14. *Thought and Letters in Western Europe, 500–900* (New York, 1931), p. 278. In this work Laistner gives considerable attention to Sedulius and his associates, pp. 201–94. Fitzpatrick, *Ireland and the Foundations of Europe*, pp. 229–56 presents a lively account of Sedulius. The poems are edited by Ludwig Traube in *Poetae Latini Aevi Carolini*, in *MGH* 3 (1886): 151–237. See also Kenney's references, pp. 553–62. Later studies include that by Nora K. Chadwick, *Studies in the Early British Church* (Cambridge, 1938), pp. 83–118.

15. The *Liber de rectoribus Christianis* has been edited by S. Hellman (Munich, 1906; rpt. 1920). It is briefly reviewed by Laistner, *Thought and Letters*, pp. 261–64, and by J. T. McNeill in *Christian Hope for World Society* (Chicago, 1937), pp. 33–37.

16. On the editions and literary style of the *Twelve Abuses* see Kenney, pp. 281–82.

17. Tommasini, *Irish Saints*, pp. 383–94; Kenney, pp. 601–2.

18. For the career and writings of John Scotus Eriugena see Kenney, pp. 569–89, and especially the research article by C. Sheldon Williams, "A Bibliography of the Works of John Eriugena," *Journal of European History* 10 (1959): 198–224. Henry Betts, *Johannes Scotus Eriugena*, (Cambridge, 1925), serves as a general introduction; Maieul Cappuyns, *Jean Scot Érigène* (London and Paris, 1933), is a searching monograph. There are valuable notices in William of Malmesbury, *Gesta pontificum Anglorum*, vol. 5; this work was edited by N. E. S. A. Hamilton (London, 1870), for the Rolls series. The comment by Anastasius, the papal librarian, is in *MPL* 127:739.

19. Richard McKeon included selections from the *De Divisione Naturae* in his *Selections from Medieval Philosphers* (London, 1928), pp. 106–24. A new stage has been reached in the editing of Eriugena in *Johannis Scotti Erivgenae Periphyseon* (*De divisione naturae*) *Liber Primus*, Scriptores Latini Hiberniae VII, by J. S. Sheldon-Williams [with the collaboration of Ludwig Bieler] (Dublin, 1968).

20. Kenney, p. 591.

21. Kenney, pp. 596–97, quoting Ekkehard IV in the *Chronicle of St. Gall*; G. G. Coulton, *Life in the Middle Ages* (Cambridge and New York, 1931), 4:50–56; Donald J. Grout, *A History of Western Music* (New York, 1960), pp. 47–50; Percy Jones, "A Survey of the Music of Ireland," *Irish Ecclesiastical Record*, 5th ser. 87 (1957): 170–78; Heinrich Zimmer, *The Irish Element in Medieval Culture*, tr. Jane Loring Edmands (London, 1891), pp. 75 ff.; Maud Joynt, *The Life of St. Gall*, Introduction, pp. 12–45. Cf. chap. 8, note 28, above. On church organs destroyed in Ireland by the Danes, see *Annals of Ulster, anno* 814.

22. Kenney, p. 596.

23. Kenney, pp. 616 ff. A *Life of Marianus*, written a century after his death, is in the Bollandist *Acta Sanctorum* 2:361–72.

24. Kenney, pp. 614 ff. The *Chronicle* is published in full in *MPL* 97:623–746; the useful third part is in *MGH, Scriptore rerum Germanicarum* 5 (Hanover, 1884): 481–564.

25. Kenney, p. 614; Charles Henry Robinson, *The Conversion of Europe* (London, 1917), p. 394. The account is taken from Adam of Bremen, *Gesta Hamburgensis ecclesiae pontificum*, in *MGH* 7 (1845): 267–389, and *MPL* 146:451–619, esp. pp. 574, 593–96; the death of John of Ireland is in chap. 166.

26. On the Schottenklöster see Joseph P. Fuhrmann, *Irish Medieval Monasteries*, pp. 73–104; see also below, pp. 190, 221, and notes 52 and 53 of chapter 12. The sequence and dates of these foundations are given with variations in different authors.

27. Kenney, p. 619–20.

28. On the foundation of the Congregation of Schottenklöster, see Fuhrmann, *Irish Medieval Monasteries*, pp. 102 ff. Cf. p. 221 below.

29. Aubrey Gwynn, "The Old Irish Missal in Corpus Christi College, Oxford," in C. W. Dugmore and Charles Duggan, eds., *Studies in Church History*, vol. 1 (London, 1964), p. 65, quoting a panegyric on Brian written in Old Irish: "He sent professors and masters . . . to buy books beyond the sea and the great ocean" in order to replace those "burned in every church" and "thrown into the water by the plunderers." Happily countless Irish scribes on the Continent had meanwhile been industriously at work. Blanche Boyer, in her detailed study "The Insular Contribution to the Medieval Latin Literary Tradition on the Continent" (*Classical Philology* 42 [1947]: 209–20, and 43 [1948]: 31–39), shows the wide prevalence and even predominance of Irish or Irish-influenced manuscripts of the eighth, ninth, and tenth centuries. See also Ludwig Bieler, "Irish Manuscripts in Medieval Germania," *IER* 87 (1957): 161–69.

30. Kenney, pp. 85–90.

31. *MGH, Epistulae* 5 (1899): 575. Ludwig Traube's remark, many times quoted or paraphased, that whoever knew Greek on the Continent in Charles the Bald's time was an Irishman or had been taught by an Irishman, may seem an overstatement, but it is the judgment of an expert: *O Roma Nobilis*! (Munich, 1891), p. 354. Cf. Wilhelm Levison, "Die Iren und die Frankische Kirche," *Historische Zeitschrift* 109 (1912): 21. Mario Esposito in "The Knowledge of Greek in Ireland during the Middle Ages," *Studies* 1 (1912): 665–83, held that the Irish who knew Greek learned it on the Continent. See Gougaud's balanced treatment of the topic in his *Gaelic Pioneers*, pp. 55–67; Robert McNally, "Old Ireland, Her Scribes and Her Scholars,"

in his Old Ireland (New York, 1965), pp. 139–40. Certainly in the days of Eriugena the teaching of Greek in northern Europe was virtually an Irish monopoly. Gougaud himself remarks: "Thanks to the Scotti, it became the fashion to talk Greek at Laon" *Gaelic Pioneers*, (p. 51). It was the judgment of Arthur West Haddan that the Irish scholars were "the leading preservers of theological and classical culture, Greek as well as Latin" (*Remains of the Late Rev. Arthur West Haddan*, ed. A. P. Forbes [Oxford and London, 1876], p. 258).

Chapter Twelve

1. Bede IV, xvii: *"praesedente Theodoro gratia Dei archiepiscopo Brittaniae insulae."*

2. Bede IV, ii.

3. Theodore, *Penitential* ix, 1–3, tr. in *MHP*, p. 206–7. The document is in Haddan and Stubbs 3:173–204.

4. Christopher Brooke, "St. Peter of Gloucester and St. Cadoc of Llancarfan," in *Celt and Saxon*, ed. Nora K. Chadwick (Cambridge, 1963), pp. 258–322.

5. Brooke, "St. Peter of Gloucester and St. Cadoc of Llancarfan," p. 313.

6. Haddan and Stubbs 2:204.

7. A. W. Wade-Evans, *Welsh Christian Origins* (Oxford, 1934), pp. 285 ff.

8. Bede V, xxii, xxiii.

9. Bede V, xviii.

10. Haddan and Stubbs 2:204–5.

11. Chadwick, *Celt and Saxon*, Chapter 10, "The Celtic Background of Early Anglo-Saxon England," pp. 335–52.

12. Asser, *The Life of Alfred*, tr. L. C. Jane (London, 1904), pp. 59 ff. The Latin text was edited with an ample introduction by W. H. Stevenson in *Asser's Life of Alfred* (Oxford, 1904); reprinted with a chapter on recent studies by Dorothy Whitelock, 1959. In Eleanor Duckett's monograph, *Alfred and His England* (Chicago, 1956), Asser's association with the king is described, pp. 108–13.

13. For the Leofric Missal, Frederick E. Warren's edition has not been replaced: *The Leofric Missal as used in the Cathedral of Exeter* (Exeter, 1883).

14. Stephen J. Williams and J. Enoch Powell have edited Howel's Laws under the title *Llyfr Blegywryd* (Cardiff, 1942), and the work has been retranslated by Melville Richards, *The Laws of Hywel Dda: The Book of Blegywyrd* (Liverpool, 1954). An older text with translation is in Hadden and Stubbs 1:211–83, based on Aneurin Owen, *Ancient Laws and Institutes of Wales*, Records Series (London, 1841).

Cf. MHP, pp. 382–83. A useful study is that by T. G. Jones, "Social Life as Reflected in the Laws of Hywel Dda," *Aberystwith Studies* 10 (1922). These laws reflect some use of the *Canones Wallici*, a document of the sixth or seventh century (MHP, p. 372–82). See Ludwig Bieler, "Toward an Interpretation of the So-Called *Canones Wallici*," in *Medieval Studies Presented to Aubrey Gwynn, S. J.*, ed. J. A. Watt et al. (Dublin, 1961), pp. 387–93. Bieler argues for a "legal syncretism" in the compiling of this document, with a strong Frankish element mediated through Brittany.

15. Haddan and Stubbs 2, pt. 2, pp. 287–88; A. Hamilton Thompson, "The Welsh Medieval Dioceses," *Journal of the Historical Society of the Church of Wales* 1 (1947): 97–111.

16. Haddan and Stubbs 2, pt. 2, p. 303.

17. Kenneth Hurlstone Jackson, "The Sources for the Life of St. Kentigern," in *Studies in the Early British Church*, ed. Nora K. Chadwick (Cambridge, 1958), pp. 273–357.

18. On the struggle over the primacy of Canterbury in Wales, see M. Richter, "Canterbury's Primacy in Wales and the First Stage of Bishop Bernard's Opposition," *Journal of Ecclesiastical History* 22 (1971): 177–87. For Giraldus' part in this controversy the chief records are in his own writings. The *Giraldi Cambrensis Opera* were edited in the Rolls Series by J. S. Brewer, J. H. Dimock, and G. F. Warren, 8 vols. (London, 1861–91). The parts pertaining to the conflict with Canterbury are translated by H. E. Butler, *The Autobiography of Giraldus Cambrensis*, with an Introduction by C. H. Williams (London, 1937), where the *De rebus a se gestis* occupies pp. 33–169. In his tangled story of ecclesiastical intrigue, *De jure et statu Menevensis ecclesiae*, Giraldus complains that the last three bishops of St. David's have been unjustly subjected to Canterbury (Butler, *Autobiography of Giraldus Cambrensis*, p. 255). See also Glanmor Williams, *The Welsh Church from Conquest to Reformation* (Cardiff, 1962), pp. 5–17. Giraldus prides himself on his fairness in criticizing Welsh and Norman wrongdoers equally: "I am sprung of the princes of Wales and of the barons of the Marche, and when I see injustice in either race, I hate it." Quoted by Thomas Jones in "The Wales of Gerald," in *Wales through the Ages*, ed. A. J. Roderich (Aberystwith, 1959), p. 105. Jones's valuable study occupies pp. 105–12 of this book. Nora K. Chadwick, in her study "The Intellectual Life in South Wales in the Last Days of the Celtic Church," in *Studies in the Early British Church* (Cambridge, 1938), pp. 121–82, takes a close look at the sources for the eleventh-century history of Llanbadarn and St. David's and interprets the roles played by Sulien, Rhygyvarch, and other leaders of that era. Cf. chapter 5 in this volume.

19. Rhys W. Hays, "The Welsh Cistercians: Recent Research and Future Prospects," *Studies in Medieval Culture* 3 (1970): 70–79. The thirteen abbeys are listed on p. 70. Other relevant studies by Professor Hays include *The History of the Abbey of Aberconway* (Cardiff, 1963) and "Welsh Students at Oxford and Cambridge Universities in the Middle Ages," *The Welsh History Review* 4 (1969): 325–61. The attitude of young Welsh churchmen to the English universities is reflected by the fact that of approximately 390 Welshmen at Oxford before 1500, Hays finds only about 130 before 1400 ("Welsh Students," pp. 326–27, 355–61. Of 38 students from Wales at Cambridge only 5 were earlier than 1400. It is clear that even after the ecclesiastical coalescence was completed, Welsh national spirit remained strong. It was not the monks who attended English universities, but a small number of secular clergy. "The Welsh Cistercians slighted the English universities for nationalistic reasons, as the Welsh secular clergy did not" (Hays, "Welsh Cistercians", p. 73).

20. For an evaluation of Llewelyn's church policy, see Glanmor Williams, *Welsh Church*, pp. 5–12. Cf. L. F. Salzmann, *Edward I* (London, 1968), chapter 4, "Welsh Affairs," pp. 65–77.

21. For Peckham in Wales, see Haddan and Stubbs 1:542–66. Glanmor Williams calls him "a just and considerate arbiter" (*Welsh Church*, p. 36; cf. p. 42, on Peckham's confrontation with Bek). Haddan and Stubbs 1:542–66; Decima Douie, *Archbishop Pecham* (Oxford, 1952), pp. 235–71, esp. 258 ff., 266.

22. Alexander R. MacEwen, *A History of the Church of Scotland*, 2d ed. (London and New York, 1915), pp. 113–14: "In religion as in politics Kenneth was distinctly a founder," since he laid the foundation of "Ecclesia Scoticana" in establishing the bishopric of Dunkeld. There is some account of the early as well as the late medieval history of the see of Dunkeld in Alexander Mylne's *Lives of the Bishops of Dunkeld*, which may be consulted in *Rentale Dunkeldense: Being Accounts of the Bishopric* (A.D. *1505–1517*) *with Mylne's Lives of the Bishops* (A.D. *1483–1517*), tr. and ed. Robert Hannay, Publications of the Scottish Historical Society, vol. 10 (Edinburgh, 1915).

23. J. H. S. Burleigh, *A Church History of Scotland* (London, 1960), pp. 32–34.

24. See Dorothy Whitelock, ed., *The Anglo-Saxon Chronicle* (London, 1961), p. 36, for a slightly different translation.

25. Cf. Richard Perry, *A Naturalist on Lindisfarne* (London, 1946), pp. 20–21.

26. A useful short book, *Iona: A History of the Island*, by F. Marian McNeill 5th ed. (London and Glasglow, 1959), presents the story of Iona through the centuries, with brief notices of the antiquities and topography of the island. For Donald Munro's visit, see p. 50.

27. *The Book of Deer*, edited for the Spalding Club by John Stuart (Edinburgh, 1969). For the legend of Drostan, see the Introduction, pp. iv ff., and text, pp. 91 ff.

28. W. F. Skene, *Celtic Scotland: A History of Ancient Alban* (Edinburgh, 1887), 2:324. Skene's translation here has been questioned, and his theory of Culdee origins in Scotland is held unacceptable by MacEwen (*History of the Church of Scotland*, pp. 131 ff.), who thinks the Scottish Culdees belong within the main development of Christianity in Scotland.

29. "Culdee, then, was a popular name for the monastic clergy, who were the only ministers of the Ecclesia Scoticana" (MacEwen, *History of the Church of Scotland*, p. 128). Burleigh, *Church History of Scotland*, p. 79, notes certain collegiate churches that apparently stemmed from Culdee organizations.

30. MacEwen, *History of the Church of Scotland*, 1:155–60; Lucy Menzies, St. Margaret, *Queen of Scotland* (Edinburgh, 1949).

31. MacEwen, *History of the Church of Scotland*, 1:163–73.

32. Ibid., 1:191; William Reeves, *The Culdees of the British Isles* (Dublin, 1864), pp. 105–17.

33. Edmund Curtis, *A History of Ireland*, 6th ed. (London, 1950), has an appreciative account of Brian Borumba, pp. 22–31: he "restored the Church and gave Ireland a new impetus in art, literature and culture not unworthy of the former Golden Age" (p. 31).

34. J. A. Watt, *The Church and the Two Nations in Medieval Ireland* (Cambridge, 1970). In chapters 1 and 2, Watt deals with Irish church affairs before and after the Anglo-Norman invasion. He indicates clearly the part played by Alexander III in relation to Henry II's involvement in Irish ecclesiastical matters. See also Annette J. Otway-Ruthven, *A History of Medieval Ireland* (London, 1968). For the Bull *Laudabiliter* and other essential documents see Edmund Curtis and R. B. McDowell, eds., *Irish Historical Documents 1172–1922* (London and New York, 1943; rpt. 1968), pp. 17–31. See also Louis Gaugaud, *Christianity in Celtic Lands* (London, 1932), pp. 151–52.

35. For this Felim, or Felimy, see Godard H. Orpen, in Walter Alison Phillips, ed., *History of the Church of Ireland* (Oxford, 1934), 2:4–7. His active career was approximately 820–40. In 833 he pillaged Clonmacnois and slew the monks. He was described, evidently by a partisan, in the *Annals of the Four Masters* as "king of Munster, anchorite and scribe, and the best of the Irish of his time."

36. The round towers were shown to be for the protection of church properties in George Petrie's still authoritative *Inquiry into the Origin and Uses of the Round Towers of Ireland* (Dublin, 1945) (also appearing under the title, *The Ecclesiastical Architecture of Ireland anterior to the Norman Invasion*).

37. Giraldus, *Topographica Hibernica* II, xxxviii. For an Irish scholar's estimate of this work see F. X. Martin, "Gerald of Wales, Norman Reporter on Ireland," *Studies* 58 (1969): 279–92. Against identification of the Kildare manuscript with the *Book of Kells* see Sir Edward Sullivan, *The Book of Kells*, 5th ed. (London and New York, 1955), pp. 21–22.

38. Giraldus, *Topographica Hibernica.*

39. See in this connection Otway-Ruthven, *History of Medieval Ireland*, pp. 38–50. The text of Gilbert's *De statu ecclesiastico* is in MPL 159:994–1004.

40. J. MacErlean, "The Synod of Rathbreasil: Boundaries of Dioceses of Ireland," *Archaeologica Hibernica* 3 (1914): 1–33; Watt, *Church and Two Nations*, pp. 28–51, with map of the archdioceses as finally determined by the Synod of Kells, 1152 (p. 30); Alwyn Rees and Brinley Rees, *Celtic Heritage* (London, 1961), p. 103, has map of Leth Cuinn and Leth Moga, divided by a low ridge from Galway Bay to Dublin.

41. Orpen, in Phillips, *History of the Church of Ireland*, 2:25–26, 45–46.

42. Bernard's *Vita Malachiae*, in *MPL* 187:1073–1118, has been translated with ample notes by H. J. Lawlor, *St. Bernard of Clairvaux's Life of St. Malachy of Ireland* (London, 1920). For further clarification see Aubry Gwynn, "St. Malachy of Ireland," *Irish Ecclesiastical Record*, 5th ser. 50 (1948): 960–78, and 71 (1949): 134–48, 317–31. Father Gwynn points out that Bernard was attracted by Malachy's personal qualities, his serviceable ways and kindly laughter. See also Gerard Murphy, "St. Malachy of Ireland," *The Month* 18 (1957): 219–37; Murphy describes the monastery of Armagh as having become more like a modern Oxford college than a typical monastery (p. 223). Light is shed on the problems of monastic property and discipline in Malachy's time and later by John Barry in "The Coarbs and the Twelfth Century Reform," *IER* 88 (1957): 17–25.

43. Kenney, pp. 770–71; Aubrey Gwynn, "St. Lawrence O'Toole as Legate in Ireland," *Analecta Bollandiana* 68 (1950): 223–40; Watt, *Church and Two Nations.*

44. See the works cited in note 34 above by J. A. Watt and Annette J. Otway-Ruthven. Watt has profited by use of a large number of special studies by the painstaking Irish scholar Aubrey Gwynn. Consult also Kathleen Hughes, *The Church in Early Irish Society* (Ithaca, 1966), pp. 197–274, and the earlier account by Archdeacon St. John D. Seymour in Walter Alison Phillips, ed., *History of the Church of Ireland* (Oxford, 1934), 2:78–168.

45. "If the world was in the church, the church was also in the world" (Hughes, *Church in Early Irish Society*, p. 250.)

46. Ibid., 273.

47. Seymour, in Phillips, *History of the Church of Ireland*, 2:148–49.

48. Watt, *Church and Two Nations*, pp. 85–107; cf. B. W. O'Dwyer's Account of the Cistercian troubles, in "Gaelic Monasticism and the Irish Cistercians ca. 1228," *Irish Ecclesiastical Record 108* (1967): 119–28.

49. Watt, *Church and Two Nations*, pp. 177–80.

50. Seymour, in Phillips, *History of the Church of Ireland*, 2:140ff.

51. Watt, *Church and Two Nations*, pp. 83–84.

52. John Hennig, "Irish Monastic Activities in Eastern Europe," *IER* 65 (1945): 394–400. Father Hennig points with approval to Fritz Blanke's reference to Columban's desire to establish a mission to the Slavs as "the earliest medieval proposal for "an unpolitical, merely spiritual mission to foreign countries." For Professor Mikhael Emmanuilovich Shaitan's "Irish Emigration in the Middle Ages" see *Srednevekoi Byt* (a Festschrift to I. M. Grevs), ed. O. A. Dobiash-Rozhdestuenskaia (Leningrad, 1925), pp. 179–205. A notice in German appeared in *Neues Archiv der Gesellschaft für altere deutsche Geschictskunde* 44 (1928): 588–89, additional note p. 601. Shaitan's "Germany and Kiev in the Eleventh Century" was published in *Letopis' zaniatii* (a serial publication of the Russian Historical Commission) 34 (1927): 3–26. I am indebted to Mr. Vaclav Laska, bibliographer for Slavic language materials in the Regenstein Library, University of Chicago, for an English summary of Shaitan's studies.

53. Fuhrmann, *Irish Medieval Monasteries on the Continent* (Washington, D.C., 1927), pp. 106–11; Daniel A. Binchy, "The Irish Benedictine Congregation in Medieval Germany," *Studies* 18 (1929): 194–210; Mark Dilworth, "Some Notes on the Religious Orders in Pre-Reformation Scotland," in David McRoberts, ed., *Essays on the Scottish Reformation* (Glasglow, 1962), pp. 185–244. The later history of St. James of Rathisbon is narrated by Ludwig Hammermeyer in "Das Regensburger Schottenkloster des 19. Jahrhunderts," *Beitrag zur Geschichte des Bistums Regensburg* 5 (1971): 241–483.

Selected Bibliography

Albertson, Clinton. *Anglo-Saxon Saints and Heroes.* Edited and translated by Clinton Albertson Bronx: Fordham University Press, 1967.

Anderson, Alan Orr, and Anderson, Marjorie Ogilvie. *Adomnan's "Life of Columba."* Edited with translation and notes by Alan Orr Anderson and Marjorie Ogilvie Anderson. London: Thomas Nelson and Sons, 1961.

Baeda Venerabilis. *Historia ecclesiastica gentis Anglorum* [*Ecclesiastical History of the English People*]. Edited by Bertram Colgrave and R. A. B. Mynors. Oxford: Oxford University Press, 1969. (Latin and English)

Baring-Gould, Sabine, and Fisher, John. *The Lives of the British Saints; The Saints of Wales and Cornwall and Such Irish Saints as Have Dedications in Britain.* 4 vols. London: C. J. Clark, 1907–13.

Barley, M. W., and Hanson, R. P. C. *Christianity in Britain 300–700.* Papers of conference in the University of Nottingham, 17–20 April 1967. Leicester: Leicester University Press, 1968.

Bieler, Ludwig. *Ireland, Harbinger of the Middle Ages.* London and New York: Oxford University Press, 1963.

———, ed. *The Works of St. Patrick* and *Hymn on St. Patrick, by St. Secundinus.* Ancient Christian Writers, no. 17. Westminster Md.: Newman Press, 1953.

———. *The Irish Penitentials.* With an appendix by D. A. Binchy. Dublin: Dublin Institute of Advanced Studies, 1963.

Binchy, Daniel A. "Patrick and His Biographers, Ancient and Modern." *Studia Hibernica,* no. 2 (1962): 7–173.

Blanke, Fritz. *Columbanus und Gallus: Uhrgeschichte des Schweizerischen Christentums.* Zurich: Fretz and Wamuth, 1940.

Bowen, E. G. *Britain and the Western Seaways.* London: Thames and Hudson, 1972.

Bulloch, James. *The Life of the Celtic Church.* Edinburgh: St. Andrew Press, 1963.

Burleigh, John H. S. *The Church History of Scotland.* London and New York: Oxford University Press, 1960.

Cappuyns, Maieul. *Jean Scot Erigène, sa vie, son oeuvre, sa pensée.* Paris: Desclée, 1933.

Carney, James. *The Problem of St. Patrick*. Dublin: Dublin Institute of Advanced Studies, 1961.

Chadwick, Hector Munro. *Early Scotland: The Picts, the Scots and the Welsh of Southern Scotland*. Cambridge: At the University Press, 1949.

Chadwick, Nora K. *Poetry and Letters in Early Christian Gaul*. London: Bowes and Bowes, 1955.

———. *Celt and Saxon: Studies in the Early British Border*. Cambridge: At the University Press, 1963.

———. *Early Brittany*. Cardiff: University of Wales Press, 1969.

———, ed. *Studies in the Early British Church*. Cambridge: At the University Press, 1968.

———, ed. *Studies in Early British History*. Cambridge: At the University Press, 1954.

Curtayne, Alice. *Brigid of Ireland*. Dublin: Brown and Nolan, 1934.

Deanesly, Margaret. *The Pre-Conquest Church in England*. London: Black, 1964.

Delius, Walter. *Geschichte der Irische Kirche von ihren Anfangen bis zum 12. Jahrhundert*. Munich: Reinhardt, 1954.

De Paor, Maire, and de Paor, Liam. *Early Christian Ireland*. London: Thames and Hudson, 1958.

Dillon, Myles, and Chadwick, Nora K. *The Celtic Realms*. London: Weidenfeld and Nicholson, 1967.

Doble, Gilbert H. *The Saints of Cornwall*. Edited by Donald Atwater. Truro, Eng.: Dean and Chapter, 1960.

Duckett, Eleanor S. *Anglo-Saxon Saints and Scholars*. New York: Macmillan, 1947.

———. *The Wandering Saints*. London: Collins, 1959. (Also published as *The Wandering Saints in the Early Middle Ages*. New York: Norton, 1959.)

Duke, John Alexander. *History of the Church of Scotland to the Reformation*. Preface by Hugh Watt. Edinburgh and London: Oliver and Boyd, 1937; reprinted 1957.

Evans, Emrys Estyn. *Prehistoric and Early Christian Ireland: A Guide*. New York: Barnes and Noble, 1968.

Filip, Jan. *Celtic Civilization and Its Heritage*. Translated by Roberta Finlayson Samsour. Prague: Czechoslovak Academy of Sciences and Arts, 1962.

Flower, Robin. *The Irish Tradition*. Oxford: Clarendon Press, 1947.

Fuhrmann, Joseph Paul. *Irish Medieval Monasteries on the Continent*. Washington, D.C.: Catholic University of America, 1927.

Godfrey, C. J. *The Church in Anglo-Saxon England*. Cambridge: At the University Press, 1962.

Gougaud, Louis. *Christianity in Celtic Lands.* Translated by Maud Joynt. London: Sheed and Ward, 1932.

———. *Gaelic Pioneers of Christianity: The Work and Influence of Irish Monks and Saints in Continental Europe (6th to 12th Century)*. Dublin: M. H. Gill and Son, 1923.

Greene, David, and O'Connor, Frank. *A Golden Treasury of Irish Poetry, 600–1200.* London: Macmillan, 1967.

Griffe, Elie. *La Gaule chrétienne à l'époque romaine.* Paris: Letourzey et Ané, 1964.

Gwynn, Aubrey, and Hadcock, R.N. *Medieval Religious Houses: Ireland.* With an appendix on early sites. London: Longmans, 1970.

Haddan, Arthur West, and Stubbs, William. *Councils and Ecclesiastical Documents Relating to Great Britain and Ireland.* 3 vols. Oxford: Clarendon Press, 1869–78.

Hanson, R. P. C. *St. Patrick, His Origins and Career.* Oxford: Clarendon Press, 1968.

Henderson, Isabel. *The Picts.* London: Thames and Hudson, 1967.

Henry, Françoise. *Irish Art in the Early Christian Period, to A.D. 800.* Rev. ed. London: Methuen. 1967.

———. *Irish Art during the Viking Invasions, 800–1020 A.D.* London: Methuen, 1965; Ithaca, N.Y.: Cornell University Press, 1965.

Hubert, Henri. *The Greatness and Decline of the Celts.* Translated by M. R. Dobie. London: K. Paul, Trench, Trubner, 1934. From Hubert's posthumous French work *Les Celtes et l'expansion celtique jusqu'à l'époque de la Tène*, edited by Marcel Mauss et al. Paris, 1932.

Hughes, Kathleen. *The Church in Early Irish Society.* London: Methuen, 1966; Ithaca, N.Y.: Cornell University Press, 1966.

Hughes, William. *The Church of the Cymry from the Earliest Period to the Present Time.* Rev. ed. London: Stock, 1916.

Jackson, Kenneth H. *Language and History in Early Britain: A Chronological Survey of the Brythonic Languages, First to the Twelfth Century.* Edinburgh: Edinburgh University Press; London: Oliver and Boyd, 1953.

Jacobsthal, Paul. *Ancient Celtic Art.* 2 vols. Oxford: Clarendon Press, 1944; reprinted 1969.

Joynt, Maud. *The Life of St. Gall.* London: S. P. C. K., 1927. Translation of Walahfrid's *De vita Cancti Galli* with introduction and notes.

Kendrick, T. D. *The Druids: A study in Keltic Prehistory.* London: Methuen, 1927. London: Cass; New York: Barnes and Noble, 1966.

Kenney, James F. *The Sources of the Early History of Ireland: Ecclesiastical.* New York: Columbia University Press, 1929; New York Octagon Press, 1967.

Knowles, David, and Hadcock, R. Nevelle. *Medieval Religious Houses in England and Wales*. London: Longmans, Green, 1953.

Laistner, M. L. W. *Thought and Letters in Western Europe, A.D. 500–900*. 2d ed. London: Methuen, 1957.

Largillière, René. *Les saints et l'organisation chrétienne primitive dans l'Armorique bretonne*. Rennes: J. Plihon et L. Hommay, 1925.

Latouche, Robert. *Caesar to Charlemagne: The Beginning of France*. Translated by Jennifer Nicholson. London: Phoenix House; New York: Barnes and Noble, 1968.

Leask, Harold L. *Irish Churches and Monastic Buildings*. Dundalk: Dundalgan Press, 1953; reprinted 1960.

Le Grand, Albert. *Les vies des saints de la Bretagne Armorique* (1636). 5th ed. Edited by A. M. Thomas et al. Quimper: Salacin, 1901.

Levison, Wilhelm. "Die Iren und die Fränkische Kirche." *Historische Zeitschrift* 109 (1912): 1–22.

Lloyd, Sir John Edward. *A History of Wales to the Edwardine Conquest*. 2 vols. 3d ed. London: Longmans, Green and Co., 1939; reprinted 1954.

———, and Jenkins, R. T., eds. *The Dictionary of Welsh Biography down to 1940*. London: Under the Auspices of the Honorable Society of Cymmrodorion, 1959.

Loyer, Oliver. *Les Chrétientés celtiques*. Paris: Presses Universitaire de France, 1965.

Macalister, R. A. S. *Ancient Ireland: A Study in the Lessons of Archaeology and History* London: Methuen, 1935.

MacEwen, Alexander R. A History of the Church in Scotland. 2 vols. Rev. ed. London and New York: Hodder and Stoughton, 1915.

McNally, Robert E., ed. *Old Ireland*. Dublin: Gill, 1965.

MacNeill, Eoin. *Phases of Irish History*. Edited by John Ryan. Rev. ed. Dublin: Clonmore and Reynolds; London: Burns and Oates, 1964.

———. *St. Patrick, Apostle of Ireland*. Edited by John Ryan. Rev. ed. Dublin: Clonmore and Reynolds; London: Burns and Oates, 1964.

McNeill, John T., and Gamer, Helena M. *Medieval Handbooks of Pennance: A Translation of the "Libri poenitentiales" and Selections from Related Documents*. New York: Columbia University Press, 1938; New York: Octagon Press, 1969.

McQueen, John. *St. Nynia: A Study Based on Literary and Linguistic Evidence*. Edinburgh: Oliver and Boyd, 1961.

Mâle, Emile. *La fin du paganisme en Gaule et les plus anciennes basiliques chrétiennes*. Paris: Hammarion, 1950.

Mélanges Colombaniens. *Actes du Congrès international de Luxeuil 20–23 Juillet, 1950*. Paris: Editions Alsatia, 1951.

Meyer, Kuno. *Learning in Ireland in the Fifth Century and the Transmission of Letters*. Dublin School of Irish Learning: Hodges, Figgis and Co., 1913.

Mohrmann, Christine. *The Latin of St. Patrick: Four Lectures*. Dublin: Dublin Institute of Advanced Studies, 1961.

Mould, Daphne D. C. Pochin. *The Irish Saints*. Dublin: Clonmore and Reynolds; London: Burns and Oates, 1964.

Mulchrone, Kathleen. *Bethu Phatraic: The Tripartite Life of Patrick*. Dublin: Royal Irish Academy, 1939.

Nash-Williams, Victor E. *The Early Christian Monuments of Wales*. Cardiff: University of Wales Press, 1950.

Oakley, Thomas Pollock. *English Penitential Discipline and Anglo-Saxon Law in Their Joint Influence*. New York: Columbia University Press, 1923.

O'Curry, Eugene. *Lectures on the Manuscript Materials of Ancient Irish History*. Dublin: W. H. Killey, 1873.

O'Hanlon, John. *Lives of the Irish Saints, with Special Festivals* . . . 9 vols. Dublin: J. Duffy; London: Burns and Oates 1875–1905.

O'Rahilly, Thomas F. *Early Irish History and Mythology*. Dublin: Dublin Institute of Advanced Studies, 1946.

———. *The Two Patricks: A Lecture on the History of Fifth Century Ireland*. Dublin: Dublin Institute of Advanced Studies, 1942.

Otway-Ruthven, Annette Jocelyn. *A History of Medieval Ireland*. With an introduction by Kathleen Hughes. London: Benn; New York: Barnes and Noble, 1965.

Parry, Thomas. *A History of Welsh Literature*. Translated from Welsh by H. Idris Bell. Oxford Clarendon Press. 1962.

Phillips, Walter Alison, ed. *A History of the Church of Ireland*. 3 vols. London: Oxford University Press, 1933–34.

Plummer, Charles. *Vitae Sanctorum Hiberniae partim hactenus inedita . . . prolegominis notis indicibus* . . . 2 vols. Oxford: Clarendon Press, 1910.

Powell, Thomas G. E. *The Celts*. London: Thames and Hudson, 1958.

Rafferty, Joseph, ed. *The Celts*. Cork: Mercier Press, 1964.

Rébillon, Armand. *Histoire de Bretagne*. Paris: A Collin, 1957.

Rees, William Jenkins, ed. and tr. *Lives of the Cambro British Saints of the Fifth and Immediate Succeeding Centuries*. London: Longman and Co., 1853.

Reeves, William, ed. *"The Life of St. Columba, Founder of Hy," Written by Adamnan . . . to which Are Added Copious Notes and Dissertations*. Dublin: Irish Archaeological and Celtic Society, 1857. (Latin text of Adomnan's *Vita Sancti Columbae*.)

Ryan, John. *Irish Monasticism: Origins and Early Development*. New introduction and bibliography. 1931; Ithaca, N.Y.: Cornell University Press, 1972.

———, ed. *Irish Monks in the Golden Age*. Dublin: Clonmore and Reynolds, 1963; London: Burns and Oates, 1964.

———, ed. *Essays and Studies Presented to Professor Eoin MacNeill . . . May 15, 1938*. Dublin: The Sign of the Three Candles, 1940.

Selmer, Carl. *"Navigatio Sancti Brendani Abbatis," From Early Latin Manuscripts*. Notre Dame, Ind.: Notre Dame University Press, 1958.

Sheldon-Williams, J. S., ed. *Johannis Scotti Erivgenae Periphyseon (De Divisione naturae), Liber primus*. With the collaboration of Ludwig Bieler. Scriptores Latini Hibernici, vol. 7. Dublin: Dublin Institute of Advanced Studies, 1968.

Skene, William Forbes. *Celtic Scotland: A History of Ancient Alban*. 3 vols. 2d ed. Edinburgh: David Douglas, 1886–90.

Simpson, William Douglas. *The Historical St. Columba*. Aberdeen: Milne and Hutchison, 1927.

———. *St. Ninian and the Origins of the Christian Church in Scotland*. Edinburgh and London: Oliver and Boyd, 1940.

———. *The Celtic Church in Scotland*. Aberdeen University Press, 1935.

Stenton, Sir Frank Merry. *Anglo-Saxon England*. 3rd ed. Oxford: Clarenden Press, 1961.

Taylor, Thomas. *The Celtic Christianity of Cornwall: Divers Sketches and Studies*. London and New York: Longman, Green and Co., 1918.

Tierney, James J., ed and tr. *Dicuili liber de mensura orbis terrae*. Dublin: Dublin Institute of Advanced Studies, 1967.

Tommasini, Anselmo Maria. *Irish Saints in Italy*. Translated with some additional notes by J. F. Scanlan. Introduction by Gregory Cleary. London: Sands and Co., 1937.

Wade-Evans, Arthur Wade. *Welsh Christian Origins*. Oxford: Alden Press, 1934.

———, ed. *Vitae Sanctorum Britanniae et genealogiae*. Cardiff: University of Wales Press, 1944.

Walker, G. S. M., ed and tr. *Sancti Columbani Opera*. Dublin: Dublin Institute of Advanced Studies, 1967.

Watkins, Oscar Daniel. *A History of Penance, Being a Study of Authorities for the Whole Church to A.D. 450, for the Western Church from A.D. 450 to A.D. 1215*. 2 vols. London and New York: Longmans, Green and Co. 1920.

Watt, J. A., et al, eds. *Medieval Studies Presented to Aubrey Gwynn*. Dublin: Printed by G. O. Lochlainn, 1961.

White, Newport J. D., ed and tr. *Libri Sancti Patricii; the Latin Writings.* A revised text. London: S.P.C.K., 1918.

Williams, Glanmor. *The Welsh Church: Conquest to Reformation.* Cardiff: University of Wales Press, 1962.

Williams, Hugh, ed. *Gildae "De excidio Brittaniae," Fragmenta, "Liber de Poenitentia," accedit et "Lorica Gildae."* [Gildas, *The Ruin of Britain*, fragments from lost letters, the *Penitential*, together with the *Lorica of Gildas.*] 2 vols. Published for the Honorable Society of Cymmrodorion. London: D. Nutt, 1899–1901.

Index

Aachen, 180
Abailard, 152
Adam of Bremen, 189
Adomnan (abbot of Iona), 88–90, 93, 94, 101, 117, 121, 124, 130, 148, 157
Aelred of Rievaulx, 23, 24
Aetheria (religious tourist), 156
Aethicus Ister, 178
Agilbert (bishop), 108, 113
Aidan (king of Dalriada in Scotland), 96, 97, 99
Aidan (missionary bishop), 105–8, 113, 114, 116, 169, 199
Ainmere (king of Ireland), 71
Alain the Great, 151
Alain IV, 151, 152
Alban (martyr), 19, 20, 29
Alcuin of York, 180, 181
Aldfrith (king of Northumbria), 100, 112, 116
Aldhelm, 116, 122, 177, 197
Alexander III (pope), 218
Alexander the Great, 4
Alfred the Great, 197, 198
Alleluia Victory, 29, 30
Allemani, 168, 173
Amhra Colum Cille (panegyric on Columba by Dallán Forgaill), 98, 133
Anastasius, on Eriugena's translation from Greek, 186
Anchorites, 85, 175, 189, 208
Andelm (commentator on Paul's Epistles), 187
Angles, 102, 103, 105
Anglo-Saxon Chronicle, 181
Anglo-Saxon invasion, 28, 118, 139, 153
Annagray, 158
Anselm (archbishop of Canterbury), 200, 201
Anthony (monastic founder), 70
Antiphonary of Bangor, 127, 131, 132
Aosta, 173
Applecross, 97
Architecture, 130
Arculf, 99
Ardach Chalice, 127
Arian controversy, 23
Arles, council of (314), 22
Armagh, 66, 70, 213
Armorica, 17, 28, 30, 138, 139
Art: Celtic, 3; Eastern Christian, 123; symbolic, 21; Irish, unity of, 127, 128
Arthur, king, 27, 28, 139, 145
Arts, the seven liberal, 178, 188
Asaph, at Llanelwy, 195

Baldwin (archbishop, in Wales), 202
Bamburgh, 105
Bangor, in Ulster, 47, 166, 213
Bangor-is-Coed, 48, 190
Bards, 9, 73, 188
Baronius, Caesare, 17
Bathildis, 171
Batz, 149
Bavaria, 174, 193
Beasts, fraternizing with, 78, 167, 168, 233, 244
Bede (Baeda Venerabilis), cited, 18–20, 23, 24, 27–30, 48, 103–7, 111, 112, 114, 115, 118, 130
Beehive huts, 77, 130
Benedict of Nursia, 156, 166, 224
Benedict (peregrinus), 171
Benedictine rule and order, 149, 193, 222
Bernard (Norman bishop of St. David's), 201
Bernicia, 104, 108

Bertha (wife of Ethelbert), 48
Bible: study of, 128, 129, 133, 158, 184, 192, 224; importance of, 121; themes of, on crosses, 128, 129
Birinus (missionary in Wessex), 108, 248
Black Death (1348–49), 222
Birr, synod of (696), 117
Blaithmac, 207
Blane, 47
Bleggwyrd (law scholar), 200
Bobbio, 124, 184, 191, 214
Bobbio Missal, 131
Boethius, 133, 179
Boite, 45, 75
Boniface IV (pope), 165
Boniface of Crediton, 115, 172, 173, 177, 193
Book of Deer, 97, 131, 208
Book of Durrow, 125, 126
Book of Kells, 125, 126, 127
Book of Kildare, 214, 215
Book of Llandaff, 200
Book of Leinster, 70
Books: copying of, 124, 189, 191; destruction of, 191
Braga, council of: (561), 153, 154; (572), 152
Breaca, 44
Bregenz, 163, 168
Brehons, 9, 73; laws of the, 89
Brendan of Birr, 76, 89
Brendan of Clonfert, 69, 76, 77, 88; voyage of, 76, 219
Brennus (Gaulish chief), 3
Breton copyists, 151, 191
Breton language, 137, 142, 152
Brian Boru (Borumbha), king of Ireland, 191, 212
Brieuc, 144
Brigid, 45, 54, 69, 79, 80, 185, 214, 223
Britain: as Roman province, 15; early Christianity in, 16–32
British monks in Germany, 173, 174
Brittany, 30, 43, 45, 60, 137–54, 158, 170; beginnings of Christianity in, 130; church origins in, 142, 147; episcopate in, 151; independence of, 150; migration from, 152; migrations and settlement of Britons in, 138–40
Brittona (bishopric in Spain), 152, 153
Brocéliande, forest of, 145, 148
Broichan (druid), 95, 96
Brunhilda, 161, 164
Brychan, 36
Brude mac Maelchon (Pictish king), 91, 94
Brynech, 223
Budoc, 44, 143, 144, 146
Burgh Castle, 105, 169
Burgundy, 158, 159, 161

Cadoc, 38, 40, 43, 72, 131, 199
Cadwallon, 104
Caesar, Julius, 1, 5, 7, 9, 137, 224
Caidoc, 170
Cain Adamnáin, 100
Canones Adomnani, 100
Canterbury: archiepiscopal see of, 48, 102, 104, 116; claims of, in the Cornish peninsula, 199; in Ireland, 216; in Wales, 194, 201–3
Carnac, 137
Carranog (Cernach), 72
Cartier, Jacques, 147
Cassain, John, 83, 84
Catalogue of Irish Saints, 72, 85, 131
Cathach of Columba, 124
Cathbad (druid), 8
Celtiberians, 5
Celtic Christianity, uncoordination of, 193, 224
Cedd, bishop of East Saxons, 107, 113, 116, 198
Cellach, bishop of St. Andrew's, 205
Chad, bishop of Mercians, 197, 116, 194, 198
Chalices, 132
Chalons-sur-Saône, synod of (603), 160
Charlemagne, 148, 149, 179, 180, 181, 183
Charles the Bald, 177, 183, 185, 187
Charles the Fat, 188
Chateaubriand, 152
Chelles, 171
Childebert II, 159
Chi-Rho monogram, 23, 128
Ciaran, 75, 76, 98
Cicero, 184
Cisalpine Gaul, 4

Index

Cistercians, 220; in Ireland, 218, 219; in Wales, 283
Clairvaux, 219
Clas (community of monks), 196
Classical literature, 121
Claudius of Turin, 181
Clonard, 75, 76, 133
Clement the Scot (of the Palace School), 180, 181
Clement the Scot (opposed by Boniface), 177
Clonmacnois, 75, 98, 180
Clontarf, battle of (1014), 212
Clovis I, 148
Clovis II, 170
Codex (codices), 123
Coelfrid (abbot), 100
Cogitosus, 54
Colchu, 180
Columba of Iona: career of, 87–101; death of, 98; hymns of, 132; mentioned, 25, 26, 47, 77, 104, 113, 124, 125; miracles of, 97; relics of, 207; rule attributed to, 85, 93; travels and missions of, 94–96
Columban: career of, 155–68; discipline and rule of, 165, 166; learning of, 157, 259; mentioned, 52, 82, 104, 121, 124; Penitential of, 166; sermons of, 166, 167; view of the papacy, 160, 164, 165
Compostella, 207
Conall, king of Dalriada, 91, 94
Conan, bishop of Cornwall, 199
Conciliarists, 165
Conlaed, bishop at Kildare, 79
Connaught, 213, 217
Constance, 169, 190
Constantine the Great, 20–22, 128, 184, 213
Constantine II of Scotland, 205
Contraries, principle of, 166
Corbelled huts, 76, 77
Corbie, 171
Cormac mac Airt (high king), 50
Cormac (missionary voyager), 96
Cornish peninsula, 116, 152
Cornwall, 36, 61, 144, 158
Coroticus, 55, 65
Crediton, bishopric of, 199
Crosses, stone, 128–30, 224
Culdees, 81, 208, 211
Culdrevny, battle of, 89, 90
Cummian of Durrow, letter of, 111, 148
Cummian the Tall, 83
Cynegils (king of Mercia), 108

Dagda (Celtic deity), 7
Dagobert I, king of Austrasia, 149, 171
Dagobert II, 171
Dagobert III, 171
Dalaradia, 27, 47, 97, 246; missionary monks from, 97
Dalriada (in Britain), 28, 91, 204
Dalriada (in Ulster), 91, 93, 97
Danes, in Ireland, 212, 215
David the Scot, 190
David I (king of Scotland), 24, 210
Deicola, 161, 162
Deira, 104, 106
Desert Fathers of Egypt, 83
Devon, 44, 116, 145, 199
Diarmit (king of Ireland), 89
Dicuil the Geographer, 182, 183, 263
Dinoot (abbot), 48
Diocletian, 19, 20
Dionysius the Areopagite, 13, 186
Dionysius Exiguus, 110
Dionysius of Paris, 13
Diuma (bishop), 109
Divitiacus (druid), 9
Donatianus (martyr), 138
Donation of Constantine, 213
Donatus (bishop of Dublin), 216
Donatus (bishop of Fiesole), 185, 220
Dol, archbishopric of, 150
Donnan (martyr of Eigg), 97
Double monasteries, 79
Drostan of Deer, 97, 208
Druids, 8, 9, 73, 95, 96
Drumceatt, convention at, 97, 98
Dublin, 215–17; bishopric of, 213, 217
Dubricius, 36
Dumbarton, 57
Dunblane, 47
Dungal, 178, 181–83
Durham, 206
Durrow, 88, 96, 111, 125

Eafrid (Eadfrith), 122, 126

East Anglia, 104, 105, 169
Easter controversy, 101, 105, 109, 194, 199; in Brittany, 148; in Cornish peninsula, 195, 216; in England, 111–16; in Ireland, 109–12; in Wales, 117, 196, 197, 199
Easter cycles, 110
Ecclesia Scotticana, 205
Echternach Gospels, 115
Eddius Stophanus, 171
Edgar the Elder (king of England), 200
Edward I, 203, 204
Edward II, 220
Edwin (king of Northumbria), 103, 104, 194
Egbert (English monk in Ireland), 116–18
"Egyptians" (Irish scholars), 181
Eichstadt, 190
Eigg, massacre of monks in, 97, 206
Einhard, 179
Eloi, bishop of Noyon, 149, 171
Elfodd of Gwynedd: called archbishop, 196; Easter reform of, 196, 197; policy of, repudiated, 197
Enda, 71, 75
Episcopacy in Ireland, 70, 216, 217; in Scotland, 210, 211; in Wales, 200
Episcopi vagantes, 172, 173
Erasmus, 184
Erchinwald, 170, 171
Erispoë (king of Brittany), 150, 151
Eriugena, John Scotus, 185–88
Ermenrich (abbot), 192
Essex, 108
Ethelberga (wife of King Edwin), 103
Ethelbert (king of Kent), 46, 102, 103
Ethelfrith (king of Northumbria), 48
Eugenius III (pope), 211
Eusebius of Caesarea, cited, 12, 19, 160
Eusebius (Irish recluse), 188
Eustace (abbot of Luxeuil), 169

Fabian (pope), 12–14
Fastidius (Pelagian bishop), 31
Felim MacCriffan, atrocities of, 214
Felix (bishop and missionary), 104
Fer léginn, 120, 133, 268
Fiacc, hymn of, 53
Fiacra, 179
Fidelis, 182
Filigree, 127, 128
Finan (abbot), 112, 130
Finnian (abbot of Clonard), 69, 72, 75, 83, 87, 88, 158, 166, 195
Finnian (abbot of Moville), 69, 71, 87, 89, 173
Fitzgerald, David (bishop of St. David's), 201
Foillan (founder of Fosses), 170, 171
Fontaines, 189
Forgaill, Dallán, 9, 98
Fortunatus (poet), 156
Fosses, 171
Frankish territories, 148–53, 157
Fredegondis, 169
Fricor (companion of Caidoc in founding Fosses), 170
Fridian of Lucca, 173, 220
Fridolin, 171, 172
Fursa (visionary and founder of Burghcastle and Lagny), 105, 169, 170, 224

Galatia, 10
Galicia, 10–11, 153, 154
Gall, 17, 141; early bishops in, 12–14
Gall (abbot), 168, 178, 224; sermon by, 169
Gallican rite, 131
Gemman (bard), 73
Geoffrey of Monmouth, 201
Germanus of Auxerre, 29–32, 35, 52, 63, 99, 139, 178
Germany, Irish foundations in, 172, 189, 190, 221
Gerontius (prince of Devon), 197
Gertrude (Polish princess), 221
Gilbert (bishop of Llanelwy), 196
Gilbert, bishop of Limerick: *De statu ecclesiae* of, 216, 217
Gildas, 16, 27, 28, 40–44, 120, 131
Giraldus Cambrensis, 80, 201, 202, 213, 214, 223, 267
Giric (king of Scotland), 205
Glasgow, 46, 47, 211

Index

Glastonbury, 17, 199
Glendalough, 78, 130, 174
Goidels, 6
Gottschalk, 185
Greek: fathers, 179; study of, 122, 186, 265
Gregory the Great (pope), 47, 49, 100, 193
Gregory II (pope), 172, 173
Gregory III (pope), 174
Gregory of Tours, 12–14, 148, 158
Guénolé (founder of Landévennec), 146, 256
Gryffydd (bishop of St. David's), 200
Gyrovagi, 156

Hadrian I (pope), 181
Hadrian IV (pope), 212, 213
Half-uncial script, 125
Hallstadt culture, 2, 137
Hanau, 171
Haroun-al-Raschid, 183
Heathfield, synod of (680), 194
Heiric, 178
Henry I (king of England), 201
Henry II (king of England), 212, 213, 218
Henry IV (emperor), 221
Henry V (emperor), 221
Hewalds, the two (martyrs), 115
Hibernicus exul, 183
Hilda (abbess), 112, 114
Hiltebold (deacon), 168
Hinkmar of Laon, 185
Hinkmar of Rheims, 179, 195
Hisperica famina, 122
Hohenburt (nunnery), 171
Honorius I (pope), 108, 110
Honorius (archbishop of Canterbury), 104
Hospices, 179
Howel the Good, 199, 200
Hubert Walter (archbishop of Canterbury), 202

Iceland, monks in, 182
Illtud (abbot), 35–37, 70, 130
Illumination of manuscripts, 123–27, 134, 191, 224
Imrama, 76
Inchcolme, oratory in, 77
Inclusi, 189
Innisboffin, 114
Innocent I (pope), 193
Innocent III (pope), 190, 193, 202, 220, 221
Iona, 88, 91–100, 104, 105, 117, 159, 184; employments of monks at, 92–94; missions from, 94–96; monastery buildings at, 92; raided and destroyed, 206, 207; royal burials at, 207
Ireland, 7, 8, 18, 27–29; Christianization of, 50–69; discord within, 212; medieval Church of, 210–21; monasteries in, 69–86, 88; Northmen and Danes in, 211, 212
Irish on the Continent, influence of, 175, 191, 192. See also *Peregrinari pro Christo*
Irish poetry, 253
Ita, 79
Italy, Irish missions in, 173, 185

James (apostle), 10, 11
James (deacon), 104, 113
Jerome, 28, 29, 89, 160
Jocelyn of Furness, 45
John (king of England), 202
John of Ireland (martyr), 189
John of Salisbury, 213
John IV (pope), 110
John XXII (pope), 220
Jonas of Bobbio, 157, 161
Joseph of Arimathea, 17, 18
Joseph of York at Aachen, 180
Judwal (Breton prince), 145, 149
Juvenal, 121

Kells, 88, 126–28, 207, 214; Book of, 125, 126, 127; synod of (1152), 217
Kenneth Mac Alpin (king of Scotland), 204, 205, 207
Kenneth [Cainnech, Canice] (founder of Aghaboe), 88, 95
Kentigern, 45, 47
Kevin of Glendalough, 78, 79, 223
Kiev, mission to, 190, 221
Kildare, 79, 80, 143, 214, 215, 218
Kilheim, 190
Kilian and companions (martyrs), 172
Kings, ecclesiastical authority of, 119

Lagny, 105, 170
Landévennec, 146, 149
Lanfranc (archbishop of Canterbury), 201
Laon, 185, 187
Lastingham, 107
La Tène culture, 3, 137
Lateran Council, Fourth (1215), 218
Latin classics, 179
Laudabiliter (papal bull), 213, 220
Laurentius (archbishop of Canterbury), 109
Lavret, 146
Learning: in British and Irish monasteries, 35, 40, 41, 93, 100, 120–22, 134, 200, 201; of druids and fili, 73, 120
Leabhar Breac, 132
Leningrad, 191
Leo I (pope), 63, 160
Leo X (pope), 222
Leofric of Exeter, 199
Liège, 183
Lindisfarne, 105–8, 112, 114, 115, 130, 169, 198, 206
Lindisfarne Gospels, 122
Liturgy, 43, 73, 131
Llancarfan, 39
Llandaff, 36, 197
Llanelwy, 195
Llantwit Major, 35–37, 39
Llewelyn ap Gruffyd, 203, 204
Loeghaire mac Neill (king of Ireland), 179
Locronan, 143
Lombards, 173
Lothar II, 182
Louis the Pious (emperor), 149, 150, 181
Lucca, 178
Lug (Celtic deity), 7, 12
Lullingstone, church shared with pagans in, 21
Luxeuil: Columban's work in, 159; his expulsion from, 162, 163
Lyons and Vienne, persecution of Christians in, 11, 12

MacConglin, vision of, 219
MacMurrough, Dermot, 213
Máel rúain, 81, 82, 208, 209
Maelrubha, 97
Maelsechlain II (Irish liberator), 212
Maenach the Culdee, 209
Mag Léne, synod of, 111
Maildulf, 116, 121
Mailoc (abbot), 152, 153
Malachy (reformer and archbishop of Armagh), 215, 217, 218
Malcolm Canmore (king of Scotland), 209, 210
Malmesbury, 116, 121
Malo (Maclovius), 147
Mansuetus (bishop), 143
Manuscripts, illumination of, 123–27, 134, 191, 224
Marianus (Mael Brigte), the Chronicler, 189, 190
Margaret (queen of Scotland), 209, 210
Martianus Capella, 133, 179
Martin of Tours, 23, 26, 27, 35, 48, 57, 69, 70
Massacre
—of monks: at Bangor-is-Coed, 48, 149; at Eigg, 97, 206; at Iona, 207; at Lindisfarne, 206
—of nuns: at Coldingham, 206
—of Patrick's converts, 65
Matmonoc (abbot of Landévennec), 149
Mauritius, as leader of mission to Kiev, 190, 221
Maximus, monastery of, 152
Maximus Magnus, 139
Mawes, 44, 144
Mayo, 114
Méen, 145, 148, 149
Megalithic builders, 77
Memmingen, 190
Mellifont, Cistercian monastery of, 215
Mendicant orders in Ireland, 219
Mercia, Mercians, 105, 198
Merwyn (king in Gwynedd), 183
Metalwork, ornamental, 127, 224
Methodist school of medicine, 84, 166
Minuscule, Carolingian, 180
Mochaoi of Nendrum, 75
Mochmolmoc, 223
Mochuta of Lismore, 4, 81
Modrá, Moravia, church in, 174
Moengall, 133, 188, 220

Monasteries, in Ireland: foreign scholars in, 121, 177; numbers in, 80, 81; violence against, 85, 86, 213; in Wales, 39, 40, 81
Monastic rules, 80, 82, 165
Monasticism, rise of, 23, 69; in Britain, 35; in Ireland, 69–86; nature of, 85
Monastirboice, 45, 75, 128
Monks, massacre of. *See* Massacre of monks
Moravia, mission in, 174, 220, 221
Moville, 69, 71, 87, 89, 173, 189, 213
Mozarbic liturgy, 131
Muirchu maccu Machtheni, 54, 65
Muiredach, cross of, 128
Music, 123

Nantes, 138, 150
Nechtan IV (Pictish king), 24, 45, 117, 205
Nechtan Morbet, 45
Nechtansmere, battle of (685), 205
Neill of the Nine Hostages (high king of Ireland), 58
Nendrum, 78
Nennius, 27, 28, 31, 196
Neustria, 164, 170
Nicholas I (pope), 193
Ninnian, 23, 27, 35, 47; influence of, 69, 71
Nivelles, 171
Nominoë, 150, 151
Norman barons in Ireland, 213
Northumbria, 101, 104, 105, 112, 117, 123, 125, 198
Notker Balbulus (monk), 180, 181, 188
Nürnberg, 190

Odilo, 171
Ogham, 123
Olaf the Red, 207
Olaf Trygvason, 174
Ollam, degree of, 73
Ollamhs of Music, 133
Origen, on Christianity in Britain, 19
Orkney and Shetland islands, 96, 134, 204
Orleans, council of (441), 148
Orosius, Paulus, 153, 154
Orthodoxy, of the Irish, 165
Oswald (king of Northumbria), 104, 107, 199
Oswin (king of Deira), 106, 107
Oswy (king of Bernicia), 106, 107, 112–14
O'Toole, Laurence (archbishop of Dublin), 218
Ouen (bishop of Rouen), 171

Padarn, 72
Palace School, 180
Palestine, 99, 192
Palladius, 31; mission of, 51–53
Paris, 170, 191; council of, (ca. 555), 145
Parker, Matthew (archbishop of Canterbury), 18
Paparo (papal legate), 217
Paruchia (*parochia*), 54, 55, 67
Patrick (bishop of Dublin), 216
Patrick (Apostle of Ireland), 50–67, 123, 131, 132, 168, 170; achievement of, 65, 66; birthplace and boyhood of, 56–68; capitivity and conversion of, 58, 59; escape and journey of, 60–62; Latin of, 63, 64; miracles of, 241; and monasticism, 69; and "the Old Patrick," 53; and the *Senchus Mor*, 74; writings of, 55, 56, 61, 62
Paul (apostle), 10, 16, 17
Paul Aurelian, 146, 147
Paulinus (missionary in Northumbria), 103, 112
Paulinus (Welsh monk), 120
Peada, 107, 108
Peacham (archbishop of Canterbury, in Wales), 203, 204
Pelagius and Pelagianism, 28–31
Penance, 42, 83, 84, 89, 93 159. *See also* Penitentials
Penda the Mercian, 106, 107, 169
Penitentials, 70, 83, 84, 166
Pepin the Short, 179
Peregrinari pro Christo (*peregrinatio pro Christo; peregrinus pro Christo, peregrini*), 43, 89, 143, 155–58, 161, 171–73, 175, 178–80, 189, 220
Perrona Scottorum, 170
Péronne, 105; Norse in, 170

Pilgrimage for Christ. See *Peregrinari pro Christo*
Pilgrims (other than *peregrini*), 220
Peter (apostle), 17, 165
Piacenza, 163, 185
Picts, 19, 24, 25, 27, 42, 44, 204, 205; "apostate," 65, 235
Plou (parish in Brittany), 141, 142
Prosper of Aquitaine, chronicle of, 29–31, 51
Protestantism, 192
Prudentius, 13, 187
Psalmody, 132, 166
Pseudo-Dionysius, 186

Quartodecimans, 110
Quiberon Bay, 138, 147

Ralph (archbishop of Canterbury), 201
Rathbreasil, synod of (1110), 216
Ratisbon (Regensburg): St. James monastery in, 190, 220; St. Peter's monastery in, 189
Reichenau, 191
Reilig Oran (cemetery at Iona), 92
Renan, 152
Rhetoricians (*rhetors*), in Ireland, 64, 122
Rhigyfarch. *See* Rhygyvarch
Rhodri Mawr (Welsh prince), 198, 199
Rhuis, 43; the monk of, 71
Rhygyvarch (Rhigyfarch; Lat. *Ricemarcus*) of St. David's, 38, 40, 201
Rieinmelth (first wife of Oswy), 194, 248
Rimini, council of (359), 23
Riocatus, 153
Riothemi, 139, 149
Rogatianus (martyr), 138
Rome, 1, 4, 155; papal 30, 37, 47, 185, 189, 202, 207, 224; siege of (390 B.C.), 4
Ronan, 143
Rosnat, 71, 236
Round towers, 214
Ruthwell cross, 128

Saekingen, 171
St. Andrew's, bishopric of, 210, 211; Culdees of, 208, 211
St. Asaph, bishopric of, 201
St. David's (Menevia), bishopric of, 197, 198, 200, 201
St. Gall abbey: chronicle of, 188; library of, 191; school of, 187
St. James of Ratisbon, monastery, 221, 222
St. Malo, port of, 188
St. Patrick. *See* Patrick
St. Patrick's Purgatory (cave), 219
Salignac monastery, 171
Salomon (king of Brittany), 151
Sampson of Dol, 37, 44, 72, 120, 144–47
Sardica, council of (343), 23
Scellig Michael, settlements on, 77–78
Schottenklöster, 189, 190; Congregation of, 190, 221, 222, 271
Scotland, medieval church of, 203–11; independence of, 211; reforms of Queen Margaret in, 210
Scotia, altered geographic meaning of, 209, 222
"Scots believing in Christ," 51
Scriptoria, 123, 124, 191
Scripture, reverence for, 192. *See also* Bible
Seal of confession, 84
Seaways and seagoing, 11, 15, 154
Sedulius Scottus, 188; *On Christian Rulers*, 184; poetry of, 183, 184
Segene (abbot of Iona), 104, 111
Senchus Mór, 74
Serf (missionary among the Picts), 47, 208
Seven liberal arts, 178, 188
Sherborne, diocese of, 116
Shrines, pagan, destruction of, 103, 168
Sigebert (king of the East Angles), 104, 105
Sigebert the Little, 107
Silchester, church of, 21
Simon Magus, 115
Sitric (Danish king of Dublin), 215
Slavs, 189, 220
Stephen of Lexington, 219
Stowe Missal, 131, 214
Strathclyde, 45, 57, 61, 118
Strongbow (Richard of Pembroke), 213
Suevi, 60, 153

Sulien of St. David's, 200
Sulpicius Severus, 23, 124
Sunniva, legend of, 174
Symbols, symbolism, 123, 126
Symphorian (martyr), 12
Syncretism, 21, 22, 130

Tallaght, 131, 188, 208
Tara, 97, 98
Teilo (abbot), 36, 37, 45
Tertullian (quoted), 18, 19
Theodore (archbishop of Canterbury), 116, 122; rejects Celtic orders, 194, 195
Theodosius II (emperor), 183
Theodulph of Orleans, 181
Tiberius (emperor), 16
Thanau (mother of Kentigern), 45
Tírechán, 52, 54, 56
Tonsure, 73, 105, 109, 114, 131, 147 148, 153, 193
Tours: archbishopric of, 143, 148, 150; council of (461), 143; monastery of, 180
Traprain Law, 45, 234
Trivium and quadrivium, 179
Trudpert, 172
Tuam, see of, 217
Turgot, 209; bishop of St. Andrew's, 211
Turin Gospel, 214
Turlough O'Connor (king of Connaught), 217
Tweed (river), 205

Ultan (brother of Fursa), 170, 171
Unity, spiritual, 44
Ursus (bishop of Aosto), 173

Vannes, 138, 150
Vergil (poet), 4, 121
Vergil of Salzburg ("the Geometer"), 174, 178
Vettius Epagathus (martyr), 12
Victorinus, 58
Victricius of Rouen, 26
Vienna, 7, 190
Vigilius (pope), 165
Viking raids, 47, 97, 128, 182, 205–7, 213
Vision experiences, 58, 100, 104, 169, 170
Vision of Adomnan (Fis Adamnáin), 100, 105
Voclut, wood of, 58

Walafrid Strabo, 178
Wales, 15, 60, 61; bishoprics, alleged, 195; church of, 15–29; and Cornwall, later church history of, 193–204; laws of, 199, 200; literature of, 198, 254; Norman pressure on, 195, 197; subjection to Canterbury, 200–203
Wends, mission to, 189
Wessex, 108, 194
Western civilization, debt of, to "Celtic fringe," 192
Whitby, synod of, 108, 109, 118; date of, 249
Whithorn and Candida Casa, 23, 24, 35, 75
Wilfrid, 109, 112–15, 148, 171
William of Malmesbury, 17, 187
William the Conqueror, 200; Bretons and, 152
Willibrord, 115, 127
Wini (bishop in Wessex), 108, 109, 194
Winyet, Ninian, 222
Worship, hours of, in monasteries, 132
Wridisten (Gourdisten), 196
Writing, art of, 120, 123
Würzburg, 172, 181, 190

York, 103, 104, 211; claims of archbishops of, in Scotland, 211

Zachary (pope), 117, 118
Zoomorphic forms in art, 124